Fly Fishing the Blue Ridge Parkway

North Carolina Section

By:

Sam R. Johnson

Outdoorsman & Author

Forward by:

Mark W. Woods

Superintendent - Blue Ridge Parkway *(Retired)*

MOUNTAIN ARBOR
PRESS

Published by:
Mountain Arbor Press
1264 Old Alpharetta Road
Alpharetta, Georgia 30005

First Published 2019

Manufactured in the United States

ISBN 1134.2351.19506.456.

Front cover image: Looking Glass Falls & the Author / Pisgah National
Forest / 2010 / Image courtesy of Brad Mast Photography

Back cover image: Northbound on the Parkway at Mile Post 420.5 near
Devil's Courthouse / 2019 */ Image by Author*

. .

This Guide is dedicated to all the fly anglers who can no longer get out there and chase trout in the wild places described in this Guide – but once did and now only dream about their escapades. Also to those fly anglers who have always fished "*assisted living*" trout waters – but dreamed of chasing trout in wild and exotic places and never did. Finally, to the rare breed of fly anglers who can still get out there and chase trout in wild and exotic places – but could use some new places to go.

Hopefully this Guide will bring some satisfaction to you all...

A minimum of five (5) percent of the net profits from the sale of this book will be donated to the *Blue Ridge Parkway Foundation*. This 501(c) (3) organization is the primary fundraising partner for the Blue Ridge Parkway. It provides support for initiatives along the Parkway's entire 469 miles in NC and VA., including historical and cultural preservation, environmental protection, visitor amenities, as well as education and outreach.

Blue Ridge Parkway Foundation
717 South Marshall Street, Suite 105 B
Winston-Salem, NC 27101

Asheville Office
322 Gashes Creek Road
Asheville, NC 28803

Contents

Forward

Mark H. Woods
Superintendent, Blue Ridge Parkway *(Retired)*

When Sam described his ideas for this guide to me, and then asked if I would consider writing its Forward, I quickly realized that he was much like me – mesmerized by the Parkway and the beautiful, magnificent mountains it traverses – and he loved to fly fish. It was immediately clear to me why he wanted to document the many known and unknown places to fish along the Parkway. After all, I too had sought these places out and enjoyed many of them over the years. I was intrigued by his passion for the Parkway and his passion for fly fishing, so I agreed to do it.

After all, I grew up in the upstate of South Carolina and fishing has always been an activity I love. I have wonderful childhood memories of fishing with my parents and grandparents. Our family owned a vacation home on Lake Greenwood in South Carolina, and I spent many cherished days from sunrise to sunset exploring the coves along the lake and fishing as much as possible.

As summer and fall approached, our family made frequent trips to the mountains of Western North Carolina, where we often ended up exploring the Blue Ridge Parkway. While I loved spending hours on the lake at our home on Lake Greenwood, there was something captivating about those cold water streams found in the mountains. Those visits to the Parkway became more frequent over the years and with each excursion I found myself at some mountain stream or river in these rugged, yet beautiful mountains. It was through these trips and the better part of four decades with the National Park Service, that I learned the Blue Ridge Parkway is much more than a roadway through an incredible landscape.

The mountain ranges of the Parkway reflect the oldest mountain-building processes in the world. The Parkway stands at the summit of many local and regional watersheds that define the hydrological patterns of much of the Eastern United States. When it was finally completed, The Parkway traversed the rugged Appalachian Mountains, spanning a full 469 miles and connecting Shenandoah

National Park to the north and Great Smoky Mountains National Park to the south. To give you some appreciation for that distance, that is approximately how far a drive it would be from Asheville, NC to St. Augustine, FL. And remember that the speed limit on the Parkway is 45 miles per hour.

The Parkway was routed across mountain plateaus and rolling pastures, open meadows to high elevation spruce-fir forests and summits of more than 6,000'. To fulfill the recreational purpose of the Parkway as a *ride-a-while, stop-a-while* Park, designers planned and developed more than a dozen recreational areas. These recreational areas vary in size from 2,000 to more than 6,000 acres, and include places like *Peaks of Otter, Rocky Knob, Doughton Park, Julian Price Memorial Park* and *Linville Falls*. There are more than 300 miles of hiking trails, lodges, restaurants, concession facilities and accommodations that serve the visitor.

Between these developed areas, overlooks and vistas allow motorists to stop, and much like visiting an art gallery, study the landscape composition of the scenery. The Parkway has become an area that is tops in the National Park System for visitation. But it's not just design and enormous visitation that make the Parkway important. The Parkway provides a carefully landscaped window from which to view Southern Appalachia at its captivating best. It is both an introduction to the region and an enduring invitation to explore, sample and savor the surroundings countryside and culture. In many respects, the Parkway only whets the appetite for discovering what lies just over the next ridge or up the next stream. It also provides a unique opportunity for anglers to pursue their passion and experience much that the Parkway has to offer.

Spanning two states and twenty-nine counties, the Parkway includes over 1,100 miles of boundary – a boundary shared with approximately 4,000 landowners, state parks, four national forests, tribal lands, and other national park system units. Land protection efforts continue as the National Park Service works with land trusts and conservation organizations to protect scenic and recreational values along the Parkway.

In August 2016, the National Park Service commemorated its 100th Anniversary and the Parkway celebrated the addition of more than 5,000 acres that included much of the spectacular views from Waterrock Knob. At 6,292 feet, Waterrock Knob is the highest peak in the rugged Plott Balsam Mountains. I can't think of a more fitting way for the public to celebrate the Centennial of the National Park Service than to observe this conservation achievement. This large landscape of rare southern Appalachian spruce fir forests visible from the visitor center and the summit of Waterrock Knob is now protected for future generations. These types of land protection efforts are critical to ensuring protection of watersheds, recreational opportunities and trout waters for future generations.

~ Forward ~

In the last decade of my career with the National Park Service I had the privilege of serving as the Superintendent of the Blue Ridge Parkway. I spent many days traveling the Parkway, and I often reflected on the millions of visitors from all over the world who come to the Parkway to explore, enjoy nature, experience the scenery and participate in recreational activities. I also had the opportunity to meet with many visitors who shared their experiences while enjoying their park. I have talked with anglers at Graveyard Fields, Linville Gorge, and other special spots. It's clear that all of these visitors are fulfilling a passion for fly fishing in a very special place. They are building memories with friends and family while enjoying the Blue Ridge Parkway.

One of the things I enjoy is admiring the beautiful handmade crafts of the artisans who are juried members of the Asheville based Southern Highland Craft Guild. Since 1930 craftspeople residing in mountain regions of Appalachia have created a network of over 900 artisans selected through a juried process for their high-quality craftsmanship and design. Members of the Southern Highland Craft Guild often demonstrate their skills for visitors at the Folk Art Center at Milepost 382 on the parkway, or at the Moses Cone Manor at Milepost 294 on the parkway near Blowing Rock, NC.

As it turns out, Sam is a member of the Southern Highland Craft Guild. His bamboo fly rods are highly prized by collectors and anglers worldwide. Each rod is handcrafted one at a time using traditional materials and methods that can take up to 60 hours. At the Folk Art Center on the Parkway in Asheville, I am always drawn to a particular display of one of his bamboo fly rods. It is a masterpiece in its own right. While that bamboo rod is a beautiful piece of art, it can also be enjoyed in the cool mountain streams found along the Parkway.

When Sam and I met in Waynesville, NC in 2018 to discuss this project, I learned we share several things in common. First is a passion for the Blue Ridge Parkway and all it has to offer. And secondly, we both have a passion for fly fishing. I'm confident you'll find *Fly Fishing the Blue Ridge Parkway* an invaluable resource as you explore the Parkway and fly fish the many spectacular locations he describes. I encourage you to enjoy the drive, but take the time to explore the lesser known areas, as they have so much to offer. Above all, have fun and enjoy the journey!

Mark H. Woods

11

~ Forward ~

Acknowledgements

Rarely does anything of any real value get created alone or in a vacuum, and this Guide is no exception. Lots of people have knowingly and unknowingly contributed their time, knowledge, talent and encouragement over the two plus years it has taken to make it come to fruition. I couldn't have done it without them.

But let me say that as I approached the end of this phase of the project, I came to the realization that one's passion to write a book can become a burden to others. It's definitely a fine line for how much to lean on people to help edit, brainstorm, provide information, suggest designs and ask favors, just for the purpose of chasing one's dream. Regardless of how important I thought it was, for everyone else, it's still just a book about fly fishing. And most of the people involved don't even fly fish, and all of them have lots of other things to do. Regardless, below are some of those who helped me along the way. I apologize to anyone I've missed simply because I'm too danged brain dead at this point to recall everyone.

At the top of this list would have to be my Parents - Roland and Clairrene Johnson. My dad was the first person to take me fishing in our newly-built family lake in Alabama back in the late 1950s. After that first outing, I was more hooked on fishing than any of the fish I hooked that day. My Mom was the reason we went to North Carolina in the first place. Thanks to her we got exposed to the Parkway - and ultimately the art of fly fishing. To both of them I owe everything!

Leesa Brandon, the Blue Ridge Parkway's Partnerships & Public Information Officer, and Jackie Holt, Museum Curator, National Park Service / Blue Ridge Parkway, both provided assistance in finding and securing permission to use several rare and seldom seen images along the Parkway. They add a lot of context to this Guide.

Gene Hyde, Head of Special Collections & University Archivist, Ramsey Library, University of North Carolina at Asheville, assisted in finding and securing permission to use some vintage images associated with George W. Vanderbilt's influence on the region, as well as the Biltmore Forest School *(the first forestry*

~ Acknowledgements ~

school in America) located in Pisgah National Forest. Those images are central to several of the watersheds in this Guide.

Jason Tomberlin at the Louis Round Wilson Special Collections Library at the University of North Carolina - Chapel Hill, helped me find and secure permission to use the vintage post card *"Night Time on the Picturesque Blue Ridge Parkway"* printed by the Asheville Post Card Co. I saw the card and it captured my fancy early on. I felt it epitomized the magic and beauty of the Parkway.

My friend and virtual fishing companion Mark Woods, the retired Superintendant of the Blue Ridge Parkway, also played a role. Aside from graciously agreeing to write the Forward, he offered insight on who to contact at the Blue Ridge Parkway and National Park Service Administrative Offices to gather information, as well as to find and secure permission to use many of the rare images I needed. He's a good guy and did a great job managing the Parkway during his tenure. I'm working on converting him to fishing bamboo fly rods!

Monte Seehorn, retired Regional Fisheries Biologist / US Forest Service Region 8, actually lived on Wilson Creek, one of this Guide's major watersheds on the south face of Grandfather Mountain. His insight, stories and enthusiasm were a huge help drafting the Wilson Creek chapter. But his vast knowledge in general spilled over into many of the other chapters. Monte speaks at our Gold Rush Trout Unlimited Chapter in Dahlonega from time to time. He's forgotten more about trout and habitat restoration than the combined knowledge of the entire chapter. He's a great guy, great angler, great friend, and an even greater storyteller!

I have to mention my Uncle Gene Roberts who was a VP with Morrison's Food Services back in the 60's and 70's. He unknowingly completed my mountain indoctrination by offering summer jobs to my brothers and me at some of the many youth camps and church assemblies in the Western NC Mountains. We worked in the mornings and morphed into *"free range"* kids in the afternoons and evenings, free to explore the mountains and other important things in life. Those summers permanently burned the mountains and Parkway into my soul's hard drive.

Finally, Betty T. Johnson, my wife and best friend, spent countless hours listening to my harebrained ideas, moaning about my trips to get just the right image, and even more time performing the primary editing duties. Her English Major knowledge and skills from the University of Houston paid off by allowing her to take my train wreck of a draft and turn it into something almost readable. As an accomplished weaver, fiber artist and Chestatee Artist Guild Member, her role in this Guide took her away from her own passions. And I appreciate it!

There's at least one other special person out there who played a big role in all this too. And you know who you are. All I can say is a heartfelt *"thank you!"*

Introduction

How this guide came about...

Serious fly fishers are always looking for new places to wet a fly. And most go to great lengths to find it. *Fly Fishing the Blue Ridge Parkway* is a two-volume, plain-spoken *"where & how to"* guide describing some of the most scenic, remote and productive waters east of the Rockies. The Blue Ridge Parkway *(hereafter referred to as "Parkway")* is perhaps the most beautiful and celebrated US highway. Aside from the vistas, it also offers great fly fishing – making it a perfect subject for a fly fishing guide! This *North Carolina Section* features waters along the 252 miles of the Parkway in North Carolina that I've fished or have first-hand knowledge of. The *Virginia Section* will be written later if I live long enough.

Kermit the Frog once said; *"I always knew what I wanted to be - even before my tail fell off."* I grew up playing in the waters on and around the Parkway and watching fly fishermen. Like Kermit, I knew even before *my* tail fell off that when I grew up, I wanted to be close to the Parkway and hopefully fly fish too!

So when I was pondering whether or not to write this Guide, I searched for similar books on the internet, visited libraries, outfitters,

An iconic Parkway entrance sign at the Hwy 276 intersection. / *Image by Author / 2018*

guides, antique book stores, and even asked some really smart people who should know. I learned no book existed that specifically covers fly fishing the Parkway. Although the Parkway runs through some of the most celebrated trout waters in the eastern US, it's been largely overlooked in serious fly fishing literature. So then you ask, why write about it now? The answer is simple... *because someone needed to do it!* And I was the tadpole who had become that someone.

~ Introduction ~

The idea to write it came from a lifetime of experiences in and around the waters of the Parkway. Those experiences started in the early 1960's when my family began traveling to Brevard, NC to visit relatives, and later to escape the oppressive South Alabama summer heat. It was a 500 mile, 12 hour trip from the flatlands of South Alabama to Brevard, NC. I could've never imagined that in 50 years I'd be writing a book about fly fishing the entire distance of a highway that itself pushed 500 miles. The Parkway is 469 miles long, and it was hard to get my head around just how to document the fishing spots on a stretch of asphalt that long. But that's exactly what the NC and VA volumes will do when completed.

In our first few trips, the fact that Brevard was sitting at the edge of the Pisgah Ranger District of Pisgah National Forest didn't resonate that much to us. After all, we lived in Conecuh National Forest in southern Alabama. We were flatlanders and knew little of the significance of this area being the *"Cradle"* of the American forestry efforts – as well as having some of the most beautiful and rugged ground and waters in the eastern half of the US. It was a new world to us, and we became fascinated by the rugged topography, the waters, and of course the exotic flora and fauna and the vistas. The Parkway became our means of escape up and down the Appalachian Chain.

When we drove on the Parkway, we'd pass over or near one clear and cascading river, stream or creek after the other – many with incredible rock

Entrance to Pisgah National Forest on Hwy 276 along the Davidson River near Brevard. / *Image by Author / 2014*

slides, pools and waterfalls. It was a new and exotic land and the clear and cold water tumbling over a labyrinth of rocks and boulders was appealing to say the least. In contrast, back at home in LA *(Lower Alabama)* the topography was flat, rivers and streams were dark and muddy, warm most of the year, and patrolled by water moccasins. Waterfalls were nonexistent. So the images and experiences of our mountain excursions became permanently saved onto my brain's hard drive. And, just as a mature salmon swims upstream to where it hatched from an egg, not a single year has passed from my early years that this ole' salmon has not returned to that area as often as possible. It's an irresistible migration I don't try to resist!

~ Introduction ~

I grew up fishing in my family's 2-1/2 acre lake in Alabama. The indigenous largemouth bass and various pan fish such as bream and shell crackers were abundant in our lake. But it was the large mouths that were the supreme predators and rulers of the lake - and by far the most fun to catch. My father taught me early on to catch grasshoppers and worms along the shore to use as bait with a cane pole. Later I learned the grown-up methods of bait casting rods and artificial lures. Our *"go to lure"* was a purple or black plastic worm with a weedless hook. My personal favorite was a 4" silver *"Rapala"* - a fishy shaped contraption made of balsa, three sets of treble hooks, and painted silver to look like a minnow. If a fish so much as looked at it, it would get snagged by at least one of its nine hooks.

But in and around Brevard and along the Parkway, we learned that even the fish were different. What were these critters? The locals called them *"trout."* They didn't look, feel, or even taste for that matter, like the warm water fish we knew. And they were stunningly beautiful in their form and color. We also learned there was a unique breed of anglers that invested a lot of time and effort trying to catch them. They were called *"fly fishermen"* and we had only seen them previously in movies and books. In the mountains, we saw them all along the streams and rivers doing what all fly fishers love to do – *fly fishing!* We were mesmerized – especially my father – by the grace and precision of their casting, as well as all the special stuff they used and wore. Fishing for trout was dang sure different from fishing for warm water fish. Little did I know that fly fishing was in my future, with one big difference: I would start out fishing for largemouth bass and pan fish in our lake in Alabama!

My fly fishing life started when I was ten. After a trip to Brevard, I took $19.59 I had earned from selling pecans to Mr. Stokes' Sporting Goods & Bait Shop and purchased what would become the most important acquisition of my life up to that time – and perhaps ever. It was a 9', 6w, 2 piece fiberglass fly rod made by Garcia. It came with an auto rewind reel and weight forward floating line - and *NO* instructions! Mr. Stokes eyed me curiously and asked, *"Sam do you know how to use that thing?"* I probably should have answered - *"No I don't. But what the heck are you doing even selling fly rods*

All that's left of the *Stokes Sporting Goods* sign in Andalusia, AL where I bought my first fly rod. / *Image by Author / 2014*

17

down here in South Alabama?" Regardless, I'm grateful he had one in stock. Through lots of trial and error *(no YouTube)*, and my visual images of the fly fishers I'd watched in the mountains, I got pretty good at casting and placing my popping bug where I wanted it. It was kinda cool to be the only kid with a real fly rod in a world dominated by cane poles and Zebco 33s.

Fly fishing in the family lake was a great place to learn the craft. It was flat and open, and the water was not crowded with laurel and rhododendron. I would eventually come to love narrow mountain streams, but to learn basic casting technique, open space was a gift. I used a yellow popping bug made of cork, six rubber legs and black eyes. The large mouths couldn't resist them and would literally explode the calm surface to get to them. I learned that bass *"strike"* and later on that trout *"take"* – a big difference in the two! Other than perhaps sex, drugs and alcohol, for me there's nothing else like the anticipation, excitement and physical pleasure of the *"strike"* of a six pound largemouth bass on a fly rod. Even today I consider it the crack cocaine of fly fishing - you can't get enough of it! The pan fish were fun too, albeit less aggressive. Yet they made up for it in numbers. So it was in my family's lake where I became hopelessly addicted to fly fishing.

The watersheds around Looking Glass Rock in the Pisgah Ranger District of Pisgah National Forest near Brevard were the first waters the Author fly fished along the Parkway. / *Image by Author / 2019*

Fast forward about twenty years. After college I moved first to Alabama, then to Atlanta, and finally to Dahlonega, GA up in the North Georgia Mountains. It was there that my fly fishing took a turn from good to great. I had to re-learn lots of what I was accustomed to in the flatlands. In the small mountain waters, casts were shorter, bugs smaller and more varied, tippets smaller, terrain more rugged, waters colder, clearer and with lots of currents and drag and often dangerous. To top it off, the trout, not bass, were far less aggressive and much more elusive and finicky. Other than that, and the fact there were no water moccasins and lily pads, it was about the same.

As luck would have it, Dahlonega was the right place and time to shorten my learning curve. I joined several other more highly-skilled fly fishers to charter the *Gold Rush Chapter of Trout Unlimited.* The sharing of techniques and experiences accelerated my transition from warm water to cold water. Guys

The Author with members of the Gold Rush Chapter of Trout Unlimited working with the National Forest Service to improve trout stream habitat. / *Image by Author / 2014*

with names like Pat, Michael, Sherman and Chris are truly great fishermen and bug tyers and can literally catch trout in an asphalt parking lot. Not only did they help me perfect my craft, but I also made some lifelong friends – and they let me bum flies off of them! Today, Gold Rush has over 100 members and is very active in cold water restoration, preservation and conservation in the Georgia Mountains.

Eventually I began venturing beyond the waters located in *Chattahoochee National Forest* and *Pisgah National Forest* by heading up and down the Parkway to additional watersheds. Over the years, I've fished hundreds of Parkway waters along its 469 miles up into Virginia - most of them multiple times. Some of those waters I found completely by chance or even by mistake. In fact, there are some I probably couldn't find again with a firm set of coordinates and a military-grade, high-gain GPS. Yet I've only scratched the surface of what's actually out there. To tell you the truth, this Guide covers but a fraction of the actual waters on and around the Parkway that's available to fish. But in my opinion it does cover many of the best of those waters. You will find many others as you study maps, get yourself lost and explore the many highways and forest service roads that crisscross the lands on and around the Parkway.

I must admit here that I don't consider myself a great fly fisher. But I make up for that by simply doing what I have to do to catch a lot of fish, and by the style of fishing I engage in. That style has evolved into a passion for fishing adventure and exploration – not necessarily large sizes and quantities of trout. I tend to seek out the small, high-elevation, out-of-the-way streams around the Parkway that don't see a lot of humans. I'm a dedicated *"blue-line stalker"* and I love the challenge and excitement of going where most people consider it too small, remote and dangerous, or requiring too much effort to get there. That's where the fish I like to catch call home. And to top it off, the fish that live there are not big – six to twelve inches on average. When one of these trout comes to hand and our eyes meet for the first time, I want that fish to look at me and think *"Holy crap – what are you and where'd you come from?"* Not *"Okay you're the 4ᵗʰ dude to catch me today – you're going to let me go aren't you?"*

Often I get asked what type of rod I use. My choice is most often one of my twelve bamboo rods. Starting as far back as fifteen years ago, I've been involved in two bamboo fly rod enterprises. *Lacey & Johnson,* and now *Rubicon Bamboo Fly Rods.* At Lacey & Johnson, we made close to 300 *"Double L"* bamboo rods for L.L. Bean, scores of Granger rods for Wright & McGill Co., and dozens of others for collectors

One of the Author's favorite L.L. Bean *"Double L"* rods he uses for small stream fishing. / *Image by Author / 2014*

and anglers around the world. We still have scores of tapers for these rods that date back to the early 1900s, as well as a dozen or more for other master makers.

My *"go to"* rods are my Granger 7042 *"Deluxe"* (7'– 4.5 oz.), and my L.L. Bean *"Double L"* #764 *(7.5'- 4 weight)*. These are my favorite makers, and I have several models of each that I've crafted and some are vintage ones. I also have Sage and Orvis graphite rods like everyone else. But I prefer fishing something that grew halfway around the world, and someone spent 40 – 50 hours turning it into a piece of functional art. Bamboo makes me feel good on the water – that alone makes me fish better.

Putting my background, bamboo rods and gear aside, let me try to sum up this *Introduction*. The Parkway offers something for every fly angler. Lots of water and fish, big and small, easy and difficult access, yet as rugged and remote as your body, experience and guts will allow you to attempt. I hope you enjoy using this guide to find new fishing spots as much as I enjoyed writing it. Perhaps we'll meet on some remote stream one day – but I hope not! Make it a local brewery instead.

Tight Lines!

Understanding & Using This Guide

What it is, what it's not, how to get the most out of it...

This North Carolina Section is about "*where*" to fly fish along the Parkway – not so much about "*how*" to fish it. I assume you already know how to do that. After reading it, I hope it inspires you to plan a bunch of "*Indiana Jones Style*" Parkway fishing expeditions. You might start on the southern end at Mile Posts *(MP)* 469 in Cherokee or at its northern end at MP 217 at the NC / VA line, and work toward the other end while fishing each watershed along the way. Or you can just cherry pick your way up and down the Parkway. Your choice!

In either event, this chapter will help you to have a working knowledge of how to get the most out of this Guide. To that end, I've outlined below a few topics to help you understand how and why I've organized it the way I did.

How the Watershed Descriptions Are Organized

The descriptions of the selected rivers, streams and creeks along the North Carolina section of the Parkway are organized in a manner that allows for a quick scan of the information, or a deep dive inspection for greater understanding. With that goal in mind, I've meticulously organized each section's descriptions of the selected waters into a format designed to make it easy. The following topics will explain my methodology and help you use this Guide more effectively.

Four Parkway Sections in North Carolina

The Parkway's 252 miles in North Carolina are sub-divided into four (4) sections *(I, II, III & IV)* of roughly sixty-three (63) miles each - starting in Cherokee and matriculating up to the NC / VA line.

Section I: *MP 469 (Cherokee) to MP 406 (north of Mt. Pisgah)*

Section II: *MP 406 (north of Mt. Pisgah) to MP 343 (above where Hwy 80 crosses the Parkway below Crabtree Falls)*

Section III: *MP 343 (above where Hwy 80 crosses the Parkway below Crabtree Falls) to MP 280 (south of EB Jeffress Park)*

Section IV: *MP 280 (south of EB Jeffress Park) to MP 217 (NC / VA state line)*

Each Section's Cover Page

Each section's selected waters are described in a single long chapter that starts with a cover page. That cover page will list the section number, Mile Post *(MP)* range, a general description of that section, and the *www.wildbearings.com* website address. Hopefully starting sometime in 2020, a page on this website will list one *(1)* sponsored *motel, brewery, fly shop, restaurant* and *campground* for each section of the Parkway. This *"trusted"* sponsor list is offered for your planning convenience and may change over time based on user feedback and participation of the establishments. This will be a work in progress as sponsors sign up.

Each Watershed's Description

The waters included in each of the four sections are the selected public trout waters along that Parkway section. The main flow and its selected tributaries and many feeders are included for each watershed. In some cases, I took the liberty to include other waters within a reasonable distance of the Parkway.

Each watershed description starts by listing its most common and generally accepted name. As you know, river or stream names can vary between maps, signs or topos based on the document's age, who produced it, mistakes, local traditions, etc. So you may see some differences, but generally, I'm pretty consistent.

Following each flow's name, two categories of data will be used to describe it in detail – *"At a Glance"* and *"Overview & Description."*

~ **Each Flow's *"At a Glance:"*** Following each flow's name are the following *"At a Glance"* data categories that provide a snapshot overview of that flow. Those categories remain constant throughout this Guide for all of the selected main flows, tributaries or feeders:

Sam's Rank: Each flow's *"general appeal"* is ranked on a five (5) thumbs-up 👍 scale: with one 👍 being *Poor*, 👍👍👍 being *Average*, and 👍👍👍👍👍 being *Excellent*. This is purely subjective based on my gut feel of the quality of experience, access to the Parkway, access up and down the flow, topography, scenery and history of the area.

GPS Fixes: Coordinates for the source and mouth of each flow are provided to help with access. They were made using TopoUSA or Garmin MapSource software. They can be Googled or put into your GPS to pinpoint and navigate to a location. In most cases, they will put you within twenty-five feet of your target - unless I really messed up.

Size: The largest section of each flow, generally the mouth, is ranked on a *Small, Medium, Large* scale. This is subjective at best and depends largely on the type of flow being observed, the season, rainfall, as well as how I see it. It is for reference only.

Gradient: This is important – *so pay attention!* This is a measurement of elevation gain over a defined beginning and ending distance. GPS fixes are used for each point - usually source and mouth. It is stated as a % and is calculated as: *the elevation gain in feet, divided by the beginning to ending distance of the flow in feet.* For example: a one (1) foot elevation gain over a ten (10) foot distance = a 10% gradient. Percentages are described as: *Flat, Mild, Moderate, Steep, Extreme.*

Effort: Based on a flow's gradient, which in most cases can be between 1% and 25%, it's ranked as: *Easy, Moderate, Difficult* or *Extreme.* The gradient % range is used to distribute the ranking consistently. I'm in pretty good shape and can handle climbing and bushwhacking – I have to get to about 15% - 18% before I get stressed. You'll have to judge what you're willing to "*suck-it-up*" for.

Pressure: This is an indication of what you can expect to see on the water as it pertains to other anglers. This "*human compression factor*" is driven by a combination of several factors: the water's classification *(such as delayed harvest, wild, hatchery supported, etc.)*, proximity to roads and population centers, size of water, reputation, fish per mile, time of year, etc. Based on my experience, I rate them as: *None, Slight, Moderate* or *Heavy.* You're probably asking, why is there a "*None?*" Well… because some of the waters in this Guide are so remote and unknown, you might fish all day and never see another human!

Fishing Quality: This is another purely subjective judgment based on my gut feel of the quality of experience, access up and down the flow, types and populations of trout, # and size of trout caught, lack of pressure, etc. It's based on a *Poor, Fair, Average, Good* or *Excellent* ranking.

Species: As best I can, I will tell you the species I have encountered or those that are posted or otherwise documented by a reliable source, to be in the flow. And if you don't already know, you can count on it being one or all of the following, *Rainbows, Brooks* and *Browns. Duh.....!* If bass and pan fish are present, which is the case in rare situations, I don't mention them.

Access: Although the GPS coordinates are provided for the source and mouth coordinates I set for each flow, the best access point may *NOT* be obvious. I will suggest access points based on my experience using: *GPS fixes, Parkway Mile Posts, general descriptions and directions, etc.* Keep in mind there are other access points that may be better than those I suggest - these are just the ones I know. Use your map and study the roads, trail systems and topography to choose the best route for you.

~ **Each Flow's** *"Overview & Description:"* Based on my experience and notes, I start by giving a general overview of the flow's significance and history, and in some cases a bit of lore. Then, I'll summarize its overall headwaters to mouth flow. Finally, I'll offer a more detailed description of the flow from its mouth up to its source. This typically includes my own twisted sense of empirical and logical thinking in terms of the flow's: *size, depth, water qualities, substrate, tributaries, distances, past fishing results, etc.* I will also offer descriptions of waterfalls and other notable topographical features I found interesting. Places of interest, Parkway history / lore, local town(s), lodging, outfitters, breweries, camping, etc. are often mentioned as a matter of convenience.

A Few Disclaimers…

While pondering just what to include in this *"How To"* Chapter, I decided to heed the counsel of my crooked lawyer neighbor I'll call Bill *(cause that's really his name)* and offer some disclaimers. After all, he's witnessed me limping home from many a trip with cuts, scrapes, bruises, bites, dents in my truck, and even worse. So he advised me to offer a few disclaimers in case you arrive at the wrong watershed and get mad, fall off a cliff, slide down a waterfall and break your neck *(which I've come close to doing many times)*, or get chewed up by a bear. I am telling you now – it's not my fault! The subtitle of this Guide clearly states - *"An Almost Accurate…"* So… let me offer the following clarifications and disclaimers.

First, let's be clear, I'm not claiming this Guide includes every prong, branch, stream, creek, seep or river on or near the Parkway. For crying out loud there are thousands of them – there's over seventy-five miles just on the Parkway right-of-way alone. I'm including only the ones I've personally fished, or that I have firsthand knowledge of from a trusted source. The ones included were because of one or more reasons: *local popularity, personal fishing preferences, good access to the Parkway, ability to be fished, and most importantly, having good trout populations.* Many flows are out of the way, remote and danged hard to get to. Others are right on the Parkway. There's something for everyone. So make no mistake about it, there's probably a thousand more flows you can discover on your own.

Second, the watershed descriptions, as well as the other topics like hydrology, trout types and Parkway history, are not intended in any way to represent an academic or scientific explanation or study. That's for the professors, government agencies and others who call themselves experts. It's simply a compilation of my personal experiences studying the topics, fishing the region, as well as thousands of hours of driving, hiking and exploring, studying dozens of topographical maps, computerized mapping programs, satellite imagery, online sites and a plethora of other sources. In fact, I've spent enough time looking at maps to qualify as a semiprofessional cartographer. For most watersheds, I supplemented my thoughts with help of a few almost reliable fishing buddies *(if there is such a thing)*, local guides, residents of the watersheds, and interviews with National Forest Service, National Park Service, Parkway and other state and federal land, fish and game personnel.

Third, all elevation and distance computations, measurements and location point references were made using GPS coordinates. In most cases they were not made in the field with handheld GPSs, instead they were made in the comfort of my office using TopoUSA or Garmin MapSource software – occasionally whilst I was drinking a cold beer. Therefore, this data is as close as I can get using a computer - in most cases within five or ten yards or less. Some may be off a little due to the effects of alcohol or careless mistakes, but not by dang much.

Fourth, I took the good time and effort to include a chapter entitled *"Cautions & Precautions."* Read it! Many of these waters are in remote areas and most have at least some measure of danger. If you have not fished these water types, you need to be aware of what can happen to you or what can get you in the wilderness. Most of these situations have happened to me at least once, and include – snake bite *(1)*, spider bites *(7)*, lightning strikes *(1)*, bad falls *(a bunch)*, and nearly being seduced by naked nymphs & wood fairies *(no comment)*.

Fifth, I strongly recommend keeping a journal to record your experiences in each watershed so you can refer back to them. This will come in handy for the waters you decide to return to and fish again. For each trip, enter the dates, times, watershed, trout species, size, flies that worked, your impressions, etc. Then, when you're too old to do this anymore or your wife / husband or doctor won't let you, you'll have something to read and fantasize about as you sit in your Lazy Boy watching Wheel of Fortune. You *WILL* get too old to do this at some point…

Here's the long and short of this darn disclaimer business. The information in this Guide is not only what Sam says, it's a compilation of what a bunch of folks *(smart and not so smart)*, many official and authoritative, have to say about the topics. But in the end, it is Sam's personal description of what he saw, heard and studied, as well as what he chose to include. So get used to the idea that it's quite possible you may arrive on a stream only to find: *"this doesn't look at all like what he described in the book..,"* or *"this is a lot harder to get to than he said it was going to be.."* or *"it ain't here...."* or *"this was a heck of a lot harder to find than he said it was going to be..."*, or even *"where's the naked nymphs and fairies?"* Well, to that I say, I described it the way I remember it the last time I was there. Besides, if you do get lost you'll probably find another stream you'll like even better. Some of the best streams I've ever fished on the Parkway were ones I stumbled across while I was lost.

Fishing Legal

My neighbor Bill, the crooked lawyer, once again reminded me to inform you that there's no attempt here to offer any *"absolute guidance"* concerning the classifications, regulations or licensing requirements for any of the Parkway's individual watersheds. Why you say? It's simple – I've found out the hard way that regulations, classifications and licensing requirements, can and often do, change with the times. So in the end, it's your responsibility to ensure you're fishing legal. Be sure to check the fishing regulations for the federal, state and private land of each Section from time to time because Parkway waters can, and often do, eventually flow through all three.

As a regulation *"primer"* for the Parkway's waters, the overriding regulations are covered by Federal Regulations set forth in **Title 36, Sections 2.3 and 7.34(b) of the Code of Federal Regulations**. The following summary provides the *"basic"* requirements, considerations and precautions for fishing Parkway waters as of the writing of this Guide:

Blue Ridge Parkway fishing license requirements conform to those established by the State in which the water is located. A fishing license from either state, Virginia or North Carolina, is valid in all Parkway waters - no special trout license / stamp is required. Persons under sixteen can fish without a license when accompanied by a licensed adult. Trout water regulations are posted at the stream bank on most streams / lakes, and are in effect for that body of water only. Be aware that many Parkway streams enter U.S. Forest Service or private land and regulations will vary as jurisdiction changes. The fishing season and hours also conform to those established by each State, except that fishing is prohibited one-half hour after sunset until one-half hour before sunrise on all Parkway waters. Creel and size limits conform to those established by each state, unless the water is listed as "Special Waters." In those cases, they are listed in each State's regulations, as well as posted on a tree on the stream's bank.

Finally, to confirm your understanding and compliance with all Parkway fishing regulations, as well as those public and private lands around the Parkway, go online or visit a local outfitter or state / federal authority to inquire about what you'll need to fish legally on and around the Parkway. If you don't and get busted – *it's not my fault!*

The Blue Ridge Parkway

The incredible story of an amazing road...

> *"This immense river waters one of the fairest portions of the globe. Nor do I believe that there is in the universe a similar extent of country. As we passed on, it seemed as if those scenes of visionary enchantment would never have an end."*

Captain Meriwether Lewis - 1804

Those eloquently written words were Captain Lewis' thoughts as he and Clark made their way up the Missouri River in 1804. He was fascinated by what he was seeing. *The Corps of Discovery* was headed into uncharted and exotic lands where almost no white man had ever been – and even if so, didn't live to tell about it. It was a land that affirmed America's great expanse and potential - a land full of beauty, surprises, treasure and danger around every curve. *It was a voyage of discovery!*

At the risk of over dramatizing these opening thoughts about the Parkway, I must admit I closely identify with Lewis' words, even though he was talking about a river and the land it passed through, and I'm talking about a road and the watersheds it passes through. They are similar in that they both allowed access to wild and beautiful places. In a way, his words perfectly describe how I felt the first time I took a ride on the Parkway with my family.

As the youngest of three boys, I sat *"shotgun"* between my parents as we drove in the big Buick. I had a perfect, unobstructed view through the windshield and side windows of the scenes beyond. Nothing missed my eye. Every mile brought new scenes of visionary enchantment for a boy who grew up in the flatlands of

Alabama. The long views into the ranges, clear and cold rivers and streams, tunnels, cool and clear air, exotic mountain plants, animals and fish, and even the roadway itself – *especially the road* – offered endless opportunities for exploration and discovery. I must admit, I still feel that same excitement each time I'm on the Parkway. It never gets old – each trip is like the first.

In this chapter, I want to offer some insights about the Parkway and why it and its waters are so special. After all, to fully appreciate your time on the Parkway and its watersheds, you need an understanding of why it came to be, how it was built, significant features and facts about it, how it gets its

Early photo of a vacationing family enjoying the vistas along the Parkway. / *Image courtesy of the National Park Service & Blue Ridge Parkway*

waters and finally, its weather. Some of what I've written here has taken a lifetime to learn – in fact I'm still learning. Other aspects I've learned from the local mountain people, Parkway officials, knowledgeable friends, as well some good ol' pick and shovel research. Consider it my version of *Parkway Cliff Notes* or for some of my fishing buddies - *The Blue Ridge Parkway for Dummies.*

Birth of a Great Idea

The idea for the Parkway was largely the result of the Great Depression. It was an example of a terribly ill wind that ended up blowing some measure of good at a time when a struggling country desperately needed it. It was built at a time when the country was destitute. Nonetheless, millions of unemployed workers, including large numbers of building architects, landscape architects, engineers and skilled tradesmen, all needed work – and were willing to do whatever they had to do to earn even a modest paycheck. Poverty was widespread, and the masses were hungry and needed work as well. This created a huge pool of desperate skilled and unskilled workers who were available for public works. This was especially true in the Appalachians.

Additionally, Shenandoah National Park and the Great Smoky Mountains National Park, authorized in the 1920s and opened in the 1930s, were being promoted in an effort to bring national parks nearer to eastern population centers. Their openings actually did attract large numbers of citizens who wanted to experience the natural beauty of those regions of the country – even at a time when those regions were suffering severely in the Depression. Another factor at play was the newly invented and increasingly reliable automobile that opened the door to a new generation of vacationing public. The Parkway would connect the two parks with a roadway on which the public could use those new machines to explore. People were looking for affordable recreation to distract them from the hard times. As it turned out, they would flock to the Parkway to find it.

But ultimately, it would be President Franklin D. Roosevelt who became the catalyst that gave wheels to the project. In 1933, the President visited Shenandoah National Park and was impressed by Skyline Drive then under construction. Senator Harry Flood Byrd of Virginia suggested a mountain road that would extend

"Night Time on the Picturesque Blue Ridge Parkway." /Published by Asheville Post Card Co. / 1930-1945 / *Courtesy of the North Carolina Postcard Collection (P052), North Carolina Collection Photographic Archives, Wilson Library, UNC-Chapel Hill*

to the Great Smoky Mountains National Park. Ironically, a scenic drive along the spine of the Blue Ridge had been proposed as early as 1906 but had not been acted upon. Now, with the Depression underway and with the public's access to cars, the timing was perfect. Roosevelt jumped at the idea of linking the two parks with a scenic motorway, and at the same time, creating badly needed jobs in the region. It would in effect kill two birds with one stone. He endorsed the concept and on November 24, 1933, Secretary of the Interior Harold Ickes announced approval of the Parkway and $4 million was allocated to begin work. The project was originally called the *Appalachian Scenic Highway* but would eventually be changed to the name we know today.

For about two years, there was the usual turf protecting, bickering and negotiations in Congress over funding, how land for the right-of-ways would be acquired, routing, management, etc. Sounds like today doesn't it? The decision was finally made that the Parkway would skirt the crest of the southern Appalachians between the two parks. Virginia was a given. The real question was between Tennessee and North Carolina - which one would be included?

As the Parkway route was being studied, a nasty competition emerged between Tennessee and North Carolina – specifically the cities of Asheville and Knoxville. Both sides realized a lot was at stake since the Parkway would bring large numbers of tourists and economic benefits to the state that won. Finally, after the dust settled from North Carolina's and Tennessee's lobbying efforts, Secretary of the Interior Harold Ickes chose North Carolina for three reasons: First, the state already had two national forests *(Pisgah and Nantahala)* that could be used as the Parkway's corridor. Second, North Carolina was more scenic. Three, Tennessee had already been awarded several New Deal projects such as the Tennessee Valley Authority *(TVA)*. In effect – it was another state's turn! Consequently, the route for the project was selected with 217 miles in Virginia and 252 miles in North Carolina. Needless to say the Volunteer State was unhappy with his decision and turned their attention to NCAA Football instead.

After more wrangling it was also decided, then agreed to by NC and VA, that the required lands for the right-of-way would be acquired by each state, and they in turn would deed them over to the federal government. Other needed lands were also to be turned over to the National Park Service by the newly formed U.S. Forest Service. Initially funded under the Federal Public Works Administration and later pulling monies and labor from other New Deal Agencies, including the Resettlement Administration, the Works Progress Administration *(WPA)* and the Civilian Conservation Corps *(CCC)*, the Parkway became one of the New Deal's signature park development projects.

One can only wonder if the Parkway could ever be approved and built in today's highly-charged environmental, regulatory and political world. I frankly don't know. But, I'm so thankful the better angels of the politicians in the 1930's stepped up to the plate and did it!

Just one of a thousand scenes along the Parkway that will capture your imagination. / Northbound along MP 420.5 near Devil's Courthouse. / *Image by Author / 2001*

Constructing the Parkway

Work began on September 11, 1935, when about 100 workers cleared and graded land on Pack Murphy's farm on the VA / NC border. This began the Parkway's initial southern stretch of 12.5 miles down to Cumberland Knob. *(A construction timeline by Section is on page 44.)* Construction in Virginia began early in 1936. On June 30, 1936, Congress officially authorized the project as the *"Blue Ridge Parkway"* and placed it under the jurisdiction of the National Park Service.

Progress was painfully slow at first. CCC crews conducting the surveying reported the project would be much more daunting than originally expected. The lack of accurate maps, extreme weather conditions, rocky and high elevation terrain, snakes, apprehensive or downright hostile property owners, etc., etc., were just some of the barriers to contend with. To top it off, many of the local mountain roads needed to support construction efforts were no more than pig trails, incapable of allowing passage for the heavy equipment and personnel required to support the construction.

Dynamiting to clear the roadway. Notice the worker placing the charge is smoking a pipe. / *Image courtesy of the National Park Service & Blue Ridge Parkway*

Parkway engineers and designers, including North Carolina State Highway Commission location engineer R. Getty Browning, National Park Service landscape architect Stanley W. Abbott, and engineers from the Federal Bureau of Public Roads, laid out a route and took extreme measures to ensure that it protected and showcased the mountain vistas.

Stanley Abbott was selected as the Chief Landscape Architect for the Parkway. He proclaimed: *"The idea is to fit the Parkway into the mountains as if nature has put it there."* Therefore, the primary goal of the Parkway design was to build a roadway that would blend into, and be a part of, its natural surroundings. Those design efforts are very evident in what we see and experience today.

Construction took place in noncontiguous segments along the selected route as land was surveyed and purchased, right-of-ways approved, and the contracts

31

On the left, Devil's Courthouse Tunnel at MP 422 under construction in the mid 1950s. On the right, as it looks today almost 65 years later. / *Construction image courtesy of the National Park Service & Blue Ridge Parkway / Image of the current state by Author / 2019*

secured. Most of the heavy construction was carried out by private contractors with federal contracts under the oversight of Harold L. Ickes in his role with WPA. The WPA did some roadway construction, and crews from the Emergency Relief Administration carried out landscape work and development of Parkway recreation areas. Some work was carried out by various New Deal public works agencies. Personnel from four CCC camps worked on roadside cleanup, right-of-way plantings, grading slopes and improving area fields and forest lands. During World War II, CCC crews were replaced by conscientious objectors in the Civilian Public Service *(CPS)* program.

Progress was steady until World War II when funds were diverted for the war effort. By the time construction halted in 1943 for the duration of the war, work had been underway on about 330 miles of the road. However, only about 170 miles had been paved and was open to public travel. After the war ended, a large portion of the funding for the road's completion came from another federal park enhancement program named *Mission 66*. This program poured $1 billion into the national parks from 1956 to 1966. The construction pace picked up!

By 1968 the only section not complete was a seven mile stretch around North Carolina's Grandfather Mountain. In order to preserve the fragile environment on the steep southern slopes of Grandfather, the National Park Service agreed to design and build a 1,200-foot *"viaduct"* section - to be called the *Linn Cove Viaduct*. Considered an engineering marvel to this day, it exemplifies how with the right goals, planning and cooperation, a road like the Parkway can be made to blend with its landscape – not detract from it. Although most sections had already been in use for decades, the 469 mile Blue Ridge Parkway was officially dedicated on September 11, 1987 - fifty-two years after the original groundbreaking!

Topography & Route

The Parkway clings to the upper ridges of the ancient southern Appalachian Mountain Range – *reportedly the oldest mountain range in North America!* This range roughly tracks from southwest to northeast and spans the distance of 1,600 miles between Newfoundland in the north, to north Alabama on the southern end. The Appalachians were formed roughly 480 million years ago during the Ordovician Period. In many locations, exposed rocks reveal elongated belts of folded and thrust faulted marine sedimentary, metamorphic and volcanic rock, as well as slivers of ancient ocean floor which provide strong evidence these rocks were deformed during violent plate collisions. At one time, the range had elevations that rivaled the Alps and the Rocky Mountains before natural erosion took much of that height into the Atlantic Ocean. In the southern part of the range, down to the Piedmonts Plain and/or out to the Atlantic Shelf, the range consists of soft and curvy ridge profiles. Even with the erosion, the range provides some of the most rugged and remote topography in the eastern US. Throughout this route, the Parkway runs through a variety of environments and vistas with elevations ranging from 650 to just over 6,000 feet. The Parkway showcases that beauty perfectly.

Aside from the Parkway being designated a *National Park,* it is also classified as a *National Parkway,* as well as an *All-American Road,* and is the most visited unit in the National Park System. A narrow, carefully landscaped, corridor of some 88,000 acres flanks both sides along its route – with a right-of-way that's only 100 feet wide in some places. It holds the record for being the longest and narrowest National Park in the world. In

Richland Balsam at MP 431 is the highest point on the Parkway at 6,053 feet *(1,845 m)* above sea level. Often closed from November to April because of snow, fog and ice. / *Image by Author / 2019*

most places it is bordered by one of four National Forests: *Jefferson National Forest, George Washington National Forest, Nantahala National Forest* and *Pisgah National Forest.* Ironically, as a National Park, it dissects National Forests lands managed by the U. S. Forest Service.

For 469 miles the Parkway's route winds down the Appalachian Range through 29 counties of Virginia and North Carolina. At the northern terminus in northwest-central Virginia just east of Waynesboro *(Rockfish Gap)*, it adjoins the southern end of Skyline Drive – the roadway traversing Shenandoah National Park. It follows the crest of the Blue Ridge Mountains southwestward for almost 220 miles through Virginia, passing near Lexington and Roanoke, before entering North Carolina. From the state line, the route continues southwestward to Blowing Rock just south of Boone, and then continues southwest to skirt the eastern edge of

Asheville. About 35 miles beyond Asheville the road climbs to its highest point on the parkway just beyond Mount Pisgah to 6,053 feet above sea level. It then makes a sharp bend to the northwest before turning west and entering the Cherokee Indian Reservation, which it traverses before crossing the Oconaluftee River and terminating at the southern entrance to Great Smoky Mountains National Park.

Notable towns and communities on, or close to the Parkway in Virginia include Waynesboro, Roanoke, Lexington and Galax. In North Carolina it runs by Blowing Rock, Boone, Little Switzerland, Spruce Pine, Asheville, Brevard, Waynesville and Cherokee. Technically, none of these are actually on the Parkway. Little Switzerland, just a wide spot in the road – *but a nice wide spot*, would be the closest at a few hundred yards, with all the others being from a mile or two, to 10 or 15 miles away.

Linn Cove Viaduct appears to be levitated over the south face of a cloudy Grandfather Mountain. It was the last section of the Parkway to be completed before being officially dedicated on September 11, 1987 - fifty-two years after the original groundbreaking. / *Image by Author / 2016*

As already noted, the mountain ranges along the Parkway are some of the oldest in the western hemisphere, perhaps even the world, and the rugged topography is reflected in the efforts required to build the road. There are 26 tunnels that were laboriously blasted through 13,271 feet or 2.51 miles of solid rock along the route – those tunnels alone make for one heck of a ride. The topographical contrast between the Virginia and North Carolina sections of the Parkway can be understood empirically by simply counting the number of tunnels in each state – twenty five in North Carolina and only one in Virginia. Obviously, the ruggedness of the North Carolina end of the Parkway wins that prize. As discussed in later chapters, those topographical differences will also be reflected in the efforts it takes to fish the watersheds along the Parkway.

There are some 168 bridges and 6 viaducts to carry the Parkway across streams, railway ravines and cross roads. More than 200 parking areas, overlooks, and recreational areas allow for easy stopping to enjoy the vistas or hike into fishing waters. Hundreds of easements and agricultural use permits ensure pastoral views, as well as minimal residential development and billboards that would spoil the views. The Parkway's right-of-way has over seventy-five miles of mountain streams, and to enhance the natural beauty even more, planners built thirteen lakes and ponds that impound over sixty-six acres of water.

Parkway Tunnels - *South to North*				
13,271 total feet = 2.51 miles of tunnel				
#	*MP*	*Tunnel Name*	*Length*	*Height*
1.	466.3	Sherrill Cove No. 6	572'	14'– 4"
2.	465.6	Rattlesnake Mountain	410'	14'– 5"
3.	461.2	Big Witch	348'	11'– 3"
4.	459.3	Bunches Bald	268'	10'– 6"
5.	458.8	Lickstone Ridge	402'	11'– 1"
6.	439.7	Pinnacle Ridge	750'	13'– 10"
7.	422.1	Devil's Courthouse	350'	14'– 2"
8.	410.1	Frying Pan	275'	13'– 8"
9.	407.4	Buck Springs	380'	13'– 8"
10.	406.9	Little Pisgah	500'	13'– 10"
11.	403.9	Fork Mountain	350'	14'– 6"
12.	403.0	Young Pisgah Ridge	400'	14'– 6"
13.	401.5	Ferrin Knob #3	323'	13'– 9"
14.	401.3	Ferrin Knob #2	231'	14'
15.	400.9	Ferrin Knob #1	360'	14'– 2"
16.	399.3	Pine Mountain	1,320'	14'– 2"
17.	397.1	Grassy Knob	600'	13'– 7"
18.	374.4	Tanbark Ridge	746'	14'– 1"
19.	365.6	Craggy Flats	335'	14'– 1"
20.	364.4	Craggy Pinnacle	176'	14'– 1"
21.	349.0	Rough Ridge	245'	13'– 9"
22.	344.7	Twin Tunnel #2	409'	14' – 7"
23.	344.6	Twin Tunnel #1	240'	16'
24.	336.4	Wild Acres	240'	13'– 1"
25.	333.4	Little Switzerland	547'	14'– 4"
26.	53.1	Bluff Mountain	630'	13'– 7"

Details of the twenty-six tunnels along the Parkway. / *List compiled and formatted by Author / 2017*

Short side roads are used to connect to other highways *(Federal & State)*, and there are no direct interchanges with Interstates. Mileposts *(MP)* along the Parkway start at zero at Virginia's northern end and count to 469 at the southern end in North Carolina. Mileposts are short concrete white posts with the mile engraved on it and are on the right side of the south bound lane. The speed limit is never higher than 45 mph and lower in some congested sections.

Large sections of the Parkway are not maintained in the winter – as detailed in the following *"Climate & Seasons"* discussion. Many sections passing over high elevations are often impassable and are closed from late fall through early spring. Sections near tunnels are also closed in winter due to seeping ground waters and freezing temperatures that causes ice accumulation inside the tunnels even when temperatures are above freezing outside the tunnel. Gates are used to restrict access to the Parkway during these seasons.

Flora & Fauna

There are multitudes of habitats along the Parkway, ranging in elevations from 649 feet at the James River in Virginia, to 6,047 feet at Richland Balsam in North Carolina, that offer home to an enormous range of plants and animals. This range in elevation has a dramatic effect on habitat. Consider that the average temperatures in the Blue Ridge decline about 5.5° F with each 1,000 foot increase in elevation. For example, the Blue Ridge near Asheville is at an elevation of about 2,000 feet, and then it climbs to 6,684 feet just north of there at Mount Mitchell. In only eighteen miles as the crow flies, that elevation gain can create an average temperature decrease of more than 22°!

This temperature range along the Parkway produces a wide variety of habitats capable of supporting a huge diversity of forest types and animal species. This diversity would include everything from North Carolina to southern Canada if they all occurred at the same elevation as Asheville. So, elevation and latitude play a key factor in the plant and animal diversity on and around the Parkway. A complete description of both would take volumes, but below is a summary.

The Flora

You'll find out very quickly that the Parkway and its waters have no shortage of trees, shrubs, vines, etc. inhibiting your casting and your travel between those casts. Spanning the Southern and Central Appalachians, the Parkway offers an exceptional sampling of Appalachian

Turk's Cap Lilies bloom along the Parkway's higher elevations in the Summer. This one at about MP 432. / *Image by Author / 2019*

flora - which is known worldwide for its diversity and beauty. All in all, over 1,400 species of vascular plants, some very rare, are known to occur along the Parkway. Some feel this number is closer to 2,000 species. In addition, more than 350 species of moss and 2,000 species of fungi live there.

This range of plant life is the result of several interactive and dynamic factors, such as elevation, climatic variability, a large geographic range and a diverse geologic substrate. Additionally there are enumerable micro-habitats tucked away in obscure areas that are supported by a variety of location specific geographic and climate factors. For example, many high elevations rock outcrops contain a fragile

Spruce, hemlock, balsam, fir, laurel and rhododendron dominate the Parkway's higher elevations creating an Alpine feel. / *Image by Author / 2013*

group of alpine species that were pushed southward during glacial times and were eventually stranded in the mountains along the Parkway. Therefore, since the Parkway covers a wide range of habitats along the Appalachian's northeast – southwest directional orientation on the compass, a unique ecosystem is created where you might find the flora on a mountain summit in Virginia could be completely different from the flora of a mountain summit in North Carolina.

Trees are everywhere - over 100 species. Generally, lower elevation zones are dominated by pine, oak, hickory and tulip trees just to name a few. Middle elevations are covered with the likes of buckeye, poplar and ash, and the highest elevations are populated with a variety of spruce, hemlock, balsam and fir among a host of others. Trees near ridges, peaks, and passes or gaps, are often broken, gnarled and contorted by the wind, and by rime ice deposited on them each winter.

Flowering trees and shrubs are distributed up and down the environmental zones based on their preferred habitat, and include serviceberries, dogwoods, mountain ashes, flame azaleas, mountain laurels and rhododendrons just to name a few. In the fall these flowering trees and shrubs create a spectacular patchwork of colors over the landscape drawing huge numbers of visitors to the Parkway. During the spring through fall, large numbers of wildflowers bloom along the Parkway's right-of-way, on the hillsides and in meadows. While the summer wildflowers are blooming in the valleys, the spectacular spring wildflowers are just beginning to bloom on the high peaks. The additional Parkway traffic in the spring and fall should be considered as you plan your fishing trips.

The Fauna

A diverse critter population calls the Parkway's rich ecosystem home as well. As with the flora, that home is generally dictated by elevation, latitude, seasons, etc. In addition to the normal population of fauna, and thanks to the effective conservation management efforts of the regulating state and federal agencies, several animals that were hunted or trapped to near extinction from the region are now making a comeback. Beavers, elk, peregrine falcons and river otters *(I'm not crazy about that one.)* that were missing from the Parkway not long ago, can now be found in healthy populations.

In all, more than 50 species of mammals call the Parkway home and include white-tailed deer, beavers, ground hogs, black bear, otters, coyotes, bats, and rodents such as many types of squirrels - including those that fly, voles and mice. At times, anglers can see entire herds of elk grazing next to them while fishing the Raven Fork and Oconaluftee River at the extreme southern end of the Parkway – a spectacular scene.

A bull elk stands guard over his herd along the Oconaluftee River just off MP 469 on the Parkway. / *Image by Author / 2016*

Over 225 types of birds live, nest or rest during their migrations on Parkway lands – including falcons, owls, hawks and numerous song birds. Several rare species of birds nest along the Parkway including Appalachian Yellow-Bellied sapsuckers, Northern Saw-Whet owls, Cerulean warblers and now even Peregrine falcons. All have begun to nest again on or around Parkway land.

The Parkway's moist climate also supports over 50 species of amphibians - including 12 species of frogs and 43 species of salamanders – including the endangered and ugly as hell *"Hellbender"* salamander. The list goes on with about 40 species of reptiles including 20 species of snakes as well as timber rattlers and copperheads, 10 turtles – including the endangered bog turtle and snapping turtle, 8 lizards, and a bunch of others.

By now you're probably thinking, okay I get it with the trees, squirrels and salamanders, but what about the blooming *FISH?* Why hasn't he said anything about the *FISH?* That's why I bought this silly Guide in the first place. Well, just hold your horses a bit longer. I've got a little more to share with you about the Parkway. There's over 99 species of fish along the Parkway, and we'll talk plenty about three of them in a following chapter.

Climate & Seasons

Elevation, latitude and topography can cause Parkway weather conditions to be extreme and fast-changing. Seasonal transitions are unique in each elevation zone, and you can literally find yourself driving up a single mountain and see climate zones as varied as those from Georgia to Canada (*Ex. Asheville to Mt. Mitchell*). Summer temperatures seldom get out of the 80°s, and winter in the same spot can bring periods of snow and ice with single digits and / or below zero temperatures.

Rain and fog occur routinely throughout each season of the year. Rain is an almost daily occurrence in the summer, slacks off a bit in the fall, often becomes snow and ice in winter, and turns to rain again in the spring. Because rain typically falls on only one side of a ridgeline, from most any high ridge top, you can see multiple weather systems in a single long view. As we'll see later, these weather systems largely drive the Parkway's hydrology.

Fog is very common and can take the form of a blowing, thin smoky mist across the Parkway, or can be so thick and heavy you can't see ten yards ahead. Once I entered Devil's Courthouse Tunnel under blue skies, only to exit the tunnel in a fog bank so thick I couldn't see twenty yards down the road – not uncommon! A frequent view from the Parkway is when fog covers the lower valleys and the higher peaks appear to be islands in an ocean of clouds. It's magical! Let's examine some of the highlights of each season.

Welcome Springs

The end of winter can have a long overlap with spring's ability to "*spring*" on the Parkway. An abundant spring rainfall allows a tremendous variety of flora to grow quickly and thickly. March can be clear and cold and an occasional heavy snow should be expected. April can remain cool and is traditionally the wettest month of the year. In April you can experience rain, quickly followed by sunshine, then rain again and followed again by sunshine, all in the course of a few hours. Frost is often seen as late as May, but the days in May and June are typically warm with chilly nights.

The last stages of spring are signaled by the rhododendron blooms in June. Spring is a time of high activity on Parkway waters. The mild weather warms the water, insect activity becomes more frequent, and trout begin feeding on the surface much more. *Fishing becomes good!*

Mild Summers

Rainfall is an almost daily occurrence given the fact that much of the Parkway runs through temperate rainforests. Cold fronts are often followed by periods of sun, but the general rule is daily thunderstorms. Lower elevations can have temperatures in the high 80°s, while higher elevations will usually be in the low to mid 70°s. The highest elevations will stay chilly all summer because of the constant misty conditions with temperatures in the 50°s to low 60°s. Parkway lands typically run at least fifteen degrees below the lower elevations nearby. This is one reason why the Parkway has become a popular destination for vacationers and summer residents. It's certainly one of the big reasons my family started visiting there. Temperatures peak in July, and the forests are fully leafed out by late May or early June except on the highest peaks.

Rainbows are common sights after the almost daily Summer showers. / Above Blowing Rock on the Parkway. / *Image by Author / 2016*

Summer slows down the fly fishing activity due to several factors. Many lower watersheds begin to suffer from higher temperatures and the seasonal dry weather causes some flows to have less volume. As water volume drops and temperatures rise, oxygen saturation in the water is also lower. With the trout's metabolism and need for oxygen at a seasonal high, they will often slow down and even seek cooler and deeper waters to escape the stress. For the big ones, you'll need to stalk them and use a bit more finesse than other seasons to get them out of their bunkers.

Colorful Falls

Fall begins with temperatures starting to creep down into the low 60°s and 50°s in late August, and the daily rains start to slack off in

The vibrant Fall foliage along the Parkway can be breathtaking. / *Image by Author / 2016*

September. By October, temperatures drop and there may be frost or even light snowfalls. These cooler and dryer days signify the start of the fall color change which usually peaks the last two weeks of October. The leaves start falling in late October and early November. Late fall is the best time for ridge views because the skies are almost always clear due to low humidity. The air is cool, the rain is gone, and there are little to no leaves to obscure views.

Fall brings an increased level of trout activity along the Parkway. The trout feed uncharacteristically aggressively – perhaps because of the cooler water with its higher dissolved oxygen content, as well as their instinctive preparation for winter. As a rule, I don't fish the waters of the Parkway much between Halloween through mid to late December because the waters are clogged with hardwood leaves, which result in large amounts of tannic acid in the water and my bugs getting hung up on leaves. *Drives me nutty - and to drinking!*

Hard Winters

Depending on elevation, winter can come as early as late October or November on the Parkway, sometimes happening within the course of one day and with little warning. With colder temperatures and leafless trees, there are usually crisp long-distance views from the ridge tops and roadways. However, during the winter months, many sections of the Parkway, as well as many access roads, will be closed due to ice and snow accumulations in and on the tunnel faces, bridges and shaded curves. Additionally, road maintenance projects can sometimes cause long-term closures. If conditions allow however, the Parkway is open to vehicle travel.

Higher elevations can experience sub-freezing temps for weeks on end – often in the single digits and even into the sub-0 ranges. Snow becomes more and more likely as winter progresses, and the heaviest snowfalls can even occur in March. It's common along many Parkway sections for the first spring rains to

Winter can come fast and furious along the Parkway - often with virtually no warning. Near Mt. Mitchell. / *Image by Author / 2016*

overlap with the end of winter's snow and ice. Waterfalls, rock faces and cliffs can be covered in sheet ice from January through mid-March. Snow may cover the highest peaks for weeks at a time, with temps well below freezing.

Winter brings a significant slowdown in trout activity levels, as well as the human activity associated with trying to catch them. The colder water slows down trout metabolisms and causes them to become lethargic - which also reduces the amount of food they need to survive. They can become very picky during these times. However, on bright winter days, trout often move into the warmth of the sunny areas to do some feeding. This can offer some really rewarding fishing to the fly angler willing to brave the elements.

Parkway Hydrology

No attempt to provide an overview of the Parkway would be complete without a healthy dose of detailed talk about the waters on and around it. After all, this guide is about trout fishing, and the trout live in water. However this topic is way too important and broad in scope to include in just an overview. So… I've reserved a dose of it in the next chapter entitled: *Parkway Hydrology - A Macro View*. Stay tuned…

On the Soap Box

At the risk of coming across as overly political, which hopefully will not be interpreted as such, I'm going to make a few comments here out of my concern for the Parkway's future well being. Just because it has survived this long, about 83 years as of the publishing of this Guide, doesn't mean it always will. If you want to protect and conserve the Parkway for your kids, grandkids and their kids, consider staying abreast of the environmental, social and political issues that can and will affect it going forward.

In 2017, the Parkway had about 16.1 million visitors, nearly 1 million more than in 2016. It is one of the top two most highly visited national parks in the nation with attendance higher than Yellowstone, Yosemite and the Statue of Liberty – even more than the Golden Gate in San Francisco. In 2017, those Parkway visitors had a combined economic benefit to the surrounding communities of $1.4 billion. Yet this level of activity puts tremendous pressures on a Parkway's budget of about $16 million that must support its management, maintenance and improvements. This budget has been relatively flat now for several years. As of this writing, the Parkway budgets about $7 million each year for maintenance, yet it has a $517 million overhang in deferred repairs / maintenance projects due to a lack of funding. That can't be sustainable!

It takes around 276 employees, 151 permanent and 125 seasonal, to keep it managed and maintained. Because the Parkway is a national park, it is funded by the *Department of the Interior*, and those funds must be appropriated by Congress. With that being the case, it can and does fall victim to the same budget cuts, de-prioritization trends and political games as any other government agency. *And its budget is already razor thin!*

So this is not a Democrat, Republican, Independent, Conservative, Liberal or Progressive thing – it's actually about any and all of them, regardless of ideology, anyone holding a seat in Congress. They make the rules and set the budgets, and we elect them. Make sure your elected officials know your expectations concerning the funding of one of our most valuable national treasures - the Parkway. Just consider the math – *a $16 million Parkway budget drives a $1.4 billion "positive" trickle down economic impact in the region!* Looks like a hell-of-a good investment of tax dollars to me. Anglers have a lot at stake here. And if we don't make an effort to ensure the Parkway survives for future generations, at some point it might not. Get informed, involved and don't take it for granted...

Park Contact Information

Blue Ridge Parkway

199 Hemphill Knob Rd
Asheville, NC 28803

Website: www.nps.gov/blri

Phone: 828.348.3400

As of this writing, the above number is the Park Headquarters main line. A recorded information line at (828)298.0398 has the most updated information on facilities schedules, road closings, etc.

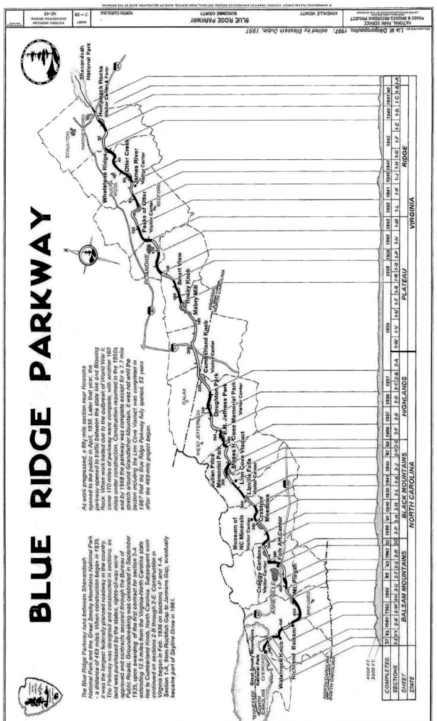

Parkway Construction Timeline / Historic American Engineering Record / National Park Service / Delineated by Lia M. Dikigoropoulou / 1997

Parkway Hydrology - *a Macro View*

How it gets water & what it does with it...

This Guide is about helping find and fish Parkway water. So what follows is my take on where all that water comes from, how it combines into the various flows, and the characteristics and features that make one flow superior trout water over another. This is not a scientific explanation *(although a good bit of science is in there)*, but rather a practical / logical explanation of Parkway hydrology. So don't go looking up *"Macro-View Hydrology"* in the dictionary because you won't find it - I coined the phrase to describe the broad-brush, 50,000 foot view I'll take.

Having said that, in addition to enlightening you on the characteristics and features of the Parkway waters we fish, I'm also attempting to help you be more interesting around the campfire - as difficult as that might be. Using words like *turbidity, gradient, pH, CFS, substrate, watershed, mean temps, etc.* will create an impression among your less enlightened cohorts that you're smarter than you might actually be. So this chapter is worth reading if for no other reason than that.

To put this hydrology discussion into perspective, it comes down to this: the Parkway was designed as a scenic drive and therefore, it runs along the ridgelines of the Appalachian Range. This puts it high above most of the surrounding lands. So what you might say? Well, it's all about the water, where it comes from, and where it goes – *and that's always downhill.* Consider the following…

The Source of Parkway Water

As you already know, the surface of this magnificent blue marble we inhabit is mostly water. The Parkway gets an almost endless supply of that wet stuff from the weather systems that pound the ridges along which it runs. Generally, those systems approach from the south-southwest out of the Gulf of Mexico and up through Alabama, Georgia, South and North Carolina, and to some degree Virginia. The systems work their way toward the southern face of the Appalachian Range while their air masses load up on moisture as they approach.

Clouds stacking up against the ridges and trying to get over the Parkway at about MP 271. / *Image by Author / 2011*

When these air masses finally reach and stack up against the mountains, they attempt to scale them. As they do, they are lifted up by the topography's increase in elevation. As they gain elevation, they begin to cool - as much as 3 - 5 degrees for each 1,000' above sea level. This cooling effect causes water vapor in the air mass to condense into clouds. As lifting continues, the on-going chilling effect causes the molecules in the air mass to compress. When a critical mass is reached, generally based on temperature, barometric pressure, saturation levels, or me washing my car for the first time in a while, the moisture is squeezed out of the clouds in the form of precipitation.

The heaviest precipitation usually occurs on the south faces of the ridgelines because each air mass has to dump its moisture load before it can get over the ridge. The faster an air mass moves and gains elevation, the more violent and dramatic its discharge of moisture and electrical charges from the clouds will be. These fast moving air masses are often the ones that bring heavy rains, accompanied by lightning and high winds. The slower an air mass travels, the more gradual and moderate its discharge.

There – that's all they taught me about mountain hydrology when I was learning to fly, and I haven't crashed due to weather yet – at least not a really bad crash where anyone got hurt. My explanation may not be absolutely scientifically accurate, but it's darn close. More importantly, you now understand why and how the Parkway gets as much rain as it does. So if you're still a doubter, look at it this way: In the end it comes down to one thing – *"does Sam catch fish or not?"* The answer to that is *"yes he does,"* and it's in large part because of my general understanding and practical application of knowledge about Parkway hydrology. There are many factors impacting an air mass that cause and accompany the scenarios above - but this is enough to understand the big picture. Now let's consider where all that water goes when it hits the surface around the Parkway.

How Parkway Watersheds Work

Now that you have the *"big picture"* of how the atmospheric component of the Parkway's hydrology delivers all that water, let's consider how that water combines to create the watersheds with all those fishy places I'm writing about and you're so anxious to find. Let me start by offering a simple and functional definition of a watershed. Basically a watershed is:

A land mass that separates and drains water into a common basin through a maze of small to large flows that collectively drain the landscape above it.

Simple enough! To make it relevant, ponder a body of water you're familiar with and apply the above definition until it makes sense. Now let's continue by illustrating how a watershed collects and organizes the water into various flows.

The *"Funnel Effect"*

As the ridgelines get pounded with rain, the water has to go someplace – *and again that someplace is downhill!* Aside from the obvious surface runoff we see after a rain, large amounts also just soak into the ground. Depending on the geology, water will permeate deeper into the ground until the zillions of tons of pressure from the mountain's sheer weight eventually squeeze it out again. This start as millions of seeps / springs oozing from under rocks, dripping off rock faces and ledges, or just moisture on the forest floor. The subsurface and runoff water flows downhill and joins other surface waters to gain volume as it loses elevation.

Along the uphill side of the Parkway you can see these small seepages running downhill toward and then under the roadway. They most often appear as dripping water off blasted rock walls, inside tunnels, soggy areas, or small water slides and cascades pouring through the underbrush. There they are collected by the Parkway's gutter or ditch system, piped under the road, and turned loose. Obviously, these seepages are everywhere – not just along the Parkway.

In other places along the Parkway, these seepages are hidden in draws and ravines after they work their way to the surface and eventually gather and run under the roadway. The volumes of these seepages are highly dependent on the rains. In wet seasons they can be deceptively large and then almost disappear during drier times. For this factor alone, the size of any trout living in these waters will be no larger than those that can survive the driest of times – which on average means small fish – if any at all.

As the seeps run down the mountain, a maze of ridge and valley features unique for each watershed create a "*funnel effect*" that gathers the water into low areas and combines it into larger flows. As these flows descend, they merge and coalesce into the small surface flows seen everywhere. The landscape's topo funnel efficiently drains huge tracts of mountain real estate based on its unique set of ridges and valleys. To complete the watershed, all you need are the countless trees, shrubs, grasses, mosses, etc., in a dense forest

Pinnacle Springs, just south of MP 354.4, is a typical free flowing spring supplying source water to the Left Prong, one of the two headwaters of the South Toe River. / *Image by Author / 2014*

and you have a pretty efficient ecosystem capable of supporting the watershed's terrestrial and aquatic life.

It's worth noting that as these waters cascade down the mountain they become infused with oxygen and are particularly clean and free of pollutants because of the elevations and lack of development around the Parkway. So by and large, as waters leave the Parkway, they are high, small, clean and cold – perfect for trout.

I find the small flows along the Parkway irresistible. I'm always looking at my GPS when driving, and when I cross a flow I can see, or even if I can't see it but it's showing on the map, I stop and check to see if it's fishable. I do this even when I'm not fishing, and it drives whoever's riding with me nutty. Over the years I've stopped at dozens of these small flows and searched up and down them like a bushwhacking fool for fishable water. Occasionally I come upon a larger than expected drop pool formed by some odd topographical formation that created a micro-ecosystem capable of supporting larger trout than the rest of the flow. These "*environmental islands*" often hold a nice trout or two fortunate enough, or unfortunate enough, to have been stranded there. That makes a stop worthwhile.

River, Stream or Creek… *which is it?*

Several years ago I was fishing with a friend in Virginia where the Parkway crosses the James River. While driving across the river I made the rhetorical statement: *"The James is a pretty good sized river."* He looked at me and with a snarky tone said: *"You call that a river?"* The debate went on for fifteen minutes with no resolution. It eventually reached the point where I considered stopping the car and making him get out and walk! I finally decided to take the comment with a grain of salt given the fact that he lives on the Mississippi River. His perspective of what is big and small, or a river or a stream, was altogether different from mine. And it showed me just how subjective defining a creek, stream or river can be.

What someone uses to describe or name one flow or the other is completely subjective since everyone has his or her opinion of what to call a body of flowing water. This is usually based on its size, signs, maps, local norms, and even the person's background - *like Mississippi Man*. For example, one person might look at a flow and call it a *stream, prong, branch* or *run*. I'd look at the same flow and call it a *creek*. Then there's the problem of differentiating between a *large creek* and a *small stream*, or a *large stream* and a *small river*. When is a branch a *branch* instead of a *prong*? When does a *creek* become a *stream* – when does a *stream* become a *river*? Who the heck knows? More importantly, aside from academia, at this point what difference does it really make?

To get us on the same page, the names below are those I use to describe the basic types of *"mountain"* flows along the Parkway. I'll use them consistently throughout this Guide. I'll start at the top of a watershed and work down:

- *Seeps:* high or low elevation, subsurface oozes to small trickles from rock faces and out of steep topography
- *Springs:* high or low elevation, free flowing subsurface trickles to small finger sized flows out of the ground, rock face and steep topography
- *Creeks:* high or low elevation, very small to small *(2' – 8' typically)*, shallow free-flowing surface water typically originating from thousands of seeps and springs
- *Streams:* mid or low elevation, small to medium *(8' – 20' typically)*, shallow to moderate depth, free-flowing surface water typically originating from one or more creeks *(feeders)*
- *Rivers:* typically low elevation, medium to large *(20'+)*, shallow to deep, free-flowing surface water typically originating from multiple streams and creeks *(tributaries)* that form a network of headwater flows capable of combining and forming the river

Classifying flowing water by size is simple in concept and print. For example, rivers by definition are large, streams are smaller, and creeks are smaller still. However, real-time classification in the field is difficult because location, geology, flow rate, etc. can be so different – and subjective. Creeks, streams and rivers can be small to large, long or short, steep or flat, shallow to deep, different in most every way – yet so much alike in so many respects. However, seeps and springs are unique in that their characteristics are more standard from one to the other. At this point, I'll assume you have a mental picture of what a small, medium or large river, stream or creek looks like and how they form inside the watershed. That's darn good enough to catch fish and communicate with cohorts.

In the end, the watersheds along the Parkway combine into segments of about 1,000 rivers, streams and creeks along the Parkway's 469 miles. Actually, I've counted over 1,250 based on my above definitions. Joined together, these waters drain into 14 major watersheds along the Parkway flowing either to the Atlantic or the Gulf of Mexico. The Parkway sits at the headwaters of most of these major watersheds, and one could argue the Parkway's waters largely define the hydrological patterns of much of the Southeast. Now let's consider the traits of the flows within those watersheds.

Traits of the Parkway's Water

When I look at a body of water along the Parkway, I naturally observe and evaluate a set of *"personality traits"* that describe flow, look and feel - and ultimately the ability to support a trout habitat. Those traits combine to create a unique personality for each flow. Again, this view is not purely scientific, but it makes perfect sense to me and has served me well over the years.

As you read the following explanations of these traits, keep in mind they can and do change as you move along a watershed. One or more can be found along the course of any flow at any elevation. You might even find all of them on the same flow. To confuse things even more, I've seen the same place on a flow have different traits the next time I fish it because of seasonal or environmental factors like rainfall, ice blockage, leaf clogging, fallen trees, landslides, etc. The medical profession has a diagnosis for this multiple personality condition – *schizophrenia!* Consider how the following traits can cause any flow to be schizophrenic.

Water Volume

This is a measure of how much water is flowing through an imaginary plane across a flow from bank to bank. It can be measured scientifically with fancy in-stream equipment that registers flow volume in *Cubic Feet per Second (CFS)*. The data is converted into various charts and graphs and then translated as *high, medium & low* for people of average intelligence like me. I can then interpret it as: *dangerous, normal,* or *safe, etc.* The data is then stored and studied by very smart people and used in all kinds of ways to better mankind.

Whenever you feel the urge to get scientific, many Parkway waters have flow measuring stations that collect and transmit flow metrics to a centralized site where they are archived and made available to the little people like us. This data is particularly useful in rainy or dry periods by allowing you to check before a trip and save a lot of wasted driving and hiking time. Check the websites of the agencies with jurisdiction over the waters you're fishing.

Another method is to use your built-in *empirical flow volume gauge* that's based on your tolerance for risk of bodily harm – *as in drowning*. In fact, most of us can look at a flow coming out of its banks and measure it as *"Dang, that water is crazy **High** – I'm sure as heck not getting in it – let's go drink a beer and wait!"* Or, we might measure one flowing well below what we normally see as *"Holy cow... that water is dang **Low** – poor trout!"* Or, if it's what we consider normal, we measure it as *"That looks pretty darn good (**Medium**) – last one in's a rotten egg."* As for scientific or empirical measurements, the latter is usually accurate enough for me for the medium to small waters of the Parkway.

Parkway waters tend to be medium to small in size with headwaters sourcing in the higher elevations of relatively large watersheds. Heavy rain coupled with the *funnel effect* gathers massive amounts of water into the creeks, streams and rivers. High water can cause gravel beds to shift around and disrupt or kill insect life. Many trout stress or die because they aren't able to find protection from the current. For instance, thunderstorms can dramatically and quickly raise volumes to the point that it's dangerous to fish. Long periods of slow drizzle can have the same effect, but not as fast. And, it can last longer because the ground is saturated. In either situation, avoid high water by heading up stream to the flow's source. This is the location where the flows will return to normal levels first.

On the flip side, dry and warm periods can cause water volumes to be excessively low and can also have a dramatic impact on trout and bugs. The most life *(fish & bugs)* a flow is capable of supporting is directly proportional to its minimal flow throughout the year. It makes no difference if the flow volume is low for only a week. The largest fish that can live in that flow in normal flows will be the largest fish that can survive for the week the flow is at its lowest level. Remember, these waters are not large in comparison to others you might fish and wet and or dry conditions impact their flows in a non-linear fashion.

When fishing the Parkway waters, I have learned that there's a happy medium between low water, enough water, and too much water. Too much water makes it difficult for me to find fish because they're trying to hide and / or stay out of the current. Too little water, especially in higher temperature seasons, creates a situation in which trout become stressed and oxygen-starved. Bad fishing! Just use your *"empirical flow volume meter"* and find water with acceptable flows – *then have at it!*

Terrain Gradient

Barring an earthquake, gradient is an unchanging measure of the steepness of the topography over which a flow passes as it heads down through a watershed. It is perhaps the primary factor impacting the many variables that define a flow's personality. It's usually measured as *degrees* or *per cents* calculated as: *# of feet of drop / distance*. The resulting % or degree can then be interpreted as: *flat, mild,* *moderate, steep* and *extreme*. This interpretation obviously influences how most fly anglers select fishing destinations based on the gradients they can physically endure.

In higher elevations toward the source, the rapid fall in elevation often creates an *extreme gradient* which allows water to drop with considerable speed and force where it can erode the substrate away to stone. The faster it falls the larger the material that forms its features. Severe gradient, high elevation Parkway streams will typically be characterized by fast water, falls and large boulders of many different sizes and shapes. *Moderate gradient*, mid elevation waters are characterized by slower flows, drop pools and a bottom composed of a wider variety of materials including large rocks and slabs, pebbles, sand and a few scattered boulders and large stones. In the lower reaches, *low gradient* waters have the least drop and the flow will be much slower with less ability to keep particulates suspended in the flow. This allow for the accumulation of the finest bottom materials such as sand, mud, decomposing bio matter, etc. – *in some cases, not the best for trout fishing!*

My experience on Parkway waters is that gradients can vary from the extreme of 20% to 28% in high elevations to as little as 1% to 5% in lower elevations. Generally, you can expect gradients to be steepest *(Extreme)* at the higher elevations, begin to flatten out *(Moderate)* in the mid ranges and be the least *(Flat)* in the foothills where the flow starts moving into valleys. You'll be surprised the number of flows around the Parkway that will have the full range of gradients.

Substrate & Obstructions

This simply refers to the type of materials on the bottom / bed of a flow *(or in it)* that water flows over or must go around. To this point, the Appalachians are about 480 million years old and over time natural forces of erosion have exposed belts of folded and thrust-faulted sedimentary, metamorphic and igneous rock in a variety of formations along many watersheds. These exposed areas can include slab rock, large / small boulders, large rocks / pebbles, etc. in an almost endless combination.

The majority of the flows around the Parkway are referred to as *freestone* water. The term freestone originates from the fact that the water flows over gravel, rocks and rubble on the bed of the flow – *the substrate*. The bed is the result of erosion. As that erosion takes place, rocks and gravel become polished and rounded. They are thus able to move around *"freely"* making them *"free stones."* The size, composition, number, and shape of these stones, as well as the gradient and volume of the flow will in large part determine a flow's personality.

Additionally, sand and mud can also work their way into the substrate – especially in lower elevations where water speeds are slower and sediments are dropped. Bad land management practices can get in the mix here too. Add to that the various obstructions like boulders, dead falls, leaf dams, etc. that cause flows to divert and eat away the substrate or riparian zones, and you have a set of factors that define a flow's personality.

All in all, you will find a wide variety of materials on the bed and in the flows of water you'll be fishing. Each one has its own advantages and disadvantages in how it affects the flow's personality, the trout's needs, as well as your ability to traverse it. Generally, I have found slab rock, boulders and gravel to be the most abundant substrate in the higher elevation Parkway waters I fish the most.

Flow Features

How the water of a river, stream or creek flows and interacts with its environment is based on several factors. These include the rate of descent or angle of the bottom *(Gradient)*, the amount or depth of the water in the flow *(Volume)* and finally, the material making up the flow bed or obstructing the flow *(Substrate & Obstructions)*. These three *(3)* factors interact to cause a flow to slowly erode its way down the mountainside in a series of bends and curves that conform to the topography. As a flow forms its course, it tends to repeat certain features that cumulatively affect the personality of the water in different ways. Those features ultimately affect if and / or how fish hang around and behave.

The water comprising the flows of the Parkway can be described as a set of eight *"classic"* water flow features – not unlike those of any flowing mountainous water. However, as easy as it is to categorize and describe them in print – or in our mind for that matter – they are not so easily recognized or perfectly placed in the watersheds. Nevertheless, understanding them will help you find and fish them better. The following are the classic mountain flow features on the Parkway's waters in ascending order of turbulence.

~ *Flats:* These can range from water that's flowing fast and shallow over a slightly uneven bed, with a slightly choppy surface, to those that are deeper and have a glassy smooth surface. But given the same size of flow, flats are generally about the same depth as riffles and shallow runs – 1' or 2' to more than 5' or 6' deep. The smoothness of the surface is a reflection of a substrate that lacks the bigger rocks and obstructions. The slope of the bed is not steep, so the flow will not be as fast. And, the substrates are typically smooth and composed of sand, silt, small rocks and gravel. Although the surface often appears to be slick, there's always at least some small surface current – but not much. Just enough to mess you up!

The relatively slow flow of most flats allows many to develop aquatic vegetation around their edges. These beds create an excellent habitat for all sorts of bugs. When this occurs, this alone makes them attractive places for trout to hang out. However, because of the slowness of the water, deceptive currents causing bad drifts, overly cautious trout, etc., flats can prove to be some of the most challenging places to fish.

~ *Runs:* This is moderate to deep water flowing evenly over a bed substrate that often tends to be slab, bedrock or sand or silt. The surface is less choppy and constant flowing. The speed of the water is slower due to the gradient not being as steep. Typically, a run's surface is unbroken. Where obstructions do break the surface or the bed's structure is so close to the surface that it boils the surface flow, there will usually be some surface choppiness. But generally the characteristic smooth substrate of a run will be reflected with a calm surface. I've observed that most runs begin with a riffle at the head and gradually slow down and deepen as it moves downstream.

A run can be from just 1' to 2' deep to 6' to 8' depending on the size of the flow. Depth and length are usually dictated by what the flow volume is capable of supporting. You will find more medium to large rocks than big boulders that are present in riffles. These smaller obstructions break the current and provide holding areas for trout. Because of this protection, trout will hold behind these obstructions or in the boundary water off the bottom of these runs even when there's no food available.

~ *Riffles:* These involve stretches of streambed that are rough or cobbled on the bed *(substrate)* yet shallow enough for this bed's roughness to be transferred or reflected to the surface. These flow features are typically 1.5 - 3 feet deep and have a relatively fast flow. When you approach a riffle, you first notice the choppy surface. The degree of chop depends on the size of the rocks or other

This twenty-five foot riffle on the East Fork - Pigeon River offers trout an excellent place to hold and feed while offering anglers a fine opportunity to catch them. / *Image by Author / 2016*

obstructions on the bed, the depth of the water, and the slope of the bed's surface. Because the bed must have a slight descent, water can flow rather quickly. In fact, some riffles are so steep they cause the water to flow so fast and shallow that trout can find it difficult to hold in them.

However given the right conditions, riffles can be among the richest areas of any stream because of the large amounts of oxygen they generate and the aquatic insect life they stir up and deliver into the water column. You will almost always find trout holding downstream of a riffle overdosing on the oxygen and feeding on the insects being delivered. When trout are in a riffle, they typically hold where they can find an obstruction or when there are so many insects from a hatch that is worthwhile to leave a holding lie and fight the current. In that case, the trout will usually be on the bed's boundary water – about 4" to 6" off the bottom. Fast and shallow riffles that lack obstructions to shield the trout from the current rarely hold trout for any reason.

~ *Pools:* In some areas a flow will slow down, deepen and spread out. Pools are created by the natural gouging out of the substrate by the water over eons, or in some cases just the natural topographical profile of the land. They are most often deeper than the waters above and below them and are usually the deepest part of the entire flow. In a small creek, a pool might be a few feet deep and 5' wide by 10' long. In a larger stream, pools can be 6' to 10' deep and 20' or 30' wide and a hundred feet long. In a river, a pool can be 15' to 30' deep and too wide and long to reach other than by boat.

The flow of a pool is usually slow and can sometimes appear to stop altogether. Where the current tongue enters the upstream end, the surface can be choppy and fast, with eddies spinning off to the side. However, the main pool body and exit point will be smooth. Because of the slow water the bottom tends to get loaded with fine sediment, leaves and sticks. Some large permanent features like boulders and logs are common and give trout a place to hold.

Because these features typically create larger waters, the ecology can support more and larger insect and bait fish the trout feed on. Some of the largest trout you will encounter on a section of water will be hunkered down in these pools. That's because there's more space and food and it's easy to hold because of the slow water. But trout like pools for another reason too. When they get spooked, they will seek the protection offered by the deeper waters of a pool. I find the entry-current tongue and side eddies, as well as the exit to be most productive water to fish. The smooth water of the main part of the pool is less productive as a rule.

~ *Drop Pools:* This is my favorite flow feature – especially ones where the pool is waist deep. After sneaking up to and fishing the pool, stand in it and fish the water entering from above while remaining mostly hidden. These features combine a small falls and a pool to form a perfect holding spot for trout – especially in small streams. Many small, high-elevation flows are a series of one drop pool after the other. The falls offer cover and extra oxygen, and the pool provides room to move around and feed. Fish the exit of the pool first, next the dark water at the base of the falls, and finally the water above the falls.

A classic drop pool on Rockhouse Creek near Looking Glass Rock offers excellent fishing. / *Image by Author / 2011*

~ *Slides:* In my opinion, slides are some of the most interesting features found on Parkway waters – or any waters for that matter. These are simply exposed bedrock substrates the flow *slides* over for long distances. Water depth is often no more than a few inches to less than an inch. These features can be from just 10' or 15' long to more than 50' or more feet. Other than swirl holes that may be found in them, these features are almost always fishless simply because there's no place for trout to hold. They should always be approached, ascended or descended with caution as they can be dangerous.

Perhaps the most notable slide on the Parkway is *Sliding Rock* on Looking Glass Creek running along Hwy 276 near Brevard. It's about 100' long and 30' wide and has a fine pool at the bottom that's full of 6" to 10" rainbows and an occasional Brookie. A few hundred yards downstream from Sliding Rock are several other lesser known slides that are just as impressive - each with fishable pools at the bottom and no crowds. Many times I've seen small trout squirming their way from the base pool to the top in their efforts to get up stream. It's interesting to watch trout swimming 50' up a rock slab in an inch of water or less. Banded water snakes have learned to take advantage of this upstream migration and can be seen hanging out on slides taking small trout with ease.

~ ***Rapids & Cascades:*** Both of these are closely related. A *rapid* will result from a sudden downward tilting of the substrate which creates a steep gradient the flow must pass over. They are typically littered with rocks, boulders and ledges and a significant increase in the speed of the flow. *Cascades* on the other hand are composed of a series of rapids strung together. Both of these features are difficult places for trout to hold and survive. They will use them only as they pass from one section of the water to the other. But both rapids and cascades produce lots of oxygenated water and often contain obstructions large enough to deflect the current and cause eddies to form. The eddy is by comparison slower water and trout can and will hold there to rest or feed.

~ *Falls:* Parkway watersheds are littered with vertical *(or dang near vertical)* flows with drops from heights that vary from just a few feet to thirty of more. Most of these features are not on the map or on a tourist *"must see"* list. They are hidden away in the backcountry where they are rarely viewed by anyone other than anglers and hikers. Apart from their beauty and the pools underneath them that hold fish, they are useless. I've yet to catch or even see a fish caught in a waterfall's falling water along the Parkway. I reckon the bears in Alaska are the only ones that can do that - although I bet even they couldn't do it with a fly rod. Always approach a falls with caution and go around them if possible.

Waterfalls of any size, especially large ones like Looking Glass Falls, offer productive fishing. The Author approaching and fishing the falls with extreme caution. / *Image by Author* / *2013*

The pools under falls are great habitats and should always be top fished and bottom dredged as a matter of habit. These pools typically hold more and larger fish because the fish tend to congregate there for several reasons. The volume and depth of the water offers cooler temps in the summer and provides more protection than the shallows. Additionally, the richly oxygenated water provides the trout with an oxygen-high buzz and the slower water flows of the pool allows them extra time to target and eat unsuspecting bugs coming over the falls. For all of these reasons and more, the pool under a falls should be top fished and dredged with reckless abandon.

Canopy

Fishing Parkway waters can be frustrating because of the wide variety of trees, shrubs, vines, etc. that overgrow and crowd its waters. This overgrowth can range from completely open overhead and sides, to partially covered, to completely covered. You'll also find that as the flow gets smaller and the overhead space closes in, the bank's vegetation will close in as well. If I had a dime for every time I've hung my dropper, and often my dry fly too, in the bushes around these waters, I'd be very rich. The stress required to get my bugs out of the bushes has caused me to use language that would make a wounded pirate blush.

The canopy and side flora density can be a challenge along many of the Parkway's high elevation flows. / *Image by Author / 2011*

Yet in the larger sense, aside from the problems of dealing with it while fishing, the canopy of hard woods and conifers contributes to the quality of the waters in terms of shade, temps, nutrients, protective cover, insect habitat, etc. As you might expect, the sources of the small high elevation waters will typically have the densest canopies. They'll be totally covered in many stretches with thickets of laurel, rhododendron, dog hobble, etc. Sometimes it's so thick you can hardly crawl through them. In fact, many old-timers in the region would call the laurel and rhododendron thickets *"Hell Thickets"* because they were so thick and tangled that it was like *"hell"* just trying to get through them.

As you work your way down the mountain and get on slightly larger waters, you'll find the canopies opening up. However, the additional light may also result in excessively large and intrusive shrubs that can crowd the banks and grab your bugs. The only permanent relief comes in the larger waters of the lower reaches of a watershed where the canopies open up really wide. Regardless of the elevation and water type, you just learn to watch your back cast and deal with it.

Water Quality

A flow can have all the positive personality traits mentioned above, but if the water is bad, it's useless as a sustainable trout fishery. Generally, Parkway flows have good / excellent water quality. One exception is the high acidic levels *(Low Ph)* caused by acid rain found in some higher elevation flows. This is the same acid rain that has helped devastate balsams and other conifers in many high elevation locations along the Parkway – Mount Mitchell being a prime example.

Water quality is generally a byproduct of all things on, or happening to, the watershed - especially the riparian zones - the narrow strips of land bordering a flow. In short, water quality cannot be separated from the quality of the overall watershed from which it flows. What follows is my layman's take on some of the basic components that define the Parkway's water quality:

~ **Chemistry.** There's a lot of technical data and explanations that could be included here – more than we could or should cover, even if I were a chemist, which I'm not. What is included are a few of the basic water quality components that will help you understand Parkway water chemistry:

   Alkalinity (pH): This is a measurement of how acidic the water is - a major factor in water's ability to provide a trout habitat. Here's the short of it; a pH of 7.0 represents neutral acidity. The more acidic the water is, the lower its pH and the less fertile it is for the entomology and the fish that eat them. For example a pH range of 6.7 – 6.0 and below is considered *less than optimal* for bug and trout production – although brook trout seem to be more tolerant to these levels than browns and bows. The higher the pH, basically the more calcium is present to lessen the acidity, the lower the acidity levels, the more conducive it is for a vibrant aquatic habitat. A pH in the range or 7.1 – 7.8 is generally considered well within that which is considered acceptable for a productive trout habitat, and the low to mid 8's can be even better. Parkway waters in both NC and VA fall mostly within these ranges.

   Rain water, or run off groundwater, is generally more acidic *(low pH)* than spring water – therefore less productive for insect life and eventually the trout that feed on them. On the other hand, spring water that has leeched through calcium rich substrates is less acidic *(higher pH)* and is usually more highly productive for bug development. Limestone *(calcium)* enriched waters carry the most usable nutrients for plant life resulting in their richness along all the links of the food chain that lead to trout production.

   Oxygen (O2): A basic need of trout is a continual source of highly oxygenated water. Although trout can survive in a range of 5 – 6 ppm *(parts per million)* of dissolved oxygen, a range of 8 to 12 is their sweet spot. Water that's constantly falling and churning over rocks infuses itself with lots of O2, and if it is cold water, it's also dense and can hold even more O2

– lots more than warm water. As a rule, NC and VA Parkway waters do a pretty good job of meeting the oxygen needs of its trout because of the rugged topography and low water temperatures in their watersheds.

It's also worth mentioning here that in the warmer seasons when water temperatures rise, a trout's metabolism will increase also, and that creates a nonlinear increase in oxygen demand. The inverse is true as temperatures drop and the trout's metabolism slows down, the demand for oxygen also decreases. So in warm weather, be sure not to over play your catches because it can put them at risk of a fatal oxygen deficit. Even after a short play, trout can actually die from the stress of oxygen deficiency.

Nutrients: Trout also need a constant source of nutrient-rich water in which to grow. These nutrients are the basic building blocks of life in a flow, and the NC and VA Parkway waters, with rare exception, do a reasonably good job of delivering a healthy dose of these life-giving substances to trout. Some of the high-elevation waters are the exception with their acidic *(low pH)* levels that interact and reduce the benefits nutrients provide.

Nitrogen, carbon, oxygen, calcium, and a variety of other trace elements, are all suspended in the water as it seeps through rock and earthen layers before it enters a flow. These elements are also *"recycled"* back into the water as a result of the decaying vegetation from the flora that stands guard over the waters. Plants absorb these nutrients from the soil and water. Then, the bugs feed on the plants, and they eventually become trout food. But it's the calcium that is especially important as one of the critical nutrients that impacts pH and affects bug development. It's the element so many waters south of the Parkway lack that prevents healthy entomology populations.

~ **Temperature.** We know how important oxygen is to trout - but so is temperature. Ironically these two components are closely related in how they interact to impact a fishery. As mentioned above, cold water holds more oxygen and this fact alone influences trout populations and behavior in a positive way.

Generally, you'll find trout most active in a water temperature range of about 45° to 65°. They'll be more active in the middle temps and less so in the extreme ends of the range. Much of their activity is feeding related because the insects they eat emerge when temperatures get into the upper 40°s and peak at between 50° and 60°. This explains the temperatures at which trout are most active because those are the times when they have the most to eat.

In reality, trout will selectively feed at 40° and below. But their ability to find food depends on the availability of bugs, and hatches are just not as plentiful below 40°. So a trout's feeding really slows down in water that's below 40°. Given the lack of food at these temperatures, as well as the fact that colder water also lowers the trout's metabolism, it's been my experience that fishing water below 40° is not very worthwhile.

So then what about high temperatures you ask? All trout start to stress when temperatures get much higher than about 70°. Rainbows and browns can survive in water as high as 80° - only if the water is sufficiently oxygenated. But even then, they become very lethargic and selective. Brookies can't get much above 75° or so before they belly up.

Whenever temperatures or oxygen levels get uncomfortable, all three species will search for better places to hang out. That can mean finding and holding at a cold ground spring, the confluence of a colder tributary, a deep pool, downstream from turbulent water that is more highly oxygenated, or in some cases even migrating upstream toward the headwater to find cooler water. A fact to keep in mind is that during higher water temperatures, you will typically find trout in and below riffles and rapids that are infusing the water with extra oxygen, even though the temps are above the trout's comfort zone.

Water temperatures along the Parkway, or any waters for that matter, will trail the *"mean"* daily air temperatures of the area by couple of days. This is because it takes water longer to warm up – or cool off. Simply put, trout waters reflect the mean temperatures of a day or two ago – a delayed effect. To predict the water temps you'll be fishing along the Parkway you need to be able to calculate the mean daily air temp of the area you'll be fishing. Do this by averaging the daily high air temp and the average nightly low air temp. The temp you come up with will be the water temperature in a day of two in those waters. Sounds crazy, but it's pretty darn close.

~ **Turbidity.** The IRS short form definition of turbidity is: *the amount of junk that's suspended in the water column.* It is one of the few factors impacting

Water clarity of the Parkway's watersheds is usually clear, and ranges from *"gin"* clear to greenish-brown caused by suspended minerals and organic decomposition. / *Image by Author / 2011*

water quality that is observable. The visual effects of turbidity can range from water that appears to be *tinted, murky, cloudy, muddy, etc.* The particulates impacting turbidity can get in the water from one or more sources such as runoff, decomposing vegetation, micro particulates, pollution, etc.

Poor turbidity can be permanent or temporary depending on several factors. For instance, all Parkway waters will have at least some temporary tinting after rains. This can actually improve the fishing by reducing the trout's visibility of your approach, presentation, line drag, etc. Some of the best days I've ever had on Parkway waters occurred after a rain that had tinted the water. If you don't like or can't fish tinted water, wait an hour or two after the rain ends, and go to the headwaters where it will begin to clear first.

Waters that consistently contain large loads of suspended particulates such as silt will cut down on light penetration. This reduces photosynthetic plant growth and that in turn reduces the vegetative base on which the bug's ecosystem depends. Over time, heavily turbid water can also deliver large loads of dirt and silt and other deposits that clog the substrate limiting the availability of places for bugs to live. It's a simple formula: *no bugs = no trout.* Silt can also clog up the gravel beds where trout spawn. This effectively destroys the sustainability of the species in that watershed. Fortunately, permanently poor turbidity is not a big problem on most NC and VA Parkway waters.

~ **Contaminates & Pollution.** As a rule, Parkway waters in NC and VA are generally free of the typical contamination and pollution threats that plague many non-protected watersheds along the Appalachian Chain. Other than an occasional Coke can or gum wrapper floating by, or a rubber flip flop washed up on the bank, the water is relatively pristine. That's because for the most part the water starts in the higher elevations of protected lands surrounding the Parkway and flows down through protected lands. There's just not a lot of contaminate or pollution sources like factories, dumps, roads, developments, runoff, etc. to pollute it on its journey to the Atlantic or Gulf. Unfortunately, as it leaves federal lands, it encounters the same threats from development, industrialization and exploitation as any other waters.

All of the traits described here, as well as some other less impactful ones, act in concert to make each river, stream and creek along the Parkway's watersheds unique. If you grasp most of this chapter you are already smarter than the average fly fisher. In the next chapter, we'll discuss the three trout species that call the Parkway waters home.

Trout of the Parkway Waters

Those critters that make fools out of us...

Most people traveling along the high elevations of the southern Appalachians would never imagine the Parkway to have much to offer as a trout habitat, or any fish species for that matter. Yet the Parkway waters are home to over ninety species of fish, including eight that aren't native to these mountains and six others considered rare. But it's the Brook Trout and two *"non-natives"* – the Rainbow and Brown Trout – that are the focus of our attention.

Of the three trout inhabiting Parkway waters, only one has a natural claim to be here. The other two *"exotics,"* as fishery biologists call them, are relative newcomers in the measurement of evolutionary time. They are here as a result of efforts in the early 1900's to reverse the impact of logging on the forests and watersheds of the region. Regardless, these many years later, all three are accepted as having a permanent place in the natural order of things.

When most people think of trout, it's the rainbow that comes to mind. Perhaps that's because rainbows are the ones most seen on restaurant menus. But for fly anglers, it's all three trout species they pursue - the native Southern Appalachian Brook Trout and all of its variants, as well as the larger and more plentiful Browns and Rainbows.

In this chapter I'll tell you what I know about all three of these trout, including where they came from, what they eat, how long they live, how big they get, what they look like and more. I've amassed much of this information empirically over the years and have grown to appreciate each one's uniqueness. There's much to know about these beautiful and elusive aquatic jewels.

Brook Trout *(Salvelinus Fontinalis)*

In my opinion, this little fellow is the most beautiful fresh water fish along the Parkway and perhaps in all of North America. No other cold water fish has the stunningly bright and interesting color patterns worn by brook trout. And aside from its natural beauty, it is elusive and difficult to locate because of the high elevation, small, overgrown creeks in which it is forced to live. They are remnants of a by-gone era. Stalking them with a six and a half foot bamboo fly rod I made gives me the ultimate fly fishing satisfaction.

Prior to the early 1900s, brook trout were the only trout *(so called)* inhabiting the mountainous waters of Appalachia. This explains why you often see the *"native"* adjective used in conjunction with their name – as opposed to *"exotics"* used with the brown and rainbow transplants. Originally from the northeastern part of the continent, the brook trout's range now extends from Hudson Bay in the north to the mountains of North Georgia.

The true Southern Appalachian Brook Trout of today is definitely a unique branch of its northeastern counterparts and is presently classified as a separate subspecies - *Salvelinus Fontinalis*. Pure southern brook trout do exist and in some locations are doing well. In many places where northeastern brooks have migrated into the same waters, or have been introduced there by man, they have interbred with their southern cousins and formed hybrids. In some areas, all three versions can be found living side by side in the same stream – southern, northern and hybrids. Other than subtle differences in the number of spots, scale patterns and bone structure, most fly fishers can't readily tell them apart. Regardless, these concerns are for wildlife officials and fishery biologist to debate and argue - not us. I just think they're beautiful, fun to catch, and if you're so inclined – pretty tasty too!

Ironically, the brook trout is not really a trout at all, but rather members of the Char family. Because they look and act like a trout, the early settlers just named them *"trout"* – a title that stuck. They were the only so-called trout the early settlers of the Appalachians found in the cold waters of the region. There were no rainbows or browns in these waters back then – brook trout had the waters all to themselves. Settlers called them *specs, speckle trout, natives, brooks, bookies* or just *trout.* Depending on the area, these names are still used today.

These days, brook trout are relatively rare unless you know where to go. But there was a time when they were plentiful in Appalachian waters. Prior to large-scale logging operations in the early 1900's which cleared much of the old growth timber in the mountains, many old timers recall stories of fishing trips when they would catch more than a hundred brook trout in a single day – and it was not a rare occurrence. I've seen dozens of antique tin, glass plate and film images showing fifteen, twenty and more brookies strung through the gills on a tree branch and held up in trophy fashion on the trip home. There was not a single rainbow or brown among them!

The brook trout's domination of the Appalachian's cold water habitats began to decline during the later Victorian Ages up through the mid-1930s. This was an era when the lumber-hungry demands of a growing nation led to the cutting of much

Brook Trout caught by Author in a Shining Rock Wilderness creek. / *Image by Author / 2011*

of the first growth forests in the east. In contrast to today's more environmentally friendly logging standards and best practices, this was accomplished with highly invasive logging techniques and poor to non-existent reforestation practices. To top it off, there was little or no regard for the long term effects on the land and waters of the areas. Entire watersheds were logged, splash dams built across streams and railroad lines and tote roads blasted out. The frequent fires that occurred from all the cut-over debris, such as the Wilson Creek Watershed on Grandfather Mountain, resulted in widespread erosion that silted in many mountain waters.

This all but destroyed the fishery habitats in many of the region's rivers, streams and creeks, and in some cases entire watersheds. The lack of canopy raised water temperatures and erosion increased turbidity to unbearable levels for the brook trout. Additionally, creek and stream beds were clogged with mud and silt from the erosion which inhibited bug life, as well as prevented the brooks from spawning even when they could. Their habitat was decimated and as a result, the only cold water Salmonoid in the Appalachians, the *"native"* brook trout, was all but eradicated.

The few brooks that survived were forced to seek the cold and clear waters of the remote, high-elevation waters - *they swam to the tall timber so to speak!* In an effort to re-populate the waters of the Appalachians, officials and concerned citizens sourced, secured and released brown trout from Germany and Scotland, and rainbows from the West Coast into the affected watersheds. This was done during the early part of the 20th century after most of the logging operations ceased. Both of these *"exotics"* were much better suited to the damaged waters of the Appalachians. They more easily adapted to the conditions resulting from the heavy deforestation and industrialization. The warm water temperatures that resulted from the cutting of the forest canopy as well as the higher siltation in the watersheds suited the browns and rainbows much better than the brooks.

In addition to the brook's habitat being lost to logging, they subsequently had to compete with the rainbows and browns that were more aggressive and better acclimated to the poorer quality waters. Over time, rainbows and browns replaced the brook trout as the dominant species in the mountain waters. This accounts for at least two of the main reasons brooks retreated to the small, high-elevation, remote headwaters of the rivers, streams and creeks they once dominated.

As a member of the Char family, brook trout coloration is consistent with their tendency to have a darkish background color with light spots and other markings. Trout on the other hand have a lighter background color with darker spots. Brooks will vary in color from dark olive to almost black along their backs. There are numerous black spots along their sides with a sprinkling of red spots, each one surrounded by a halo color that can range from various shades of pale and powder blue, all the way to shades of lavender. Perhaps the most defining attribute of the brook trout is the vermicular *(worm shaped)* tracks along the darker upper parts of their back and up and into the very beautiful translucent dorsal fin. Another distinctive marking is their pectoral, pelvic and anal fins which have a leading edge trimmed in a vibrant white. As mentioned previously, there are some subtle differences in coloration, number of spots, etc. between the native, northern, hybrid and hatchery raised brookies. But I can hardly tell the difference.

Brook trout habitat is generally restricted to very clean, cold waters with lots of oxygen and a minimum of other aggressive fish with which they must compete – like the rainbow and brown interlopers. Brooks spawn between September and December and during this time coloration becomes even more vivid. The ideal year-round water temperature range they prefer is from 56° to 60°. Temperatures of 77° or higher can be lethal. This is why they are typically found only in the headwaters of small high-elevation shaded creeks and streams. Plus, this higher elevation helps them avoid other aquatic predators that don't like smaller waters.

In addition to being very finicky about their water quality and temperatures, brooks don't normally live very long. This short lifespan, along with the small waters they inhabit and the smaller number and size of bug hatches, might account for the fact they rarely attain large sizes. In the Parkway waters, they typically live four to seven years and reach a size of only 4 to 6 inches. Other than Delayed Harvest fish, which can be much larger, catching a wild brookie over 6 to 8 inches is reason to celebrate and take pictures to show your buddies. In fact, several studies have shown that for every 10,000 brook fry that hatch, only one will live to an age of six years. These dismal statistics cause me great distress…

Perhaps another contributing factor to the high mortality while still young fish, is that brooks seem always to be hungry. This makes them bolder and less selective or careful in their quest to satisfy that big appetite. They are therefore easier prey and more easily caught by people like you and me. I suspect this constant hunger is in part due to the lack of entomology variety and volume in the high elevation waters they inhabit. I can't blame them though; I do some pretty stupid things when I'm hungry too!

When brooks do get to eat, they tend to feed on a variety of aquatic insects including stoneflies, mayflies and caddis flies. Because of where they live, they don't see the large insect hatchings that lower elevations fish see. Therefore, they tend to be subsurface feeders – yet they are not opposed to taking surface flies. It's just that they don't have the opportunities for surface feeding on big hatches like rainbows and browns enjoy in the larger lower elevation waters. Terrestrials are also taken and include everything from ants, flies, bees and grasshoppers. The fact is bookies are aggressive eaters and will eat just about anything they can get their mouth around. As an example of this *"eat anything and everything"* tendency, a few years back I caught a seven inch brook just off of the Parkway near the NC / VA state line. When I pumped its stomach, a six inch black snake came out. I can only imaging the scene as that beautiful little brookie and that nasty snake wrestled in a life and death struggle.

Since the early part of the last century, the native Southern Appalachian Brook Trout has experienced some danged rough times. But thankfully, it seems to be making a comeback. This slow recovery is due largely to the efforts of many federal and state wildlife agencies and other well-meaning private and public organizations like Trout Unlimited. These groups have launched well-funded and manpower supported programs to help re-establish brook trout in protected waters.

In conjunction with, and/or as part of these programs, bans and restrictions for catching or killing brook trout have been implemented and enforced in many waters throughout the region. In some watersheds, key headwater streams representing prime habitat have been closed to fishing altogether to protect brook trout in hopes of giving them a chance to recover faster. Trout Unlimited's *Back the Brookie Program* is just one of many such programs that works in concert with state and federal agencies to find, improve and manage brook trout habitat. Through the highly coordinated efforts of a lot of passionate and committed stakeholders, many of these programs have been successful in helping the brook trout recover lost habitat. In fact, because of the success of some of these programs, many of the bans and restrictions have been lifted or removed altogether. The future of the brook trout is still not certain, but it's a heck of a lot more certain than it was just twenty years ago.

Rainbow Trout *(Salmo Gairdneri)*

Today, the rainbow is the species most likely to be caught in the majority of the Parkway's waters described in this Guide. Of the three trout, rainbows are the undisputed champs in terms of sheer numbers and aggressive agility during the fight. Among their fighting skills, they are best known for their gymnastic leaps when they are on the take. Many times I've seen seven inch rainbows behave like Flipper and jump a full four feet out of the water – time after time. It's enough to make your heart jump for joy almost as high. For that reason alone they are fun to catch.

As mentioned previously, Rainbows are not native to Appalachia. They originally came to the region as a result of an initiative to re-establish healthy cold water habitats after logging destroyed so many of the watersheds in the early 1900's. Along with browns, they are considered to be *"exotics"* by fishery biologists – *documented / green card* toting immigrants so to speak. As proof of their adaptability, the majority of the primary trout streams along the Parkway – as well as the entire Appalachian Range – support reproducing wild populations of these colorful interlopers from the west coast.

Rainbows were transported to the Appalachians from the Sierra Mountains of California. Out west they enjoyed a natural range that extended from California all the way up to Alaska. Upon arriving in the east, they were released in selected waters throughout the affected Appalachian watersheds. Their success is attributed to their hardy nature and a keen ability to adjust to an environment – perhaps more than any of the three trout discussed in this chapter. This is because of several unique traits, most notably their ability to tolerate warmer water temperatures than either the brook trout they was replacing or the brown trout for that matter. The rainbow can tolerate water temps in the low to mid 80°s for short periods of time, although it prefers 50° to 60°.

Other factors contributing to the rainbow's success include being able to live in waters with a wider turbidity range than other trout. Its long lifespan of seven to eleven years is not uncommon as compared to a brook trout's four to seven. Age allows rainbows to attain larger sizes, and the larger size allows them to push their weight around and be more aggressive and competitive. This ability to grow old and get bigger could also be attributed to its preference for moving water with rapids and riffles that create a broken surface that's more difficult for predators to see through. The moving surface serves as a safety feature for the rainbow – a feature that's lacking in the still waters preferred by brook trout. Opaque water ultimately makes rainbows harder to prey upon and so consequently allows them to live longer and get bigger.

Rainbows, especially wild ones, are particularly beautiful fish. An Appalachian rainbow's color scheme ranges from light to dark green / dark blue on a back that

A colorful Rainbow Trout caught by the Author on the Raven Fork. / *Image by Author / 2015*

is heavily covered with black spots and specs, with a gray to off-white belly. An irregular or "*blurry*" reddish stripe runs along the lateral line of each side – which is the bow's signature identifier. This stripe on a wild bow can run from the gill plate to its tail and is often stunningly bright blood red in appearance. In some watersheds, the area in front of the gill plate will also have a patch of bright red coloration. Stock rainbows on the other hand often show little or no sign of red hues on any portion of their bodies and are predominantly silver. The side stripes, if visible at all, will be a light pink hue with possibly some shades of blue bordering it.

Rainbows will take a variety of insects common to the waters they habitat including mayflies, stoneflies and the other usual line-up of aquatic and terrestrial insects. With the exception of those waters being protected for brook trout, rainbows inhabit practically every other river, stream and creek around the Parkway. This gives them the advantage of a wide range of water - from small creeks and streams to the large rivers. In the midsized to larger waters, the rainbows encounter a large variety and quantity of insects. This offers the advantage of frequent and larger hatches and more elbow room to go after them.

Rainbows spawn in the spring with runs usually beginning in February. In most of the streams, I see wild fish in the 7" to 10" range with a few over 12". Occasionally, it's possible to take a 12" to 17" bow from a larger pool or run. A wild bow over 17" from most of the waters around the Parkway is considered a wall hanger. In the waters that are hatchery stocked, rainbows will average in the 7" to 12" range. Delayed Harvest fish can be much larger.

Brown Trout *(Salmo Trutta)*

Generally speaking, browns tend to be the biggest, baddest and oldest trout in the waters they inhabit– and that's most of the lower and mid-level waters along the Parkway. In some of the larger waters of the lower elevations, browns can attain *"Typhoon Class"* sizes that will cause any angler to freeze in his tracks and just marvel at the scene. Hooking a big one is like hanging-up on a log – except the log starts to move! If you have ever hooked a good-sized brown and it turned and started its typical downstream run at a high rate of speed, you know what I'm talking about! They are formidable opponents in a fight at any size - and one heck of a lot of fun to catch.

The brown trout is of European descent and is known simply as a brown trout or brownie. From what I've learned, they came to America around 1883 from the rivers and lakes of Germany's Black Forest Region. They were transported as eggs across the Atlantic to a hatchery in New York State. There they were hatched, raised and released into selected local waters where they thrived. Others from Scotland and England arrived soon after. Those browns from Germany have been appropriately referred to as *German Browns* and those from Scotland as *Loch Leven Browns*. For years, records listed different names for the two fish. However, over time both have become known simply as *"brown trout."*

There's evidence that suggests browns have been present in Parkway waters since the early 1900s. However, there's also evidence to suggest they were around even earlier than that, although I have not been able to confirm it. Regardless, browns along with rainbows came to the Appalachians as part of the efforts to re-establish populations of cold water fish after logging destroyed much of the habitat previously inhabited only by the brook trout. As with rainbows, the browns adapted well to the slightly warmer and less than pristine waters where brook trout could no longer survive. But browns prefer slightly better water qualities and lower temperatures than do rainbows.

The overall appearance of a brown's body is a golden / brassy brown to just brown on the back, fading to a yellowish / mustard lower side and a white belly. Its signature coloration trait includes a multitude of large black spots that start in front of the gill plate and run along both sides of the lateral line to the tail fin. The spots often fade into the dorsal fin as well as the tail fin. Many of the black spots are surrounded by halo rings of coloration ranging from gold, light yellow or off-white. A number of red spots are scattered about with halo rings. The color, especially the yellowish / mustard lower sides, becomes particularly vivid in October through February when spawning takes place.

Browns prefer water temperatures in the 54° to 63° degree range - temperatures in the mid 80°s can be lethal. On average, browns live from seven to eleven years. However, some fish upwards of fifteen to an astounding twenty years old have

A Brown Trout caught by the Author on Bull Head Creek / *Image by Author / 2011*

been recorded. The average browns I've encountered in the waters around the Parkway tend to be in the 7" to 12" range. Occasionally, a 16" fish may be found in some streams. Given the right conditions, a few browns will attain what I call a *Typhoon Class* status I mentioned previously. Keep in mind these trout grow to this size because they dominate their waters. They eat when and what they want. And, big trout know how *NOT* to do stupid things like get caught.

In the lower elevations where they have larger waters, they are known to be highly aggressive and territorial. They all but eliminate their competition by eating it once large enough to do so. When a brown attains approximately twelve inches, it becomes the major predator in its space. The carnivorous brown will eat just about anything in the stream. Its diet is primarily of other fish, including other browns, salamanders, crawfish, as well as other large invertebrates and terrestrials.

Aside from eliminating its competition, the brown has a reputation for becoming a picky eater. It can be difficult to entice it to take a hook, unlike the rainbows and brooks. It likes deep protected areas with dense cover and lots of shade. In fact, the harder it is to get a bug to a promising looking spot, the better the chance you'll find a big brown. This is why you will generally catch three to five times more rainbows than you will browns of any size.

Another factor accounting for their age and size might be that larger fish eat larger prey. And after eating a larger meal, browns will find a safe place to rest a spell – the "*Lazy Boy Effect*" so to speak. During this rest the majority of their food is converted to weight, as opposed to being expended on energy-draining currents looking for more food. The smaller rainbows and brooks eat smaller foods and are continually using energy while feeding instead of using energy to grow. As the brown gets larger, it lives in large slower pools. And with its larger size, feeding patterns change too. It tends to become nocturnal and feed on even larger prey. For that reason, the best time to put a hook in one is late dusk or early dawn.

To Eat, or Not to Eat? That is the Question…

I'm sure this is going to tick some folks off, but while we're on the topic of trout, I've got to be honest about something. Occasionally I actually eat some of the trout I catch! There… I said it!

Whenever I'm talking to folks about fly fishing, inevitably the question always seems to find its way into the conversation about what I do with the trout I catch. The question always sounds something like: *"Do you turn the trout loose?"* Or something to that effect.

My answer depends on how I read that person. If I read them as an unenlightened, environmental zealot, never catch and keep a fish, save the

Trout dinner caught along the Parkway near Blowing Rock / *Image by Author / 2000*

world kinda person, I answer them with something like: *"Oh yes I keep them all – if they can bite my fly, and I can get them into my net, they're going back to my camp to a hot frying pan."* I know it's twisted and sick, but I do it for the sheer pleasure I get from the avalanche of abusive responses and name calling I am pelted with. I revel in the abuse!

On the other hand, if I read the person as being reasonable and just curious as to what I do with the trout, I answer with something like: *"Ninety-nine point nine per cent of the time I release them. But occasionally, I want to keep one or two to eat, so I do."* Which is true, and they always seem to be okay with that answer.

In the end, I'm an informed, responsible and reasonable conservationist. I've spent a ridiculous amount of my adult life standing in the fifty degree water of a trout stream trying to improve fish habitat by dragging logs, piling rocks, driving rebar, and building structures. *And*, especially when you consider the non-linear relationship between a healthy and sustainable trout population and the reasonable harvesting of trout – it just doesn't hurt to keep a trout every now and then. So, I believe I've earned the privilege to keep and eat a trout when I want one – and when it's legal. If you haven't, you ought to give it a shot. There's nothing like the taste of fresh caught, wild trout, cooked and eaten over a campfire!

Cautions & Precautions

Stuff that can go wrong...and how to prevent it

As the saying goes, *"trout don't live in ugly places,"* and the mountain ranges along the Parkway's 469 miles are some of the most beautiful places they live. However, keep in mind that those waters and the terrain that surround them represent risk levels that range from nominal to extreme and can cause some pretty bad things to happen. To put it into perspective, you're actually in no more danger than you would be walking in the alley of a large city after dark in short sleeves wearing a Diamond Presidential Rolex, or walking across a busy interstate at night wearing a blindfold, or bungee jumping drunk and naked in Tanzania. In the end, it's all relative to your personal perception of risk...

I've lived most of my life with my safety clicked off, and when I consider all the things that could have gone wrong, I'm amazed I'm still around! I haven't even lost any of my fishing buddies on Parkway waters – at least not any good buddies. In either event, my neighbor Bill the crooked lawyer, has once again advised me to mention a few of the bad things that can happen in the wilds of the Parkway's watersheds, as well as offer suggestions to prevent or minimize their impact. So here's Sam's list of the *"Deadly 15."*

Cautions – Sam's *"Deadly 15"*

1. **Bad Judgment.** You probably don't smoke a cigar while pumping gas, drive after you've been drinking, or tell your neighbor just how good looking you think his wife is... all examples of bad judgment that will most likely lead to bad outcomes. Yet, if you're like me and believe you're invincible, you probably slip on your waders, get in the stream as quickly as you can, and that inadvertently can cause bad things to happen. We all get in a rush to get on the water and occasionally forget what we're doing.

    I've made crazy decisions about where to fish, what to wear, what falls to climb, wading belt – no wading belt, supplies to take, chances to take, etc., etc. Sometimes a single bad decision leads to another bad decision, and another,

73

etc. Taken together, this chain of poor decisions can lead to a disastrous rubicon – a line that when crossed permits no return. In other words, an unavoidable and/or serious calamity. And each time it happens to me, I recall earlier decisions that inevitably lead to the disaster. At any time I could have injected some good judgment and broken the event chain. These days I'm more careful with my decision making than I once was because of what I've seen and what has happened to me over the years.

Judgment plays a critical role in all of the factors that follow because most are the result of bad judgment – a decision about whether to do something or not. Take your time, keep your head about you and be aware of what's going on around you and what can happen to you. Remember, "*A man / woman, has to know his / her limitations.*" Well punk – do you?

2. **Waterfalls.** Those beautiful waterfalls are everywhere - big ones, small ones, and in those in between. And we always believe there are schools of trout living at their base, sometimes inside of them or in the edge on top. So that means we need to climb them right? Wrong!

All falls to one degree or another, involve a combination of height, slippery rocks and rushing water. When combined with #1 above, that's a deadly combination. All waterfalls represent a hazard that can hurt you or even worse. Rule of Thumb: *When it looks like it could be too high, steep or difficult - go around!* But then, that's a judgment call isn't it?

More times than I care to admit, I have climbed or descended a waterfall to save time or because I felt like a stud and believed I was invincible. I invariably reach that rubicon point where I can't go forward or backward. I was in that exact situation last year at Yellowstone Falls on the West Fork of the Pigeon. I slipped and fell 25 feet into the pool below, bouncing on the rocks as I went. I was lucky. But there have been times when I was not so lucky. If this happens to you, don't waste time hoping or praying it won't hurt when you hit - because it danged sure as heck will. Rather, concentrate on where you'll throw your rod so you don't fall on it and break it too. It's better to break a leg than your favorite bamboo rod.

3. **Slick Rocks & Slides.** It goes without saying that every stream you get in will have slippery rocks to one degree or another. I don't know what it is, but in some creeks the rocks are more slippery than others. So, be aware and make sure your felt bottoms or studs are up to the task and consider using a wading stick. Since many of these streams are remote, falling can have dire consequences; to say nothing of the time it will take for rescuers to extract your mangled body. Additionally, you will be navigating around lots of long and slippery rock slides. To be safe, I recommend going around them if you can. There was a time when I tried to go up *all* of them, but I learned my

lesson at Sliding Rock on Looking Glass Creek. It was a 37 degree January day. I slipped, got soaked to the bone, was two miles from my truck, and it was getting dark. If a passing car had not picked me up, I would have dang sure frozen to death.

Low gradient slick rocks in most Parkway waters represent big slip and fall hazards. This one is on West Fork of the Pigeon. / *Image by Author / 2017*

4. **Terrain Falls.** Access to many of the streams and rivers in this guide requires cross-country navigation to one degree or another. That's a two-sided coin because remote places are where you find some of the best fishing. But on the flipside, it involves traversing steep grades with ledges, rock slides, drop-offs, narrow trails, etc. What else needs to be said here? Just be careful and watch your footing and always carry your rod with the tip pointed backwards. If you fall, you have less of a chance of breaking it. I've done that too!

5. **Flash Floods.** Take it from me, I've been involved in two flashfloods, and both were harrowing experiences to put it mildly. One was on the West Fork of the Pigeon River in the Shining Rock Wilderness Area. The other was on Wilson Creek on the south face of Grandfather Mountain. Here's the long and short of it: be aware of what's going on upstream and pay particular attention to the weather in the higher elevations of the watershed you're fishing. If you see or hear lightning, see dark clouds and heavy rains on the top of the mountain, there's a darn good chance the water levels you're standing in will be rising soon. Depending on the topography and the rainfall, the rise in water level can be dramatic and fast.

When this has happened to me, I was mildly aware of the storm above me, but was busy catching fish and not paying attention to the increased chatter up the hill. Eventually, in both cases, I noticed several cues that signaled imminent danger: 1. A bunch of scared birds flying from the upstream direction, 2. An increasing sound of rushing water, 3. Some movement of foliage upstream, and 4. The hair on the back of my neck stood up as the little guy on my shoulder said: *"Forget the fish, let's get the hell out of here you fool!"* Both times I made it to the shore and climbed through the dog hobble in time to see the water rise 3 to 4 feet in a matter of seconds.

So stay aware that it can happen and move swiftly. It's all about being quick or getting dead. Listen to the little guy / gal on your shoulder – when he or she says "*RUN*" don't over think it! Just run!

6. **Getting Lost.** What can I say here? Don't get lost! You're in the mountains for crying out loud. You will be on trails and sometimes bushwhacking your way across country. Regardless, you can get turned around and get lost, especially early morning or late afternoon when the sun, or lack thereof, and the shadows play games with your senses. If you have high-quality magnets in your head like I do, you probably have a fair sense of direction. But it's still a good idea to have a GPS that's fully charged or at least a good map and compass. Getting lost in hot or cold weather can lead to less than favorable outcomes to your mortality! Know where you are and pay heed to #1 on this list.

7. **Snakes & Spiders.** There are critters out there that can hurt you – and I'm convinced they want to! For starters, snakes are the worst of the lot and they are plentiful. You pass them every time you go into the woods in the spring, summer and fall. The good news is there are only two poisonous snakes in the region that can really mess up your day - *Copperheads* and those exceptionally nasty *Timber Rattlers.* Although there are lots of other snakes in the woods, these are the two to watch out for. Both are beautifully colored and marked with incredible camouflage. They are virtually impossible to see unless you focus your eyes directly at them on the forest floor.

I was bitten by a copperhead several years ago. My elbow swelled up; I had a high fever, foamed at the mouth,

Many Copperheads inhabit the lands along the Parkway and its waters. This one was at Stone Mountain State Park. / *Image by Author / 1999*

hallucinated, and reportedly spoke in tongues. Apparently my bite was a "*semi-dry*" bite, and I survived. But it wasn't a pleasant experience, and I still have a knot on my elbow. So be careful. And if you do get bitten, take the recommended first aid measures, and then get your butt to the nearest hospital.

As for spiders, they are out there as well. Black Widows and Brown Recluses are the primary villains you need to be aware of. Take it from me, they will bite you and the results are not good. Several years ago I was bitten seven times behind my left knee by a Brown Recluse that had crawled into my waders to spend the night. I did not even feel the bites. The resulting wounds took months to heal with a lingering question as to whether I needed plastic surgery to close the wounds. It was nasty!

In the woods, there are countless opportunities for these vicious little eight-legged, poisonous, fang-toting insects to get you. Be cautious sitting on rotting logs, leaving your tent and/or sleeping bag unzipped, laying your waders and vest on the ground or hanging them on or against a tree or log and forgetting to check them out before putting them back on. Reread #1.

8. **Bears.** Generally speaking you don't have to worry about bears… *generally.* But one thing is for sure, if a bear does get after you, that little bit of worry will quickly turn into sheer terror, and you'll probably have several awful months following the encounter. Assuming you're lucky enough to tell about it at all! If you've seen the movie *"The Revenant,"* you understand just how bad it can be. But yes, these big and potentially bad critters are out there in numbers and are definitely at the top of the food chain. Awareness and knowledge means you don't have to fret as much as some people – especially if you're packing a 470 Nitro Express caliber or larger like me.

Depending on the time of year, elevation of the stream you're fishing, proximity to campsites, fish in the creel, cubs, etc., the chances of seeing a bear are still pretty slim. In all the years I've fished these mountains, I can count the bears I've seen on two hands and still have a finger or two left over. I wish I had a really scary story of a bear encounter on a stream – but I just don't. But then that's a good thing and probably why I still have ten fingers to count with.

If you encounter a bear, just keep a level head and think logically. These are wild and powerful animals that belong here – you don't. Give them their space and don't approach or spook them – especially if cubs are in the mix. When you're camping, make sure all your food is hung in a trapeze, not in your vehicle or tent. If you're keeping fish and a bear approaches, get rid of the fish immediately. If you have a fish on and a bear approaches, cut the fish off and retreat. Again, keep a level head, be deliberate and logical, become as big as you can be, show confidence – *not fear!* And by all means don't panic. Remember most bears, *(and I say most)*, are just as leery of you as you are of them. As for pepper spray, I guess it's better than nothing. But not better than a 470 Nitro Express. You decide.

9. **Lightning.** Get zapped by lightning and you're toast – literally. In fact, in my opinion, lightning is more dangerous than all the other factors combined. This is especially true in higher elevations where storms can creep up from behind a ridge and you are considerably exposed.

    Keep in mind that all of the dead stand hemlocks where we fish can function as lightning rods directing lightning to the ground and water. When a storm approaches, get out of the water; get away from tall trees as much as possible. Keep your graphite rod tip down, and find a rock overhang or depression to get into. Tuck yourself into a small ball and pray for God's salvation for the duration of the storm.

    This has happened to me several times on waters up and down the Parkway. Most recently, it was on a small stream north of Boone, and I could find little cover to protect myself. I ended up crawling as far into a hollow log as I could get – which was not far enough. All the time I was worried about snakes and spiders that were surely there running from the storm as well. It was a hell of a religious experience with lightning stabbing the trees and ridges all around me for about 45 minutes. Now, I have a renewed respect for lightning, a stronger faith, and pay much closer attention to the warning signs of its approach.

10. **Dead Tree Bridges.** Nearly all the waters in this book will have trees that have fallen across it. Many times, I have mistaken these trees for a foot bridge for me to use having been placed there by a wood fairy. But as we will discuss in #15 below, wood fairies can be mean as hell and could have set the bridge as a trap! So walk across them with a heightened degree of caution because bad things can happen.

Fallen tree bridges are tempting, but can be slippery and dangerous. / *Image by Author / 1998*

They can be very slick because of moss and algae and you might slip and break your neck. The tree bridge can break and dump you into the water and you break something or at a minimum get wet. You can lose your balance and fall and break something or get wet. And, worst of all, many of these trees have short broken limbs that stick up and can act as bungee stakes. If you slip and fall just right, you could impale yourself like a piece of sausage in a smokehouse rack – I saw that happen in a movie once and it was downright horrific! So be careful when using tree *"bridges."*

11. **Widow Makers.** Speaking of dead hemlocks, take a look at all the limbs lying on the ground in the forest. And also notice the millions of other dead trees and high hanging dead or broken limbs that surround you. Where do you think they come from? Widow makers are large branches or tops of dead trees that fall to the ground at high velocity with the potential of striking the unsuspecting angler and injuring, or in extreme cases, killing him or her. *(In the case of it being a her, it would be called a "widower maker.")* More than once I have been bushwhacking cross-country and have wandered into an area of dead stands where one or more large branches crashed through the canopy near me. I've been lucky and have learned to scan the trees ahead for threats. Do the same as you walk, and always keep one eye on the top of the big trees around you to spot this danger.

12. **Heat Stroke / Hypothermia.** Depending on the time of year and the elevation of the stream you're fishing, both of these conditions can ruin your day or even be a killer. And both can slip up on you before you know what's happening. Factor #1 above is in play for all seasons.

    Be sure you are appropriately dressed and protected. Keep in mind that the average temperatures along the Parkway decline about 5.5 degrees Fahrenheit with each 1,000 foot gain in elevation. So it might be 48 degrees in Brevard, but it might be 28 degrees where you're going on that high elevation stream. Have a contingency plan if you take a plunge in January like I did. I did not have one and that's why I've included it! And in every season, carry plenty of water – your body needs it year round.

13. **Getting Shot.** Geeezzzz…. what? Get shot! Yes, it can dang sure happen – and does happen. Hunting deer, bear and other critters is allowed in many of the watersheds in this Guide. Check the seasons carefully, plot your access points, and be sure to wear blaze orange while hiking or bush-whacking cross-country in and out of a watersheds. I don't do well with bullet or arrow holes in me, and I'm sure you don't either. So don't be mistaken for a critter and come home in a body bag.

    Okay… these last two *"Cautions"* almost cost me my publisher. And I'm sure even you'll laugh, roll your eyes and think Sam has lost it. I assure you I have not. I know both of these last two exist. I have been thoroughly convinced of their existence after repeated consumption of large quantities of beer or single malt while sitting alone around my campfire. So don't laugh – how do you know they don't exist? After all, you once believed there was a Santa Claus, Easter Bunny, Tooth Fairy, and that love was forever!

14. **Green Men.** The old saying, *"these hills have eyes,"* or in this case, *"these trees have eyes"* is true. Reports of these critters living in the lower Appalachians have been around for centuries – from Native Americans to the

early European settlers. These *"tree men"* take the form of leaf covered, human like faces on the trunks of some trees and even on buildings. I believe in them because in one dead fall instance where I almost got impelled by a falling limb, a scowling Green Man appeared on a tree. When I returned through the same area on the trip out, that face was gone. It moved! I even think I've seen them looking at me through the campfire smoke at night. I believe they are up to no good. I'm scared of all of them.

Originally they were thought to be confined to the lower Pisgah Forest District. But after the Parkway was built, they found it easy to use the road to migrate at night to the south as well as further north - all the way to the Shenandoah Valley. They seem to be particularly numerous in the Asheville area, appearing on the corners of buildings. And one of the more enterprising *"Green Man"* even started a brewery by the same name that has become wildly popular. If you don't think they exist, some night while you're in the middle of nowhere sitting by the fire, just ask yourself *"do you really know what's looking back at you beyond the light of the fire?"*

15. **Nymphs & Wood Fairies.** I've danged sure seen with my own eyes adolescent female nymphs at Skinny Dip Falls in Shining Rock Wilderness. And my eyes don't lie! I was approaching from downstream and heard a loud ruckus long before I got there. I eased into an obscure position behind a large boulder where I observed a dozen or so butt naked, beautifully shaped, female nymphs, sitting in the trees and on rocks, sun bathing, braiding each other's hair, and diving off rocks into the deep blue pools. They were acting just about like I would have imagined nymphs would act. I was mesmerized. But keep in mind, as cute and appealing as they are, they should all be approached and treated with respect and extreme caution. My wife reminds me of that each time I head out to mountains to chase trout.

A wood fairy will engage in trickerations that can lead to bad outcomes for fly anglers. / *Image from anonymous source*

As I understand it, nymphs don't have a bad bone in their rather cute and appealing little bodies. But as they reach the age of 18, their bodies begin to develop and some of them morph into Division 1 College cheerleaders. The ones that don't make the cheerleader squad become white squirrels and move to Brevard. Regardless, make no mistake about it: if you are a married man, they represent a grave danger that could cost you your marriage, treasure, life - or all three. If you are a single man, they could be an opportunity for a lifetime for pure happiness – unless you fall in love with one that turns into a squirrel.

On the other hand, I've only seen one wood fairy *(see the accompanying image)*, a young female with huge dragon fly like wings. She was near the summit of Grandfather Mountain – not even on a stream. But I understand they are around where we fish and reportedly engage in deeds of trickery and mischievous acts like setting tree bridge traps, cutting tent strings, breaking bamboo fly rods while you sleep, tangling tippets, eating your food and drinking your beer, causing your fly lines to tangle or hang up in trees, spooking fish, teasing you in your dreams, and the like. I can't attest to that being true because the one I encountered at Grandfather was quite pleasant – and very pretty. But just to be safe with wood fairies or nymphs - approach and handle with caution. Or have a good lawyer!

Precautions

Geeezzzzz.... now you know some of the bad things – or in the case of messing around with nymphs and wood fairies – lapses of good judgment that can happen to you. So if you still want to fish the Parkway, have at it! Just keep in mind the things that can go wrong, use your head, and keep your life insurance paid up. Let's now turn our attention to some precautions you might take to minimize the risk of bodily harm.

1. **Have a *"Plan A"* & *"Plan B."*** I know this sounds rhetorical, but if you are going into the mountain wilds of Appalachia, it's a good idea to have a Plan A. Be sure you have a general idea of exactly where you are going, when you'll arrive, how you will access the water, and when you will be returning. Then be sure someone else knows that plan other than you. See # 6 below: *Location Markers & Rescue #s.*

   If you're like me, Plan A doesn't always work out – or it works out really badly! I've gotten myself into a lot of tough situations that started out in a seemingly innocent and harmless way. But there I was, standing or laying in a heap asking myself: *"What the hell happened? What do I do now?"* or *"Geeezzzz..... that was stupid!"* So count on this - if it happened once, it will happen again. Always have a Plan B to fall back on. Think of everything that could impact Plan A and have a general idea of what to do about it. Your choices may not be attractive – but one of them might be your only way out. You'll want to know what those *"out"* options are while you still have a clear head.

2. **Emergency Stuff.** This is my list of stuff that should be in your fishing vest / pack at all times when in the wilds of Appalachia. They don't take a lot of

room and can save your life if you're lost or stranded: *map, compass (Learn to navigate with either), whistle, micro filter for water, micro light, knife (larger the better), sawing device (wire type), waterproof matches, scotch,* and *cigars.* Any more is overkill – any less can kill...

3. **GPS and/or Map.** You may know where you're going, but can you get there with the least effort, time and risk? For me, either one is acceptable, but both are better. Just be sure the map has enough detail for effective navigation, and that you can use the GPS effectively. Both can be life savers in a crisis or can get you to and from your fishing spot over the most efficient route.

4. **Transponders & Trackers.** These devices are now affordable, effective and easy to use. They can be put on your hat or pack and they allow someone at home or camp to pinpoint your exact location and even track your progress. They are GPS based, so phone signals are not needed. This is a good thing since most of the places we fish don't have cell service. I recommend getting one that has an "*emergency*" transponder capability. If you fall and break your neck, or a bear chews your leg off, you can activate the feature and send a distress signal with your exact location uplinked to a satellite and then downlinked to several locations that can coordinate your rescue. They are worth the money. If your significant other won't let you spend the money – well then I'd be worried all the more.

5. **Buddy Fishing.** For all the obvious reasons, whenever possible, it's a good idea to have another person with you. They might be able to provide the good judgment you lack. This holds true unless that person is a drag or a lousy fisherman who takes too much time to manage. If that's the case, consider finding a sweet-spirited nymph or wood fairy – just have a good alibi. And hope they're not growing up to be a white squirrel.

6. **Location Markers & Rescue #s.** If you are going to be hiking in, be sure to leave your GPS coordinates or map locations with someone, along with the times you should be back in communication. Also, have the emergency phone numbers for the local NPS or NFS offices, as well as local fire / rescue centers. If you don't come home, you'll at least know there's nothing more you could have done.

Section I

63 miles
MP 469 *(Cherokee)* to MP 406 *(just north of Mt. Pisgah)*

This section includes many notable watersheds in Smoky Mountain National Park and the Qualla Reservation. It also includes several other waters on and around the highest elevations on the Parkway, as well as many located below Mt. Pisgah in some of the most historical and geographically significant lands in the entire Pisgah National Forest.

www.wildbearings.com will have *lodging, campsite, outfitter, restaurant* and *brewery* recommendations to help plan your trip along this Section of the Parkway.

Oconaluftee River

At a Glance

Sam's Rank: 👍👍👍👍👍

GPS Fixes: This mouth fix below is not the official *"mouth"* – that's about twelve miles downstream on the Tuckasegee River. The fix below is about 2.6 miles north of Cherokee at MP 469 on the Parkway. The *source fix* below is the actual undisputed source of the river:

- Source fix: N35 35.274 W83 21.742 @ 2,800'
- Mouth fix: N35 30.362 W83 18.009 @ 2,020'

Size: large at mouth

Gradient: flat 1.8% source to mouth average *(8.2 miles / 780')*

Effort: lower section - easy / upper section - difficult

Pressure: lower section - moderate / upper section - slight

Fishing Quality: both sections - good to excellent

Species: Rainbows, Brooks, Browns, Goldens

Access: US 441 / Newfound Gap Road parallels the Oconaluftee along the 8.2 miles from mouth to source – within five to twenty yards in most places. There are plenty of pullouts, side roads and parking all the way up. Along lower elevations below Smokemont, access is easy. But as you gain elevation, getting to river level requires some hand over hand descent and / or bushwhacking. In these cases, you might reread the chapter entitled *Cautions & Precautions* to avoid becoming a statistic or the subject of a late night campfire story with a bad ending.

Overview & Description

There's a certain irony in the fact that the Oconaluftee River, one of the few really large rivers the Parkway actually crosses along its 469 mile route, is the first river in this North Carolina edition. There's irony in that it's also one of my favorite places on the Parkway to fish. Whether it's an *"assisted living"* step out of the car and into the river – or a *"high-octane"* backcountry style that flicks your switch, there's something for everyone. It has every water type and trout species this guide covers. I like that variety, along with its extremely rich history. What follows is my description of this great watershed.

According to local tribesmen, *Oconaluftee* comes from a Cherokee root word *Egwanulti*, meaning *"by the river."* Its waters were sacred. Cherokees were the dominant Native American tribe in the area and were primarily farmers and gatherers. During the infamous period of the 1840s when Cherokees were being removed from the area *(an event known as the "Trail of Tears")* a small band of Cherokees refused to leave and hid in an area that's now called the Smokies. Survivors eventually returned and found a way legally to acquire their land. The area became the *Qualla Reservation* – known today as *"Cherokee."* This story could go on – but let's get back to the river and fishing.

The Oconaluftee sections included here are contained entirely in Great Smoky Mountains National Park *(GSMNP, Smokies or Park)*, save a few miles of Raven Fork in the Qualla Reservation. The Smokies encompass 800 square miles / 512,000 acres of which 95% is forested in second growth timber and some old growth timber. There are over 2,115 miles of streams and 750 of those support trout. Many are accessed by pulling off the road – but a good many of the best ones require hiking and / or bushwhacking.

The Park is world renowned for its diversity of flora and fauna and is one of the more biologically diverse areas in the US. In 1976 it was designated an *International Biosphere Reserve.* More species of trees grow in the Park than all of Northern Europe, an area 1,000 times larger. The Park has over 100,000 acres of old growth forest. As far as its fauna, it's not uncommon to see elk, deer, turkeys, black bear, groundhogs, etc. while fishing. Elk are spotted frequently during the rutting season along the lower Raven Fork and Oconaluftee Visitor Center area.

Aside from the Cherokee's influence and history, it's also home to many other historical happenings and places – many to be discussed in the watershed segments in which they occur. These include places like the Civilian Conservation Corps *(CCC)* and Work Progress Administration *(W.P.A.)* Camps, decommissioned fish hatcheries, working grist mills, abandoned settler farmsteads, saw mill towns, and cemeteries as well as road, trail and bridge construction projects, etc., etc. The area's history can enhance your experience if you pay attention to it – the past is all around you.

The river's main run is considered large by Smokies' standards and is classic freestone trout water. Along with its tributaries, it constitutes one of the best, if not *THE* best, trout habitats in the Smokies. Its gentle gradient creates a steady flow rate that's not too turbulent in periods of normal precipitation. The flow types are mostly riffles, long slow runs and a variety of pools and drop pools. The headwaters are a different story.

The Oconaluftee comes to life as the result of *Beech Flats Prong* and *Kephart Prong* - two high elevation streams that ramble down the Smokies' south slope and converge. Both start as seeps and descend at steep gradients while picking up feeders that transform them into streams when they converge at 2,800'. That convergence is where the Oconaluftee officially comes to life and is about 8.2 miles north of the Parkway – a few yards east of US 441 / Newfound Gap Road.

From its source, the river's *Upper Section* loses elevation in the first 3.9 miles at a flat 2.8% gradient. Along there it's still small and shrouded in a thick canopy. Boulders form large pockets with deep holes and sections of shallow and deep runs and riffles combine to create good feeding and holding lanes. As it continues southward, it gains added flow from *Collins Creek* and *Bradley Fork* – Bradley being the larger. At the bottom of the *Upper Section*, the river has grown larger

The Oconaluftee River flowing under the Parkway at MP 469 and continuing down into Cherokee and beyond. / *Image by Author / 2015*

and has cut a wide valley between *Richland Mountain* to the east and *Thomas Ridge* to the west. Upon reaching *Bradley Fork*, the river becomes a large stream.

Below *Bradley Fork* the river continues into what I consider its *Lower Section*. From there it flows at a flat 1% gradient for about 4.3 miles to its mouth at 2,020' at the Parkway. Along the way it gathers water from *Mingus* and *Couches Creeks* and finally *Raven Fork*, its largest contributor enters just above the Parkway. This section has spread out and created a huge mountain meadow – where deer, elk and turkey are common. This section's mild gradient, soft flowing water and open canopy offer easy casting and wading. The *Lower Section* ends at the Parkway.

Below the Parkway the river assumes another personality. Aside from entering civilization, it's now a full-fledged river, entering the *Qualla Indian Reservation* and then on into *Cherokee* some three miles down. Approaching Cherokee you will see several fishable streams - *Lambert Branch* and *Owl Branch*. They're fishable and if you want to try them, knock yourself out. I never have.

From Cherokee, the river continues another 10 miles until it converges with the *Tuckasegee River, (better known as the "Tuck")* just east of *Bryson City, NC*. Just beyond Bryson the Tuck enters Fontana Lake.

Moving upstream from the mouth at the Parkway, the *Lower Section* up to *Bradley Fork* is large, has open canopies and sides, flat gradients - and larger trout! There are lots of places for big browns and rainbows to hide in the undercut banks, roots balls and rocks that provide cover. Distance casting is much easier – including roll casts.

Up the *Lower Section* .5 miles, *Raven Fork* enters river right, at 1.2 miles *Mingus Creek* enters river left, and about 2.5 *Couches Creek* enters river left – all very fishable. In my opinion, this stretch of the *Lower Section* is the most overlooked stretch of the river – probably because most anglers drive along US 441 looking for more scenic and secluded water. Also, the highly-stocked waters in the Qualla Reservation draw attention away from this section of the river in the Park. That's just my opinion.

The *Upper Section* starts with *Bradley Fork* entering river right at about 4.3 miles above the Parkway. Here the river begins to get much smaller, gradients steeper, canopies tighter, and the trout smaller. This section has lots of runs, riffles and pools and a canopy and sides of dense foliage. You'll find yourself bushwhacking your way up the stream while using short casts and even "*sling shotting*" for good presentations to the trout hiding underneath all those Rhododendrons. At 5.9 miles up, *Collins Creek* enters river left – also fishable. At 8.3 miles you reach the source at the confluence of the headwater flows *Beech Flats Prong* and *Kephart Prong*. This section is full of trout and is fun to fish.

As for trout populations along the main flow, the Oconaluftee is known for robust brown trout populations in the *Lower Section* – often yielding Typhoon Class specimens in the 18" – 24" range. In fact, as of this writing, it holds the NC record for a brown - weighing in at 15.9 lbs. Nonetheless, rainbows are the primary inhabitants throughout the watershed, with some in the 6" to 14" range – all the way into many headwaters. The Park's efforts to restore brookies now has them prospering in many high elevations. Most of these tend to be in the 4" - 6" range with some surprisingly larger.

The Oconaluftee's distribution of trout is like all mountain watersheds. As source water leaves the higher elevations and starts descending, changes in gradient and flow channels combine with changes in water chemistry, substrate composition and temperatures to effect the distribution of trout. In the lower section's big water, especially below the Parkway and Raven Fork's trophy section, trout are large and smart due to pressure. These fish see a lot of fake bugs, and many are hair-lipped from being caught so many times. This makes fly selection and presentation more difficult. Conversely, in the upper section's smaller waters, where there's less pressure, trout aren't as spooky or selective, and are typically more eager to eat the standard fare of caddis flies and bead heads. I've had as many as four missed takes on the same caddis, by the same trout, in the same pool, before I finally caught it. Whether that speaks of my persistence and / or poor skills, or perhaps how hungry and desperate that poor trout was, I can't say for sure. But it was probably the latter!

In concert with healthy trout populations, the river also boasts some of the best insect populations in the Park – over 100 species in most streams. In the Park's slightly acidic waters, mayflies, caddis and stoneflies are important aquatic food chain players. This results in some good hatches and is the key reason for a thriving trout population – even in these wild, non-stocked waters. Regardless, I rarely fish with more than three to five different bugs – wet or dry. In the upper sections, as with most Appalachian streams, the fish just seem to be hungry most of the time, and one of my standard imitators will most likely fool them. For the lower sections where fish are more selective, I always check with a local outfitter and ask what the "*sure fire*" bug selection is for the section I'm fishing.

As a heads up, the *Cherokee Fisheries & Wildlife Management* does stock the section of the Oconaluftee beginning at Raven Fork where it enters just above the Parkway and downstream into Cherokee. In fact, it's some of the heaviest stocked waters in all of the Southeastern US. At last count, I understood yearly stocking to be in the 300,000 - 500,000 range. Brook, brown, rainbow and golden are stocked in the section below the Parkway into Cherokee, as well as in the trophy section of Raven Fork – *more detail in the Raven Fork Chapter*. Some other easily accessible streams on the Reservation are also stocked. Special Qualla Cherokee Reservation permits are required for *ALL* waters within its boundary. Be sure to check the regulations specific to the waters you plan to fish.

As I understand it, Park waters don't get stocked, but there are plenty of wild trout throughout the Oconaluftee watershed. And, there are some larger stockers that escape the reservation waters up the Oconaluftee and its tributaries waters.

Oconaluftee Tributaries

Beech Flats Prong
One of Two Oconaluftee Headwaters

At a Glance

Sam's Rank: 👍👍👍
GPS Fixes:
- Source fix: N35 36.422 W83 26.087 @ 4,780 ft.
- Mouth fix: N35 30.362 W83 18.009 @ 2,780 ft.

Size: small at mouth
Gradient: moderate 8.4% source to mouth average *(4.5 miles / 2,000')*
Effort: moderate to difficult
Pressure: none to slight
Fishing Quality: average to good
Species: Rainbows, Browns & Brooks
Access: About 8.4 miles up US 441 / Newfound Gap Road from the Parkway, Kephart and Beech Flats Prongs converge about 200 ft. off the right side of the road. The road continues, paralleling Beech Flats from its mouth for about 3.2 miles to where the creek goes under US 441 for the first time – right to left. Along

that stretch the road is about 200' to 400' from the creek, but requires a 100' descent to get to it. Getting to the water can require serious bushwhacking and fancy foot work. There are numerous places to park most of the way up. After the prong goes under the road for the second time – left to right, it starts a 1.2 mile assent to its source at Luftee Gap. Access to this remote section can be found up US 441 another .3 miles to a NPS trail on the right. This trail parallels the prong all the way up, but getting to it requires a steep hike of about 300' – 500'.

Overview & Description

This prong is a beautiful and rugged little stream and well worth the effort to fish. With that said, you should know it's not the most productive fishery on the Oconaluftee due to an unfortunate chain of events that started years ago during the building of US 441 / Newfound Gap Road. As fate would have it, Beech Flats flows through an ancient formation of acid bearing shell called the *Anakeesta Formation*. Over the eons, the stream leached out and sealed the formation making the stream tolerable to aquatic life. As the story goes, early in the 1900s when US 441 was being built, the Anakeesta Formation was blasted into and the stream was re-exposed to a fresh dose of the toxic stuff. This re-exposure once again dramatically changed the pH and damaged the aquatic life. Over time the stream healed to some degree, and the aquatic life adapted. Yet as fate would have it again, a decision was made to widen US 441 some years ago and another dose was released. Recovery is ongoing, but the damage is done for our lifetime. You'll catch fish, but just imagine what this fishery would be like if those projects had been thought through and managed more efficiently. This account was

Beach Flats Prong emerging from under Hwy 441 after leaving its source. / *Photo by Author / 2015*

confirmed by NPS personnel, some of the locals, as well as writings I've seen. Considering its unfortunate history, Beech actually has a decent population of browns and bows, with a few specs high up.

As one of the two headwaters forming the Oconaluftee, Beech sources way up under *Luftee Gap* at about 4,780' and plunges down the mountain at a moderate 8.4% average gradient for about 4.5 miles. Starting as a seep, it descends quickly while being fed by nine or ten tiny feeders along the way. Only *Kanati Fork* is worth fishing - I'll explain below. The feeders transform it into a small stream by the time it converges with *Kephart Prong* at about 2,780'.

Moving upstream from *Beech Flat's* mouth, it's most fishable feeder, *Kanati Fork*, crosses under US 441 / Newfound Gap Road and enters Beech about 100' above where it joins *Kephart* to form the source of the Oconaluftee. *Kanati* sources at about 4,638' and screams downhill at a smoking 20.4% extreme gradient for about 1.4 miles on its way to meet *Beech Flats.* It starts small and is still small when it goes under US 441 and joins Beech Flats at about 2,800'.

A Brook Trout caught high up on Beech Flats Prong above the first Hwy 441 crossing. / *Image by Author / 2011*

Per the locals, Kanati in Cherokee means "*lucky hunter.*" I prefer the now extinct *Pig-angler* language interpretation of "*lucky angler.*" It's definitely one of the more widely written about brook trout streams in the Park. For the angler willing to work, it offers an excellent opportunity to catch a brookie. Yet most anglers overlook it because it is so tiny, over grown and difficult to fish. Even though on paper it's Beech Flat's largest tributary, don't be deceived. It is tiny! In fact, years ago when I was driving around looking for it, I drove over it several times before I finally realized it was there. This was way before GPS.

Kanati is extremely tight, steep and requires aggressive climbing to fish. I've fished it about .5 miles up three times and had to use the stream bed to get in and out – bushwhacking and rock hopping excessively. You'll definitely employ some refined small stream casting tactics such as high stickin', sling-shotting, dapping, flick casts, etc. to present your bugs. I have not fished above .5 miles – way too tight and hard to fish beyond that. It's been my experience that every now and then you'll encounter a larger than normal drop pool holding a larger than normal brookie in the 5" – 8" range. That's huge considering my understanding is that brookies on average only live about three to five years in the Park. Most of what I've caught were 4" fingerlings. Kanati is a fun little trout stream and if you need to catch a brookie to complete your grand-slam, you can probably do it there.

Moving on up Beech's main flow from Kanati, the entire 3.2 miles up to where Beech goes under Hwy 441 for the first time is littered with pools and runs that hold one or more hungry trout. This entire stretch is fishable, as well as much of the 1.3 miles above that up into the headwaters.

Rainbows and browns tend to hang out in the lower section along US 441. Brook trout are more likely found in its headwaters above Hwy 441 and its feeders. I've fished nearly all of Beech Flats and even though it is close to the road, it is still difficult fishing given the elevations, hiking and bushwhacking required. This is especially true as it leaves US 441 and heads up to its source. But I have grand-slammed there several times. And given the history of the area, I have been pleasantly surprised by the size of the fish– many in the 7" – 10" range.

Kephart Prong
One of Two Oconaluftee Headwaters

At a Glance

Sam's Rank: 👍👍👍👍
GPS Fixes:
  - *Source fix:* N35 37.838 W83 23.210 @ 5,866 ft.
  - *Mouth fix:* N35 30.362 W83 18.009 @ 2,780 ft.
Size: small at mouth
Gradient: steep 14.2% source to mouth average *(4 miles / 3,069')*
Effort: difficult to extreme.
Pressure: slight to moderate
Fishing Quality: average to good
Species: Rainbows, Browns & Brookies
Access: About 8.1 miles up US 441 from the Parkway, Kephart and Beech Flats converge about 200' on the right – creek access is easy. Kephart Prong Trail starts at a foot bridge on the right side of the road and offers parking and access up the creek for about 1.8 miles. Other trails offer access to its headwaters.

Overview & Description

Kephart Prong, along with its hiking trail, shelter and even the mountain itself, was named after *Horace Kephart*. Horace was a writer who lived in Bryson City in the early part of the 1900's. He authored *Our Southern Highlanders*, an excellent account of the culture of the Southern Appalachians, as well as the outdoorsman book *Camping & Woodcraft*. More importantly, he was a major influence and champion in helping to establish *Great Smoky Mountains National Park*.

Horace's namesake creek, *Kephart Prong*, is a small freestone stream that's typical of the high-elevation, bush streams so common in the Appalachians. The stream's higher elevations hold brookies, with bows and even an occasional brown near its confluence with Beech Flats. As usual, bows are dominant in lower waters, and specs tend to hang out in the higher elevation waters.

Kephart Prong starts at *Icewater Springs* on *Mt. Kephart* at over a mile above sea level. At 5,866', its source is the highest elevation headwaters of the Oconaluftee watershed. Starting very small, it descends quickly for about 4 miles at a steep 14.2% average gradient to its mouth. Along the way it adds eight or ten tiny feeders - the largest being the fishable *Sweet Heifer Creek*. These feeders turn Kephart into a small stream by the time it converges with Beech Flats at about 2,780' to form the Oconaluftee.

Along the first 1.8 miles upstream from its mouth, the creek is about 6' – 10' wide, not steep, and mostly brush covered plunge pools. Although the trail is close to the creek, getting on, off and up can be

The original sign frame for the Civilian Conservation Corps (*CCC*) camp on Kephart Prong from 1933 to 1942. / *Image by Author / 2015*

challenging due to the canopy and side foliage. However, this entire stretch offers productive fishing for the bows that occupy the endless chain of small pools.

As you start up the trail, you soon realize the area is steeped in history. About ¼ miles up you'll reach the stone ruins of a *Civilian Conservation Corps (CCC)* camp whose 200 members / Company 411 occupied the spot between 1933 and 1942. Stonework remains include a stone camp sign frame, terracotta water / sewage piping, a barracks chimney, water fountain and scattered piping. This CCC camp worked on Newfound Gap Road, trails, bridges and other area infrastructure projects. This Company also built most of the footbridges on the trail – many still have the original stone buttresses that were hand crafted eighty-five years ago.

Just upstream are the remains of a *Works Progress Administration (W.P.A.)* fish hatchery. I've looked for depressions that indicate the trout runs similar to those which can be seen in the upper Davidson River, but never found any. I have seen pipes and valves which probably carried water to those runs. Further up are some narrow-gauge railway rails from the *Champion Lumber Company* narrow gauge train used to carry logs out of the valleys during the logging era of the 1930's.

At about 1.5 miles, *Sweet Heifer Creek* enters creek left. This creek is fishable – although I have never fished it. Kephart gets even smaller along here - about 5' – 8' wide and very tight in spots. On up at about 1.8 miles is *Kephart Shelter* at the junction of *Kephart Prong, Sweet Heifer Trail* and *Grassy Branch Trail*. This is a great place to hang out and poach food and beverage from the well - stocked day hikers - or even stay the night.

Sweet Heifer Trail serves the *Sweet Heifer Creek* tributary, and *Grassy Branch Trail* tracks up Kephart into its high elevation feeders *Hunter Creek* and *Upper / Lower Grassy Branch*. As you gain

Kephart Prong about a mile above its confluence with the Oconaluftee River. / *Image by Author / 2015*

elevation, the headwaters become more difficult to reach and fish because of the extreme 18% gradient. It requires excessive physical exertion. So if you've got someone who's always bugging you to take them fishing and you don't like them - take them on the "*Kephart Headwater Rubicon*." I guarantee they'll never bug you about anything again! But there are lots of trout up there! Your efforts will likely be rewarded with hefty quantities of 4" – 6" spec fingerlings in bright colors.

Collins Creek
A Tributary of the Oconaluftee

At a Glance

Sam's Rank: 👍👍👍
GPS Fixes:
- Source fix: N35 32.764 W83 21.995 @ 4,546 ft.
- Mouth fix: N35 34.039 W83 20.050 @ 2,385 ft.

Size: small at mouth

Gradient: steep 14.6 % source to mouth average *(2.8 miles / 2,158')*
Effort: moderate to difficult
Pressure: none to slight
Fishing Quality: average to good
Species: Rainbows, Browns & Specs
Access: About 5.8 miles up US 441 / Newfound Gap Road from the Parkway, Collins Creek glides under the road and converges with the Oconaluftee about 250' off the road's right side. Parking is at the Collins Creek Picnic Area across the road. Collins Creek Trail offers access up the creek for about 2.6 miles.

Overview & Description

Collins Creek is very small and somewhat overgrown much of the way up the valley. Yet to reward your efforts, it offers pretty good trout fishing and provides some absolutely spectacular views of the old growth forest surrounding you. Although the fishing is difficult, it'd be worth it just for the views, even if you didn't catch anything – *but you will!*

The creek dives off *Newton Bald* and *Thomas Ridge* from about 4,546' and flows about 2.8 miles to its mouth on the Oconaluftee. As it rushes down the valley at an attention-getting 14.6 % average gradient, it adds four or five feeders –

Newton Branch and "*No Name*" *Creek* being the largest and most fishable. I use the term "*no name*" because no map sources show it as having a name. By the time it reaches its mouth at 2,385' a very small trout stream has been born.

The first 150' from its mouth up to US 441, Collins is darn near vertical. Above the road, the first .9 miles of Collins is small and shallow – about 5' – 7' wide and 6" – 12" deep. Some drop pools and runs are deeper and more open. It is typical blue-line pocket water fishing in thick foliage all the way up the steep topography. You will

Collins Creek passing under Hwy 441 just north of the Parkway. / *Image by Author / 2011* fight hard for small bows, browns and specs in the 6" – 8" range.

At about .9 miles *"No Name" Creek* enters creek right. It looks fishable. The first time I fished Collins, I clawed my way up to *"No Name"* using the stream bed as a trail. It was slow and frustrating – so much so that I managed to create a whole new vocabulary that day that would make a seasoned pirate blush.

Newton Branch, Collins' other feeder of any size, enters creek left at about 1.3 miles. I have not fished *Newton* or *"No Name"* for that matter. I was too beat each time I finally reached them. So forget the headwaters - I imagine they would be an exercise in self torture.

The second time I fished Collins I got smart and used *Collins Creek Trail* to drop in and out of the creek all the way up to Newton. This was much less physical, and I covered more water than wading and bushwhacking. Although I've only fished Collins a couple of times – I did get lucky and *grand - slam* both times. My experience says Collins fishes best in the spring and early summer.

Bradley Fork
A Tributary of the Oconaluftee

At a Glance

Sam's Rank: 👍👍👍👍👍
GPS Fixes:
- Source fix: 35 38.039 W83 19.790 @ 3,400 ft.
- Mouth fix: N35 33.337 W83 18.741 @ 2,200 ft.

Size: large at mouth – about the same flow as the Oconaluftee
Gradient: flat 3.3% source to mouth average *(6.9 miles / 1,200')*
Effort: lower section - moderate / upper section - difficult to extreme
Pressure: lower section - moderate to heavy / upper section - slight
Fishing Quality: good to excellent - entire creek
Species: Rainbows, Browns & Specs
Access: About 4.3 miles up US 441 / Newfound Gap Road from the Parkway, Bradley enters the Oconaluftee about 200' off the right side of the road - just above Smokemont Campground Road. The river is accessible from its mouth to the upper side of Smokemont Campground via that road. About .8 miles up the campground road a gate restricts access to foot / hoof only. Parking is available there. From that point a road / trail system follows the Bradley almost to its source.

Overview & Description

A while back I turned my friend Chris on to Bradley. He had a twenty trout day - and a *"grand-slam"* his first and second time on it! Not surprisingly many feel this creek is one of the best rainbow and brown trout fisheries on the Oconaluftee, if not in the entire Smokies. And, there's a large population of brookies in its headwaters and much of its main flow. I tend to agree with this notion – there are many reasons why this is true.

For the assisted living folks, there's almost seven miles of low gradient trout water paralleled virtually the entire length by a road / trail system. For people like me who like "*full-contact fishing*," several miles of its upper section / headwaters churn through some of the most rugged areas of the Park at a blistering 18.9% gradient. Top this off with campgrounds conveniently located where you can limp back, sit by the fire, light up a good cigar and indulge in libations while telling lies about all those 16" specs you caught on a #20 BWO. Easy / hard water, lots of all three species and a convenient campground - what else could you ask for?

Aside from great fishing, Bradley is also loaded with history. Smokemont Campground is located on the original site of *Bradleytown* - named appropriately after the "*Bradleys*" who settled the area. It is also the site of a massive saw / pulp mill that operated in the early 1900s by *Champion Fibre Company* of Canton, NC. At that time, Champion's paper mill was the largest of its kind in the entire free world – and I believe still operates today as *Blue Ridge Paper Company*. The lumber mill included a sawmill, commissary, homes and businesses, community house, school, church, hotel and even a narrow gauge railroad that hauled logs and lumber. In the early 1920s, the saw mill was producing 45,000 bd. / ft. of lumber daily, plus large quantities of pulp wood to feed the paper mill.

In 1931, Champion sold 90,000 acres, including the Bradley watershed, to the N.P.S. to create the Park. That amounted to 140 of the 781 square miles the Park

Bradley Fork *(right)* entering the Oconaluftee River *(left)* just below Smokemont campground along Hwy 441. It is about the same size as the Oconaluftee. / *Image by Author / 2015*

needed. The lumber mill, locomotives, railroad cars, miles of tracks, and the buildings and homes were all removed. *"Lufty"* Baptist Church survived, and only a few brush choked clearings and foundations offer evidence of the once vibrant community. Okay, enough history...

From about 4,900' *Chasm Prong* and *Gulf Prong*, two small high-elevation headwater streams crash down the south side of the Smokies to birth the Bradley. As usual, both start tiny and descend rapidly while gathering the water that transforms them into small streams by the time they convergence in about 2.2 miles at 3,400 ft. to form the Bradley.

From its source, Bradley loses elevation over the next 6.9 miles at a mild 3.3% gradient as it passes between the rugged slopes of *Richland Mountain* and *Hughes Ridge*. Along the way, it's joined by feeders with names like *Bearwallow Branch, Louie Camp Branch, Tennessee Branch, Taywa Creek* and *Chasteen Creek* – with Chasteen being the largest. At about 6.9 miles from its source, it passes Smokemont Campground, and at about 2,200' kisses the Oconaluftee's main flow alongside US 441.

Moving upstream from its mouth, Bradley is rather large the first couple of miles, 25' – 30' wide in most places and easy to fish. Its moderate gradient makes for flat hiking and wading, and the flow is relatively calm and wide open. This makes for easy navigation and open casting. Bradley's lower main flow stretch and its lower feeders are easy to fish if you're in reasonably good shape.

About 1.6 miles from the mouth, *Chasteen Creek* enters creek right – backcountry Campsite # 50 is also located here. From about 4,670' up on *Hughes Ridge*, Chasteen fights its way down between *Mine Ridge* and *Beck's Bald* at a steep 13.6 % average gradient for about 3.2 miles. It converges with Bradley at about 2,370'. It is a typical small, high-gradient, freestone mountain creek that's definitely worth investing time on. It's known for healthy populations of small rainbows, occasional browns in the lower reaches, and brookies in the headwaters. Being the closest feeder to the campground, it gets more pressure than the others because of the easy 1.6 mile hike from the campground.

At *Chasteen's* mouth, it's about 8' across and shallow with the typical drop pool, run, riffle and pool features where trout gather. The main flow is rather steep, brushy and tight with lots of plunge pools. At about 1.7 miles further up are several small cascades, including *Chasteen Creek Falls* – roughly 30' tall. I've caught some nice trout in this stream – most in the 7" to 10" range. *Chasteen Creek Trail* follows it for about 2.3 miles to its source and Backcountry Campsite # 48 and then on to the top of *Hughes Ridge*. From there, it probably goes on to Anchorage for all I know!

On upstream at about 4 miles on Bradley's main flow, *Taywa Creek* enters creek right. Taywa is very small but has a vibrant population of rainbows in the lower sections and mostly specs in its upper half and headwaters. Being further up Bradley and away from the campground, and being small and overlooked, this feeder gets far less pressure than Chasteen or lower Bradley.

Taywa starts on the slopes of *Hughes Ridge* from about 4,100' and runs for about 1.8 miles down between *Mine Ridge* and *Long's Ridge*. It converges with Bradley at about 2,855'. As you move upstream, be ready for tight fishing with rhododendron and laurel choked plunge pools and runs. The creek is only 6' – 7' wide, shallow and steep, so fishing can be technical. About .5 miles up, *Taywa Creek Trail* joins and offers headwater access. I've only fished this stream once, and it was hard. But I had a productive outing that netted a dozen or more brightly colored bows and specs in three hours. All of them were in the 6" to 8" range.

Continuing up Bradley's main flow to about 4.6 miles, you'll arrive at the confluence of *Tennessee Branch* on the left. The trail splits there and the left fork follows Tennessee for a while, and then on to who knows where. The right fork follows Bradley another .7 miles. At about 5.3 miles above Bradley's source, you'll arrive at Backcountry Campsite # 49. Past this campsite the trail ends and so will civilization as you know it. From there, you're on your own for the next 1.6 miles to where *Chasm Prong* and *Gulf Prong* converge to form Bradley's source. The only way to get there is to *WADE* it - *good luck with that!* Wading that 1.6 miles takes me about 2.5 hours - your exact time will depend on how much you fish, how determined you are, and above all how fit you are.

At about .6 miles into that wade *(5.9 miles above Bradley's mouth)* you'll encounter tiny *Louie Camp Branch* entering creek left. I've not fished this feeder, but I've pondered its topos and satellite images and threatened to because its remoteness and extreme topography probably makes for some exotic fishing. The times I've waded past it, I was on a

A Brown Trout caught high up on Bradley Fork just below Tennessee Branch. / *Image by Author / 2010*

mission to get to Bradley's source, and I just kept going. Coming back down I was just too tired. Based on memory and topo / satellite imagery, *Louie's* main run looks fishable. One day! In the meantime, if you do, I'd appreciate a report.

Wading on up Bradley for another mile *(about 6.9 miles above its mouth)*, you'll finally reach its source - *Chasm Prong* and *Gulf Prong*. Although maps vary, it's *Chasm Prong* and *Gulf Prong* that I consider Bradley's source – if for no other reason than they're the highest and largest of the headwaters. They're amongst the most remote, rugged, beautiful and hard to get to streams in the Park. And you might as well be trying to fish the dark side of the moon – they're that hard to get to! If you fantasize about combining exotic fishing with self-punishment, these creeks are a dream come true! I don't recommend fishing either of these alone - bring a buddy, or better, someone you don't like and want to punish. You'll be in a very remote area and will *NOT* see another hiker or fisherman for a while. Backcountry Campsite # 49 is a good base camp to stay while you fish and explore – *believe me you will need a place to crash and rest when this is over!*

Chasm Prong comes off *Porter's Gap* and *The Sawteeth* from about 4,900'. From there it runs for about 2.2 miles at a steep 12.9% gradient before converging with *Gulf Prong* at about 3,400' to form the Bradley. Its twin *Gulf Prong* comes off *Laurel Top* and *False Gap* from about 4,600'and runs for about 2.4 miles at a moderate 9.4% gradient to that same 3,400'convergence point. Both of these creeks pick up small feeders along the way – all but possibly one are "*non fishable*" in my opinion. Gulf Prong's *Frowning Rock Prong* is the largest and is possibly fishable. When I've been there, I didn't have the energy to fish it.

You'll find *Chasm* and *Gulf* to be typical high-elevation, headwater streams with steep / extreme gradients. Neither has improved trails that follow them, although you'll see some evidence of those that came before you in the faint paths and occasional primitive campsites and fire rings. Both streams are 5' – 7' wide - enough for reasonable casting and presentations to the trout occupying the endless drop pools. Brook trout rule these waters, and they are all I have caught the two times I have fished about .5 miles up each one. All the trout were in the 4" to 7" range – impressive for a small, high-elevation Park stream. Every trout I caught seemed surprised to see me when our eyes met for that brief encounter before the release. They don't see a lot of people – or artificial bugs!

Generally, as far as Bradley's main flow goes, Chris and I have found fishing to be good up the entire run. All three trout species are present in abundant populations – mostly in the 7" – 12" range, with some in excess of 16". Although the lower stretches can be crowded due to reputation, ease of access and proximity to campgrounds, as you approach and get above Backcountry Campsite N.P.S. # 49, that pressure disappears. In my opinion, the fishing is best on the approach to Backcountry Campsite N.P.S. # 49 and above that up to the source. You'll catch lots of fish; but you'll work your butt off doing it!

Mingus Creek
A Tributary of the Oconaluftee

At a Glance

Sam's Rank: 👍👍👍
GPS Fixes:
- Source fix: 35 32.558 W83 21.363 @ 4,630'
- Mouth fix: N35 31.236 W83 18.465 @ 2,050'

Size: small at mouth
Gradient: moderate 11.6% average *(4.2 miles / 2,580')*
Effort: moderate to difficult.
Pressure: none to slight
Fishing Quality: average
Species: Rainbows, Browns & Specs
Access: About 1.2 miles up US 441 / Newfound Gap Road from the Parkway, Mingus Creek slides under the road and converges with the Oconaluftee about 200' on the road's right side. Parking is across the road at Mingus Mill parking. Access up much of the creek's 4.2 mile flow is via Mingus Creek Trailhead or the Jeep trail across the creek.

Overview & Description

Upon arriving at Mingus you're soon aware of the valley's history. For starters, about fifty yards to the right of the gate that leads to *Mingus Creek Trailhead* is a slave cemetery with several unmarked fieldstones. *Stop in and pay your respects!* Next is *Mingus Mill*, an impressive wooden structure across the creek. It's well worth checking out.

The mill and trail both take their names from John Jacob Mingus *(1774-1852)*. In the 1790s he was among the first white settlers in the Oconaluftee Valley. The mill was built in 1886, and it used a water-powered, cast iron turbine rather than a water wheel which was common in that era. The turbine developed up to 11 horsepower – enough to run the entire mill. It was considered high tech for the times and was also the largest mill in the Smokies. The N.P.S. bought the mill in the 1930s during the Park's formation, and it still operates from mid-March through mid-November where you can watch corn being ground into cornmeal.

Mingus seeps out of *Newton Bald* at about 4,630' and flows down between it and *Mt. Noble* for about 4.2 miles to its confluence with the Oconaluftee at about 2,050'. Along the way, it loses elevation at a steep 14.6% average gradient while picking up several small feeders – *Madcap Branch* being the largest.

The first 1.3 miles above the mouth, the creek is about 6' – 8' wide, shallow, with lots of sand and choked with foliage. About 200 yards above the mill, a small dam diverts water from the creek into the mill's sluice. Above the sluice, the creek enters a semi-open area that was once a Civilian Conservation Corps *(CCC)* base camp. You can make out the foundations of the officers' quarters, workshops, barracks, dining hall, and other buildings. This area was once a beehive of human activity. Fishing is usually worthwhile along this relatively flat stretch.

Historic Mingus Mill and its sluice - worth a stop while you're fishing. / *Image by Author / 2014*

Past the CCC Camp, the creek winds about 1 mile through overgrown farmsteads and open forest. It then reaches its largest feeder *Madcap Branch* on the left about 1.3 miles above its mouth. At this intersection, *Mingus Creek Trail* bears left and follows *Madcap Branch* to its source - *don't get confused by this*. Mingus Creek and the Jeep trail continue to the right. Up the Jeep trail about another .7 miles, a trail leads about eighty yards to the *Mingus Creek Cemetery* - again… stop in and pay your respects! The Jeep trail tracks the creek another .6 miles and then stops. From there the creek continues another 1.7 miles to its source.

I've fished Mingus two times, but not beyond the end of the Jeep trail 2.6 miles up. After passing the mill, the moderate gradient and wider stream bed makes for easier wading and casting. I've caught lots of hungry bows and browns in the 5" to 7" range, but only a few specs just inside Madcap's mouth. I'm sure there are specs up Madcap. I just didn't bushwhack more than a hundred feet or so.

Raven Fork

At a Glance

Sam's Rank: 👍👍👍👍👍

GPS Fixes:
- Source fix: N 35 38.688 W83 15.727 @ 4,250'
- Mouth fix: N 35 30.706 W83 18.127 @ 2,000'

Size: large at mouth

Gradient: flat 2.6% source to mouth average *(16.6 miles / 2,250')*

Effort: lower section - easy to moderate / upper & headwater sections - difficult to extreme

Pressure: lower section - moderate to heavy / upper & headwater sections - none to slight

Fishing Quality: good to excellent

Species: Rainbows, Browns & Specs

Access: Depending on which part of the Raven you plan to fish, there are in my opinion, only a few logical access points. To simplify it, I've divided the river into the "*Lower Section*" and the "*Upper Section & Headwaters.*" *And,* to clear my conscience, and on the advice of my crooked lawyer friend Bill, I'll offer a few cautions about the "*Gorge*" that's in between.

~ *Lower Section:* Big Cove Road parallels the river 10.7 miles upstream from where Raven Fork enters the Oconaluftee along US 441 / Newfound Gap Road, to where it leaves the Park and enters the Qualla Reservation at its northern boundary. From US 441 / Newfound Gap Road, take Big Cove Road *(below the Parkway)* along Raven for 9 miles to where Straight Fork enters river right. Big Cove Road bears left and continues 1.7 miles to just below where Raven comes out of the Park and enters the Reservation. Parking areas are all the way up – stay off private property.

~ *Upper Section & Headwaters:* This access will put you in the middle of the upper 5.9 miles of Raven in the Park above the Qualla Reservation. To get there, turn right off of Big Cove Road onto Straight Fork Road *(some maps note it as Balsam Mountain Road and/or Round Bottom Road)*. In about 1.1 miles you'll pass a fish hatchery and enter the Park Boundary *(Gated)*. At about 3.4 miles you'll arrive at the trailhead of Hyatt Ridge Trail. This trail starts a tortuous 1.7 mile / 1,462' / 16.2% gradient hike to its junction with Enloe Creek Trail. It begins by paralleling Hyatt Creek *(a good spec fishery)* for about .9 miles, then crosses it and begins a .8 mile ascent to the junction of Enloe Creek Trail. Here you'll take the left fork onto Enloe Creek Trail and start the .9 mile / 750' downhill hike to just above the confluence of Enloe Creek and Raven. The last .9 mile leg is easier, and Backcountry Campsite # 47 is located there. After that death march, you'll be hating life *(and me)* and will be glad to see it. Access to Raven's source 4.1 miles above the campground is by wading and trails branching off Enloe Creek Trail near the camp.

~ *The "Gorge:"* Forget it – don't even think about it! This southernmost part of the *Upper & Headwater Section* just above the Qualla Reservation boundary is a dangerous gorge that's extremely tough to get into and fish. Besides, you can get killed or worse in there. I've never fished the gorge, but have talked to some who have and lived to regret it. If you feel like a stud or particularly lucky, go for it. I'm sure it's loaded with trout!

Overview & Description

Raven Fork is actually a major tributary of the Oconaluftee. However, because of its size, complexity, popularity and the fact that it flows in and out of both the Qualla Reservation and the Park, I'm treating it as its own watershed. Those reasons will become clearer later on.

According to local lore, Raven Fork was named in honor of Chief Kalanu – a legendary Cherokee war chief who lived on its banks – exactly where, we don't know. This namesake is perfect since Raven's *Upper & Headwaters Sections* are some of the most remote, rugged and hazardous places in the Park to get to, fish and hang out. This contrasts starkly with its *Lower Section* in the Qualla Reservation, which is easy to get to and fish. Raven's waters flow directly out of the Park from the south slope of the central Smokies and are as clean and clear as any water you'll find in the Park. Cold year round, fast and turbulent flows, adequate bug populations, and remoteness, make for healthy and energetic trout.

Raven's *Upper Section* is considered by many to be *THE* finest brook trout fishery in the Oconaluftee Watershed, if not the entire Park. I agree! I think it's the result of several factors that by a twist of fate, combined to make a superb spec fishery. *First,* the section is so rugged it prevented roads from being cut in. This minimized trails and generally reduced development during and after the logging era. Access is restricted only to those willing to expend the time and effort required to get there. *Second,* the ruggedness protected the watershed from the heavy logging of the early 20th century that damaged / destroyed many watersheds. Because of the lack of access, only choice Chestnut, Cherry and Oaks were selectively cut. This left much of the watershed intact – *as well as the specs that lived there.* Raven provides a snapshot of what the forest, and the fishing for that matter, would have looked like before the logging era. *Third,* in the post logging era, fewer than 2,000 rainbows were stocked in the upper Raven to repopulate / boost numbers. Today, Raven has low bow populations. It appears as though those stockers weren't able to establish the same dominance they enjoy in other

Raven Fork *(upper left)* entering the Oconaluftee River's main flow from the east just behind the Oconaluftee Visitor's Center on Hwy 441. / *Image by Author / 2012*

watersheds. Brookies didn't lose habitat – in fact they flourished into the great spec fishery we enjoy today.

Three streams source over a mile up on the ridges of *Mark's Knob (5,582')* and *Mt. Yonaguska (5,725')* and become Raven's headwaters. *Left Fork, Right Fork* and tiny *Middle Fork*, seep out and descend at mild gradients while gathering enough feeders to become small streams before converging at about 4,250'. This convergence forms a large round pool that was about 25'- 30' across when I was there and is the Raven's official source and start of its *Upper Section.*

From "*The Pool*" Raven begins a 5.9 mile *Upper Section* ramble down the central Smokies at a flat 4.8% gradient. Along that first 5.9 mile stretch it picks up some feeders - the largest and most fishable being *Enloe Creek.* Just before exiting the Park and entering the Qualla Reservation, it flows through a "*gorge.*" The *Upper Section,* especially the gorge, is amongst the Park's most remote and treacherous places.

As Raven exits the Park, it enters its *Lower Section.* There it flows through the *Qualla Reservation* for about 9.1 miles at a flat 1.5% gradient while picking up more feeders – *Straight Fork* and *Bunches Creek* the two largest. This section is also home to the famous Trophy Section *(more below).* By the time it re-enters the Park at 1.6 miles above its confluence with the Oconaluftee, the Raven has become a small river.

Moving upstream from the mouth, along the 10.7 mile *Lower Section,* the river leaves the Oconaluftee and the Park, enters the Qualla Reservation and then at the northern boundary of the Reservation, re-enters the Park at 10.7 miles up. Along the 9.1 miles in the Reservation, Raven is flat, wide open water, easy wading and open casting – an *"assisted living"* personality paralleled by *Big Cove Road.*

About 7.3 miles above the mouth, *Bunches Creek* enters river right – very fishable. On up at about 8.3 miles, *Straight Fork* enters river right – also very fishable. As you continue, at about 10.7 miles Raven departs the Qualla Reservation and re-enters the Park. Road service ends there. There are parking pull-offs along Big Cove Road all the way up offering access to the river.

The 9.1 miles of Raven flowing through the Reservation are stocked by the *Eastern Band of the Cherokee Indians* with rainbow, brown, brook and palomino (*Golden*) trout. Additionally, a 2.5 mile *"Trophy Trout Fly Fishing Only"* section of Raven Fork / Oconaluftee has been carved out. This trophy section starts at the Parkway *(which includes .4 miles of the Oconaluftee – which is not in the reservation)* and runs 2.5 miles upstream to just below the first campgrounds on Big Cove Road. This stretch is managed as *"Fly Fishing / Catch & Release Only."*

It's possible to catch trout that exceed 20" in the trophy section - some in the mid-30" Typhoon Class. This stretch of Raven, as well as the .4 mile section of the Oconaluftee, features long pools separated with some faster and more shallow waters in between that are easy to wade and fish. This section is popular and has hosted professional fly fishing competitions, including the *2011 Team USA Fly Fishing National Championships,* as well as the *Rumble in the Rhododendron.* The largest rainbow I've ever caught was on this section of Raven – 23.75".

All Cherokee Reservation *"general waters"* require a Cherokee Enterprise fishing permit. Additionally, the 2.5 mile Trophy Section requires a second permit. According to my DNA results, I am 1.6% Cherokee, but that did not qualify me as a Tribesman. I tried, but I still had to purchase both permits, dang it!

Above the Qualla Reservation / Park boundary, you enter Raven's *Upper Section.* Fishing this section requires a *"full contact"* mentality - you will get scratched and banged up! For starters, the first 1.8 miles inside the Park passes through one of the steepest and most foreboding gorges in the Park. As previously noted this gorge is virtually impossible to get into and out of and is downright dangerous. I don't recommend fishing it as one can get hurt or worse in there! And many people have…

Above the gorge at about 12.5 miles above the mouth, highly-prized *Enloe Creek* enters creek left. *Enloe Trail* also crosses here *(the access trail noted above),* and it's the site of Backcountry Campsite # 47. The area above the gorge and downstream from the campsite can also be dangerous due to topography and lack of safe access. The gradient is steep, and the stream is full of huge rocks and fast water. A rough trail tracks downstream, but it's high up and stream access is tricky.

Around the campsite Raven is surrounded with what looks to be old growth timber, car-sized boulders, large plunge pools and fast currents that make upstream fishing difficult. The whole area is beautiful and offers a glimpse into what the Smokies might have looked like

A typical Brown Trout dressed up in Fall colors caught on the Upper Section of the Raven Fork. / *Image by Author / 2010*

500 years ago. This section is very fishable, but with the steep gradient and fast waters, you must take care. *You can get hurt!*

For the next 4.1 miles above the campsite to its source, Raven passes through what many believe *(including yours truly)* is the best *"wild trout"* fishing in the Park – abundant specs with big appetites! About a mile upstream at the confluence of *Jones Creek*, Raven flattens out a bit and becomes a mix of rough / calm water. Fishing is good along here with specs being the dominant catch.

At 16.6 miles above its mouth, the *Left, Middle* and *Right Fork* headwaters join to form *"The Pool"* – Raven's source. The pool is home to many trout. But when I was there I was so taken by the beauty of the place that I put my rod down, stripped off, jumped in and just soaked up the wilderness. I believe I attained a heightened degree of cosmic consciousness in that pool, but lost it pretty quickly. Chief Kalanu and his squaw(s) probably experienced the same thing – but retained their cosmic consciousness and probably some physical consciousness too.

Getting up to the cosmic pool requires a lot of wading, or locating and working your way up the unmaintained trail that branches off *Enloe Creek Trail* at the campground. In either event, if you want an adventure, fish upstream from the campsite to the three forks pool. It's challenging – but you'll be glad you did.

Almost all the trout you'll catch in the Raven's *Upper Section* will be *Southern Appalachian Specs.* You'll also find a few rainbows left over from the *"post logging"* era. All the fish seem hungry and eager to attack your flies; catching lots of them is not difficult. I've found average sizes for specs to be in the 6"- 8" range. However, the watershed's very structure and quality ensures you will regularly bring to net those in the 8"-10" range. And it's not uncommon to net one in the 12" to 15" range.

The *Upper Section* is rugged and that's precisely why it's one of the better streams in the Park – *very few people fish it!* It is gin clear water, littered with steep plunge pools, small waterfalls and deep holes. These combine to make it a perfect wild trout habitat. You can hike in and out in one day. But considering the effort required to get there, you'll need more time to really fish and experience this special place. Use Backcountry Campsite #47 as your base camp and a place to crash.

Finally, you need to be determined, experienced and in good physical shape to fish the *Upper Section* safely. This section requires what can only be described as: *one part wading and two or three parts crawling and climbing.* Once again, I advise against fishing the *Upper Section* alone. Always let someone know exactly where you're going, how you'll get there, where you'll stay and when you'll return. Always check the local weather before going in, and keep an eye on the sky and listen for thunder up on the ridges above you - flash flooding is common in this extreme terrain. Lastly, reread the *Cautions & Precautions* chapter.

Raven Fork's Tributaries

Right Fork & Left Fork
Raven Fork's Two Headwaters

At a Glance

Sam's Rank: 👍👍👍👍 *(Based on the fishing & the exotic nature of the location.)*
GPS Fixes:
- Right Fork's source fix: N35 40.633 W83 14.573 @ 5,582'
- Left Fork's source fix: N35 41.537 W83 15.147 @ 5,725'
- Mouth fix for both: N35 38.688 W83 15.727 @ 4,245'

Size: both are small at their mouths
Gradient:
- Right Fork: mild 6.6% average *(3.9 miles / 1,350')*
- Left Fork: mild 6% average *(4.7 miles / 1,480')*

Effort: both - difficult to extreme
Pressure: both - none *(Are you kidding...?)*
Fishing Quality: both - average to good
Species: Specs
Access: There are two ways to access the headwaters. Both start out by using the same basic directions to get to Raven's Upper Section. Start by turning right off Big Cove Road in the Qualla Reservation onto Straight Fork Road *(some maps note it as Balsam Mountain Road and/or Round Bottom Road).* In about 1.1 miles,

you'll pass a fish hatchery and enter the Park Boundary *(Gated).* At about 3.4 miles, you'll arrive at the trailhead of Hyatt Ridge Trail. This trail starts a butt-busting 1.7 mile / 1,462' / 16.2% gradient hike to its junction with Enloe Creek Trail. It begins by paralleling beautiful *Hyatt Creek (a good spec fishery)* for about .9 miles, then crosses and begins a .8 mile ascent to the junction of Enloe Creek Trail. At this junction on the ridge you have two choices:

~ *To fish up Raven Fork from Backcountry Campsite # 47 to the headwaters:* Take the left onto Enloe Creek Trail and in a .9 mile hike you'll arrive at Backcountry Campsite # 47 just above the confluence of *Enloe Creek* and *Raven Fork.* The final 4.1 miles from the campground to Raven's headwaters requires a combination of wading or hiking the unmaintained trail that branches off of Enloe Creek Trail near the campground.

~ *To hike directly to the headwaters:* Take the right and stay on Hyatt Ridge Trail. After a 2.3 mile ridge-running hike, you'll arrive at Backcountry Campsite # 44. From here you're about 1.8 miles to the Right and Left Fork's confluence pool via an unmaintained trail. This campsite is a convenient place to hang out.

Overview & Description

Right Fork, Left Fork and *Middle Fork* form the headwaters of Raven Fork. Even though the Middle Fork is there, it's so small I don't really count it even though I mentioned it. Its bigger cousins, *Right* and *Left Forks*, ooze out of the rocks at well over a mile above sea level. Each is extremely remote, rugged, beautiful… and darn hard to get to! But once there, you'll be amazed by the fishing and scenes of visionary enchantment.

It is an exotic place, and if you like fishing remote and exotic places… these creeks and their confluence pool are about as remote and exotic as anything in this part of the country. However, as with most remote headwaters, this is one place you don't want to fish alone. I did it once, but won't make the mistake again. Bears, Green Men and spirits of some kind were out there in the dark beyond my campfire – *I'm danged sure of it!*

Right Fork and *Left Fork* are different streams in name only. They are virtually identical in structure, size, gradient, and difficulty level and trout type. The slightly smaller *Right Fork* comes off *Mark's Knob* from about 5,582' and runs about 3.9 miles at a mild 6.6% gradient before converging with Left Fork at about 4,245' to form a beautiful round pool serving as Raven's source. The slightly larger *Left Fork* comes off *Mt. Yonaguska* from about 5,725'and runs about 4.7 miles at a mild 6% gradient to the same pool. Both pick up small feeders along the way, but Left Fork's *Raven Creek* is the only one I consider even marginally fishable.

I have only fished a few hundred yards up *Right Fork.* I caught several spec fingerlings. As for the *Left Fork*, I was determined to fish the 1.5 miles up to

Raven Creek. For my efforts I was rewarded with a lot of small specs as well as one 7" spec caught in a larger than average drop pool under a rock ledge. At that point, I didn't have the energy to climb and crawl any further. Both streams are hard fishing for small fish, but well worth the experience.

You'll find fishing in the confluence pool to be rewarding, with about the same size fish as in the three headwaters that feed it. I have seen much larger fish in the 8" – 12" range in that pool, but didn't catch any of them.

This is not a day trip so plan to stay at Backcountry Campsites #47 or #44 – both good base camp locations. These two streams are hard to get to and hard to fish, and you'll need a place to crash. If you make it up there, the *"pool"* is well worth the time to fish. Or, just strip off and jump in and soak up nature just like the Native Americans most assuredly did.

Enloe Creek
A Tributary of Raven Fork

At a Glance

Sam's Rank: 👍👍👍👍👍
GPS Fixes:
- Source fix: N35 39.149 W83 18.389 @ 5,200'
- Mouth fix: N35 36.556 W83 15.542 @ 3,571'

Size: small at mouth
Gradient: mild 5.4 % source to mouth average *(5.4 miles / 1,629')*
Effort: difficult to extreme
Pressure: none
Fishing Quality: good to excellent
Species: Brookies
Access: In my opinion, Enloe has only one logical access route, and it's the same as my preferred access to Raven's Upper Section. Others you'll hear or read about such as Chasteen Creek Trail or Hughes Ridge Trail will be longer and more difficult. The following access will take you to Enloe's mouth, roughly in the middle of the upper 5.9 miles of Raven's Upper Section. To get there, turn right off Big Cove Road in the Qualla Reservation onto Straight Fork Road (some maps note it as Balsam Mountain Road and/or Round Bottom Road). In about 1.1 miles you'll pass a fish hatchery and enter the Park Boundary *(Gated)*. In about 3.4 miles you'll arrive at the trailhead of Hyatt Ridge Trail. This trail starts a tough 1.7 mile / 1,462' / 16.2% gradient hike to its junction with Enloe Creek Trail. It begins by paralleling Hyatt Creek *(a good spec fishery)* for about .9 miles, then crosses and begins a .8 mile ascent to the junction of Enloe Creek Trail. Take the left onto Enloe Creek Trail and after a .9 mile / 750' downhill hike you'll arrive just above the confluence of *Enloe Creek* and *Raven Fork*. Backcountry Campsite # 47 is

located there. Enloe Creek Trail continues across Raven Fork and parallels Enloe for about 1.4 miles. After that you'll wade, bushwhack and hurt until you come to your senses and turn around.

Overview & Description

Nestled in perhaps the most remote and scenic watershed in the Park, *Enloe Creek* is one of the Park's most hidden fly angling treasures. It's nothing short of incredible for someone hoping to experience a Southern Appalachian Brook Trout Stream. Nevertheless, just like its larger brother the Raven Fork, it's hard to get to and difficult to fish when you do get there. But it'll reward anyone willing to put their hiking, fishing, rock climbing, endurance and survival skills to the test. The hike-in offers incredible views. And when you make it to the upper end of the gorge, you'll see the Park as it would have been hundreds of years before the invention of saws, skidders, dynamite and logging trains.

Enloe starts and ends in the Park. It sources up on the south slope of *Peck's Corner* at about 5,200' between *Katalsta Ridge* and *Hugh's Ridge*. From there it works its way downhill for about 5.4 miles at a mild 5.7% average gradient before converging with Raven at about 3,571'. During its decent, it's supplied with water from a few feeders - only one, *Hideaway Creek*, is even close to being fishable.

At its mouth, the stream is much smaller than Raven Fork – about 10' wide with large boulders, drops and slides making navigation through the deep plunge pools and runs difficult. However, fishing upstream from the mouth / campsite always produces fish – mostly in the 6" - 7" range.

The stream's topography, water quality and quantity and size of fish stay about the same as you continue upstream until you approach Enloe's only fishable feeder, *Hideaway Branch,* coming in at 1.4 miles creek right. I fished less than 100 yards up it and caught several spirited specs in the 4" to 5" range. Above Hideaway, Enloe starts getting tight and is choked with laurel, rhododendron and other brush. The fishing gets harder and the fish get smaller. Wading and casting to the occasional run or pool large enough to hold trout becomes a challenge.

If you fish Enloe, plan to invest a whole day - and for sure don't do it alone. The required wading and climbing is dangerous, and that danger factor is magnified by the remoteness if something goes wrong.

Straight Fork
A Tributary of Raven Fork

At a Glance

Sam's Rank: 👍👍👍👍
GPS Fixes:
- Source fix: N35 41.499 W83 14.687 @ 5,515'

- Mouth fix: N35 33.959 W83 14.691 @ 2,480'

Size: small at mouth
Gradient: mild 5.3 % source to mouth average *(10.9 miles / 3,035')*
Effort: lower section - moderate / mid section–difficult / upper section - difficult to extreme
Pressure: lower section - slight / mid section - none / upper section - none
Fishing Quality: average to good - all sections
Species: Rainbows, Browns & Specs
Access: The creek access is divided into three (3) sections:

~ *Lower Section:* From its confluence with Raven Fork, the first 4.8 miles of Straight Fork's 10.6 mile flow is paralleled by Straight Fork Road *(some maps note it as Balsam Mountain Road and/or Round Bottom Road).* Take Straight Fork Road off of Big Cove Road and at about 1.1 miles you'll pass a Fish Hatchery - just past it you'll cross the Park boundary *(Gated).* At about 4.3 miles you'll pass Round Bottom Campground on the left. At about 4.8 miles the road crosses the stream via a metal bridge, veers right and begins tracking away from Straight Fork. Above the bridge about .2 miles the road becomes *"One Way Only"* from the downhill / opposite direction. Park anywhere along the first 4.8 miles.

~ *Mid & Upper Sections:* These two sections above the bridge are only accessible by hiking in through heavy brush and / or wading. I know of no improved trails into these areas. Park anywhere around the bridge, and look for unimproved trails heading upstream.

Overview & Description

This is a beautiful stream that's probably one of the most under-rated streams in the Park given its size, quality of fishery, and ease of access – at least for its *Lower Section*. It is a vast watershed. The *Mid* and *Upper Sections* are remote and difficult. Generally, I've found Straight Fork to have healthy populations of both stocked rainbows and brookies in the *Lower Section* and mostly wild versions of specs in the *Mid* and *Upper Sections*.

Straight Fork comes off the south slope of *Balsam Mountain* in the Park from about 5,326' and starts its decent from between *Balsam High Top* and *Hyatt Ridge*. It flows downhill at a mild 5.3% average gradient for about 10.9 miles before converging at about 2,480'with Raven in the Reservation. All 9.8 miles of its initial flow are in the Park. The last 1.1 miles are in the Reservation. On its way to Raven, it gathers many feeders – four I consider fishable, others are questionable.

From its mouth upstream, the 3.5 mile *Lower Section* has a mild gradient and is known for great road access and easy fishing. Most of it has open skies with lots of room for casting and maneuvering. From its mouth below the hatchery all the way

This metal bridge crosses Straight Fork about 4.8 miles up Straight Fork Road above the hatchery. / *Image by Author / 2018*

up to *Round Bottom Camp* and the bridge above, it offers great rainbow fishing with an occasional spec.

Its first feeder, *Stillwell Creek*, is up .3 miles creek right and is a good-sized stream that offers some surprisingly fine fishing. *Hyatt Creek*, up 3.4 miles creek left, is a very small spec stream. I have found it difficult to fish due to the tightly enclosed rhododendron canopy – but it's still worth the effort. *Ledge Creek* enters creek right at 4.3 miles and is the third fishable feeder, although I've never fished it. I'm sure there are trout to be caught in it. It is paralleled a good bit of its flow by the one way, downhill only, *Balsam Mountain Road*.

The *Mid Section* is represented by the next 2.1 miles above the steel bridge, up to *Balsam Corner Creek*. This section features a flat 5% gradient and is full of small rainbows and specs in the 6' – 8' range. Some say there's a trail that parallels the creek above the bridge, but I have never found anything even resembling a real trail. Much of this section is tightly enclosed in canopy and side brush, with occasional open stretches that make the pocket water fishable.

At about 2.1 miles above the bridge, or 7.1 miles from the source, the fourth fishable feeder, *Balsam Corner Creek,* enters creek right. It's a small flow, but I've found it to be rewarding with the size and number of specs found there. I guarantee none of them have ever seen a human being. I have only fished a few hundred yards past *Balsam Corner Creek*.

The 4.2 miles of the creek above Balsam, or the *Upper Section*, has a moderate average gradient of about 9% - however the last two or so miles are in the steep 12% range. On topos and satellite images, this section appears to get even tighter and steeper and would require more climbing than fishing. This *Upper Section* is for the hard core adventurist with a desire for pain.

Bunches Creek
A Tributary of Raven Fork

At a Glance

Sam's Rank: 👍👍👍
GPS Fixes:
- Source fix: N35 34.476 W83 10.466 @ 5,326'
- Mouth fix: N35 33.556 W83 14.897 @ 2,400'

Size: small at mouth
Gradient: mild 6.9% source to mouth average *(8 miles / 2,926')*
Effort: lower section - easy to moderate / mid section - extreme / headwaters–difficult.
Pressure: lower section - slight / mid section-slight / headwaters - none
Fishing Quality: average to good
Species: Rainbows, Browns & Specs
Access: Bunches is accessible from three points depending on which part of the stream you plan to fish:

~ *Lower Section in Qualla Reservation:* From Big Cove Road, take Bunches Creek Road to parallel all but the last .7 miles of the first 4 miles of the creek before it leaves the reservation and enters the Park. The .7 mile stretch just below the Park boundary is accessible via an obscure dirt road to the left just as Bunches Creek Road veers away from the creek. This dirt road fords the stream several times on the way to the Park Boundary and the start of the Mid Section.

~ *Mid Section:* This 1.9 mile stretch starts at the Qualla Reservation / Park Boundary and goes upstream to its headwaters. It's accessible via the dirt road mentioned above. From the Park Boundary upstream to where Flat Creek enters creek left, I know of no trails or roads penetrating this section.

~ *Headwaters Section:* The upper 2.1 miles of Bunches Creek's headwaters as well as its first real tributary, *Flat Creek,* can be reached by taking Balsam Mountain Road, also called Heintooga Ridge Road, at Wolf Laurel Gap on the Parkway. Drive 5 miles to Flat Creek trailhead on the left. An easy .2 mile hike takes you to Bunches Creek about .6 miles above where *Flat Creek* joins it.

Overview & Description

Bunches Creek is a typical freestone mountain creek that is known by the locals but overlooked by most everyone else. It's well worth the effort to explore and fish. In late 2018, my friend Chris and I fished the first few hundred yards of its Mid Section beyond the Park Boundary. Because of the recent heavy rains and high flows, we didn't have much luck in that section. We saw little sign of others fishing the area. So.... given the elevations, remoteness and lack of pressure, in normal flows I bet the fishing is crazy good fishing up there.

Bunches Creek comes off the south slope of *Cataloochee Balsam Mountain* from about 5,326' and flows downhill for about 8 miles at a mild 6.9% average gradient before converging with Raven at about 2,400'. Almost ½ of its 8 mile flow from its source to its mouth is located in the Park. The other half is in flatter low elevations of the Reservation. Along the way, it's joined by feeders – three are fishable, some others look like they might be. It has good populations of both stocked rainbows and brooks in the *Lower Section* and wild versions in the headwaters. I feel certain that holds true for the *Mid Section* as well.

The 4 miles of the *Lower Section* flowing through the Reservation is the easiest to fish but has more pressure due to access and stocking. Two of its three most fishable tributaries, *Heintooga Creek* and *Redman Creek*, source up in the Park above the Reservation Boundary and flow south back into the *Lower Section* of Bunches Creek in the Reservation. This section yields larger rainbows and specs due to aggressive stocking programs – some migrate into the higher elevations.

As for the *Mid Section*, I had never fished it until Chris and I tested it in the fall of 2018. Even though we didn't have much luck, it had a beautiful emerald green, mossy landscape with very appealing creek features – there has to be trout there! This section is unreachable except by the dirt road mentioned above, and once there, you'll find no trails. It has a rather steep average gradient of about 10.9% which makes for some good runs and drop pools. Given its remoteness and lack of pressure and the fact it's just above the Lower Section with a lot of stocked fish, I believe it could be really good fishing. *Chris and I will return!*

Although rugged and remote itself, the *Headwater Section* is more accessible than the *Mid Section*. You'll see no one else other than a few hikers while you're there. But like many brook trout streams, it can be rather steep, brushy and tight fishing, making getting on and off the water difficult at times. There are lots of plunge pools and hungry specs in the 6" to 8"range.

Flat Creek is Bunches' third sizeable tributary. It starts at a very high elevation and can be accessed by continuing down *Flat Creek Trail*. It's very small and tight and although at a high elevation, the stream's gradient isn't extremely steep. I like this creek because it's loaded with specs, and I've never seen anyone else fishing while I was there.

North Fork
of the French Broad River
At a Glance

Sam's Rank: 👍👍👍👍👍

GPS Fixes:
- Source fix: N35 15.956 W82 53.341 @ 3,210'
- Mouth fix: N35 08.561 W82 50.327 @ 2,210'

Size: large at mouth *(At its confluence with the West Fork of the French Broad)*

Gradient: flat 1.5% source to mouth average *(12.7 miles / 1,000')*

Effort: section 1 - easy / section 2-easy / section 3 - difficult to extreme / section 4-difficult to extreme / section 5 - easy / section 6 - difficult

Pressure: section 1 - moderate to heavy / section 2 - moderate to heavy / section 3 - none to slight / section 4 - none to slight / section 5 - slight Section 6: none / slight

Fishing Quality: good to excellent - all sections

Species: Rainbows, Browns & some Brookies

Access: As the crow flies, access to the North Fork is relatively easy. But then we aren't crows. Hwy 215 may be close to the river, but there can be huge differences in stream / road elevations, as well as no trails to traverse those elevations. For ease of access and description purposes, I've divided the North Fork's 12.7 mile flow into six *(6)* sections.

Note: Some access and extraction points can leave you far away from your vehicle. Avoid long walks by learning to "*limp*" off the trail and onto the right-of-way, play lame and pitiful, and a tourist or local will almost always stop and offer a ride. Shameful - but it works every time!

~ *Section 1:* Hwy 215 parallels the river along the 1.9 miles from the mouth at Hwy 64 to just above Lazy Jay Campground at the NFS Boundary. Parking is easy with minimal stream / road elevations.

~ *Section 2:* Hwy 215 parallels the river along the 1 mile from the NFS Boundary above the campground to the confluence of Big Bearwallow Creek on the right. There's lots of pull-offs for parking. Getting to the water can be a pain due to road / stream elevations. Put in at the NFS Boundary and through fish to extraction at Big Bearwallow Creek. There's supposedly a trail on the right leading up to Hwy 215, but I've not found it - so just bushwhack.

~ *Section 3: (Best NOT fished alone.)* Access to the "*Gorge's*" mouth is difficult. Find and hike down the same trail mentioned above on the left of Hwy 215 about 1.6 miles above the campground. If you can't, just bushwhack down to the gorge's mouth where Big Bearwallow Creek meets the North Fork. Through fish 2.1 miles to the "*Lake*" at Big Mountain

Branch entering river right. Extract by hiking up to Hwy 215 using the .1 mile trail to the right of the lake. This point will be about 3.2 miles above the campground. You can also hike up the power line easement – a bit further but not as steep.

~ *Section 4: (Best NOT fished alone, too.)* Access by hiking down the same .1 mile trail mentioned above from Hwy 215 to where Big Mountain Branch enters the North Fork at the "*Lake.*" Or, take the power line easement trail mentioned above. Through fish the 1.8 miles to an easy extraction at the bridge at Hwy 1379 / Macedonia Church Road. Extracting anywhere else involves serious hiking. Satellite imagery shows trails / roads on private lands bordering to the west, but I haven't found them.

~ *Section 5:* Hwy 215 closely parallels the stream for the entire 4.6 miles from the bridge at Hwy 1379 / Macedonia Church Road to the bridge on Hwy 215 at FSR 140. Park anywhere.

~ *Section 6:* At about 5.6 miles above Hwy 1379 / Macedonia Church Road, FSR 140 comes in on the right and parallels the last 1.5 miles of the river to its source. Parking and access is easy along most of this entire section.

Overview & Description

Four headwater streams converge to form the source of the *French Broad River (Proper)* flowing from NC up into TN. The *East Fork, Middle Fork, West Fork,* and the focus of this chapter, the *North Fork,* are those four headwaters. Three are good-sized, high-elevation streams, but the *Middle Fork* is a tiny low elevation flow hardly worth mentioning. The other three are good trout water. The upper North Fork in the *Game Lands Section* is managed as *Wild Trout Waters.* Most of the water below to the mouth is managed as *Wild Trout / Natural Bait Waters.*

Several of my younger buddies who, like me, enjoy bushwhacking for wild trout, consider the North Fork a favorite. Each section has a different identity in terms of access, topography, difficulty, flow features, trout populations, risk, etc. Its "*Jekyll & Hyde*" personality will be disguised at times as flat, serene and easy to fish. Then, just around the bend it becomes a rubicon of cascading, dangerous, heart-pounding, hang-on-for-dear-life waters. The only constants are a wide open stream bed with easy casting and healthy populations of wild trout!

One or more of these personalities can satisfy my psyche on any given day. But then my psyche is a bit twisted by some accounts, and what I think is fun can be downright dangerous and crazy to others. At least two sections fit the "*crazy*" designation. Make no mistake; these sections aren't for the casual angler and take planning, guts, endurance, and in some cases pure athletic ability to fish.

In addition to the fishing, this watershed has some interesting things around it tucked away in the mountains. One of these is the so called *Pisgah Astronomical Research Institute* located about halfway up the main flow. Here you'll see a

Pisgah Astronomical Research Institute located about halfway up North Fork's main flow. Notice the open gate that allowed entry for the Author. / *Inage by Author / 2019*

bunch of giant 20 meter antenna dishes pointing to the sky surrounded by large government-looking buildings with no windows. *"Officially"* it's for educational / research purposes. But it has *"Area 51"* written all over it, so I don't believe that story for a minute. It looks sinister to me, and I'm betting they have the bodies of those bug-eyed Martians on ice that crash landed in Area 51. Or, it could be some other top secret skunk works / black ops project... Who the heck knows?

One day the guard gate to the complex was unmanned and like an idiot, I just drove in and started looking around. It took all of about one New York minute for a big bad security dude in a black Suburban to find me and escort me to the gate. And he was *NOT* friendly! I just think it's kinda spooky to see a NASA / DOD / NSA looking complex with a bunch of satellite dishes, black Suburbans and sunglass-wearing security dudes in a remote mountain valley. Who'd a thunk?

Back to fishing - since this guide is about *"trout waters"* close to the Parkway, and the French Broad's main flow and much of its headwaters are some distance from the Parkway, we're going to examine only one of its headwaters – *North Fork*. It's the closest to the Parkway and the pick of the litter in my opinion. To offer a wider perspective, I'll give a detailed overview of the entire French Broad River Watershed, along with its other three headwaters in *Section 2*. But for now, we'll focus on North Fork.

The North Fork's source results from the convergence of two high-elevation headwater streams that come down from just under *Devil's Courthouse* on the Parkway. *Courthouse Creek* and *Kiesee Creek* start their journey to meet each other and when they do meet at 3,210', the North Fork comes to life. From that source point, it begins a 12.7 mile run at a low 1.5% gradient. Along the way it is fed by several large feeders with names like *Beetree Fork, Tucker Creek, Long Branch* – all fishable. It finally arrives at its mouth under Hwy 64 near *Rosman* at about 2,210'. It's then joined by the West Fork and then downstream by two other headwaters. Together, the four form the *French Broad River's (Proper)* source.

Moving upstream along the 1.8 miles of *Section 1* above the mouth at Hwy 64, the river runs mostly through private land and is basically flat with no more than .4% gradient. There are very few large obstacles to obstruct its flow. At about 1.1 miles, *Diamond Creek* enters river left. It is fishable for a ways, but small and entirely on private land. At 1.8 miles, the river flows past *Lazy Jay Campground* then on to the *Pisgah NFS Boundary* at about 2,250'. Up to this point, the river holds a decent population of wild bows and browns. It is very wide open and can be accessed, waded and fished with relative ease.

Section 2 starts at the Pisgah NFS Boundary just above the campground, and runs one mile to the confluence of *Big Bearwallow Creek* entering river right at 2,320'. Between these points, the section has no sizeable tributaries adding water volume. *Big Bearwallow* is small, but home to some rainbows. As with Section 1, this section has an open canopy along with a wide stream bed and is relatively flat with a 1% average gradient that makes it very easy to fish. Numerous long, slow and deep runs with undercut banks provide the trout ample places to hide.

This section can be fished in a long morning or afternoon. An ideal place to sample the North Fork is by starting at the NFS Boundary and fishing one mile up to where at *Big Bearwallow Creek* comes in river right – which is also the mouth of the gorge in *Section 3*. The main run has lots of wild rainbows and browns in the 9" to 12" class. Although it's paralleled by Hwy 215 – it can be a pain traversing the elevation differences if you access or extract other than the section's beginning or end. My advice - fish through to *Big Bearwallow*, then bushwhack out.

According to Bill my crooked lawyer friend, Sections 3 & 4 need some *"disclaimer"* comments due to the fact the river's *"Jekyll"* personality can be particularly nasty. The difficulty in fishing them is in the ruggedness of their flows and the lack of good access points. All of the access points require a steep rappel-style hike or bushwhack to get from the road to the water. And then you have to get out! The other challenge is the scarcity of trails needed just to get around.

For the above reason, if you start at one point and don't know where you're going to extract, you're in for a tough time – so plan your start and extraction points carefully. For both sections, reduce backtracking and cross-country hiking by through fishing to an extraction point. This requires a serious commitment in time and effort between those two points since the shortest distance is about 2 miles in these sections. I recommend dedicating a long day for each one.

Section 3 is described by most people who fish it as *"The Gorge."* The 2.2 miles from where the access trail from Hwy 215 and *Big Bearwallow Creek* meet, all the way up to the *"lake"* where *Big Mountain Branch* enters river right, is a bust-ass, contact sport, fishing experience. After the access trail reaches the river, it crosses it and continues about .5 miles to *Long Branch* entering river left - this section's only sizeable tributary. From there the trail leaves the river and tracks up *Long Branch* for about 1.2 miles. It's fishable, with all but its headwaters in the National Forest.

From the top of the gorge to its bottom, the bed drops about 250' in elevation producing an average 2.2% flat gradient. But don't let that fool you! This gorge is deep and rugged and is home to some fast water and incredible scenery - and an excellent wild trout habitat. As with lower sections, its canopy is wide open for easy casting. There are many stretches where you'll need to climb over Volkswagen-sized boulders, navigate over or around waterfalls and drop pools, get around long, deep pools with no bank, etc. – all with no trail. The natural lake on the north end where *Big Mountain Branch* enters is rare for a mountain stream. A natural topographical depression, along with the entry of *Big Mountain Branch*, creates a beautiful pool worthy of changing flies and doing some dredging. It is popular with locals who dare the steep hike in. Some big trout live there. The largest I've caught on the North Fork was here – a 16.5" brown I dredged off the bottom with a #12 black Woolly Booger.

The gorge is difficult to get into and navigate, and I don't recommend it for the casual fly angler. But if you are willing to risk the rugged topography and wild water, your angling and visual expectations will not be disappointed. I guarantee you will not see another

A natural "*lake*" on the North Fork where Big Mountain Branch joins at the top of the gorge. / *Inage by Author / 2019*

human in the gorge. Not many people are willing to expend the energy and risk the dangers to catch the average-sized fish that live there. The river runs fast through this section and there are many runs, waterfalls, slides, pools and dark holes that are home to some respectable browns and bows in the 9" to 12" class.

Section 4 is described as "*The Wilderness*" section because it flows further away from Hwy 215 than any other section – over .6 miles at the furthest – making access difficult. It flows for 1.8 miles from the bridge at Hwy 1379 / Macedonia Church Road, down to the "*Lake*" at *Big Mountain Branch*. Between those points, this section is similar to the gorge in terms of structure, fishability and open canopy. Its only sizeable tributary, *Lamance Creek*, enters river left about 1.3 miles above the "*Lake*." It's fishable for a short distance before entering private land.

This section of the river flows at an average gradient of only .5%. But again, don't be fooled. It is very rugged with remote fishing conditions. It's loaded with stretches where you'll be climbing over huge boulders, navigating around or over waterfalls, pondering how to get by several large, long and deep pools with no banks, etc. You'll use the stream bed as your trail or bushwhack most of the way. Be sure to fish the pools really hard. As with the Section 3, this section is also home to many browns and bows in the 9" to 12" class.

Section 5 is a section of the stream with "*issues*" in terms of legal access – it's mostly private! Starting at the bridge at Hwy 1379 / Macedonia Church Road, the river immediately enters private land and is posted through most of its run through *Balsam Grove* until just north of there at the bridge on Hwy 215 at FSR 140. Only a short .6 mile stretch starting about .5 miles above Hwy 1379 / Macedonia Church Road at the bridge is in the National Forest and is open to the public.

This section runs for about 5.6 miles at a flat 1.6% average gradient from the Hwy 1379 / Macedonia Church Road bridge at 2,625' up to the bridge crossing Hwy 215 / FSR 140 at 3,010'. As far as fishing, I don't know, I haven't done it. But I haven't asked permission either. I don't like being shot or cursed at, so I've just skipped that section in favor of all the other open water in the area.

Tucker Creek comes in on the left about .4 miles above Hwy 1379 / Macedonia Church Road. It is medium sized and located on private and National Forest lands, but fishable for about 1.5 miles past the fish hatchery located at its mouth. *Shoal Creek* and *Indian Creek* are two other small tributaries coming into Section 5, but they flow mostly in private land, and I just haven't taken the time to explore them.

About 1.5 miles or so up Hwy 1326 is the *Pisgah Astronomical Research Institute* reference above. Also, there are several trout hatcheries in Section 5, including one on *Tucker Creek* on the left just off Hwy 215, and another beside Hwy 215 on the left just north of Balsam Grove. Some time ago my buddy Chris and I sat in his truck and watched trout jumping up the drop pools from one run to the next – "*just like wild Salmon... I thought to myself.*"

Section 6 is the North Fork's northernmost section. It starts where the river goes under the bridge on Hwy 215 at 3,010' and up to its source at about 3,210'. FSR 140 parallels the entire flow making for excellent access and crosses it in several places on newly-built bridges. Along this section, the stream is small / medium sized and loses elevation at a flat 3.9% gradient. Other than *Beetree Fork* cascading in on the left at .3 miles up FSR 140, there are no sizeable feeders entering Section 6. Beetree is very accessible and highly fishable.

The area this section runs through is quite beautiful with gin clear water and a typical drop pool, run and riffle flow. The gradient is just steep enough to maintain a good flow of churning water with ledges and boulders that form nice pockets with pools, as well as shallow and deep runs and riffles. There are many drop pools that allow you to stand waist deep in the lower pool and fish the flow above it with great stealth – one of my favorite stream structures. The floods of recent years have scourged some runs down to bed rock almost as smooth as a dinner plate. There are plenty of wild rainbows as well as a few browns in the 6" to 9" class.

North Fork Tributaries

Courthouse Creek
One of Two North Fork Headwaters

At a Glance

Sam's Rank: 👍👍👍👍

GPS Fixes:
- Source fix: N35 15.956 W82 53.341 @ 5,020'
- Mouth fix: N35 18.094 W82 53.978 @ 3,210'

Size: medium at mouth *(At its confluence with Kiesee Creek)*

Gradient: moderate 11.1% source to mouth average *(3.1miles / 1,810')*

Effort: moderate to difficult

Pressure: none to slight

Fishing Quality: good to excellent

Species: Rainbows, Browns & Brookies

Access: From Hwy 215, FSR 140 parallels the uppermost stretch of North Fork to its source about 1.5 miles up at the bridge where Courthouse Creek and Kiesse Creek meet. FSR 140 then tracks away from Courthouse and follows Kiesse upstream for about .5 miles. There it departs Kiesse to the left and then runs another .8 miles along the ridge until it reaches a bridge and it re-joins Courthouse. Along those .8 miles, Courthouse is only accessible by fishing upstream or bushwhacking. There's a trail from the bridge at 2.8 miles with access to Courthouse Falls. At the bridge above the falls, the road continues for about .8 miles and then turns into a trail and follows the creek up to Devil's Courthouse. Take it from me: it's a 1.7 mile death march up that mountain to the Parkway!

Overview & Description

Charlie Daniels once sang about the *Devil Coming Down to Georgia*. But he apparently came down to North Carolina first and held court just off the Parkway at a place he named - *Devil's Courthouse*. It should be no surprise then that the stream sourcing up under that spot is appropriately named "*Courthouse Creek*." The fact that it is named Courthouse Creek, is loaded with wild trout, is one of the North Fork's two headwaters, comes off the Parkway from the highest elevation of any of the French Broad's headwaters, and finally, sources at a place called Devil's Courthouse, excites me to no end. I am compelled to fish it every time I'm in the

A brightly colored Rainbow caught on Courthouse Creek just down the ridge a ways from Devil's Courthouse. / *Image by Author* / *2019*

watershed. As one of the North Fork's two headwaters, Courthouse is by far the highest and largest.

Courthouse starts cold and high at about 5,020'and then screams down from under *Devil's Courthouse* below the Parkway between *Courthouse Ridge* and *Brushy Ridge*. Its average gradient along the 3.1 mile run is a moderate 11.1%. Along the way, it gathers water from several small feeders and becomes a good-sized stream by the time it converges at about 3,210' with *Kiesee Creek* to form North Fork's source. *Mill Station Creek* coming in creek left at .6 miles above its mouth and *Chestnut Creek* at about one mile are Courthouse's two largest feeders. Both are fishable for a distance – although the going gets tough and the fish are small.

There are several waterfalls on this stream - *Courthouse Falls* is the largest at about 25' and is about .6 miles above the mouth. Up to and above those falls are lots of smaller falls, long slides and deep pools that can be six to eight feet deep and make for challenging, yet rewarding fishing. Below Courthouse Falls, the stream is open and easy to wade and cast. Above the falls, the landscape and gradients are more challenging. Up there it's a small stream run and drop pool, close canopy environment.

Courthouse is known for cold, crystal clear water with good populations of wild rainbows and browns in the 5" – 10" range, as well as a few brookies in the 3" – 6" range in higher elevations. Courthouse may be small in comparison to other area creeks, but it delivers more fish than a lot of larger streams. As a personal challenge, I once tried to see how far I could fish up Courthouse and still catch fish. Using FSR 140 and the trail at its end, I fished another .7 miles up to 4,200' before the fishing ended. At that point, I hiked on up to the Parkway and hitch-hiked back down to my truck on Courthouse. I won't do that again.

Kiesee Creek
One of Two North Fork Headwaters

At a Glance

Sam's Rank: 👍👍👍
GPS Fixes:
- Source fix: N35 18.086 W82 52.956 @ 4,680'
- Mouth fix: N35 15.956 W82 53.341 @ 3,210'

Size: small at mouth *(At its confluence with Courthouse Creek)*
Gradient: moderate 10.3% source to mouth average *(2.7 miles / 1,470')*
Effort: moderate to difficult
Pressure: none
Fishing Quality: fair
Species: Rainbows
Access: From the bridge on FSR 140 at the confluence of Courthouse and Kiesee, the road parallels the creek for .5 miles. Beyond that first .5 miles, you'll be bushwhacking or using the creek bed as your trail.

Overview & Description

Even though Kiesse Creek is one of the two headwaters of the North Fork and offers some great hiking and water fall destinations, in my opinion it's insignificant in terms of its size, fish populations and ease of fishing. For that reason, I'll just cover the basic information about it here, and you can explore it further if you like. With all the other highly-productive water around, it's hardly worth devoting too much time to it given the effort required and the minimal rewards earned.

Kiesee starts way up under *Silvermine Bald* on the Parkway at about 4,680' and blasts its way down the mountain for about 2.7 miles between *Chestnut Ridge* and *Shuck Ridge* at a blistering 10.3% average gradient. It descends quickly while being fed by numerous feeders that transform it into a small stream by the time it converges with Courthouse Creek at about 3,210'. None seem to be really fishable.

It's a small but scenic stream with lots of water falls. Passage is difficult above where FSR 140 departs it. However, there are some reports of rail beds and logging roads for upstream access to and above the falls. But I've never found any access trails close to the stream that can be used reliably for fishing purposes.

I've fished up the .5 miles along FSR 140 from the confluence of Courthouse and Kiesee. With its mild gradients and tight canopies and sides, this stretch can be difficult. I continued fishing, hiking and climbing my way to just under the base of *Lower Kiesee Falls* - I could also see the *Upper Falls* just above. These two-tiered falls end with a small yet deep pool that held the largest trout I caught – a 9" bow. Others along the way were in the 5" – 7" range. Getting around the Lower Falls to the Upper involves slipping and sliding up a lot of wet and steep rocks. That was not worth the risk for me. I turned around and called it quits for Kiesee.

Beetree Fork
A Tributary of the North Fork

At a Glance

Sam's Rank: 👍👍👍
GPS Fixes:
- Source fix: N35 16.586 W82 55.134 @ 4,700'
- Mouth fix: N35 15.071 W82 53.408 @ 3,000'

Size: small at mouth *(At its confluence with the North Fork)*
Gradient: moderate 11.9% source to mouth average *(2.7 miles / 1,700')*
Effort: difficult to extreme
Pressure: none to slight
Fishing Quality: average
Species: Rainbows & Brookies
Access: Take Hwy 215 above Balsam Grove to the bridge at the entrance to FSR 140. At .3 miles past the bridge on Hwy 215, the North Fork veers away and parallels FSR 140; Beetree joins the North Fork from the left. Hwy 215 parallels Beetree its first mile and access is easy. At 1 mile it comes under the second Hwy 215 Bridge from the right. A trailhead on the right of the bridge tracks Beetree for about .8 miles to about 3,600'. The trail then leaves the creek, heads up Big Fork Ridge and eventually rejoins Beetree at its source at Cold Springs Gap.

Overview & Description

It's an understatement to say that Beetree Fork is my kinda stream. The combination of high elevation, good flow, nice fish variety and sizes, very low pressure and easy access, make it ideal for chasing wild trout. With the exception of a few other small seeps and creeks, Beetree is the North Fork's first sizeable tributary. And in my non-humble opinion, it's the best. Still, Beetree is under-fished given its access and attractive attributes. No visit to the North Fork is complete without spending at least a few hours on Beetree.

Beetree Fork begins life on the uphill side of Hwy 215 at *Cold Springs Gap* at 4,700'. This source is about 2.7 miles south of the Parkway on Hwy 215, and is just a stone's throw from the *Nantahala / Pisgah National Forest Boundary* to the west. From there it seeps under Hwy 215 and averages a blistering 11.9% descent for the next 2.7 miles between *Big Fork Ridge* and *Tanasee Ridge*. At about 1.4 miles above its mouth, *Bald Knob Branch*, the largest of a handful of feeders enters

A tiny Brook Trout fry caught high up on Beetree Fork with a bug almost as big as it is. / *Image by Author / 2016*

creek left. None of the feeders seem worth the effort to fish. By the time it crashes into the North Fork at 3,000' Beetree is a full-fledged small mountain trout stream.

I've fished Beetree from its mouth up about 1.8 miles until the trail that parallels it pulls away and heads up the ridge. Along that lower section, the creek has stretches wide enough for casting into the many fast-flowing drop pools and runs. In places, a *"drop pool ladder"* runs for a hundred yards or more up the mountain. I find most hold trout that are waiting for food sources coming down the water column. Brookies and bows in the 4'to 7" range seem to be the norm here, and I caught my share each time I've fished it. Typical small stream tactics such as slingshots, roll casts and high sticking are in order here. It's a fun creek to fish!

Tucker Creek
A Tributary of the North Fork

At a Glance

Sam's Rank: 👍👍
GPS Fixes:
- Source fix: N35 13.217 W82 55.671 @ 3,210'
- Mouth fix: N35.12.463 W82 51.579 @ 2.630'

Size: medium at mouth *(At its confluence with the North Fork)*
Gradient: flat 2.6% source to mouth average *(4.5 miles / 620')*
Effort: easy to moderate
Pressure: slight.
Fishing Quality: fair

126

Species: Rainbows & Browns
Access: From the bridge on Hwy 1379 / Macedonia Church Road, go .4 miles up Hwy 1379 to Hwy 1325. Turn left onto Hwy 1325 at the fish hatchery. About .3 miles past the hatchery, the next 1.5 miles of creek up to just below Hwy 1324, is on NFS land. You can fish anywhere along that stretch. Parking is plentiful.

Overview & Description

If the North Fork had a bunch of good tributaries, Tucker probably wouldn't have been included. But it doesn't, so it made the cut because it's one of the larger tributaries that are actually fishable. Even though Tucker flows for about 4.5 miles, only about 1.5 miles is on NFS land and open to fishing. Most of it is on private agricultural lands, so there's not much reason to fret about the private sections. The only part of this creek I'll cover is the lower 1.5 miles on NFS land.

Tucker starts on private land on the east face of *Bald Rock Mountain* at about 3,250'. From there it heads downhill at a flat 2.6% average gradient for about 4.5 miles to its convergence with North Fork at about 2,630'. About 2.2 miles below its source it receives water from its largest tributary *Johnnies Creek*, which also is on private land. Regardless, I'm not even sure if it is fishable. Other than several other small feeders, it receives no other fishable water along the way. At its mouth just past the hatchery, it's about 15'– 20' wide and very shallow.

From its mouth at the hatchery on NFS land, the first 1.5 miles upstream starts out flat with a lot of canopy obstruction. Along the lower stretches, there has been a lot of domestic refuse dumping. As the gradient gets steeper, the dumping stops, and the canopy opens up and the stream bed becomes more like a mountain stream with small falls, runs and pools. Ironically, the steeper section is relatively open and wide and offers easy casting and wading all the way to just below Hwy 1324.

I found lots of long shallow runs followed by riffles between shallow pools and drop pools. Rainbows dominate these waters, and I caught them mostly in the 7" - 10" range. I have fished most of the 1.5 miles and the upper higher-elevation stretch is by far the best fishing comparatively speaking. To me, it is a marginal trout stream at best. And given its elevations, gradient and flows in its lower section as well as the development all around it, I question its future as trout water.

West Fork
of the Pigeon River
At a Glance

Sam's Rank: 👍👍👍👍

GPS Fixes: The *mouth fix* below is at Lake Logan and is not the West Fork's actual *"mouth."* The official mouth is another 8.8 miles downstream where it converges with the East Fork to form the Pigeon River's source. The fix below is the southernmost starting point for the sections of the river featured in this chapter. The *source fix* noted here is the West Fork's undisputed source:

- Source fix: N35 18.248 W82 55.024 @ 5,340'
- Mouth fix: N35 24.448 W82 55.871 @ 2,910'

Size: large at mouth *(As it enters Lake Logan)*

Gradient: lower section-flat 1.7% average *(4 miles / 365')* / upper section-mild 6.7% average *(5.9 miles / 2,085')*

Effort: lower section - easy to moderate / upper section - difficult to extreme

Pressure: lower section - moderate / upper section - none to slight

Fishing Quality: good to excellent all sections

Species: Rainbows, Browns & Brookies

Access: The stretch of the river featured here is divided into an *Upper Section* and *Lower Section*. Both are paralleled by Hwy 215. Parking is easy along the lower section with some improved parking, as well as shoulder parking. There can be significant differences in stream / road elevations along the upper section. Be prepared to shoulder park, hike and bushwhack.

~ *Upper Section:* From the Parkway just south of MP 423.3, head up *(North)* Hwy 215 for 7 miles to Tom Creek – the start of this section.

~ *Lower Section:* From Tom Creek, head up Hwy 215 for 3.9 miles to Lake Logan – the start of this section.

Pigeon River *(Proper)* Watershed Overview

Although this chapter is only about the *West Fork*, let's put it into perspective by first considering just where it fits into the greater Pigeon River watershed. *If you've already read the East Fork chapter, skip the next two paragraphs.*

The *West Fork* is one of two headwaters of the Pigeon River *"Proper"* – a large and storied river that runs up into Tennessee. The West Fork rises entirely within Pisgah National Forest in the high elevations just north of the Parkway and runs the border between *Middle Prong Wilderness* and *Shining Rock Wilderness* to its confluence with the *East Fork* – the other Pigeon River headwater. The *East Fork*, the second headwater, also rises within Pisgah National Forest in Shining Rock Wilderness just north of the Parkway. As it leaves Shining Rock, it flows along

Hwy 276 on a northern course. Since the East Fork is a unique watershed itself, it is the subject of a standalone chapter.

Both of these *"forks"* meet just south of the paper mill town of Canton to form the Pigeon River's source. From there the Pigeon flows north-northwest, paralleling I-40 as it cuts through the Appalachians along the eastern boundary of the Smokies. About halfway up I-40 between Canton and the Tennessee line, it's impounded by Progress Energy's Walters Dam before continuing its ramble northward through gorges and wild country. At about 70 miles from its source, it flows into the French Broad River at the top of Douglas Lake near Newport, TN.

Here's some campfire trivia about the Pigeon – and not the usual paper mill *"pollution"* stories. The Pigeon River actually took its name from the now extinct *Passenger Pigeon* whose migration route once included the river's watershed. The name stuck even though I've never seen any kind of pigeon near that river – even under its bridges on Hwy 276 and I-40. Your guess is as good as mine about who chose that name, why they thought it would be cool, and when it was formally adopted. Being the great watershed it is, I believe it is deserving of a more regal sounding name – like the *"Pileated Woodpecker"* or something obvious like the *"Red Tail."* Okay back to the West Fork.

West Fork Overview & Description

Although the *Upper* and *Lower Sections* of this river share Hwy 215, each one is distinctly different in terms of topography, access, wild vs. stocked trout populations, pressure, etc. From a low elevation *(relatively speaking)* assisted-living *Lower Section* with wide, flat water, excellent in-and-out access, and lots of stocked trout with hair lips, to a high-elevation *Upper Section* with deep gorges, dangerous waters, sketchy access and wading, and wild fish with *NO* hair lips – there's something for everyone.

In normal flows, West Fork's water is cold with crystalline clarity and with most runs and pools so transparent you can see fish holding on the bottom six - eight feet down. The effects of past storms have extended the stream's banks quite a bit and even in the higher elevations, the *Upper Section's* banks and canopies are pretty open most of the way up. Generally, the river holds rainbow and browns in the *Lower Section* and a great population of brookies in the *Upper Section* and most tributaries.

From its source of well over a mile above sea level at about 5,340', the West Fork's *Upper Section* begins as a small, high-elevation flow just off the Parkway from between *Mount Hardy* and *Beech Gap*. Its first tributary, *Bubbling Springs*, starts even higher at 5,430. The West Fork screams down the slopes while gathering additional water and becomes a large stream by the time it reaches Lake Logan at about 9.9 miles. Over the first 5.9 miles *(Upper Section)* from its source, it loses elevation at a mild 6.7% average gradient as it runs the boundary between

Several arched stone bridges built by the CCC on Hwy 215 cross the West Fork in Middle Prong Wilderness and Shining Rock Wilderness. The pool offers good fishing. / *Image by Author / 2018*

the rugged slopes of *Middle Prong Wilderness* and *Shining Rock Wilderness*. The *Upper Section* is fed by several tributaries with names like *Bubbling Springs, Flat Laurel Creek, Sam Branch (I'm honored)* and *Tom Creek* – Sam Branch and Flat Laurel being the largest.

At 5.9 miles from its source, the *Lower Section* starts and runs for about 4 miles down to the head of *Lake Logan* at 2,910'. Along the way, its average gradient of a flat 1.7% is about a fourth of the *Upper Section's* – making for easier access and fishing. Along those 4 miles, it flows between *Fork Mountain* and *Lickstone Ridge* as it works its way through the beautiful *Great Balsam Mountains* – with their numerous mile high peaks. Along the *Lower Section*, tributaries with names like *Middle Prong, Queen Creek* and *Big Creek* provide more volume. Middle Prong, with its really nice feeder *Right Hand Prong*, is the largest entering either of the river's two sections. Finally, at 9.9 miles below its source, it enters Lake Logan at 2,910' and becomes impounded for the first of two times on its run to Tennessee.

Starting at the mouth and heading upstream, the West Fork's *Lower Section* starts at the head of Lake Logan at a place called "*Sunburst.*" Perhaps we should pause here for a short history lesson. Sunburst is an interesting place and a Federal plaque there describes Sunburst as having been a "*model*" logging town that supplied the needs of the *Champion Paper Company* in Canton in the early part of the last century.

After the area timber was harvested, the sawmill was moved to another location and Sunburst, the company town, became a ghost town. Company President, Reuben Robertson, convinced his Board that if the Pigeon was dammed to form a lake, it would assure a reserve water supply for Champion's paper mill just downstream in Canton. So the town was disassembled, a dam was built, and the water of the West Fork impounded to form Lake Logan - named for Mr. Robertson's brother-in-law, Logan Thomson.

Robertson, being the visionary he was, created a family compound called *Sit 'n Whittle Village*. It consisted of a main lodge and six log cabins moved from the Great Smoky Mountains National Park and reconstructed on the lake's shore. Sit 'n Whittle soon became Champion Paper Company's Executive Retreat and could accommodate 80+ visitors. In the late 1990s, Champion was sold to its employees, and in 2000 the Retreat was divested to the Episcopal Diocese of Western North Carolina for use as a conference center. Much of the surrounding timberland was acquired by the North Carolina Land Conservancy and eventually transferred to State and Federal ownership. It's a neat place and has rooms to rent and good food for the weary and hungry fly angler. Enough history…

The *Lower Section's* average gradient drops just enough to create a solid base of deep runs, enough current to offer fish plenty of feeding lanes and places to hide, and enough surface occlusion to keep trout from being spooked. It is also a pretty large trout stream and allows plenty of room to wade and cast. Most stretches of this section feature abnormally wide gravel beds and banks that provide great access and nothing to obstruct your back casts. Many of the gravel beds are wide and dry during summer months and resemble western streams. The first 2.8 miles above its mouth up to just below the Campgrounds, the West Fork is mostly surrounded by private homes, farms, open pastures, etc. Even so, the stream is open to fishing.

At about .9 miles up, *Big Creek* enters river right and at about 2.3 miles *Queen Creek* flows in on the right. Both flow through private land, are very small and appear only marginally fishable – especially the *Queen*. Finally, the larger and very fishable *Middle Prong* enters river right at about 2.8 miles. It creates a large convergence pool at the Hwy 215 Bridge that can be congested with swimmers in warm months. Middle Prong is entirely surrounded by federal lands and drains a huge watershed off the Parkway.

This first 1.75 miles of the *Lower Section* just above Lake Logan is managed as *Delayed Harvest*. This stretch runs upstream to about *Queen Creek* which enters just downstream of the Sunburst picnic and campground entrance. This *Delayed Harvest* stretch is stocked with a large mix of rainbow, brown and brookies, and those in the 14" – 16" range and bigger are not uncommon. There's also some natural reproduction going on as well as interlopers from the *Hatchery Supported* water upstream. Because this section is out of the way and not widely known, it doesn't get the pressure some more popular *Delayed Harvest* waters get. Even outside of the *Delayed Harvest* season, you can find good fishing there.

~ **West Fork of the Pigeon River** ~

The 1.2 miles above Middle Fork to the top of the *Lower Section* at *Tom Creek* transitions from private to NFS lands. This upper stretch of the *Lower Section* finally starts to take on the look of an Appalachian trout stream. Along this stretch the river is exiting a deep gorge, cascading from one huge drop to the next, squeezing between boulders and granite cliffs and collecting in large and deep plunge pools. But it is still wide and open. At about 4 miles up from the mouth, *Tom Creek* enters river right. Some say it's fishable, but it looks small to me.

The upper part of the *Lower Section* from *Queen Creek* upstream to about *Tom Creek* is managed as *Hatchery Supported*. It is also about 1.75 miles of water and other than the first ¼ mile, most of this *Hatchery Supported* section runs through NFS land. It receives monthly stockings of rainbows, browns and brook trout even when the *Delayed Harvest* does not. This probably accounts for the goodly numbers of trout along the *Lower Section* pretty much year-round. The trout I've caught along here are nicely sized in the 12" – 14" range.

At about 4 miles above the mouth, the *Upper Section* starts at *Tom Creek* at an elevation of about 3,265' and runs the next 5.9 miles to its source just north of the Parkway. This section is managed as *Wild Trout Water*. Along this section, you'll be dazzled with a variety of deep gorges, large and dangerous waterfalls and slides, fast and turbulent runs rushing between boulders, sheer granite walls, large and deep drop pools, minimal trail access, beautiful stone arched bridges, etc., etc. This section of the stream is wide-open fishing most of the way up.

The *Upper Section* becomes noticeably tighter and steeper with not many trails. And getting upstream from one run to the next can be strenuous. Although the streambed is not as wide, past floods have scourged the vegetation back and there's lots of room to cast and navigate. The entire section is mostly a series of steep drops and large plunge pools interspersed with steep pocket water.

This section has a well-deserved reputation for wild browns, with a healthy number of rainbows, mostly in the 6" – 10" range. Additionally, the far upper stretches of the creek's headwaters are home to at least 40 known populations of brook trout. Adequate riparian buffers and a denser canopy keep these streams clear and cold year round, and barrier falls prevent browns and rainbows from poaching the little brookies. The fact that these headwaters remain cool all summer keeps the trout active and the fishing good year round.

Upstream from *Tom Creek* at about 6.8 miles, *Sam Branch (I'm still honored)* flows in river left. It's a tight little creek, but very fishy. Just above the point where the *Sam* enters, Hwy 215 crosses a historic single arched stone bridge built by the CCC in 1937. Above and below it are a series of cascades that includes *Sunburst Falls* – a great fishing spot. As you continue up at 7.8 miles, *Flat Laurel Creek* enters river left - also tight, but good brookie fishing. Just below where *Flat Laurel* enters is another arched stone bridge built by the CCC – this time with three arches. Finally, at 9 miles above its mouth at the lake, *Bubbling Springs*, the West Fork's first and highest elevation tributary, flows in from the left from about 5,435' – just a stone's throw from the Parkway. At this point *Bubbling Springs* actually seems larger than the West Fork and is a worthy fishing destination.

West Fork Tributaries

Bubbling Springs Branch
A Tributary of the West Fork

At a Glance

Sam's Rank: 👍👍👍👍
GPS Fixes:
- Source fix: N35 18 031 W82 55.330 @ 5,430'
- Mouth fix: N35 18.825 W82 54 608 @ 4,840'

Size: small at mouth *(At its confluence with the West Fork)*
Gradient: mild 6.2% source to mouth average *(1.8 miles / 590')*
Effort: moderate to difficult
Pressure: none
Fishing Quality: average
Species: Brookies and Rainbows
Access: From the Parkway just south of MP 423.3, head north on Hwy 215. About .5 miles down, Bubbling Springs comes in from the left, and follows the road for about another .7 miles. At that point, the West Fork approaches from the left and Bubbling Springs from the right. Parking is easy. At about .8 miles down from the Parkway are primitive camp sites on the right. From there road / trail # 346 fords Bubbling Springs and heads deep into Shining Rock Wilderness.

Overview & Description

This first tributary of the West Fork is a nice little stream to fish for several reasons. *First*, it sources up within a stone's throw of the Parkway. *Second*, it's a beautiful, very high-elevation stream *(over a mile up)*, surrounded with big and fragrant Black Balsam, Fir and Spruce conifers. *Third*, it's paralleled by Hwy 215. Fourth, it's very secluded and not fished much. And *fifth*, it has a healthy population of hungry wild brook trout living in it. Those are good enough reasons to fish any stream.

Bubbling Springs comes to life at about 5,430' just north of the Parkway at *Mount Hardy Gap* between *Mount Hardy* and *Beech Gap*. It starts small and remote as it begins its 1.8 mile plunge to its confluence with the West Fork at 4,840'. Along the way, it attains a mild average gradient of about 6.2% while collecting volume from only one small and insignificant feeder. Even so, by the time Bubbling Springs reaches the West Fork, it's actually the larger of the two.

As the highest elevation West Fork tributary, Bubbling Springs Branch is within sight of Hwy 215 most of its flow and offers excellent trout angling opportunities. / *Image by Author / 2015*

For the first .5 miles or so above its mouth up to the campground and road / trail #346, Bubbling Springs features lots of runs, small falls and drop pools that average three to six feet deep. All of these hold lots of wild fish and make for some challenging and yet rewarding fishing. To be a small, high-elevation stream, this first .5 mile is generally open and relatively easy to cast and navigate. On up .3 miles to where it goes under Hwy 215 and into the higher elevations and gradients, it becomes a bit more challenging. Up there it is the typical small stream with runs and drop pools and a very close canopy – but still adequate populations of wild brookies. All along the stream's 1.9 mile run are several notable long and open slides with swirl pools that trap fish. These are fun to fish and several can be seen from the road. They're also handy to strip off and cool off in during hot weather.

Bubbling Springs is noted for clear and cold waters with healthy populations of wild brook trout. I have found them to be in the 4" – 8" range just above the mouth and in the higher elevations in the 2" – 6" range. It is a small stream in comparison to some others in the area, but is worth the time and effort to fish for sure.

Flat Laurel Creek
A Tributary of the West Fork

At a Glance

Sam's Rank: 👍👍👍👍
GPS Fixes:
- Source fix: N35 19.170 W82 53.075 @ 5,575'
- Mouth fix: N35 19.648 W82 54.537 @ 4,530'

Size: small at mouth *(At its confluence with the West Fork)*
Gradient: steep 12.4% source to mouth average *(1.6 miles / 1,045')*
Effort: difficult to extreme
Pressure: none
Fishing Quality: average
Species: Bows & Brookies
Access: From the Parkway at about MP 423.3, head up *(North)* Hwy 215. At about 3 miles, Flat Laurel Creek enters from the right and joins the West Fork – which is paralleling the road. Parking is plentiful on paved pull outs and shoulder. About 500' upstream from the mouth, a trail crosses the creek from the left and tracks upstream for about .8 miles through a gorge section – then departs the stream. For most of those .8 miles, it is far above the creek and not much use for fishing. Also, as a shortcut to the headwaters, head up Hwy 215 from the Parkway for about .8 miles to where road / trail #346 fords Bubbling Springs on the right. It continues into Shining Rock Wilderness and at about 1.9 miles will parallel Flat Laurel. At 2.2 miles ford it again just above where it splits into two prongs. The headwaters are supported by a maze of trails.

Overview & Description

   This second *"fishable"* tributary of the West Fork is a highly respectable trout stream. However, it has two distinct topographical zones. Its lower half is in a gorge and can be a challenge to fish. I say this because the first .8 miles above its mouth averages a gut busting 21.1% gradient. It's half Alpine climbing and half fishing at the same time. On the bright side, that topography means lots of stream structures full of native trout. It also means you won't be harassed by other anglers. The gorge section is about a mile high and surrounded with big, fragrant Black Balsams, Firs and Spruces. As a contrast, when you get above the gorge, the stream flattens out and opens up to what resembles a calm and easy to fish western high meadow. The two sections could not be more different.

   Flat Laurel Creek begins its steep 1.6 mile run to the West Fork from the north face of *Pisgah Ridge* and *Black Balsam Knob* just north of the Parkway at about 5,575' and then down and between *Sam Knob* and *Little Sam Knob*. *(I am honored yet again.)* It seeps out and runs through the *Pisgah Game Lands* at a steep average gradient of 12.4% *(the final .8 miles above the mouth is 21.1%)* before plunging into the West Fork at 4,530'. Along the way, it collects more volume from two feeders – neither has significant fishing potential. By the time it reaches the West Fork, it's still a small stream in terms of depth and width – but it's big on character.

From the mouth up through the first .8 miles, it grinds through the gorge, and it will take a toll on your mind and body. Countless large / small falls, drop pools, runs and slides create challenging, yet rewarding fishing if you're willing to pay the price. Along much of this section you'll be surrounded on two sides with near vertical walls of granite or ridges too steep to climb. Many truck-sized boulders, falls and pools will need to be navigated during this assent. But to be a small, high elevation stream, it's still generally open and pretty easy to cast most of the way up. Much of your navigation will need to be in the stream bed due to the trail being so far up the ridge. The fishing is productive in this section with brook trout being what I've found to be the dominant resident - all in the 5" – 8" range.

Above the gorge at about .8 miles from the mouth, you'll break out of the gorge and onto a relatively level mountain meadow in the shadow of *Pisgah Ridge* and *Black Balsam Knob*. Grasslands and the ever-present and fragrant Black Balsams, Spruces and Firs punctuate the landscape. In about .2 miles you will reach a point where the creek splits – one small *"no name"* tributary heads to the right, and *Flat Laurel*, the larger of the two, heads left. Take the left for the best visual and fishing experience up to the source. Along this stretch, the creek widens and becomes docile in nature. Calm water dotted with boulders, runs and pools hold easily spooked brook trout. Many pools are large with calm surfaces, and the brookies tend to be very cautious. I've found them to be in the 4" – 6" range, and they will hit most anything you throw at them at least once before running for cover.

All around this meadow are scores of deep cut trails from the animals and many hikers you'll often encounter from the *"free range people"* camped up on *Black Balsam Knob*. As you might expect, many of them will ask you; *"are you catching anything…"*, then the; *"do you keep them or let them go?"* I always respond with; *"yes I am catching trout, and I keep and eat every one of them!"* I don't of course – but it's worth it just to see the expression on their faces. In either event, this is a special spot and well worth the effort to get there.

Middle Prong
A Tributary of the West Fork
At a Glance

Sam's Rank: 👍👍👍👍👍
GPS Fixes:
- Source fix: N35 19.659 W82 56.616 @ 4,315'
- Mouth fix: N35 22.438 W82 56.260 @ 3,130'

Size: medium at mouth *(At its confluence with West Fork)*
Gradient: mild 6.1% source to mouth average *(3.7miles / 1,185')*
Effort: moderate to difficult
Pressure: first 1.4 miles up road–moderate / next 2.3 miles up trail–none to slight
Fishing Quality: good to excellent

Species: Rainbows, Browns & Brookies

Access: About 2.8 miles up Hwy 215 above Lake Logan, Sunburst picnic / primitive camping is on the right - turn right on to FSR 97. It parallels the stream for about 1.4 miles before starting several switch backs and leaving the stream. Park anywhere. With the exception of where elevations are steep, access is easy.

In the curve of the second switch back on FSR 97, Trail #142 begins a 2.5 mile trek to the stream's source. From there it tracks up *Haywood Gap Creek (a Middle Prong headwater)* and then to the Parkway at Haywood Gap *(MP 426.5)*. The trail starts high above Middle Prong, then at *Big Beartrap Branch*, descends to stream level up to the source. The trek up *Haywood Gap Creek* and on up to the Parkway is at a gut busting 16 – 19% gradient. *Go for it – it'll make a good campfire story!*

Overview & Description

If you only have the time and energy to fish one of the West Forks' tributaries and want easy access and good fishing, the Middle Prong is it. This stream is the West Fork's largest tributary above Lake Logan. With its headwaters starting just north of the Parkway, it drains most of the 7,900 acres of the *Middle Prong Wilderness* on its run to its confluence with the West Fork. This wilderness area lies just west of the *Shining Rock Wilderness* – with both being in the *Pisgah Ranger District of the Pisgah National Forest*. The Parkway forms a *"U"* shape border around these two wilderness areas from the south, and Hwy 215 dissects them. The Middle Prong is a medium-sized, wild trout stream that provides almost 4 miles of trout water where you can drive in and fish or hike in to more remote water.

The smallest Brookie I've caught in the Middle Fork's headwaters - most are much bigger. / *Image by Author / 2018*

Two small headwater streams form up high under the ridge lines of *Mount Hardy (6,122')* and *Parker Knob (5,407')* on the Parkway and scramble down to form the Middle Prong's source. Tiny *Buckeye Creek* and *Hayward Gap Stream* seep out and start descending at a blistering 16% gradient. Along the way, they collect enough water to transform into small streams when they finally converge at about 4,320'.

From that convergence point, the Middle Prong starts losing elevation over the next 3.7 miles at a moderate 6.1% average gradient as it makes its way between the towering slopes of *Fork Ridge* to the east and *Beartrail Ridge*. Along that distance, it is joined by several feeders of varying sizes such as *Grassy Ridge Branch, Big* and *Little Beartrap Branches,* and finally *Right Hand Prong,* its largest and most fishable. At about 3.7 miles from its source, it passes through the Sunburst primitive campground and picnic area and then under Hwy 215 at 3,130' where its mouth meets the West Fork. This confluence creates a large pool next to the road that's a popular fishing spot and swimming hole.

From its mouth at Hwy 215 and upstream for about 1.4 miles, the Middle Prong is a medium-sized flow. Its moderate gradient makes for easy hiking and the water is relatively calm with wide-open canopies that help navigation and casting. This stretch offers good brown and bow fishing with many in the 8" – 13" range and larger. As usual, the browns prefer late afternoon or after a rain when the water is up and with more color. In either case, the lower section of this stream offers superb fishing.

In this *Lower Section* about .4 miles up from the mouth, the small but highly fishable *Right Hand Prong* flows in on the right. Of all the feeders, I think it's the best in terms of fish populations and fishability. It crashes down the mountain from almost 2.8 miles up on the ridge at a steep average gradient of about 14.3%. Eventually it opens up a bit in the lower stretches and becomes a nice stream that's fun and easy to fish – and productive! Expect lots of small 6" – 10" rainbows in the lower reaches and brookies in the 4" – 6" range in the upper parts of the flow and its one feeder – *Boomer Inn Branch* at about 1 mile from its mouth.

At about 1.4 miles up Middle Prong, *Little Beartrap Branch* enters river right. This is a very small flow and is marginally fishable for about .1 miles before it goes vertical. On up at about 2.3 miles, *Big Beartrap Branch* flows in river right from about 1.5 miles up. As its name implies, it's bigger and is fishable for a ways if you're up to the steep climb. Bows and brookies in the 6" – 8" range is all I've caught. But some claim much bigger fish are up there. Other than the feeder streams just mentioned, that's about all the Middle Prong has to offer for *blue line* fishing on your way to the source.

At about 3.7 miles from the mouth, you'll reach the Middle Prong's source. Here the two headwater streams *Buckeye Creek (left)* and *Hayward Gap Stream (right)* converge. Both source up on the ridges above you from about a mile above sea level. From its source, *Buckeye* flows for about 1.4 miles and *Haywood* flows for about 1.7 miles to where they converge. Both streams are quite small and fishable, but are extremely steep with an average gradient of about 16%. Throughout much of their flows you will find abundant falls and plunge pools. Both of these streams seem to contain brook trout almost exclusively.

East Fork
of the Pigeon River
Also known as *"Big East Fork"*
At a Glance

Sam's Rank: 👍👍👍👍👍

GPS Fixes: The *mouth fix* below is not the East Fork's *official* mouth. That's another 13.4 miles downstream at Hwy 276 where it converges with the West Fork to form the Pigeon River's *(Proper)* source. The fix below is the southernmost starting point for the section of the river featured in this chapter. The *source fix* noted here is the East Fork's undisputed source:

- Source fix: N35 19.639 W82 49.793 @ 4,230'
- Mouth fix: N35 21.930 W82 49.091 @ 3,380'

Size: large at mouth *(As it goes under Hwy 276)*
Gradient: flat 3.9% source to mouth average *(4.1 miles / 850')*
Effort: moderate
Pressure: slight
Fishing Quality: good to excellent
Species: Rainbows, Browns & Brookies
Access: Access is best gained from either end of the stream. The Parkway parallels it most of the way, but in many places stream / road elevation differentials can be 800' – 1,000'. It's a bushwhacking nightmare to climb in and out of any location other than the mouth or source.

~ Access from its mouth is 2.6 miles north of the Parkway where the East Fork comes under Hwy 276. Parking is plentiful. Upstream access is via the Big East Fork Trail #357 which follows the stream for about 3.3 miles to Greasy Prong, then becomes #607 and continues another .6 miles to just under Yellowstone Prong and Dark Prong's convergence point – the East Fork's source. From there it climbs to the Parkway at Looking Glass Rock Overlook at MP 417. The trailhead for #357 starts south of the culvert / bridge under Hwy 276 and heads up the creek.

~ Access from its source begins at Looking Glass Rock Overlook on the Parkway at MP 417. At the trailhead, just past *"Deer Head"* tree, take the right onto Trail #607 down to the East Fork's source point mentioned above. From there, continue downstream on Trail #357 to its mouth.

Pigeon River *(Proper)* Watershed Overview

Although this chapter is about the Pigeon River's *East Fork*, we'll put things into perspective by examining how it fits into the greater Pigeon River watershed. *If you've already read the West Fork chapter, skip the next three paragraphs.*

The *East Fork* is one of two headwaters of the Pigeon River "*Proper*" – a large and storied river that runs into Tennessee. It rises entirely within Pisgah National Forest on the eastern face of Black Balsam Knob just north of the Parkway, then runs east just under the north side of Pisgah Ridge and along the southeastern boundary of Shining Rock Wilderness. As it leaves the wilderness area, it flows north for about 13.4 miles along Hwy 276 on its way to meet the West Fork. Most of those 13.4 miles are on private land, and none of it is considered good trout water. In fact, most of it is not even designated trout water by the state.

The West Fork, the Pigeon's other headwater, rises just north of the Parkway in the high elevations of the Middle Prong Wilderness and Shining Rock Wilderness. It then runs the border between Middle Prong Wilderness and Shining Rock Wilderness down to its confluence with the East Fork just below Canton. The West Fork is a unique watershed and is the subject of another chapter.

Both "*forks*" meet just south of the paper mill town of Canton to form the Pigeon River's source. From there it flows north-northwest, paralleling I-40 as it cuts through the Appalachians along the eastern boundary of the Smokies. About halfway up I-40 between Canton and the Tennessee line, it's impounded by Progress Energy's Walters Dam before continuing its ramble north through gorges and wild country. At about 70 miles from its source, it flows into the French Broad River at the top of Douglas Lake near Newport, TN. Okay, back to the East Fork.

Some of the old timers tell great East Fork stories. One story is about a 100 ton boulder lying next to the East Fork with several 2" holes drilled through it. Its name is "*Holy Moley Rock*" and it lays up the creek a ways above Hwy 276 mostly covered in moss and Rhododendron these days. It's supposedly good luck to stick a finger in one of the holes and scream "*Holy Moley.*"

The story goes something like this. Back when the stretch of Parkway above the East Fork was under construction, crews were blasting to clear the right of way. On one particular day, an old timer was camped out hunting squirrels in the valley below on the East Fork. When the construction crew torched off a dynamite charges, it dislodged the boulder in the image on the next page. It started rolling slowly down the side of the mountain toward the river creating a path of destruction not often seen by humans this side of Hell. Entire 12" chestnut oaks and everything else in its path were being mangled and shredded beyond recognition as the rocky behemoth picked up speed on its way downhill from 700 feet above.

The old timer could hear the commotion above and even feel the earth shaking as it was getting closer, but he couldn't see what was coming because of the thick summer foliage. For the old timer, the wait felt like forever – with the fear of being killed by something that he might never see. Fear quickly turned into sheer terror as suddenly, the crashing, splitting and crushing sounds became deafening and the forest before him exploded in a storm of rocks, splinters and dust. The 100 ton boulder crashed into the stream bank just 30 feet in front of him in an earth shattering roar and a cloud of leaves and mud.

As the dust settled, the old timer caught his breath, and shouted; *"Holy F--king Moley." (The "F" verb was later*

"Holy Moley Rock" below the Parkway on the East Fork of the Pigeon River. / *Image by Author / 2018*

dropped...) I'm sure I would have cussed like a wounded pirate too – probably worse. After regaining his composure, he reportedly staggered up to the rock and put a shaking finger into the hole – later claiming that he could feel the heat of the dynamite's ignition flash. *Hmmmm.....*

I've fished past that rock with its holes several times and have no reason to doubt the story. When there, I stick my finger in the hole for good luck – I believe I catch more fish because of it too. I wonder, after the old timer changed his pants, did he keep on squirrel hunting? Or did he just sit down and ponder what had just happened? Well, that's enough local lore. Back to fishing the East Fork.

East Fork Overview & Description

The East Fork is managed as *Wild Trout Waters* and offers some of the most scenic, challenging and rewarding fishing of this entire Guide. The stream's main flow and two headwater streams could not be more different. The river's main flow passes through *Shining Rock Wilderness*, with some of the most remote and hard to get to real estate along the Parkway. But, when you do get there, it's relatively flat and easy to wade and fish for the browns and bows that call it home. It's fed by several highly regarded brookie streams, and there are the two headwater streams with names like *"Dark Prong"* and *"Yellowstone Prong."* They pass through the exotic *"Graveyard Fields"* and offer everything from wide open Wyoming style topography, to rugged stretches with 100' waterfalls, huge plunge pools, boulder / rock gardens and long stretches of runs and riffles. If you like fishing for all three trout in one exotic watershed – *this fork's for you.*

The water of the East Fork is without equal in purity, gin-clear clarity, and year-round cold temperatures. In fact, in the winter, the highest elevation waters can be so cold the trout become very lethargic and slow down their feeding. All of its waters originate in *Shining Rock Wilderness* – which provides the cleanest and purest

Several overlooks offer parking, good views and access to the East Fork's watershed. All are crowded on weekends. / *Image by Author / 2018*

water around. I've seen pools 12' deep, and the water is so clear you can easily see a 6" trout on the bottom.

As far as the trout go, most of the headwaters, tributaries and feeders are hold-outs for brook trout. My buddy Chris and I have caught some of the most beautifully colored brookies there. Their unique dark tint, accented with bright orange, white, yellow, red and green, makes them special in my book. The river's main flow also supports a healthy population of rainbows and browns. Along many access trails it's not uncommon to see 14'–16" browns and bows holding in the deep pools and runs below. All in all, it's great trout water surrounded by breathtaking beauty!

The East Fork comes to life as its two headwater streams converge just below *Bridges Camp Gap* just north of the Parkway. *Yellowstone Prong* seeps out of the east slope of *Black Balsam Knob*, and *Dark Prong* starts on *Tennent Mountain*. Both start at over a mile above sea level and

Deer Head Tree at Trail #607 trail head leading down to the East Fork's source. / *Image by Author / 2016*

converge at 4,220' to form the East Fork. From there, the East Fork forms and starts a 4.1 mile run to its mouth at Hwy 276. Along the way it picks up volume from several fishable tributaries. From source to mouth it has a flat 3.9% average gradient making for some easy wading, a wide-open stream bed and an open canopy for easy casting most of the way up. From headwaters to mouth, I consider the East Fork unsurpassed in beauty and wild trout fishing.

Starting at the East Fork's mouth at the giant arched culvert under Hwy 276, it's about 60'–75' wide. For several hundred yards the river is littered with large boulders, long and fast runs and deep pools. On up a quarter mile or so the stream shrinks to about 24'–30' across but still has nice runs, pools and an occasional large drop pool. The entire lower stretch has a flat gradient, spacious banks and open canopy, and paralleled by good trails. Along this lower stretch, the river holds vibrant populations of wild bows and browns and is waded and fished with ease.

At about 1.2 miles up *Shining Creek*, the first large tributary enters river right. This stream drains a large watershed and is steep, rugged and very fishable. It holds lots of brookies in the upper stretches in the 5" class. From Shining Creek up to about 2.1 miles, the stream gets smaller but is still fairly easy wading and casting. Healthy numbers of browns and bows in the 6" – 10" range and an occasional

Pools like this one are common along the East Fork and all hold good populations of hungry trout. / *Image by Author / 2011*

brookie in the 4"- 6" range "*wash down*" and populate this stretch.

At about 3.3 miles from the mouth, *Greasy Cove Prong* enters river right. This is a small stream at its mouth, but is home to good brookie fishing. It has no trail, only in-stream navigation or bushwhacking. For some reason unknown to me, I really like this stream – perhaps because it's so remote and rugged, and the fishing is always good. Most of what I have caught here are brookies in the 5" class.

Along the next .8 miles upstream, the stream narrows even more, but is still easily fishable. At .8 miles above Greasy is the East Fork's source – a point about 4.1 miles above Hwy 276. At this point, *Yellowstone Prong (left)* and *Dark Prong (right)* converge. *Yellowstone* flows down from above through 3.1 miles of some of the most diverse and beautiful topography of any water in this Guide. *Dark Prong* flows about the same distance through slightly less beautiful topography to converge with the *Yellowstone* at 4,230'. These are polar opposites in terms of everything, but both are very fishy and contain brook trout almost exclusively in the 4"–7" range.

East Fork Tributaries

Yellowstone Prong
One of Two East Fork Headwaters

At a Glance

Sam's Rank: 👍👍👍👍👍
GPS Fixes:
- Source fix: N35 19.434 W82 52.385 @ 5,690'
- Mouth fix: N35 19.639 W82 49.793 @ 4,230'

Size: small at mouth *(At its confluence with the Dark Prong)*
Gradient: moderate 9% source to mouth average *(3.1 miles / 1,470')*
Effort: upper section - easy to moderate / lower section - difficult to extreme
Pressure: upper section-slight / lower section–none
Fishing Quality: upper section - good to excellent / lower section - excellent
Species: upper section - Brookies / lower section - Brookies, Rainbows & Browns
Access: The Parkway parallels the entire stream. However the road / stream elevation differentials can be as much as 300'– 700'. Because each end of the stream has completely different characteristics and access points are so different, I have divided the stream into *Lower* and *Upper* sections.

~ The *Lower Section* starts at the top of Second Falls *(a wooden bridge crosses there)* and goes downstream about 1.3 miles to the confluence with Dark Prong. To get to the mouth, go to Looking Glass Rock Overlook on the Parkway. Paved parking is available across the road from the trailhead. At the trailhead, take the right onto Trail #607 and continue down for .6 miles to just under the point where Yellowstone Prong and Dark Prong converge. A maze of other trails crisscrosses the area you can also use.

~ The *Upper Section* starts at the source point at the Upper Falls and continues 1.9 miles down to the wooden bridge just above Second Falls. To gain access, park at Graveyard Field paved parking at about MP 419 on the Parkway. Next to the restrooms, Trail #358C begins a .2 mile decent to the wooden bridge crossing the stream just above Second Falls. The trail continues all the way to the source at the Upper Falls. This entire basin is a maze of trails offering additional access.

Overview & Description

The old saying: *"trout don't live in ugly places"* definitely applies to Yellowstone Prong! Of the East Fork's two headwaters, Yellowstone is by far the more scenic, exotic, topographically unique, fishable and difficult / dangerous of the two. It's managed as *Wild Trout Waters* and is one of my top three most favorite Parkway fishing destinations in North Carolina. It's also a favorite of a huge numbers of Asheville day trippers and other trout anglers who know its secrets and have the same affinity for it.

Because of the differences in the landscape through which Yellowstone flows, I consider it to have two different topographical, flow and forest zones. The *Lower Section*, starting at its mouth upstream to the trail bridge just above the Second Falls, is mostly in a steep and rugged gorge with several large waterfalls. Its water is constantly churning and the canopy is heavily forested with hardwoods, brush and a mix of conifers. This makes for difficult navigation and fishing. Much of the Lower Section, especially the falls, is visible from the Parkway.

By contrast, the *Upper Section* from the trail bridge above Second Falls to its Upper Falls source is flat and open in what resembles a western high-meadow stream. It's easy to fish. Almost the entire Upper Section's flow is through Graveyard Fields and is within sight of the Parkway. The two sections couldn't be more different - the only similarity being they both are beautiful beyond words.

Yellowstone Prong sources high up on the east slope of *Black Balsam Knob* at 5,690'. From there it starts a 3.1 mile slow run through *Graveyard Fields* between *Pisgah Ridge* and *Graveyard Ridge*, then into a gorge and on to its convergence below *Bridges Camp Gap* with *Dark Prong* at 4,220'. Along its *Upper Section*, it has a moderate 7.5% average gradient through *Graveyard Fields*. Below the bridge, it plunges into the *Lower Section* and its gradient increases to over 15% for its final run below *Skinny Dip Falls* to converge with *Dark Prong*. Along its entire run, it collects no significant volume from any other feeders. By the time it converges with the *Dark Prong* to form the source of the East Fork,

The Yellowstone is fishable all the way to its Upper Falls just below its source on Black Balsam Knob. / *Image by Author / 2018*

it's still a small stream in terms of depth and width – but big on fishability.

Moving upstream from its mouth, the .4 miles under *Skinny Dip Falls* has a mild gradient and is relatively open. Banks are steep, especially on the Parkway *(south)* side and foliage is very thick along this stretch, although the canopy is open. Casting is easy to the rainbows and browns and the occasional brookie residing there. In-stream navigation is the best option along here. In warm months, as you approach *Skinny Dip Falls*, you'll hear swimmers and rock hoppers before you see them. This unique and aesthetically pleasing series of falls, deep pools and runs makes the area immensely popular with locals and anglers alike. I've seen as many as 200 scantily clad humans, as well as a pack of female wood fairies, in this place having the time of their lives. I try to ignore them and fish up between them. These waters have lots of fish and even with the activity, the water here is productive.

If you are a fly angler among skinny dippers, you'll be treated as a celebrity with dozens of pictures taken of you as you fish through. Several years ago I was fortunate enough to hook an 18" Hellbender in the middle of this mass of humanity. When I hoisted that ugly critter out of the water, you would have thought it was a 10' alligator. The stream emptied in about 10 seconds. Women were screaming, babies crying, dogs barking, men reaching for weapons, cameras snapping, etc., etc. I unhooked it and returned it to the water. No one got back in after that. It was kinda funny, and it left them perplexed and dumbfounded.

The Second Falls on the Yellowstone is large with a deep and very fishable pool at its base if you can get past the swimmers and rock hoppers. / *Image by Author / 2014*

The .5 miles above Skinny Dip up to *Yellowstone Falls* enters what amounts to a gorge and becomes a whole lot steeper and more difficult to fish. The average gradient along this half-mile stretch is a heart pounding 19%, and the stream constricts as you move up into the gorge. However, the extreme topography creates lots of drop pools and stair-step falls that hold trout. *Yellowstone Falls* is two-tiered. The downstream tier is the highest at about 75'. Truck-sized boulders and slabs litter the stream for a hundred yards below the falls and offer endless

146

hiding places for trout. But be prepared to do some climbing and bushwhacking. And be careful along here – lots of folks have gotten hurt and killed here.

From *Yellowstone Falls* to the *Second Falls* at the top of the *Lower Section* is about .4 miles. Above Yellowstone, you leave the gorge and the gradient lessens to about 9.5%. Although tight, this stretch between the two falls is very fishable. The fifty yards below the 50'- 75' Second Falls are strewn with the same large boulders and slabs as the approach to Yellowstone. Its plunge pool is large and deep and offers a fine habitat to some of the stream's larger trout as well as swimmers and rock hoppers that congregate there. My largest catch on this stream was here – a 16" brown on a # 16 Bead Head Prince dropped under a huge # 14 Golden Caddis.

At the top of *Second Falls* you'll be on solid slab rock all the way to the wooden bridge and the start of the *Upper Section*. This is a truly magical place to fish. It's 60'-75' wide, solid rock, runs and pools, wash holes, and a huge rock / boulder garden sitting on slab rock. Just before the creek rolls off over Second Falls to the pool below, there is a small pool cut latterly into the slab rock. It's dangerous, but I always rappel down to fish it, and it never disappoints!

The first 1.1 miles of *Upper Section* starts at the bridge on Trail # 358C accessing from the *Graveyards Fields* parking lot. At nearly any point, you can stop, look up, and see the parking area on the Parkway. It's an enchanting visionary experience made better by some great brookie fishing. Just above the bridge the creek runs through a solid rock trough into a pool and then under the bridge. There's always trout there – and lots of gawking day hikers.

The next 1.1 miles up to the *Upper Falls* is at a mild 3.1% gradient. The first .6 miles is different from any other section of the watershed. Since it is through the flat topography of the *Graveyard Fields*, it spreads out to 30' or more in places. Small quartz rocks, a gravel and slab rock substrate and very wide gravel banks make it feel like a Western stream. Only until you get to about .5 miles below the *Upper Falls* do the stream and vegetation start to constrict. This entire section is prime brook trout water and the most beautiful brookies I've ever seen were caught here by my buddy Chris and me. I recommend putting in at the start of the Upper Section at the bridge on Trail # 358C and fishing up to the *Upper Falls*. It's a good four hours of fishing. I have not fished the .7 miles above *Upper Falls* up to the source just under *Black Balsam Knob*. But I have had some memorable times there…

Dark Prong
One of Two East Fork Headwaters

At a Glance

Sam's Rank: 👍👍👍👍
GPS Fixes:

- Mouth fix: N35 19.645 W82 49.784 @ 4,220'
- Source fix: N35 19.969 W82 52.229 @ 5,525'

Size: small at mouth *(At its confluence with the Yellowstone Prong)*
Gradient: moderate 9.9% source to mouth average *(2.5miles / 1,305')*
Effort: difficult to extreme
Pressure: none
Fishing Quality: good
Species: Brookies & Rainbows
Access: This stream is hard to access and move around on due to its remoteness. Mouth access is the best option. Go to Looking Glass Rock Overlook at MP 417 on the Parkway. Parking is across the road from the trailhead. At the trailhead, take a right onto Trail #607 and continue for .6 miles to just under where Yellowstone Prong and Dark Prong converge. A short upstream hike puts you in Dark Prong's mouth on the right. Fish the main run by wading upstream from the mouth, then backtrack out the same way.

Overview & Description

Dark Prong is managed as *Wild Trout Waters*. It runs from source to mouth in a gorge located in some of the wildest parts of Pisgah National Forest. Despite its remoteness, getting to its mouth is relatively easy, but that's the only thing easy about this stream! You'll need to navigate upstream using the path of least resistance, and most of the time that's in the middle of the creek. Along its 2.5 miles flow, it's littered with an endless series of large / small falls, long rock slides, boulders and an occasional dead stand that's fallen across. Given the stream's structure, it can be difficult, even technical at times, and progress will be slow. I've only fished the lower 2 miles and it took a long day! I just skimmed the most attractive water and barely got out of there before darkness fell.

Its water is perfectly clear and very cold. Many pools can be 8' deep but you can see the bottom. Even after a rain, turbidity normalizes quickly due to the lack of trails and other runoff sources. Fishing is always good, and it's common to net brookies in the 8" class here. If you're looking for true wilderness fishing and solitude, you'll find it on Dark Prong.

Dark Prong springs to life from just over 5,500' between the peaks of *Black Balsam Knob* and *Tennent Mountain*. It flows its entire 2.5 miles run between *Graveyard Ridge* and *Ivestor Ridge* before converging with *Yellowstone Prong* at 4,220' to form the East Fork's source. Along the way it maintains an average gradient of about 9.9% although its ruggedness makes that gradient seem higher. It does not receive any volume from sizeable feeders, and by the time it converges with the *Yellowstone*, it is still the smaller of the East Fork's two headwaters.

Moving upstream from its mouth, the first .5 miles is deceptively small, tight and "*dark*" with numerous large / small falls, slides, pools and boulders to

A typical Brookie caught on Dark Prong - they are all this beautiful. / *Image by Author / 2018*

negotiate. But after the first .5 miles, it opens up and gets wider. Even so, that next 1.5 miles is a labyrinth of large and treacherous waterfalls, deep plunge pools, and long and slick rock slides. Several of these falls will cause you to take pause as you approach. And it's a good idea to spend some time figuring out just how you will get over, around and through them – while simultaneously trying to fish safely the pocket water in and around them.

The middle stretches of the creek are often obstructed by huge granite slabs and boulders, dead falls and with steep or no banks. Occasionally, the canopy creates a tunnel approaching some of the falls, and some areas look as though the forest has burned and allowed the canopy to open up. In other places, erosion appears to have modified the stream's geometry with slides and / or small alluvial fans of sort. Be careful on the rock slides and falls – many are larger than you'd imagine for a creek this size. Navigating them takes time, finesse, and to a degree – guts.

As you approach about 2 miles up at about 5,200', the creek becomes choked with bushes and low canopy. Fishing gets danged hard! Last time I was there, I bushwhacked up to *Graveyard Ridge Trail,* connected with *MTS Trail* and high-tailed it back to the parking area just as darkness fell. It's not a place to be after dark – flashlight or not.

The entire stream is loaded with wild brook trout in the 8"–12" range and even a few in the 14" class have been reported. The going is tough but it's worth it when you can catch wild trout of this size. All in all, Dark Prong never fails to deliver a productive and memorable day of fishing.

Greasy Cove Prong
A Tributary of the East Fork

At a Glance

Sam's Rank: 👍👍👍👍👍
GPS Fixes:
- Mouth fix: N35 20.241 W82 49.623 @ 4,000'
- Source fix: N35 20.506 W82 51.434 @ 5,085'

Size: small at mouth *(At its confluence with the East Fork)*
Gradient: moderate 10.8% source to mouth average *(1.8 miles / 1,085')*
Effort: difficult to extreme
Pressure: none
Fishing Quality: good
Species: Brookies & Rainbows
Access: Due to its extreme remoteness, this stream is more difficult to access than Dark Prong. The logical access point is where it converges with the East Fork. Get there by going to Looking Glass Rock Overlook at MP 417 on the Parkway. Parking is across the road from the trailhead. At the trailhead, take the right onto Trail # 607 and continue down about .6 miles to just under where Yellowstone Prong and Dark Prong converge. Continue down along the East Fork another .6 miles to Greasy on the left. From there Trail #362 tracks up the Prong for about 1.1 miles before pulling away and ascending to Grassy Cove Ridge. The only way I know to fish Greasy is wading upstream from its mouth – then backtracking out.

Overview & Description

In my opinion, Greasy Cove Prong is a smaller version of Dark Prong. I've fished the first mile of it several times, and caught a bunch of brookies each time. The last time I fished it, I was about a mile above its mouth and it was getting late, and it was there that I had a *"close encounter of the first kind"* with a sow bear and two cubs. They were up stream about fifty yards. Fortunately, the wind was in my favor and they didn't detect me. For forty-five minutes I watched them as they hung out at the top of a small falls while the cubs roughhoused. Since it was late afternoon, I decided to call it quits and head out. No reason to push my luck.

Greasy runs through some of the most remote and wild country Pisgah National Forest has to offer. The biggest difference from Dark Prong is that there is a trail along about a mile of it. This is handy when negotiating the numerous waterfalls, slides, boulders and dead stands that litter its lower section. It took me almost five hours to fish that first mile where the trail peeled away before the bear encounter caused me to hightail it out of there. If you want a wilderness fishing experience on a small stream loaded with brookies, Greasy fits the bill.

Greasy oozes from between the peaks of *Tennent Mountain* and *Grassy Cove Top* at about 5,085'. From there it rambles downhill at a serious 10.8% gradient for about 1.9 miles between *Ivestor Ridge* and the exceptionally steep slopes of *Grassy Cove Ridge* before plunging into the East Fork at 4,000'. That mouth point is where *Nobreeches Ridge*, *Chestnut Ridge* and *Ivestor Ridge* all converge. Along the way, no other sizable feeders add any volume. When it reaches the East Fork, this Prong is the smallest of all the East Fork's main tributaries.

Years ago I was on my way down the East Fork when I passed through that point on the trail where the three ridges mentioned above meet. What I would describe as a group of "*free range*" humans were there having a ceremony of sort - chanting, singing, burning incense *(or something)*, dancing, etc. It was kinda creepy. I asked one of them named Star: "*what's up?*" In a breathy voice she said; "*Oh... this special spot on Mother Earth's surface focuses the free energy from distant stars, and our leader has found a way for us to capture and absorb that energy and live a more aware, peaceful and accepting life.*" The hair stood up on the back of my neck... and I thought really? I could use a dose of that, but there were fish to be caught first, so I excused myself.

I returned later that afternoon determined to get a dose of that enlightenment. Instead I found half the group passed out on the ground – butt naked. Others were arguing and fighting like banshees. Several couples were in the bushes doing something to each other; one couple was sitting in the stream talking in tongues – all naked! And one dude was sitting by the fire ring in the lotus position. I approached him with a friendly: "*hey, what's up?*" He glanced at me and responded with; "*f - - k off dude...*"

I guess all that enhanced awareness, peacefulness and acceptance they were supposed to be getting didn't happen. I figure they got either too much energy or not enough – or maybe some bad energy from a black hole. I think about that experience when I'm in the area and wonder if all that focused energy affects trout in some manner. Okay, back to the normal world and trout fishing.

From its mouth moving upstream over the first 1.1 mile, Greasy's path is best described as through a gorge. Along that section, the stream is gin clear and very cold year round. It is steep, has tight banks and canopies, and an endless flow of drop pools, small falls, slab slides and runs. I found this section to be tough to fish – but the trail helped. I have used it to hasten my portage around the larger and more risky obstacles. Several of these will cause you to take a deep breath in awe of their seductive beauty before you make the calculated decision to get out and go around them. The times I've been there the fishing was excellent. All I caught were brookies in the 8" – 12" range – although I've heard of rainbows being caught here as well.

The gorge seems to open up a bit at about .8 miles through about 1.1 miles where the trail leaves the stream. After that point, my observations, as well as maps and satellite imagery, seem to indicate the gorge closes in again with the usual stream features that accompany that topography. Above that, it looks much like Dark Prong's impressive features - albeit smaller. As with Dark Prong, several areas appear to have burned some time ago. But I'm not sure if this is fact or just my impression. As with my warning for Dark Prong, be careful on this stream. Many of the obstacles are beautiful but downright nasty. Navigating them takes good judgment, ability and time.

Shining Creek
A Tributary of the East Fork

At a Glance

Sam's Rank: 👍👍👍👍

GPS Fixes:
- Mouth fix: N35 21.272 W82 49.106 @ 3,485'
- Source fix: N35 21.476 W82 50.700 @ 4,365'

Size: small at mouth *(At its confluence with the East Fork)*

Gradient: moderate 9.3% source to mouth average *(1.8 miles/880')*

Effort: moderate to difficult

Pressure: none

Fishing Quality: good

Species: Brookies & Rainbows

Access: Head north of the Parkway on Hwy 276 for 2.6 miles to where the East Fork goes under the road. Parking is on both sides of the road. From there, upstream access to Shining Creek's mouth is via Big East Fork Trail #357. This trail follows the East Fork upstream for about 1.2 miles to Shining Creek's mouth. The Trail #357 trailhead starts south of the huge arched culvert / bridge going under Hwy 276.

An alternate route is to take Trail #363 from the end of the parking area on the north side of the creek along a .5 mile hike to a point about .4 miles up from Shining Creek's mouth on the East Fork at Shining Creek Gap. From there it continues on up to the creek's source and then on to the North Prong - one of Shining Creek's two headwaters. If you want to fish the upper sections of the Shining Creek, this trail will save you time and provide access all the way.

Overview & Description

Shining Creek is the largest tributary for the segment of the East Fork included in this guide. Its watershed drains no less than twice as much land as any other tributary. Even so, at its mouth it's still not even a medium-sized stream. In fact, it is small. But given its small size, the ruggedness of the topography of the land it flows through creates an inordinate number of big water features – most with brook trout in them. Generally, from its headwaters to its mouth, Shining is surrounded by high peaks and flows through some of *Shining Rock Wilderness's* most steep and rugged areas. This makes for one heck of a trout fishing experience – if you're able and willing to pay the price.

With that said, I find Shining desirable for several reasons. *First* and foremost, it has what seems to me an above average population of fish for a stream of its size. I have fished the entire flow and caught as many as four to six fish per hour. *Second*, it's very remote and wild – which automatically puts it at the top of my list. And *third*, other than the first .4 miles above its mouth, it has an excellent trail system. The trail allows you to cover a lot of high-elevation, remote and wild water by scouting the falls, runs and pools from the trail above, deciding which ones to invest effort in, and then drop in and fish – then move on. To sum it up, as trout streams go, it has a lot going for it! But easy is not one of them. Even with a trail it is hard fishing.

Shining Creek's source is created as the result of the convergence of two remote headwaters streams at 3,485'. From over a mile above sea level *North Prong* and *South Prong* flow through *Shining Rock Wilderness* to that convergence point. It's worth noting here that these two headwaters have the highest average gradient of any of the other headwater streams in this watershed – *by far!* From that source, Shining explodes to life and starts a 1.8 mile rampage at an average gradient of 9.3% down between *Chestnut Ridge* and *Raven Cliff Ridge* to where its mouth kisses the East Fork at 3,485". Along that run only two small feeders offer any added volume – neither are notable by any measure.

Starting at its mouth and moving upstream, I have found the first .4 miles up to where Trail #363 joins at *Shining Creek Gap* to be the mildest terrain on the stream. Even so, the stream is small and difficult to fish due to the many large and deep pools, falls and slides with little room on the banks and slopes to get around them and no improved trail to help. However, the initial .4 miles is some of the best fishing on the entire stream – probably because the water is larger and some bigger fish from the East Fork wander up there. The water is very cold and clear and brook trout seem to dominate. Nearly every run and pool you'll encounter will have at least one hungry trout. If you approach with stealth, you'll actually see trout rise through the clear water and take your bug under the reflection of a blue sky. It's a sight those of us addicted to fly angling never tire of seeing.

Beyond where Trail #363 comes in at .4 miles, the slopes on both sides of the creek close in and get steeper, and the canopy and side brush close in. The stream's features are exaggerated due to the topography causing several falls and pools to appear too large for a stream this size. But unlike the first .4 miles, you at least have a trail to help navigate the rugged stream bed. At about 1.1 miles from the source, the small feeder *Bell Collar Cove* enters creek left. In my opinion, it's too small to deal with. On up at about 1.5 miles, *Daniels Cove* enters creek right. Although it's a bit larger, it's still too small for me to expend effort on. The stream's entire main run above the first .4 miles, all the way to its source, has a good population of trout. But those trout are well protected in one of the most steep and rugged streams in the watershed. It's danged *HARD* fishing for sure!

At about 1.8 miles above its mouth, you'll reach the confluence of Shining Creek's two headwater streams at 3,485'. Both are very similar in structure, flow and difficulty in fishing. *North Prong* on the right is slightly larger and boasts the highest source of 5,735" on the east slope of *Shining Rock* itself. From there it screams downhill for 1.2 miles at a punishing 21.4% average gradient to its confluence with its twin. *South Prong* is on the left and starts on the east slope of *Grassy Cove Top* at about 5,485' where it runs for only .9 miles to that confluence point – but at an incredible 23.4% average gradient. Both of these steams flow down from between *Bearpen Ridge* to the north and *Grassy Cove*

The East Fork flowing through the huge culvert under Hwy 276 at its mouth fix - an interesting place to fish. / *Image by Author / 2018*

Ridge to the south where they meet to form Shining Creek.

I have not attempted to fish *South Prong*. But I have fished up *North Prong* for about .7 miles before the 21.4% gradient got the best of me. I only caught brookies in the 4" class – in diminishing numbers as I gained elevation. I did catch one 7" spec in a pool formed at the base of two huge boulders that squeezed the creek through a 12" crack before plunging 8' into a larger than average pool. Generally, these headwaters are very small with the usual drop pools and occasional runs that are just big enough to hold fish. These headwaters are *EXTREMELY HARD* to fish!

Generally I find anything to do with Shining Creek a pain in the butt. If it weren't for the good populations of brookies and a passable trail along its banks, I would have fished it only once. But it does have a lot of fish, and if you like high-elevation, technical hiking and rock climbing to catch small brook trout, Shining Creek is it.

Davidson River

At a Glance

Sam's Rank: 👍👍👍👍👍

GPS Fixes: The mouth fix below is not the actually the *mouth* of the Davidson. That's another 1.8 miles downstream where it converges with the French Broad River. This mouth fix is the southernmost starting point for the 10.8 miles covered by this chapter. Basically, it's at the intersection of Hwy 276 / Hwy 64 in Pisgah Forest.

- Source fix: N35 17.537 W83 50.725 @ 2,900'
- Mouth fix: N35 16.384 W83 42.329 @ 2,125'

Size: large at mouth

Gradient: flat 1.4% source to mouth average *(10.8 miles/775')* / lower section-flat .5% average *(5.4 miles/160')* / mid section-flat 1% average *(2.2 miles/105')* / upper section-flat 3% average *(3.2 miles/510')*

Effort: lower section-easy / mid section-moderate to difficult / upper section-moderate to difficult

Pressure: lower section-moderate to heavy / mid section-moderate to heavy / upper section-none to slight

Fishing Quality: good to excellent in all sections

Species: Rainbows, Browns & Specs - especially in the headwaters

Access: The elevations and topography of the watershed's flows create three unique river personalities. To describe them, I've divided the river into three *(3)* sections: *Upper Section, Mid Section* and *Lower Section*

~ *Lower Section:* This 5.4 mile section starts at the intersection of Hwy 276 / Hwy 64 in Pisgah Forest and continues to the bridge where Looking Glass Creek and FSR 475 meet. Hwy 276 parallels this entire 5.4 mile section. There is plenty of paved and unpaved roadside parking available.

~ *Mid Section:* This 2.2 mile section starts at the bridge on Hwy 276 where Looking Glass Creek enters creek right. Take the left onto FSR 475 and continue along for 2.2 miles to its ending point where Rockhouse Creek enters on the right across from the hatchery. Plenty of roadside parking is available. Some stretches require a short and easy hike to the water.

~ *Upper Section:* This 3.2 mile section starts on FSR 475 where Rockhouse Creek comes in on the right across from the hatchery and continues up to where a bridge crosses the Davidson and Laurel Fork enters river left. As you progress, FSR 475 will go from asphalt to dirt at Cove Creek. From the bridge crossing the Davidson, access for the remaining 1.2 miles to the Davidson's source is via FSR 137 *(Gated).* About .7 miles up, the road ends and Trail #105 will take you the final .5 miles to the source. Both FSR 137 / Trail #105 have mild gradients making for an easy hike. Primitive camping is available from the junction of FSR 474 / FSR 137 up to the source. Roadside parking is available at the junction of FSR 474 / FSR 137.

Overview & Description

It's been dang near 60 years since I first laid my eyes on the Davidson River. My family was camping next to the river at Coontree Campground. At that time in the early 1960s, Coontree was a campground, not the picnic area it is now. My mother's cousin Bob, who was a local from Brevard, had joined us on this trip to be our guide. Our campsites were located on the water. It was a great place to base camp, and a fun part of the river for a kid of seven years old.

One day we visited the hatchery up the river at Camp John Rock. For the first time, I saw how trout were raised for release into the local rivers and streams. We were wonderstruck! During that visit we also learned that the trout's diet was being supplemented with day old bread from local bakeries. Most of the time, it was just plain sliced white bread. But as soon as the bread hit the water, the fish went crazy and the water was whipped into froth until every crumb was gone. It reminded me of the Tarzan movies when piranhas would devour a poor African native who had fallen into *(or been thrown into!)* an infested river. For this reason, it was in fact illegal to use bread as bait – *the fish couldn't resist!* It turned fishing into harvesting…

The *"Pool"* at Coontree Picnic Area *(originally Coontree Campground)* on the Davidson River where my family caught contraband stockers in the early 1960s. / *Image by Author / 1997*

Well, the illegal thing didn't stop cousin Bob. Apparently, it was common place for the locals wanting a *"mess of trout"* to press white bread into a dough ball around a hook to use as bait. No sooner than when we got back to the campsite, Bob was pulling out the line, hooks and bread. Of course, as soon as the bread ball hit the big pool in front of the rock face at Coontree, a trout gobbled it up – one after the other. In no time at all, we had a serious stringer of trout.

As fate would have it, a US Forest Ranger pulled up about that time and began a walkthrough of the campground, making small talk with the folks at each site while also looking for *"poaching"* offenders. Panic set in at our site. So, before Mr. Forest Ranger Sir got to our site, Bob had stuffed the fish – which were still alive – into a huge Dutch oven on the picnic table. When the ranger came by to chat with the adults, the trout began floundering around in the Dutch oven and rattling its top. It was so obvious, but the Ranger either overlooked it, or just didn't notice. My father was also a Federal employee and was a real straight shooter – so much so that he was the sort of guy who would get out of the shower to pee. Years later he confessed that he was sweating blood until the ranger had left our campsite.

Later that evening, the adult "*criminals*" fried the contraband trout on the campfire. For first time, we Alabama flatlanders ate fresh trout from a mountain stream. Even today, it ranks as the best tasting illegally caught, or legally for that matter, trout I have ever eaten. Every time I pass Coontree, I think of that experience – *every time!* But that's enough about me and mine – back to fishing.

There are several reasons this watershed is a favorite of mine. *First,* it has something for everyone. Whether it's a flat and laid back "*easy boy*" access for big stocked trout you seek, or a "*nose bleed*" high-elevation bushwhack in to small water and wild fish, it offers both. *Second,* I like the watershed's history – the Cradle of Forestry, fish hatchery(s), Civilian Conservation Corps *(CCC)*, Looking Glass Rock, Sliding Rock, George Vanderbilt's forest lands, etc. *Third,* I like the little town of Brevard – multiple breweries, folk art, mountain music, good restaurants, lodging, fond memories, etc. It's just fun to hang out. *Fourth,* as a kid, it was the first mountain stream I ever played in – a "*first love*" so to speak.

Few rivers in the Southeast have more name recognition than the Davidson. Yet the Davidson hasn't always been called the Davidson – it started out as the *Rolling River*. Following the Revolutionary War, *Benjamin Davidson* was granted 640 acres along the lower part of the river for his services. He opened a mill and drained the lower ground so he could farm. Eventually the river's name changed to *Davidson Creek* and finally the *Davidson River*. Not only has it been featured in scores of travel publications and outfitters within 150 miles, it was also named as a "*Top 100 Trout Streams in America*" by Trout Unlimited. The Davidson is not only an extremely productive freestone river that supports a trophy-class trout population, but it also has lots of natural attractions and amenities. It's very accessible to several population centers – *Asheville, Brevard, Hendersonville, Atlanta, Greenville, Waynesville, Dahlonega, etc.* For those reasons, the river is a year-round destination. And, it's just as popular in the summer with kayakers, tubers, swimmers, rock hoppers, campers, wood fairies and the like.

Several years ago, North Carolina Wildlife Resources Commission surveyed trout populations along the river and found an average of 216 bows, 64 browns and a goodly number of brookies for each water acre. This density, and ease of access, has made the Davidson one of the most heavily fished Southeastern streams. Another popularity factor is the trout hatchery upstream dumping lots of oxygen and nutrient filled water into its flow. The river also lies at relatively low elevations in Pisgah National Forest and it does not experience the colder temperatures as seen in many higher elevation flows. Despite the fact that cold winter water slows down trout feeding activity a bit, winter fishing on the Davidson is still respectable because the water is not excessively cold. Likewise, because its watershed is not as large as some other rivers, its low water volumes and warmer water temperatures in the summer can combine to make the Davidson a bit more challenging to fish.

For the most part, I have found spring and fall to be the best times to fish the Davidson. On most of these days, empty parking places are hard to come by along the entire 5.1 miles of U.S. Highway 276 along the Lower Section. Scores of anglers, rock hoppers, picnickers, tubers, canoeists, kayakers and swimmers can make the area a congested mess. Even so, thanks to the hatchery and excellent management, the Davidson fishes well year after year even with all this attention.

The Davidson's source is the result of two headwater streams that flow south from between *Shuck Ridge, Fork River Bald* and *Oaklog Gap* on the Parkway. *Daniel Ridge Creek* and *Right Fork* start from relatively low elevations just below the Parkway and eventually converge at about 2,900' to form the Davidson's source. As mentioned, this lower elevation sourcing accounts in part for the Davidson's slightly higher water temps in the winter and summer months.

From its source, the Davidson begins a 10.8 mile run to its mouth at 2,125" at Hwy 276 / Hwy 64 – just north of Brevard. A few miles below the source it enters a gorge, passes a NC State Fish Hatchery and Pisgah Center for Wildlife Education, and then shoots the gap between the iconic and towering *Looking Glass Rock* and the slightly smaller and lower *John Rock*. From there it becomes the wide and docile river it is known for in its lower two sections. Along the way it receives volume from tributaries with names like *Looking Glass Creek, Avery Creek, Rockhouse Creek, Cove Creek* and *Laurel Creek* - the largest being Looking Glass. From source to mouth it averages a low 1.4% gradient which makes for some really easy wading in most stretches. Its especially wide stream bed and open canopy allow for easy casting from source to its mouth.

Lower Section: The 5.4 miles of this section above the mouth at Hwy 276 / Hwy 64 starts just below of what's left of the original stone Pisgah National Forest boundary sign *(put up in the early part of the last century)* on Hwy 276, and ends upriver at the bridge on Hwy 276 / Looking Glass Creek's confluence. At its mouth the river is almost 30'- 40' across. The first couple of miles upriver is very flat and shallow and features long and slow runs, with the occasional deeper run or undercut bank that hold large fish. The Lower Section's entire 5.4 miles has a very low .5% average gradient with wide and spacious banks and an open canopy that make for some easy access and fishing for the nice population of stocked trout that are under fished. Few obstacles obstruct the flow along that section.

The Lower Section's initial 2.3 mile stretch up to Avery Creek is managed as *Hatchery Supported* and is stocked periodically with a thousand or so of all three trout. Surprisingly, this lower stocked stretch doesn't get much attention by serious

Hwy 276 Bridge at the confluence of the Davidson River *(left)* and Looking Glass Creek *(right)* emerging from under bridge. The pool is loaded with huge trout. / *Image by Author / 2018*

fly anglers due to its tendency to be crowded with campers, bait casters, rock hoppers and an armada of tubers in the warmer months. But the fish don't seem to mind! So by all means fish it, and you'll be surprised by the trout and impressed by some of the eye-candy distractions that float past you...

At 1.4 miles upstream from the source, a bridge crosses to provide access from Hwy 276 to the Schenck Job Corps Civilian Conservation Center and Davidson River Campground. This is a good place to stay while fishing the area – my Trout Unlimited Chapter does so several times a year. Across from the campground at about 2.3 miles, the Davidson's first sizeable tributary, *Avery Creek*, enters river right. Although several small flows enter below it, Avery is the first one I consider worthwhile to fish. It is highly prized as a favorite by many local old timers.

The next 3.1 miles above Avery up to Looking Glass Creek, the river is still about 25'- 35' wide in most places. Along this stretch it is flat and slow and features long, smooth runs with many wide and calm pools that magnify your casting and mending mistakes. In many places the river flows around dead falls, and the banks next to the road are undercut, deep and offer exceptional fishing. The stretch from Avery Creek to Looking Glass's confluence is managed as *Catch and Release - Artificial Fly Only* – and is known for wild browns and rainbows averaging 12" or more. This portion is also home to the occasional wash downs from the upstream hatchery that can reach *Typhoon Class* size. These fish tend to be cautious and picky, and fishing for them can be very technical.

~ Davidson River ~

In the Lower Section, I've noticed many anglers using the typical dry / nymph patterns and rigs on the deepest, fishiest pools and runs. These obvious stretches do hold trout, and those rigs will catch them. But often these anglers unknowingly stomp right through some of the best lies trying to get to the next obvious spot. Pay special attention to shallow edges and boundary waters along the banks! Even if there is just a shallow current flowing over them, I've seen and caught large trout holding in water shallow enough to barely able to cover their dorsal fin. A local outfitter taught me that secret, and I've never forgotten it.

Mid Section: This 2.2 mile section starts where the Davidson's second sizeable tributary, *Looking Glass Creek*, enters river right at the stone bridge *(built by the CCC)* on Hwy 276 and continues along FSR 465 to where *Rockhouse Creek* crosses the road in front of the hatchery. Where Looking Glass enters at the bridge, there is a very large and deep pool created by the confluence. On sunny days you can walk out on the bridge and see ten or more Typhoon Class trout patrolling the flow. It's inspirational – and frustrating! Many times I've stood there and spotted for my buddies – all to no avail. We've tried everything short of C-4 and electric shock, and those trout made fools of us every time! And we'll do it again…

Above the confluence of Looking Glass, the Davidson narrows to just 15'- 20' due to the reduction of flow. The 1.5 mile stretch upstream to just below the NC State Fish Hatchery and Pisgah Center for Wildlife Education is known as *Horse Cove* - after a small, sandy and marginally fishable feeder that enters river left. This part of the river is in the gap between *Looking Glass Rock* and *John Rock* – the two highest peaks in the area. Yet for the most part, it flows in a flat and wide floodplain of meadows, beaver ponds and open forest, and eventually slows down to long runs and calm pools with eddies and stretches of undercut banks, downed timber, rock ledges and walls. The river can be up to .2 miles from the road in places, but good trails are everywhere – which tells you something.

This stretch of the Mid Section is home to mostly rainbows and a browns in the 10"–12" range, with a few up to twice that size. Many guides in the area consider this section the river's best fishing, and you'll see them and their clients in some of the best spots. Keep an eye on them and move in after they leave. In either event, try using a guide the first time you fish this section – they understand the fish and know the spots. The well-packed trails are evidence of my claims.

Now let's consider some history of the area around the Davidson. The next .7 miles up to Rockhouse Creek flows past a *NC State Fish Hatchery* and the *Pisgah Center for Wildlife Education*. But long before they existed, the land was occupied by one of *George Vanderbilt's Black Forest Lodges*. These were used by his Forest Rangers who managed and protected his forests holdings of about 68,000 acres. After that, the *Carr Lumber Company* used it as a base camp for their logging operations in the Davidson watershed, and eventually it was renamed *Camp John Rock*. Camp John Rock was a *Civilian Conservation Corps (CCC)* work camp designed to provide work relief during the Great Depression to men ages eighteen to twenty-five. In time, some three million men were hired by the CCC at an average salary of thirty dollars / month – or a dollar a day. Described as *"Roosevelt's Tree Army,"* the CCC initiated site development and improvements in 2,082 national, state and private forests and parks across the US. Their accomplishments are all around you!

In North Carolina the CCC had sixty-six camps employing 13,600 men in forty-seven counties. *Camp Pisgah Forest* was built on this site. It was the first CCC camp built on National Forest land in NC. Men arrived from Fort Bragg as early as May 5, 1933 to construct over 25 buildings including barracks, a mess

A monument to the men of Camp John Rock at the NC State Fish Hatchery & Pisgah Center for Wildlife Education. / *Image by Author / 2018*

hall, school, officers' quarters, pit latrines, bathhouses, and many other buildings. It was assigned the number *"F-1"* and occupied on May 18, 1933. In early 1934 the name was changed to *Camp John Rock* after the nearby peak overlooking the camp. Local legend has it that John Rock was not named after a person at all. Apparently an early settler's horse named John slipped and fell to its death and forever after the mountain was called *"John Rock."* Personally, I think the horse was so depressed by being called John that he jumped off the mountain. Who names a horse John? And why was he on top of that rock in the first place?

Eventually, 220 workers were assigned to the camp. Their projects included fish and deer rearing stations, road building / maintenance, trails, reforestation, fire protection and forest conservation. The camp closed in 1936 and the CCC program was shut down by Congress in 1942. A life-sized bronze statue stands at the entrance in honor of all those CCC workers. Today, this site is home to *NC State Fish Hatchery* and *Pisgah Center for Wildlife Education*. Back to fishing…

The Mid Section's *"Hatchery Run"* is flat with an average gradient of only 1%. Just below the confluence of *Rockhouse Creek* the flow passes over the dam and water intake for the hatchery. Thousands of gallons per minute are diverted, infused with oxygen, funneled into the raceways, and then released back into the river. Although this section is not stocked, a few trout manage to escape. But they are in the minority because wild trout own the water and grow big and fast as a result of the oxygen and nutrient-rich effluent from the hatchery. This is evident when flipping rocks and observing the midge and caddis fly larvae, mayfly nymphs, worms, and other invertebrates that thrive on the rich oxygen and nutrients. The hatchery impacts the entire river – everything downstream benefits from the improvements it contributes. It's danged near like a river on steroids!

Given the hatchery's positive influence, the Mid Section might be the closest thing to a spring creek in the region. The ease of access and wading, plus lots of large visible fish, results in this stretch receiving massive pressure. Most any time you can see from five to fifteen anglers pounding the water. With all this action, trout have become jaded to the

The Davidson's most popular stretch runs beside the hatchery. Notice the water outlet on the left. / *Image by Author / 2019*

constant appearance of flies hitting the water and have predictably become selective about where and what they eat. Along here the fish are highly pressured, ultra-selective and extremely large. Pigs in the 24"–28" range, weighing in at 8 pounds have been hauled in. I have found the secret is using small flies that closely match the trout's natural prey, small indicators, small tippet, staying low, drab clothing, and presenting your flies, drag free, precisely in the feeding lanes.

Upper Section: This 3.2 mile section starts on FSR 465 where *Rockhouse Creek* enters across from the hatchery and continues for 2 miles up to the bridge crossing the Davidson and *Laurel Fork* entering river left. It then goes on up a final incredible 1.2 miles to its source at 2,900'. Of the three sections, Upper is my favorite due to its varied topography, smaller-sized, wild fish and less pressure.

About .2 miles above *Rockhouse Creek* to the confluence of *Cove Creek* one mile above that, the Davidson passes through a deep gorge. Along the gorge the river drops only 125'. But along that run it plunges over numerous small and large cascades, pools and slides – some too risky to traverse. It's like fishing a gauntlet! The flow constricts to about 10'-15' in places. The walls close in and are steep and slippery to climb, and the river bed is littered with boulders – many the size of cars. The water is exceptionally clear and the fish wild and spooky. I've found rainbows and browns in the 8"-12" range – but there's some big fish in there too!

Fly fishing the gorge can be difficult and dangerous due to lack of access, along with the ruggedness and danger of flash flooding. I've also heard reports of the abundance of Timber Rattlers and Copperheads – but I've never seen any. In any event, unskilled waders, climbers, hikers and couch potatoes should stay out. The gorge section

A wild rainbow caught in the gorge above the hatchery on the Davidson River. / *Image by Author / 1997*

is paralleled by Trail #650 which runs above it to the north. Getting on and off the river using the trail is hard. Your best bet is to fish the entire mile.

At the top of the gorge, just below where *Cove Creek* enters river right, the Davidson constricts down to just a few yards at *Whaleback Rock Swimming Hole*. There, the river plunges through a 40' long, 10' deep trough with slab rock on each side. It's loaded with fish! About .3 miles above Cove Creek, *Long Branch* enters river left and offers more fishing – albeit very small and overgrown.

The .7 miles above the gorge up to the bridge crossing the Davidson at *Laurel Fork's* confluence is more like a typical mountain stream. Along this stretch the river is about 10'–15' wide with wider than expected canopies that make casting easy. Its features include fast runs, small plunge pools and pocket

The Davidson's *Upper Section* just below its source is plenty big and wide enough for easy fishing. / *Image by Author / 2007*

water. All the trout I have caught along this stretch are bows and browns and a few brookies in the 6"- 8" range. Access is easy as FSR 465 follows the river.

The upper 1.2 miles of the Davidson above the bridge on FSR 475 at Laurel Fork's confluence to its source is the most beautiful section of the Davidson. Along this stretch it is wider than you'd expect, typically 10'–15' across in most spots, with a wide and open canopy. Along the 1.2 miles, it loses about 260' of elevation creating a mild average gradient of about 4.1% - which makes for relatively easy wading. About .7 miles up FSR Road / Trail #137 from the bridge are the remains of an old fish rearing station built by the CCC that includes concrete dams, cables, pipes, canals, dry ponds, telephone poles, drains, etc. It's hard to imagine the activity that must have been at this place almost a hundred years ago. At that point, FSR Road / Trail #137 ends and Trail #105 picks up along the final .5 miles to the source. A foot trail along the bank parallels the river more closely. Further up is another dam closer to the source – not sure how it was used. There are several waterfalls, one over 25'– 30', as well as some smaller ones. I can't express just how beautiful and fishy this stretch is.

Along this upper stretch, falls, runs, ripples and pools are common, with the occasional larger drop pool. Even though this stretch is so close to the source, the river is still relatively big and open. This makes casting to the small, wild rainbows and brookies easier than expected. Most of what I have caught were in the 5"- 8" range, with the occasional 9" - 12" brown in the bigger pools.

At 1.2 miles above the bridge, *Daniel Ridge Creek* and *Right Fork* converge at 2,900' to form the Davidson's source. This point is about 10.8 miles above the Davidson's mouth at Hwy 276 / Hwy 64 in Pisgah Forest.

Davidson Tributaries

Daniel Ridge Creek & Right Fork
The Davidson's Two Headwaters

At a Glance

Sam's Rank: 👍👍👍
GPS Fixes:
- Daniel Ridge Creek source fix: N35 18.691 W82 51.894 @ 4,720'
- Right Fork source fix: N35 18.800 W82 51.345 @ 4,625'
- Mouth fix for both: N35 17.537 W83 50.725 @ 2,900'

Size: both small at their confluence point
Gradient:
- Daniel Ridge Creek: Steep 19.2% average *(1.8 miles / 1,825')*
- Right Fork: Steep 19.2% average *(1.7 miles / 1,725')*

Effort: both - difficult to extreme

Pressure: both - none
Fishing Quality: both - fair
Species: Bows & Specs
Access: Start at FSR 475 where the bridge crosses the Davidson and Laurel Fork enters river left. From the bridge, start the 1.2 mile hike up river via FSR Road / Trail #137. About .7 miles up, #137 ends and Trail #105 starts and continues the last .5 miles to the confluence point / Davidson's mouth. Trail #105 and Trail #106 provide access up Right Fork for about another .8 miles. Daniel Ridge Creek seems to have no improved trail. Parking is available around the bridge area on FSR 475 and at the campground parking area.

Overview & Description

The Davidson's source is the result of two small headwaters converging - *Daniel Ridge Creek* and *Right Fork*. Both seep out of the ground just under the Parkway on the south slope of *Pisgah Ridge* at well under a mile above sea level – low for a major Parkway headwater. Generally, these streams represent nothing remarkable, other than the pleasures one gets from fishing the headwaters of such a storied river. And… if nothing more than just to say you did it!

The main difference in these streams is their name – they are almost identical in structure, length, size, gradient, difficulty level and trout. The slightly larger *Right Fork* comes off the south slope of *Pisgah Ridge* at about 4,625' and runs down between *Lanning Ridge* and *Fork River Ridge* for about 1.7 miles at a

The Right Fork flows through a trestle abutment just before meeting Daniel Ridge Creek to form the Davidson's source. / *Image by Author / 2007*

very steep 19.2% gradient before converging with *Daniel Ridge Creek* at about 2,900' to form the Davidson's source. About .9 miles up from its mouth, it picks up additional flow from only one feeder – I consider it non-fishable. About 300' above its confluence with *Daniel Ridge*, it flows between two huge stone abutments of the old narrow gauge railroad trestle that was used to log the area. Other than the trestle being removed, the stonework looks as if it were set yesterday. It's a cool spot to catch a trout knowing its ancestors actually swam under that same trestle when logging was going on.

The smaller *Daniel Ridge Creek* starts on the same slope just to the west at about 4,725' and crashes down between *Fork River Ridge* and *Daniel Ridge* for about 1.8 miles at a 19.2% gradient until it meets the *Right Fork* at 2,900'. About .3 miles up from its mouth it receives additional volume from *Shuck Ridge Creek* – I consider it marginally fishable.

Each creek is relatively easy to get to but can be extremely rugged to fish because of the gradient and other than a short distance up Right Fork, the lack of a good trail system. Both are wider than you might expect and allow for precision casting to the trout that occupy the endless progression of pools and runs up the mountain. As you get higher, many stretches become increasingly difficult to fish due to the canopy. There's also a fair amount of climbing and high sticking from one pool to the next.

I have fished stretches of these streams several times. I've fished about a mile up Right Fork to *Lanning Branch* – only because the trail made it easier. As for Daniel Ridge Creek, I've fished about .5 miles up to *Shuck Ridge Creek*. Each time on both I was rewarded with bows and brookies in the 4"–7" range – common for streams like these. I did catch one 9" spec up Daniel Ridge Creek. I was shocked – so was it! This trout was hunkered down under a Chestnut Oak's root ball that created a large pool. Above these points, I haven't had the energy needed to go any further. Both streams are hard fishing for small fish, but well worth the effort.

Laurel Fork
A Tributary of the Davidson

At a Glance

Sam's Rank: 👍👍
GPS Fixes:
- Source fix: N35 16.682 W82 51.777 @ 4,275'
- Mouth fix: N35 17.023 W82 49.690 @ 2,640'

Size: small at mouth
Gradient: steep 14.7% source to mouth average *(2.1 miles / 1,635')*
Effort: moderate
Pressure: none to slight
Fishing Quality: average
Species: Bows
Access: Start on FSR 475 where the bridge crosses the Davidson and Laurel Fork enters river left. From the bridge, FSR 475 parallels the creek to where the bridge crosses one mile up. Continue .4 miles to where it crosses Laurel Creek's only feeder. Parking is available all along FSR 475.

Overview & Description

My most memorable experience fishing the Laurel Fork has nothing to do with fishing. On my last trip, I was hitchhiking back to the truck when I was given a ride by a pack of free range, purple-haired, pierced and tattooed Millennials packed into an old Jeep Wagoneer. They insisted I join them at their communal camp about a mile downstream – a place that resembled a mini-Woodstock!

For several hours we sat by the fire, ate some unusual, but really great "*organic*" food, and shared many assorted libations – some of which I had never heard of. I finished my meal and lighted up one of my Arturo Fuente Chateau cigars I'd been craving. They were smoking something else that didn't look like a Marlborough and were passing it around among the group. I guess they couldn't afford store-bought smokes. All the time the females were dancing around the fire and singing. All in all, it was an interesting end to an average day of fishing.

I'll come clean here and admit that after fishing Laurel Fork several times, it is not my favorite Davidson watershed. As the Davidson's first tributary of any size, Laurel's lower stretches are small, choked with flora, flow rates seem to vary widely between the seasons, and the trout are small. All this combines to make it only marginally productive in my opinion.

Laurel Fork squirts out of the ground at about 4,275' on the east slope of *Sassafras Knob*. From there it descends for about 2.1 miles at an average gradient of 14.7%, and at 2,635' it dumps its anemic volume into the Davidson. About .7 miles up from its mouth, Laurel Fork is joined by its only sizeable "*no name*" feeder – it's not really fishable in my opinion.

For me, fishing the Laurel Fork is all about focusing on its pocket water and not worrying about the real estate in between. The first time fished it, I speed fished only the first mile up to where the bridge on FSR 475 crosses. That is the flattest part of the creek by far *(4.3% gradient)*, and I moved between pocket waters to sample what the creek offered. What it had to offer each time were rainbows in the 5" – 8" range and not in large quantities. Along this stretch, it's obvious how the creek got its name. Mountain Laurel grows everywhere, but it grows especially well here – well enough to choke the creek. It is difficult fishing for small fish.

On several subsequent trips, I fished only above the upper bridge about a mile up from its mouth. I found that to be the best fishing. There the gradients are higher, the stream's structure is more conducive to hold trout, and the canopy is open forest as opposed to laurel thickets. This is in contrast to the lower stretches that are too flat, sandy and choked with flora.

Cove Creek
A Tributary of the Davidson

At a Glance

Sam's Rank: 👍👍👍
GPS Fixes:
- Source fix: N35 18.854 W82 50.368 @ 4,295'
- Mouth fix for both: N35 16.929 W82 49.010 @ 2,540'

Size: small at mouth
Gradient: moderate 11.1% source to mouth average *(3 miles / 1,755')*
Effort: moderate
Pressure: slight
Fishing Quality: average
Species: Bows & Specs
Access: Start at the Looking Glass Creek Bridge on Hwy 276. Take the left onto FSR 475 and continue past the hatchery to where Cove Creek crosses the road at about 3.1 miles - the road turns to dirt past that bridge. Parking is available on the left side of FSR 475. Cove Creek's mouth on the Davidson is about 50 yards downstream. FSR 809 *(gated)* parallels Cove Creek upstream and leads to several large group campsites about .3 - .5 miles up. Two trails at the first camp clearing, Caney Bottom Trail *(Trail #361)* & Cove Creek Trail *(Trail # 340)* offer access up the best fishing stretches of Cove Creek and its feeder Caney Bottom Creek.

Overview & Description

Cove Creek is a quaint little trout stream located in the western shadow of *Looking Glass Rock*. It's known more for its group camping sites, hiking trails and beautiful waterfalls than for fly fishing. I've fished it numerous times and attended bamboo rod gatherings at one of the group campsites. Its ease of access and good populations of rainbows and brookies above its waterfalls are worth exploring.

Cove Creek sources on the south slope of *Pisgah Ridge* just below the Parkway at about 4,295'. From there it begins a 3 mile run between *Lanning Ridge* and *Seniard Ridge* at a moderate 11.1% gradient. The upper reaches of Cove Creek are steep all the way down to 50' *Cove Creek Falls* at about one mile above its mouth. Further down at about .6 miles above its mouth, it collects volume from its only fishable feeder - *Caney Bottom Creek*. It reaches the Davidson at about 2,540' at a place called *Whaleback Rock* – a great swimming and fishing hole.

Whaleback Rock is about 150' below the parking area where Cove Creek goes under FSR 475 and reaches the Davidson – a popular spot with bathers, rock hoppers and fishermen alike. There the Davidson constricts down to a few yards and plunges through a 40' long / 10' deep trough-pool surrounded by shelf rock. It's loaded with fish. Although *Whaleback Rock* is technically on the Davidson, not Cove Creek, the fishing is excellent with 6" - 12" bows and browns common.

Fishing all along Cove Creek and Caney Bottom is productive with fish averaging 8". However, I tend to focus on just three areas. *Cove Creek Falls* has an excellent pool at the base that offers habitat to some larger than normal trout - I've

Stalking at Whaleback Rock Swimming Hole on the Upper Davidson. / *Image by Author / 2000*

caught several 12" – 14" bows there. About .7 miles up *Caney Bottom* is another sizeable waterfall / slide with a nice pool at its base with larger than normal trout. Below both falls, the gradient flattens to about 7% and becomes easier. Above the falls, wading and casting is difficult. I've not fished higher up, but I hear brookies do reside up there. *Whaleback Rock* is the third area I like to fish on Cove Creek.

Rockhouse Creek
A Tributary of the Davidson

At a Glance

Sam's Rank: 👍👍
GPS Fixes:
- Source fix: N35 18.546 W82 48.164 @ 3,020'
- Mouth fix for both: N35 17.074 W82 48.006 @ 2,390'

Size: small at mouth
Gradient: mild 6.3% source to mouth average *(1.9 miles / 630')*
Effort: moderate
Pressure: none
Fishing Quality: poor to fair
Species: Rainbows
Access: To access the mouth, start at the Looking Glass Creek Bridge on Hwy 276. Take a left onto FSR 475 and continue for 1.5 miles to where FSR 475b *(Headwater Rd.)* enters on the right across from the hatchery. FSR 475b provides access for the entire 1.9 miles of the creek, although some stretches may require a short hike to the water. Access from the source's end can be had by entering FSR

475b from where it meets Hwy 276 just below the Cradle of Forestry. Plenty of parking is available up and down FSR 475b. There are campsites along the way.

Overview & Description

This creek is included only because of where it is and its ease of access – not for the quality of fishing. With its flow in the western shadow of legendary *Looking Glass Rock*, it's not remarkable in any way other than its three or four small waterfalls and the occasional pool that is best fished in the spring and fall when water levels are sufficient. During the drier months, the stream's flow can be so low that it is not worth the effort. It seems to me that much of Rockhouses' flow has excessive levels of sedimentation covering its bed that distracts from the ecosystem's support of a healthy trout population. At least that's my impression.

Rockhouses' source is at about 3,020' on the northwest slope of *Looking Glass Rock* between *Gumstand Gap* and *Bennett Knob*. From there it begins a 1.9 mile run at a mild 6.3% gradient to its mouth at 2,390' on the Davidson. From source to mouth it has no sizeable feeders to add volume.

With so much great water in the Davidson's watershed, this creek is not at the top of my list. The three or four times I've fished Rockhouse, it was in the late fall when all the leaves were off the trees, and I drove up and down FSR 475b looking down at the stream and spotting falls and drop pools to fish. I caught rainbows, mostly in the 6" class and that was about it. And I burned a bunch of gas doing it.

Looking Glass Creek
A Tributary of the Davidson

At a Glance

Sam's Rank: 👍👍👍👍👍
GPS Fixes:
- Source fix: N35 20.381 W82 47.393 @ 3,100'
- Mouth fix: N35 17.479 W82 46.208 @ 2,280'

Size: medium at mouth
Gradient: flat 3.1% source to mouth average *(5 miles / 820')*
Effort: below falls - easy / above falls - moderate to difficult
Pressure: below falls - moderate / above falls - none to slight
Fishing Quality: good
Species: Rainbows, Browns & Brookies - headwaters & feeders
Access: From the Looking Glass Creek Bridge on Hwy 276, the road parallels the creek 5 miles up to its source just below FSR 475b entering from the left. Parking is available at paved / unpaved pull-outs.

Overview & Description

It's hard to express in mere print just how much I like this creek. I've spent many a happy day as a kid playing at the base of Looking Glass Falls and slipping and sliding up and down Sliding Rock just up the creek. Since then, I've spent even more of my adult days standing in those same runs and pools chasing trout. I can't think of a stream anywhere that has more great memories for me, or one I would rather invest a day on, than Looking Glass. Mostly known for its 50' waterfall and natural waterslides, it's always a fun and productive day of fishing.

Looking Glass has about everything a trout stream should have. To start with, it sources and flows through the historic southwestern edge of the *Cradle of Forestry in America.* National Forest Service, the CCC, the Biltmore and George W. Vanderbilt history hides behind every tree. If that's not enough, it offers miles of low gradient water with open canopies, healthy populations of trout and excellent access along its five miles. It also has iconic waterfalls with deep plunge pools, some long rock slides with pools at their base, as well as some challenging upper stretches with high gradients, tight banks and canopies. You can lose yourself in a secluded wild stretch, or be amongst hoards of scantily-clad swimmers and picture-taking

Entrance sign on Hwy 276 for the Cradle of Forestry in America Center. / *Image by Author* / *2007*

tourists and still catch twenty trout a day. It's a unique stream. It's also an excellent place to get away from the Davidson's crowds and spooky hair-lipped fish.

Official topos, satellite imagery and a litany of other sources are fuzzy as to which streams are the official headwaters of Looking Glass. However, *Poundingmill Branch* and *Cherry Cove* seem to be the two most likely to me. They source up about a mile apart just south of the Parkway between *Cherry Gap, Bennett Gap* and *Pigeon Gap*. From there they flow down and converge at about 3,100' to form Looking Glass's source. That source point is right beside Hwy 276 about 400' south of the Hwy 276 / FSR 475b intersection. This point is the extreme southwestern edge of the Cradle of Forestry. *Poundingmill* is the only headwater actually sourcing inside the Cradle Boundary – and only then by just a few yards. Both of these streams and some of their feeders offer blue-line pocket water fishing - albeit tough going for small bows and an occasional brookie.

From its source at 3,100', Looking Glass begins a five mile rubicon through the *Pisgah Ranger District* to its mouth at the bridge on Hwy 276 / FSR 475. Along that run the road crisscrosses the creek numerous times via a series of beautiful stone bridges built by the CCC in the 1930s. Be sure to fish underneath all of them. About 1.7 miles below its source, it is joined by *Big Bearpen Branch* – its largest and most fishable feeder. On down another .5 mile, the wildly popular *Sliding Rock* formation is where the creek flows over a huge stone slab. Just below it, another even larger lesser known slide and pool can be found. About 4.7 miles below its source, the creek flows over iconic *Looking Glass Falls*. This is a popular destination for tourists and anglers alike. At 5 miles below its source, Looking Glass enters the Davidson River at 2,280'. From source to mouth, Looking Glass averages a low 3.1% gradient making for relatively easy fishing.

At its mouth, a large deep pool has been created below the Hwy 276 Bridge by the creek's

Sliding Rock attracts many *"sliders"* as well as anglers in the off hours. / *Image by J. R. Johnson / 2018*

convergence with the Davidson. Be sure to explore and fish it if for no other reason than there are some huge, visible trout holding there. Good luck. I've never caught one – even with a guide!

Moving upstream above the bridge, the first .3 miles up to Looking Glass Falls receives the most attention from anglers. The mouth is small, but the creek opens up to about 30' all the way up to the falls. This stretch is flat and has several pools, runs and dead falls where wild rainbows, browns, and an occasional spec can be found – most are less than 8". When approaching the falls, fish the run leading up to the huge boulder river left, then the shallow run against the rock wall river right up to the fall's plunge pool. These are full of wild rainbows and browns in the 5" to 8" range.

The Author dredging the pool at Looking Glass Falls. / *Image courtesy of Brad Mast / 2003*

The falls plunges into a large and deep pool. I top fish the edges and then dredge the bottom each time I'm there. I never fail to catch several bows or browns – several have been in the 14" to 16" range. The wave action and gusts coming of the base of the falls can make casting and drag an issue. You'll need to be creative with casting and mending techniques.

The next 1.1 miles up to the bridge at *Moore Cove Creek* is, in my opinion, not the best trout water on the creek. It's wide, shallow, flat, relatively featureless and not fun or productive – so I just skip it. The next 1.5 miles above *Moore Cove* up to *Sliding Rock*, the creek is still wide, but deepens a bit and flows over some excellent topographical features that create lots of fishy plunge pools, cascades, long rock slides and pocket waters. The pools at the base of *Sliding Rock*, as well as the big rock slide downstream, are loaded with trout in the 6" to 8" range. Once, I even caught a trout in one of the secluded swirl holes on the right side of Sliding Rock. When I was unhooking that trout, he was staring at me. I bet he thought I was God, and I was releasing him from Purgatory. I never even got a thank you note… now I wish I'd eaten him.

Above Sliding Rock for the next .5 miles up to *Big Bearpen Branch* entering river left, the creek gets smaller and more like a mountain stream. But it's still wide enough, and although choked with rhododendron, laurel, alder and hemlock, its canopy is relatively wide and open. Most every drop pool or run will yield one or more trout. When you reach *Big Bearpen*, it's about the only Looking Glass

173

feeder worth investing your fishing time on. It's small but always offers some interesting challenges and a few trout.

The 1.7 miles above *Big Bearpen* to Looking Glass's source is what I'll describe as hard-core blue-line water. Most of the way up it is shallow and narrow – yet the canopy is still open enough to cast. Fishing the pocket water delivers the best results, but requires a stealthy approach to the wild trout living there.

At 5 miles above the bridge at Hwy 276 / FSR 475, you will reach the point where *Poundingmill Branch* and *Cherry Cove* converge at 2,280' to form Looking Glass Creek's source. Both of these headwaters hold lots of trout.

Avery Creek
A Tributary of the Davidson

At a Glance

Sam's Rank: 👍👍👍👍
GPS Fixes:
- Source fix: N35 20.104 W82 46.407 @ 3,285'
- Mouth fix: N35 17.208 W82 44.159 @ 2,160'

Size: very small at mouth
Gradient: low 4.8% source to mouth average *(4.4 miles / 1,125')*
Effort: moderate to difficult
Pressure: none to slight
Fishing Quality: good
Species: Rainbows, Browns & Brookies
Access: Travel north along the Davidson for 2.2 miles from the Hwy 276 / Hwy 64 intersection. Turn right onto FSR #477 *(Avery Creek Road / Pisgah Horse Stables Road)*. This road parallels all of the creek's 4.4 mile flow with the exception of the upper 2 miles above Clawhammer Creek. The road continues for miles above that and eventually circles back into HWY 276 just inside the southern boundary of the Cradle of Forestry.

At 2.4 miles above the mouth when FSR #477 leaves Avery Creek at the confluence of Clawhammer Creek, Trail #327 starts tracking up Avery for the remaining 2 miles to its source. About .8 miles up that trail, Trail #103 crosses it and follows Henry Branch *(Avery's 1st tributary)* 1.3 miles to its source. These two trails make it possible to fish these upper waters.

Overview & Description

Avery Creek is a small tributary of the Davidson that many Brevard and Pisgah Forest old timers claim as their favorite creek in the watershed. I've heard many stories about how this creek was *(and still is)* their "go-to" choice for a mess of trout. They fondly recount memories of fishing it as kids in the mid part of the last century and returning home with stringers of 25 to 40 fish – mostly brook trout. This stream is managed as *Wild Trout Waters* today. However, having fished it many times, I cannot imagine how Avery could ever have been the special creek the locals claim it was. However, it can be an attractive alternative when the Davidson is too high to fish and/or too stained from rain.

From a relatively low elevation of about 3,288', Avery sources in the gap between *Buckwheat Knob* and *Rich Mountain*. From there it runs for 4.4 miles to its mouth and along the way loses elevation at a flat 4.8% average gradient. It runs between *Black Mountain* on the east and *Coontree Mountain* and *Bearpen Mountain* to the west. Along the way, it's joined by feeders with names like *Henry Branch, Clawhammer Creek, Maxwell Cove, Pressley Cove,* and others – most are too small to worry about. At 4.4 miles below its source, Avery flows under Hwy 276 and enters the Davidson at 2,160' across from Davidson River Campground.

Moving upstream from its mouth, Avery is about 6'- 8' wide. That doesn't change up to the culvert under Hwy 276 almost 400' away. Over the next 1.9 miles it stays small as it flows through *White Pines Camping Area* and then up to *Pressley Cove Creek*, its first small tributary coming in river right – too small to fish. On up at about at 2.1 miles *Maxwell Cove Creek*, another small tributary enters creek right – also too small to fish.

Over the next .8 miles Avery flows through what amounts to a flat valley with minimal in-stream habitat structures that hold trout. I don't consider it very productive. At about 2.9 miles further up, it reaches *Clawhammer Creek* entering creek right. I've fished Clawhammer several times and caught small 6" class rainbows – but it is full-contact fishing. Up to this point, the road crisscrosses Avery about 4 – 5 times and beyond *Clawhammer* the road departs the creek.

The 2.4 miles of creek up to *Clawhammer* gain only 310' of elevation – a flat gradient. It's wide and open in most places and wading is easy between the fishable pockets. Most stretches have adequate structures to hold trout. But it can be shallow, sandy and crowded with flora. Above *Clawhammer* up to *Henry Branch*, the gradient gets even flatter, and the creek closes in quite a bit.

At 3.7 miles up, *Henry Branch*, Avery's highest feeder enters creek right from its source 1.3 miles above. This feeder is fishable and is paralleled by a good trail that also provides access to the small falls located on it. I've caught bows and brookies all the way to the falls. The gradient for this section is a heart-pounding 21.9%. From the confluence of *Henry Branch*, Avery continues another 1.2 miles to its source point at 3,285'. This headwater stretch is very small and tight but does contain small specs. Fortunately, it is serviced by a trail that makes fishing it easier.

South Fork
of Mills River
At a Glance

Sam's Rank: 👍👍👍👍👍

GPS Fixes:
- Source fix: N35 21.091 W82 46.492 @ 3,240'
- Mouth fix: N35 23.567 W82 36.603 @ 2,120'

Size: medium at mouth *(At its confluence with the North Mills River)*

Gradient: flat .9% source to mouth average *(23.9 miles / 1,120')*

Effort: lower section - moderate / mid section – moderate to difficult / headwater section – easy to moderate

Pressure: lower section - slight / mid section - none to slight / headwater section - slight

Fishing Quality: good to excellent all sections

Species: Rainbows, Browns & Brookies in some headwaters

Access: See below for the best way to get to each section:

~ *Lower Section:* This section starts at the South Fork's confluence with Mills River and heads up river for about 9 miles to the point where Turkeypen Road meets the river at the suspension bridge. For downstream access, turn left off of Hwy 280 onto Hwy 191. In about .3 miles turn left on Hwy 1338 *(Mills River Road)* and in about 2.2 miles you will cross the South Fork. The mouth is about .5 miles on the right. Continue about 5.8 miles to Nellie Cove for parking. Just upstream the river enters NFS land. Wading is about the only access for the first 1.3 miles upstream until you come to Bradley Creek river right. From there, Trail #115 follows the river up to Pea Gap. Then switch to Trail #351 and follow it to Turkeypen Road – the section's northern access point. Upstream access is via Turkeypen Road off Hwy 280 just south of Mills River. Roadside parking is available.

~ *Mid Section:* This section starts at Turkeypen Road and goes up river for 12.1 miles to just above the gauging station at FSR 476 / Cradle of Forestry's boundary. Downstream access is via Turkeypen Road off of Hwy 280 to Trail #133 which parallels the river up to FSR 476 / Cradle of Forestry boundary. A 1.6 mile stretch of river between Glady Branch and Billy Branch doesn't have trail access. Upstream access is by turning off of Hwy 276 onto FSR 1206 and driving about 3.2 miles across the Cradle of Forestry basin to FSR 476. Turn right and go about 1.2 miles to the boundary marker and South Fork entering from right. Pick up Trail #133 and head south on the river.

~ *Headwater Section:* Starts at the Cradle of Forestry boundary / FSR 476, and goes upstream for 2.8 miles to its source just below the Pink Beds picnic area. Downstream access can be had by turning off of Hwy 276 onto FSR 1206 and driving about 3.2 miles to FSR 476. Turn right and go 1.2 miles to the boundary marker / South Fork on right. Trail #118 follows the river to its source, and then continues to the Pink Beds off Hwy 276. Upstream access is via the Pink Beds. Then pick up Trail #118 and head south.

Overview & Description

If easy Parkway accessibility is a key criterion for including a watershed in this guide, why then has the South Fork been included? Other than its headwaters, its main flow hardly meets the standard. But I'm stretching the rules for several reasons. *First*, it's great trout water – especially brown trout. *Second*, all of its headwaters do come directly off of the Parkway. *Third*, those headwaters flow down through the Cradle of Forestry – a historically significant piece of real estate. *Fourth*, it flows for almost 24 miles through some wild and remote country that takes stamina and planning to traverse and fish. And *fifth*, because I don't want to get nasty cards and texts from folks whining about how it should have been included - and that Sam doesn't know what he's talking about, etc., etc. So... to keep everyone happy, it's included. Let's consider a bit of the history of this place.

George W. Vanderbilt, III, grandson of railroad tycoon *Cornelius Vanderbilt*, reportedly once said something to the effect of: "*I can stand on the terrace of my Biltmore Estate, and everything I can see, I own.*" I can make the same claim about the 100 yard view line from my deck across the six acres I own. The difference between me and George *(other than the fact that he was worth a gazillion dollars)* is that his view line was over 20 miles as the crow flies. His view encompassed almost the entire 86,700 acre *Mills River (Proper)* and

George W. Vanderbilt, III owned Pisgah Forest where the forestry school was located. / *Image courtesy of Special Collections, UNC Asheville*

Davidson River watersheds! Vanderbilt named the entire tract *Pisgah Forest*, in honor of the biblical mountain from where Moses looked over into the Promised Land. Not only was it part of his original holdings, but it eventually became the foundation for the *National Forest Service in America*.

~ South Fork of Mills River ~

Today's *Cradle of Forestry*, originally the *Biltmore Forest School*, was the site of the first school of forestry in the United States. Started by Vanderbilt, the forestry education offered at Biltmore was taught by Vanderbilt's Chief Forester, Dr. Carl Schenck. Schenck was a native German who was referred to Vanderbilt when Gifford Pinchot resigned from the position to operate the newly formed Division of Forestry.

Based on European models and concepts, Vanderbilt and Schenck created an American model for scientific, sustainable forestry. They conducted testing, established best practices and refined the technique of generating revenue through selective harvesting. After his death, Vanderbilt's wife Edith sold the property to the National Forest Service, and it became the core of Pisgah National Forest.

Today, Pisgah National Forest covers about 513,000 acres of mountainous terrain in North Carolina. Elevations reach over 6,000 feet and include some of the highest mountains in the eastern US. Management is divided into three Ranger Districts: *Grandfather, Appalachian* and *Pisgah*. The *Grandfather Ranger District* lies in the northernmost mountains south of Boone. The *Appalachian Ranger District* stretches along the Tennessee border from the Great Smoky Mountains National Park north to Hot Springs. *Pisgah Ranger District* is located in the southernmost mountains below Asheville, down to Brevard and over near Hendersonville.

Years ago, in virtually every watershed of the Pisgah Ranger District, a group of mounted forestry students would have ridden past you surveying and

Biltmore Forest School students preparing for a mounted field trip into Pisgah Forest to study all things forestry. / *Image courtesy of Special Collections, UNC Asheville*

conducting experiments. George Vanderbilt no doubt spent many a day with Head Forester Dr. Carl Schenck roaming the watersheds or camping / staying in one of the many Black Forest Lodges he built to accommodate his forest management team. The area is steeped in a history that's had far-reaching implications on forestry and recreation in America. Each time I'm there fishing, I feel the presence of these men who laid the foundations for modern forest management in America. Without them and their pioneering efforts, our forests would not be what they are today. This is a great topic for your next campfire! Now back to fishing.

Mills River *(Proper)* is one of the first sizeable tributaries of the French Broad River – the Davidson being another of similar attributes. The *"Mills"* forms when the South Fork *(the headwater examined in this chapter)* and its twin the North Fork *(examined in Section II)* converge. From that source to its mouth on the French Broad, it is only 6 miles – not very long for a river. For most of those 6 miles it flows slowly through flat, private truck farming land with restricted access. Trout are scarce along that main flow because they prefer the clean, cold, highly-oxygenated waters upstream in the *South Fork* and *North Fork*.

Both the *North Fork* and *South Fork* are good-sized flows that form up and drain the south face of *Pisgah Ridge* on the Parkway. From there they flow through some of the most remote and historically significant forests in the Eastern US. The imaginary line at MP 426 on the Parkway separating the 63 miles of *Section I* and the 63 miles of *Section II* of this guide, actually bisects the watersheds of these two headwaters.

Plaque on Hwy 276 commemorating George Vanderbilt's first forestry school in America. / *Image by Author / 2007*

The South Fork is managed as *Wild Trout Waters* and is known as an excellent brown trout fishery. Its rugged access keeps fishing pressure down, and the numerous deep, dark and shaded pools throughout its central flow provide a perfect habitat for browns to grow up unchallenged, dominate their waters and grow *BIG!* Many attain *"Typhoon Class"* sizes capable of testing any angler's skills. In between those slower pockets of water are miles of faster, more challenging waters where the nimble rainbows flourish. However, getting to them is difficult, and other than the headwaters and the lower water towards the mouth, getting on and off this wilder and remote central section can only be done by hiking. So…. be prepared to do a bunch of walking if you fish the best trout waters in the central part of this river.

The South Fork's topography, elevations and difficult access create three unique sets of characteristics. To describe them, I've divided the river into three sections: *Headwater Section, Mid Section* and *Lower Section.* I usually start at the mouth and work upstream with my descriptions. But in this instance, I'll start with the South Fork's headwaters and matriculate downstream to its mouth.

Headwater Section: The way I see it, the South Fork's headwaters include five high-elevation streams flowing off the Parkway: *Pigeon Branch, Bearwallow Brook, Barnett Branch, Poplar Creek* and *Thompson Creek.* Each one forms up just under the south face of *Pisgah Ridge* between *Green Knob* and *Little Bald Mountain* at about 4,500'. From their sources below the Parkway they dive off the ridge and enter an area known as the *Cradle of Forestry National Historic Site –* also known as the *Pink Beds*. This unique, almost flat basin is rectangular shaped with a southwest to northeast axis - about 3.5 miles wide *(east to west)* and about 2.5 miles *(north to south)*. All five headwaters enter this basin and form the South Fork's source at about 3,245' on the west end of the basin between the *Pink Beds Picnic Area* and the *Cradle of Forestry Visitors Center*. The entire basin is surrounded by peaks with only one gap for the South Mills to escape to the south.

Most of these headwater streams are small, but fishable to some degree – at least where they meet the South Fork. The 2.8 miles of the *Headwater Section* run across the bottom of the *Cradle of Forestry*. The section is flat with only a .5% gradient and is dotted with numerous beaver ponds that are full of small, wild browns. Between these ponds are long, slow runs with occasional pocket water –

especially where a headwater enters from the north and adds volume and turbulence. These create small pools that are deeper and full of wild trout.

Most of what I've caught in the *Headwater Section* has been in the 4"- 8" range – with an occasional 10"-12" ringer. Many stretches are too shallow, narrow or tight to hold fish. Fishing is made easier by the FSR roads traversing the upper runs of all five headwaters and by trails that offer access along the first 2.8 miles from the source on the west side of the Pink Beds. Then it turns south at 3,165' on the east corner and enters the remote *Mid-Section*.

Pigeon Branch seeping out of Pink Beds Picnic Area is one of five South Fork headwaters. / *Image by Author / 2011*

Mid-Section: If fishing for easily-spooked wild browns and bows flicks your switch, then the *Mid-Section* is for you. At the point where FSR 476 ends at the southeastern boundary of the *Cradle of Forestry*, the South Fork turns south and goes wild. After passing an old gauging station used by the Forest Service to measure water depths, the river opens up a bit. It begins a 12.1

mile ramble through some incredible and remote back country. In those 12.1 miles, the river loses about 765' in elevation. This results in only a flat 1.2% gradient, which makes wading and getting around easy for such remote and wild country.

The lower you get in the *Mid-Section*, the larger the water, and the canopy opens up to allow full casting and open mending. You can wade or use Trail #133 to enable you to move around. The trail follows the river through the entire run of the *Mid-Section* except for a short 1.6 mile stretch between *Glady Branch* and *Billy Branch* near the top of the section.

Along the *Mid Section*, each mile is a mix of large, deep drop pools, runs and slides. You'll also need to navigate several waterfalls, cascades and cataracts of varying heights along the way, including *High Falls* – the largest waterfall on the river as far as I can tell. There are also several steep gorges that test your fishing and in-stream navigation skills and endurance. The gorge fishing is always great.

As mentioned earlier, this section is known for some huge browns lurking in many of the larger pools. I've never caught one but I've caught browns and bows in the 12' – 16" range on a regular basis. Because of its remoteness and trail-only access, fishing this section requires an "*endurance*" mentality – so be prepared to get banged and scratched up. About 14.9 miles below the South Fork's source, the *Mid-Section* ends at about 2,400' where *Turkeypen Road* meets it above Hwy 280.

Lower Section: This lower 9 mile section from *Turkeypen Road* at 2,400' to its mouth is roughly 50 / 50 on public / private lands. From Turkeypen Road downstream about 4.5 miles to *Nellie Cove* at the foot of *Hammett Mountain*, the river is still flowing through NFS lands. Along that stretch it's wide and open canopied – much like the lower stretches of the *Mid-Section*. About 3.1 miles below *Turkeypen Road*, the South Fork's largest tributary *Bradley Creek* enters from the north. This large flow begins up under the parkway, has a good trail system, and is a worthwhile fishing destination. Because of reasonably good access from roads, suspension bridges and trails, this stretch of the South Fork gets more pressure than the other parts. Still, it fishes well with a good mix of browns and bows in the 8" – 14' range and a few Typhoons making cameo appearances.

The 5.5 miles from *Nellie Cove* to its confluence with the North Fork at 2,120' is almost exclusively on private land – except for the last .5 miles or so. You'll be tempted by sexy water and good access, but get permission first.

South Fork Tributaries

Bradley Creek
A Tributary of the South Fork

At a Glance

Sam's Rank: 👍👍👍👍

GPS Fixes:
- Source fix: N35 24.110 W82 44.385 @ 4,700'
- Mouth fix: N35 21.338 W82 38.576 @ 2,290'

Size: small at mouth
Gradient: flat 5.1% source to mouth average *(8.9 miles / 2,410')*
Effort: moderate to difficult
Pressure: none to slight
Fishing Quality: good
Species: Bows, Browns and a few Specs in some of the headwater and feeders
Access: Below are my recommended access points:

~ *Lower Section:* This section includes roughly 4.1 miles between the mouth and Yellow Gap Creek. Mouth access is via Turkeypen Road off of Hwy 280 just south of Mills River. Drive to where Turkeypen Road meets the South Mills. Limited parking is available. A suspension bridge is there as well. Pick up Trail #351 and follow it downstream a mile or so to Pea Gap. From there, follow Trail #115 downstream about 2.6 miles to the Bradley's mouth. There are several other trails, but I think this one's best.

~ From the mouth, upstream access is via Trail #115 which meets Trail #351 a mile up. From there Trail #351 follows the stream 3.2 miles up to FSR 1206 at Yellow Gap Creek – which parallels the creek almost to its source. The trails cross the creek twenty or more times via fords and log bridges.

~ *Upper Section:* This section includes roughly 4.8 miles between Yellow Gap Creek and the source. Access from the top is via turning off of Hwy 276 onto FSR 1206 *(Yellow Gap Road)* and driving through the Cradle of Forestry basin for 3.9 miles *(just past Grassy Lot Gap)*. There is parking there. The road crosses the Bradley and parallels it for the next 3.4 miles downstream to where Yellow Gap Creek enters. The Bradley turns south away from the road there. Trail #351 provides downstream access.

Overview & Description

Bradley Creek runs through the eastern half of George Vanderbilt's experimental Pisgah Forest. If you're looking for a great stream on which to chase wild trout with a blend of Pisgah history, water size and types, numerous feeders, access and remoteness, look no further than the Bradley. Its upper, docile flow is very accessible via a NFS road. It's lower and more challenging stretches are accessible by trails. Because of remoteness and the fact that it is over shadowed by the main flows of the more accessible and popular *South Fork* and the *North Fork*, this creek is off the radar and gets little pressure other than hikers and bikers.

Bradley oozes out of the rocks on the south face of *Little Bald Mountain* just south of the Parkway at about 4,700'. From there it begins its 8.9 mile descent from between *Dividing Ridge* and *Pilot Rock* down through Pisgah National Forest to its mouth at 2,290' on the South Fork. Throughout that entire run, it averages a flat 5.1% gradient, making most of its water easy to wade and navigate. Along the way, it receives additional flow from no less than twenty tiny feeders – with *Slate Rock Creek* being the largest and most fishable. For description purposes

One of several fat Browns caught about halfway up Bradley Creek. / *Image by Author / 2016*

I've divided Bradley into two sections: *Lower Section* and *Upper Section.*

Lower Section: At its mouth, Bradley's stream bed is about 15' wide. Moving upstream, the first 2.5 miles is a continuous gauntlet of riffles and runs, plunge pools and some flats. Several unremarkable feeders enter the flow, but none of which I've been compelled to waste time fishing. At about 2.5 miles up is a small decommissioned reservoir dam that supplied the City of Hendersonville with drinking water. There is a similar dam on the North Fork – Mills River with the same purpose. Both are about the same size, and both damage the stream's hydraulic properties in the same way with higher water temps and lower oxygen levels. That's just *MY* opinion. Over the next 1.6 miles above the dam up to *Yellow Gap* and FSR 1206, the river doesn't change much except that it passes through a more winding topography surrounded by steep mountains.

The Lower Section is prime trout water and is managed as *Wild Trout Waters.* It's my favorite section on this stream. You'll find mostly bows in the 6" – 14" range and because the canopy provides filtered light to the water, I've caught a goodly number of browns as well. I know there are bigger fish in there; I just haven't caught them yet – *but I will!* I've also not caught any specs in the main flow or in any of its fishable feeders. This section's stream bed is relatively wide and has a flat 1.8% gradient. The canopy is open enough to allow for easy casting. Most of where I've fished is in the bigger water below *Yellow Gap.* This is truly wild water with an endless number of riffles, runs, cascades, pools and plunge / drop pools that all hold fish. My kinda fishing!

Upper Section: The 3.5 miles along FSR 1206 from *Yellow Gap* to *Grassy Gap* also has a flat gradient of only 3.5%. Along the entire section, the creek is small and comprised of a continuous mix of excellent in-stream structures that create the types of pocket water that trout like. Up about .6 miles above *Yellow Gap* is the Bradley's largest feeder, *Slate Rock Creek* entering creek right. It's small and fairly open. I believe it to be the most fishable of any of the other feeders – at least for the

.5 miles I've fished. Near the top of that half mile, I did lots of bushwhacking between assorted types of pocket waters for small rainbows in the 4" – 7" range.

I've not fished above the *Grassy Gap Bridge* / parking area up to the source. I'm sure there's a big 12" spec up there with an attitude just smacking its lips waiting for my #14 Elk Hair Caddis. But he'll have to wait for another day!

The best thing about fishing the *Upper Section* is that FSR 1206 allows you to drive between water features and then drop in and fish them without bushwhacking and climbing. I appreciate being able to do that when I can, especially at the end of the day when I'm tired. There are also lots of primitive camping sites all along the road to set up a base camp – but pick one out and make camp early because they go quickly.

Section II

63 miles

MP 406 (just north of Mt. Pisgah) to MP 343 (just north of where Hwy 80 crosses the Parkway below Crabtree Falls)

This section includes some storied watersheds in the Mt. Pisgah and Asheville areas that offer excellent fishing opportunities, as well as numerous watersheds of various sizes on and around Mt. Mitchell. Several of these watersheds have significant historical importance pertaining to the US Forest Service, Pisgah National Forest, Asheville, George W. Vanderbilt, III and the Biltmore Estate. The Swannanoa and French Broad Rivers are included because of their proximity to the Parkway, as well as their size, general popularity and history. This is despite the fact that their main flows are not considered great trout waters. But there're plenty of others that are!

www.wildbearings.com will have *lodging, campsite, outfitter, restaurant* and *brewery* recommendations to help plan your trip along this Section of the Parkway.

North Fork
of Mills River
At a Glance

Sam's Rank: 👍👍👍
GPS Fixes:
- Source fix: N35 25.195 W82 40.496 @ 2,485'
- Mouth fix: N35 23.565 W82 36.600 @ 2,120'

Size: medium at mouth *(At its confluence with Mills River)*
Gradient: flat 1.2% source to mouth average *(5.7 miles / 365')*
Effort: lower section – easy / upper section – moderate
Pressure: lower section - moderate to heavy / upper section - slight
Fishing Quality: lower section - average to good / upper section - fair to average
Species: Rainbows, Browns & Brookies
Access: below are my recommendations for getting to each section:

~ *Lower Section.* This section starts at the North Fork's confluence with the South Fork, *(Mills River's source)* and goes up river about 2.8 miles to the North Mills River Campground where Rocky Fork enters river left and North Fork makes a 90 degree right turn under the FSR 1206 bridge. There's plenty of parking and a day fee when you enter the campground.

- *Downstream access:* In Mills River turn off Hwy 280 onto Hwy 191 north. At about .9 miles turn left on Hwy 1345 *(North Mills River Road)*. At about 2.5 miles the mouths of the South Fork and North Fork meet to form the Mills River's source about .2 miles on the left. Continue on and as you enter Pisgah National Forest, the road changes to FSR 1206 and parallels the North Fork to the North Mills River Campground. At 2.8 miles the river makes a ninety degree right turn under the bridge – that's the top of the *Lower Section.*

- *Upstream access:* Below the Parkway turn off of Hwy 276 at the Cradle of Forestry onto FSR 1206 and follow it across the basin to the North Mills River Campground. As you enter the campground, North Mills will flow from the left and Rocky Fork is on the right.

~ *Upper Section:* The bottom of this section starts where the North Fork makes its ninety degree turn under FSR 1206 in the North Mills River Campground. From there it heads up river for 2.9 miles to the decommissioned Hendersonville Reservoir.

- *Downstream access:* From the North Mills River Campground, wade upstream .3 miles to pick up Trail #353 and follow it up to FSR 142. This road parallels the river up to the section's start at the reservoir.

- *Upstream access:* Pick up FSR 5000 *(Wash Creek Road)* at the south entrance to the North Mills River Campground and follow it about 1.9 miles up to the parking area at FSR 142 *(gated)*. Park and hike down FSR 142 for about 1.8 miles to the reservoir. FSR 142 parallels the river much of the way.

Overview & Description

The South Fork of the Mills barely scooted under the wire for inclusion into *Section I* because of its poor Parkway accessibility. And the *North Fork* is even less accessible. Additionally, it has the disadvantage *(in my opinion)* of being managed as *Delayed Harvest* and with the exception of its headwaters above the reservoir, is not a good wild trout fishery. But, I yielded to pressure and bent the *"Parkway Accessibility"* rule once again. *First* and foremost, George Vanderbilt's favorite sylvan get-a-way, *Buck Springs Lodge,* was perched high up on Pisgah Ridge. From his backyard overlook he could gaze directly down the entire North Fork watershed – more on that below. *Second,* even though North Fork's main flow is not known as great wild trout water, both of its headwaters do come off of the Parkway and do have healthy populations of wild trout. *Third,* I didn't want to get beat up on fishing blogs and in Trout Unlimited meetings by the Delayed Harvest crowd about how it should have been included – *so I caved!*

To put the North Fork's watershed as well as its neighboring watersheds into proper historical context, let your mind wander back to the late Victorian Age of the early 1900s. It was a time when George W. Vanderbilt owned about 125,000 acres of Western NC – including the entire Mills River watershed and the surrounding peaks. He'd often stand on his *Buck Springs Lodge* overlook and gaze at the expansive Pisgah Forest below – *he owned it all!* It was a grand panoramic view of the entire watershed from his beloved Buck Springs Lodge which is located high up on Pisgah Ridge at present day *Buck Springs Gap* on the Parkway. The Adirondack Style lodge had a commanding 180 degree view of the North Fork watershed as well as the South Fork and Pink Beds. In fact, the view encompassed much of the 86,000 acres of his Pisgah Forest holdings. George Vanderbilt and his Chief Forester Dr. Carl Schenck had set up an experimental forest in this acreage which would become the first forestry school in America – *The Cradle of Forestry.*

After George's death from an appendectomy in 1914, his wife Edith offered to sell 86,000 acres of the 125,000 total holdings to the National Forest Service. The government eventually purchased the property and on October 17, 1916 it became the centerpiece of the new *Pisgah National Forest* - the first National Forest in the eastern US. Edith Vanderbilt carved out 471 acres around Buck Springs Lodge and continued to frequent it until her death in 1955. The Parkway then took possession and demolished the buildings. Unfortunately, only a few foundations, an overlook,

Buck Springs Lodge had a commanding view of George Vanderbilt's entire Pisgah Forest holdings - especially the North Mills Watershed. / *Image courtesy of Special Collections, UNC Asheville*

and the spring house survived. The spring house is beside the Parkway as you turn into Pisgah Mountain parking area. You can still drink the cold pure water from the same spring as George! *Back to fishing...*

Given the rich history of the place, no description of the North Fork's watershed would be complete without considering the Mills River *(Proper)*. The main flow of the Mills is one of the first sizable tributaries of the French Broad River – the Davidson being another similar in size. Mills forms when the North Fork *(the headwater this chapter examines)* and its South Fork twin *(examined in Section I)* converge. From that source to its mouth on the French Broad, it flows only 6 miles – not long for a river. Most of those 6 miles flows slowly through flat, private truck farming land with restricted access. But that doesn't really matter because trout are scarce along that main flow anyway. They prefer the clean, colder and highly-oxygenated waters upstream in the *South Fork* and *North Fork*.

Both *North Fork* and *South Fork* are good-sized flows that drain the south face of *Pisgah Ridge* on the Parkway. From there, they flow through some of the most remote and historically significant forests in the Eastern US. The imaginary line at MP 426 on the Parkway separating the 63 miles of *Section I* and the 63 miles of *Section II* of this guide actually bisects the watersheds of these two headwaters.

The North Fork's headwaters are composed of two high-elevation streams sourcing just below the Parkway on the south face of *Pisgah Ridge* between *Buck Springs Gap* and *Beaverdam Gap*. *Big Creek* and *Fletcher Creek* seep out of the ground at about 4,000' and flow down to an old decommissioned reservoir at

2,485'. As their combined waters escape the dam, the North Fork's source comes to life and begins a 5.7 mile flow to its convergence with the South Fork. Along the way, it picks up volume from several tributaries with names like *Wash Creek, Rocky Creek* and *Seniard Creek* – all fishable. From source to mouth, North Fork sports a flat 1.2% average gradient. At about 2,120' it reaches its mouth as it joins the South Fork to form the source of the Mills River *(Proper)*. Because of the North Fork's variety of flows, topography and access, I've divided it into two *(2)* sections to describe it more easily: *Upper Section* and *Lower Section.*

Lower Section: Moving upstream from the mouth at about 2,120', this section runs upstream 2.8 miles to the bridge on FSR 1206 in the campground. Along that run, it loses only 110' giving it a flat average gradient of .7%. The river is about 20'– 30' wide in most places with wide open canopies and a series of slow runs and pools. This makes for easy wading and casting all the way up. The start of this section is on private land before it enters National Forest and the campground. Make sure you know where the boundaries are. *Seniard Creek* enters river right about 1.6 miles up and *Rocky Creek* enters river left at about 2.8 miles up in the campground. Both feeders contribute additional flow and are fishable. *Rocky* is small, and I have fished it with some success. *Seniard* is also small, and I have not fished it because it's on private property.

The *Lower Section* is managed as *Delayed Harvest* and receives the most pressure virtually year round. It has become one of North Carolina's newest and best known *Delayed Harvest* streams. As of this writing, about 11,000 rainbows, brooks, and browns are stocked each year along the section – mostly inside the National Forest boundary. Some brood fish are reportedly set free too. And so you'll find the typical 10"- 12" stockers and an occasional 18"- 20" pig in the mix.

Aside from the *Delayed Harvest* season, this river is open to fishing under general regulations the rest of the year as well. The campground's accessibility to regional communities and the local *"kill & grill"* crowd keep it busy much of the year. In spite of that, because there is so many trout being dumped in, it fishes well even in the cooler months. There is a good mix of browns and bows in the 8" – 14" range, with the occasional *"big-un."* That said, I don't fish this section more than every couple of years – and then only in mid-week. But if you're a Delayed Harvest person – you'll love it.

Upper Section: Moving upstream from the bridge in the campground at about .3 miles up, the section's only sizeable feeder – *Wash Creek* – enters river right. It's definitely fishable. Along the next 2.6 mile stretch up to the decommissioned Hendersonville Reservoir, the river loses about 235' in elevation - a flat 1.5% gradient. Wading and getting around is easy and trails, bridges and roads make it even easier. This section averages about 10'- 15' wide and has a relatively open canopy. The water is a mix of plunge and drop pools, slides, runs and stretches of

Rocky Creek *(left)* entering the North Fork *(right)* at the campground's upper end below the bridge on FSR 1206. The confluence pool offers good fishing opportunities. */ Image by Author / 2018*

long slow flows. Some Delayed Harvest fish are up here too and find refuge in the usual places. On average I catch a mix of all three species in the 8"- 14" range.

At 2.9 miles above the campground, you will reach the North Fork's source at the old 1.5 – 2 acre *Hendersonville Reservoir*. This source point is unusual for a mountain trout stream, and it greatly impacts the quality of fishing in the waters below. The Hendersonville Reservoir is a small, silted-in, 15' deep decommissioned water impoundment for the City of Hendersonville. The impoundment is formed by the confluence of the North Fork's two headwater streams – *Big Creek* and *Fletcher Creek*. The concrete / stone dam forces its water to exit over the top rather than coming out cold from underneath the dam. The warmer surface water makes it difficult to support trout during the hot summer months and does nothing to enhance the water's fertility or oxygen properties. As a result, the North Fork fishes good until about June when water temps warm up in excess of 70 degrees. The impoundment has no negative impact on the two headwaters or the other tributaries entering North Fork. That's why the wild fishing is productive. And, a big reason the North Fork got included in *Section II*.

North Fork Tributaries

Big Creek
One of Two North Fork Headwaters

At a Glance

Sam's Rank: 👍👍👍👍

191

GPS Fixes:
- Source fix: N35 24 803 W82 44.725 @ 4,420'
- Mouth fix: N35 25.192 W82 40.491 @ 2,485'

Size: small at mouth *(At its confluence with Fletcher Creek at the reservoir)*
Gradient: moderate 8.5% source to mouth average *(4.3 miles / 1,938')*
Effort: difficult
Pressure: none
Fishing Quality: average
Species: Rainbows, Browns & Brookies
Access: To get to Big Creek's mouth at the Hendersonville Reservoir Dam, pick up FSR 5000 *(Wash Creek Road)* at the south entrance to North Mills River Campground and follow it about 1.9 miles up to the parking area. Park and hike down the FSR 142 *(gated)* for about 1.8 miles to the dam. FSR 142 parallels the river much of the way. To get to the headwaters from the Parkway, pick up Trail #102 at MP 406.9 near Buck Springs Gap. It will descend the ridge and then parallel Big Creek most of the way to the dam.

Overview & Description

There was a time in the early part of the last century when fishing up Big Creek would have afforded you an opportunity to rub shoulders with George and Edith Vanderbilt plus a Who's Who of international blue bloods. They might have been sitting on their overlook at Buck Springs Lodge looking through their spy glasses and watching you fish. George's Buck Springs had a perfect view down the entire Big Creek watershed. In fact, the creek sources only about 1,000' in front of Buck Springs Gap. If you've not visited and soaked up that site on the Parkway, you're missing something special and something very few people are even aware of. It's accessed from the Mount Pisgah parking area at about MP 407.3. Follow the signs to the trailhead that leads about 300' to the ruins and overlook. Be sure to visit the original spring house sitting on the Parkway. It's worth a special trip.

As one of the two North Fork headwaters, Big Creek seeps out just under *Buck Springs Gap* at about 4,420'. From that source, it begins an easterly 4.3 mile downhill run from between *Little Pisgah Mountain* and *Little Bald Mountain* at a moderate 8.5% gradient. During its run, it gathers more volume from several feeders – with *Bee Branch, Horse Cove* and *Boby Cove* being the largest and most fishable. These feeders transform it into a worthy trout stream as it reaches the reservoir at about 2,485'.

Big Creek's mouth is at the reservoir's upper left corner. Moving upstream from there, the creek flows at a flat 2.7% gradient over the next 1.9 miles – which is the stretch of the main flow I've fished most. Along that stretch, the creek is a typical headwater stream with numerous long, slow runs with pocket water, faster runs with drop pools and small falls, to stretches that are very tight and choked with flora. Along several stretches, the ridges on both sides get steep and close in a bit. I've fished this entire stretch and caught bows and browns in the 6" to 8" range all the way up. Several times I've lucked up and snagged a 12" overachiever in some of the larger pools. Fishing is made easier if you use Trail #102 that runs between Buck Springs Gap and the reservoir.

About 1.8 miles up, *Boby Cove* enters creek left, and then at 1.9 miles *Horse Cove* enters creek right. Both are fishable, and I've fished them both for about .5

The spring house for George Vanderbilt's Buck Springs Lodge at about MP 407.3 on the Parkway. / *Image by Author / 2018*

miles and caught small bows and a few specs in the 4"- 6" range. They were fun but you need to be prepared to do some climbing and bushwhacking. Each one starts out relatively flat and then gets steeper as you move up.

Bee Branch enters high up at about 2.4 miles creek left. I have hiked past and pondered this creek several times, but I have not fished more than a few yards into its mouth. It looks really fishable, and I'm sure it would be worth the time and effort. I've just been too beaten each time I've been there.

Aside from the history of the Big Creek watershed, if you want to fish for wild bows and browns and a few specs mixed in, this backcountry headwater is the best the North Fork has to offer in my opinion.

Fletcher Creek
One of Two North Fork Headwaters

At a Glance

Sam's Rank: 👍👍👍

GPS Fixes:

- Source fix: N35 26 .868 W82 42.426 @ 3,395'
- Mouth fix: N35 25.192 W82 40.491 @ 2,485'

Size: small at mouth *(At its confluence with Big Creek at the dam)*
Gradient: mild 5.9% source to mouth average *(3 miles / 913')*
Effort: difficult
Pressure: none
Fishing Quality: average
Species: Rainbows, Browns & Brookies
Access: To get to Fletcher Creek's mouth at the Hendersonville Reservoir Dam, pick up FSR 5000 *(Wash Creek Road)* at the south entrance to the North Mills River Campground and follow it for about 1.9 miles up to the parking area. Park and hike down FSR 142 *(gated)* for about 1.8 miles to the dam. The road parallels the river much of the way. At the dam, pick up Trail #600 and follow it up the creek to the Middle Fork where it connects with Trail #350. Trail #350 continues up into Fletcher's headwaters and eventually intersects FSR 5097 *(Never ending Road)* higher up. Other trails offer access up some of its feeders.

Overview & Description

As the other North Fork headwater, Fletcher Creek oozes out from under *Glady Fork Gap* at about 3,395'. It runs for 3 miles at an average gradient of about 5.9% down to the Hendersonville Reservoir. Along the way, it gathers water from just two sizeable feeders – *Middle Fork* and *Spencer Branch*. Middle is the larger of the two, but both are fishable. By the time it reaches the reservoir at about 2,485', it has transformed into a respectable trout stream.

Fletcher Creek's mouth is at the reservoir's upper right corner. As you move upstream over the first 1.3 miles, the creek flows at a very flat 2.5% average gradient. Along the way, it has many large to small drop pools and falls, as well as some stretches with bigger than expected runs and riffles that all hold fish. As with Big Creek, there are stretches where the sides and canopy become so tight and choked with foliage that fishing is difficult. At about .8 miles up the main flow, *Middle Fork* enters creek left from its source 2.7 miles up just below Parkway. At about 1.3 miles up, *Spencer Branch* enters creek right from its source 1.3 miles up – also just below the Parkway. Fletcher's main flow continues up the valley for another 1.7 miles to its source point just under the Parkway.

One of my buddies and I have fished up the first 1.3 miles of the main flow only once as well as about .5 miles up *Middle Fork* and *Spencer Branch*. Along the main flow we caught rainbows and a few browns in the 5"- 8" range. For a small creek the main flow fishes rather easy because of its low gradient. The lower stretches of the two feeders are also relatively flat, but both became tight and difficult the further up we fished. Both of these fished about the same with the exception of catching a few brookies and the more plentiful bows, all in the 4"- 8" range. Fishing was easier because of the trail system that services all of the Fletcher water we fished. This is a remote creek and fun to fish if you like a challenge. It's hard fishing but worth the experience.

Wash Creek
A North Fork Tributary
At a Glance

Sam's Rank: 👍👍👍
GPS Fixes:
- Source fix: N35 27 068 W82 40.652 @ 3,180'
- Mouth fix: N35 24.639 W82 39.004 @ 2,280'

Size: small at mouth *(At its mouth on the North Mills)*
Gradient: flat 4.3% source to mouth average *(4 miles / 900')*
Effort: moderate
Pressure: none
Fishing Quality: average
Species: Rainbows, Browns
Access: Except for the first .3 miles or so, FSR 5000 *(Wash Creek Road)* at the south entrance to the North Mills River Campground tracks almost all the way up Wash Creek's flow. As it reaches the headwaters, it turns eastward and eventually reaches Bent Creek Gap on the Parkway at MP 400.3. There are several gates along this road so check access first.

Overview & Description

I'll confess that I haven't fished a lot on Wash Creek. What I did fish of it were several stretches along the first 1.8 miles of FSR 5000 *(Wash Creek Road)*. I was on my way up to the parking area at FSR 142 just above where *Bear Branch* enters Wash Creek and then on to hike to the Hendersonville Reservoir for some headwater fishing. The extent of my fishing involved stopping several times to explore the deep pools, runs, and small falls and drop pools seen from the road. Each time I was rewarded with rainbows and a few browns in the 6"- 8" range but none bigger. I'll go back and fish the entire creek sometime. But on previous trips, I was on a mission to fish other *"agua."*

Wash sources on the south slope of *Ferrin Knob* just under the Parkway at about 3,180'. From there it works its way just east of *Trace Ridge* for about 4 miles on the way to its mouth. From source to mouth it averages a flat 4.3 gradient. During that run it receives flow from just a few feeders – *Bear Branch* and *Bad Fork* being the larger of these. At about 2,281', its mouth meets the North Fork at .3 miles above North Mills River Campground.

From its mouth above the campground and moving upstream 1.5 miles to *Bear Branch*, the ridges on both sides of the creek are steep. The road from the campground joins and parallels the creek about .5 miles above the campground. But even then, getting from road to creek requires quite an effort to negotiate elevations differences. A friend and I have done this particular stretch up to *Bear Branch* three or four times and were so beaten by the time we finished, we had to rest a spell and drink a beer or two before starting the hike to the reservoir. However, given the topography, Wash has a lot of structures that hold trout, and we caught bows and browns in the 6"- 10" range. Not bad for a small creek.

A small Brown caught on an Adams about a mile up Wash Creek. / *Image by Author / 2016*

At about 1.5 miles up, *Bear Branch* enters creek right and on up at about 2 miles, *Bad Fork* enters creek right. Both are small and although we did not fish them at that time, from what we saw, they both looked "*kinda*" fishy. Above *Bear Branch*, the road / creek elevation differences moderate and make for easier access – *we should have fished along there instead!* The remaining 1.1 miles above *Bad Fork* up to about 3.1 miles above the campground is paralleled by the road. The creek is still attractive and looks fishable to me.

French Broad River
An Overview of Its Main Flow

At a Glance

Sam's Rank: N/A

GPS Fixes
- Source fix: N35 08.192 W82 48.660 @ 2,190'
- Mouth fix: N36 01.888 W83 11.494 @ 1,010'

Size: very large at mouth *(At its confluence with the Holston River to form the Tennessee River's source.)*

Gradient: very flat .001% source to mouth average *(218 miles / 1,180')*

Effort: N/A

Pressure: N/A

Fishing Quality: N/A

Species: First few miles below its source at Rosman down to the Davidson River: Rainbows & Browns. Downstream from the confluence of the Davidson River: bass *(large, small & rock mouth)*, pan fish, chain pickerel, catfish, chub, even claims of muskie, etc.

Access: Data for all 218 miles would be overkill. The river is paralleled by major and secondary roads practically its entire length. A basic road map is all you need for any access point.

French Broad *(Proper)* Watershed Overview

The French Broad River's main flow is being included not because it's such a great trout fishery – *because it is NOT!* It's simply out of respect for several of its headwater streams that *are* great trout habitats. The other reason is that the Parkway actually crosses the French Broad in Asheville. And even though it doesn't have much of a sustainable wild trout population below its headwaters, I included it because I didn't want to hear any whining about it *not* being included.

The *North Fork* of the French Broad River is examined in detail in *Section I*. It's the only one of the French Broad's four headwater streams that is easily accessible from the Parkway. So at this point I'll offer just an overview of the entire French Broad *(Proper)* watershed, as well as mention the other three headwaters I don't cover in *Section I*. After that you can decide if you want to fish them, or decide instead to chase bass and pan fish in the French Broad's main flow. Keep in mind that this is just the kind of knowledge you need to talk about around the campfire! It will help you sound wiser than you probably are, and you might even impress a few of your buddies with your newly acquired wisdom.

In its whole, the French Broad system represents one of the more "*broad*" and impressive rivers in this part of the country. It is a big river that drains a huge watershed and offers most any kind of water and fishing you might want. Besides the fact that its headwaters provide dozens of miles of trout water, this watershed

197

includes waters of all sizes and types for other fish as well. From trout fishing in fast and furious high-elevation headwaters, to bass and pan fishing in the flat and slow and lower elevation waters of its main flow – there's something for everyone. Specific to trout fishing, whether an angler wants an easy limit, a catch-and-release experience, or even wild trout in a remote setting, somewhere along the French Broad system will fit the bill.

Contrary to what some of my perverted fishing buddies swear as being the truth, the French Broad was not named after a French settler woman with loose morals. It was named so because the English settlers of the area considered it to be one of the two *"broader"* rivers in western North Carolina – which it actually is. The one flowing north into the lands claimed by France was named the *"French Broad River."* The other, which flowed south into lands claimed by England, was named the *"English Broad River"* - later the English was dropped, and it was renamed simply the *"Broad River."* Both have huge watersheds that drain thousands of square miles. Before white man arrived on the scene, the Cherokee used several names to describe each of the river's distinct sections: *"Agiqua"* *(broad)* in the mountains, *"Tahkeeosteh"* *(racing waters)* from Asheville down, and *"Zillicoah"* above Asheville. The French called it the *"Agiqua,"* based on their interpretation of one of the Cherokee names.

As with nearly all of the major flows in this Guide, the French Broad's source is the sum total of several headwater streams. In this case, four flows converge to form its source - three good-sized, high-elevation streams, and one tiny lower elevation flow that's not really worth mentioning beyond this reference. The *North Fork,* which is covered in Section I in detail, is the only one directly accessible from the Parkway. Here's a brief overview of all four:

~ *East Fork*, the first of those headwaters, is a good-sized flow, and one I'd recommend fishing when you are in the Rosman area. Unfortunately, it's not directly accessible from the Parkway. It sources up at about 2,915' near *Sassafras Gap* east of Rosman and flows northwesterly for about 10 miles at a gentle 1.4% average gradient to join the French Broad's source in Rosman at about 2,200'. The East Fork has become one of the area's most popular *Delayed Harvest* waters given its ease of access and aggressive stocking program. The state stocks about 20,000 rainbow, brown and brook trout along 4.8 miles of *East Fork Road* between *Gladys Fork Road* and the French Broad's source at Rosman. The stream is paralleled by road much of the way – although some stretches are on private lands.

~ *Middle Fork*, the second headwater, is very small and in my opinion not worth wasting time on given the fact that much of it is on private lands and the abundance of much better water all around. However, it does get some stocking by the state. About 1.7 miles of its flow is accessible by US 178.

The West Fork of the French Broad *(upper)* joining the North Fork *(right)* at the bridge on Hwy 64 in Rosman, are two of the French Broad's four headwaters. / *Image by Author / 2018*

~ *West Fork*, the third headwater is a sizeable stream that's a notable trout fishery – although it's not directly accessible from the Parkway either. It sources up northwest of *Lake Toxaway* at about 3,240' between *Big Pisgah Mountain* and *Round Mountain*. It flows for almost 11.7 miles at a gentle 1.7% average gradient to the French Broad source in Rosman at about 2,210'. This stream is a relatively fertile trout habitat and produces some especially big browns. However, it is overshadowed by the North and East Forks because of their heavy stocking programs and ease of access. The state does stock some portions of this stream, and the populations are definitely helped by the periodic water releases from several trout farms in the headwaters. This creates favorable environments for aquatic bugs – especially large hatches of mayflies. There is some road access along several stretches, but much of the stream is not road accessible except by foot. This is especially true for the National Forest Service section since much of it is located in a gorge with no road.

~ *North Fork*, the fourth headwater stream forming the French Broad is in my opinion, the "*pick of the litter*" of these four headwaters. I'll save the ink here, and you can read about it in its own chapter in *Section I*.

To describe a river's main flow, I typically start at the mouth and work upstream with my descriptions. But for this *Overview* of the French Broad's main flow, I'll start at its source and matriculate downstream to its mouth – which is actually to the north. The French Broad's *official* source per most authorities is just west of the *Eastern Continental Divide* in Rosman. At the bridge on Hwy 64 where Hwy 215 comes in, two of its headwaters, the *North* and *West Forks* converge. The other two headwaters – the *East* and *Middle Forks* – join about 2.5 miles downstream. It's here that the French Broad officially comes to life in the middle of a darn cow pasture – *and a private cow pasture to boot!*

From its source at about 2,190' it flows for about 218 miles in a north – northwesterly trajectory to its mouth at about 1,010' near Knoxville. Over those 218 miles, it drops in elevation only about 1,180' – or .001% gradient – an extremely flat trajectory for a river flowing through mountainous topography. Along the way it cuts across the Appalachian Chain and flows through some of the most beautiful landscapes in Western North Carolina and Tennessee, while draining a large portion of Pisgah National Forest and Cherokee National Forest.

As it begins to follow a north / northeasterly path through *Transylvania County* and *Brevard*, it picks up the waters from its first major tributary - the *Davidson River* – discussed in Section I, then the *Mills River*. It then passes through *Henderson County* and on into *Buncombe County* where it flows through the city of *Asheville*. In Asheville, it passes the *Biltmore Estate,*

The Swannanoa *(left)* entering the French Broad *(right)* at the Amboy Road bridge near the Arts District in Asheville. / *Image by Author / 2019*

picks up the *Swannanoa River (a sad river),* and flows past two major breweries. More than once I've fished for bass along the shoals in front of these breweries and ended the day by celebrating with more than a few pints of draft!

Through Asheville, limestone ledges run the entire width of the French Broad in most places making for difficult wading. If you do fish it, be sure to use studded soles, or even better, experience the river from a boat. A float trip through the *Biltmore Estate* section allows you to drift past forests that George W. Vanderbilt planted. You'll also pass stables and vineyards while casting to the smallmouths that live among the shoals. Muskie is caught along here too, but the excellent small mouth fishing and scenic vistas are what draw anglers to this part of the river.

As it leaves Asheville, the river starts a northwesterly arch as it passes through the mountain resort of *Hot Springs*. It then leaves North Carolina and enters *Cocke County, Tennessee*. In Cocke County, the *Pigeon River* enters the French Broad just north of the Cocke County seat of *Newport*. The river then enters the impounded waters of the *TVA's Douglas Lake* where the *Nolichucky River* also joins the flow. Douglas Dam in *Sevier County* was built on the lower French Broad

The French Broad is about sixty yards across as it passes through Asheville. Here in the Art District, New Belgium Brewery can be seen on the opposite bank. / *Image by Author / 2019*

by the TVA during the 1940s and is about 31 miles upstream from the river's mouth. North of *Sevierville,* the French Broad is joined by the flow of the *Little Pigeon River,* which drains much of the Tennessee section of the Smoky Mountains. As it continues northeasterly, it enters *Knox County* where it joins the famed *Holston River* just east of Knoxville to form the *Tennessee River.*

As far as trout fishing below the headwaters on the main flow goes, the river is rather large, flat and sluggish through most of its 218 mile run – as evidenced by its source to mouth gradient of only .001%. The 20 mile stretch from its source to the Hwy 276 Bridge south of Brevard, the French Broad is managed as *Hatchery Supported Trout Waters.* But even these waters are marginal at best and in turn are only marginally stocked along the 20 mile section. As you head north from that Hwy 276 Bridge, the river becomes too warm and silted to provide a sustainable wild trout habitat. Therefore, only about the first 20 miles of the French Broad's 218 mile flow can be considered even marginal trout fishing. The remaining 200 miles to its mouth is a good bass and pan fish habitat.

With all that negativity said, I love the French Broad for the simple reason that virtually all of its headwaters start high in the mountains – mostly within Pisgah National Forest. These headwaters have dozens of tributaries and feeders with adequate populations of wild and stocked trout, including brookies in most cases. In short, the real trout fishing is in the French Broad's headwaters.

201

Swannanoa River
An Overview of Its Main Flow

At a Glance

Sam's Rank: N/A

GPS Fixes:
- Source fix: N35 37.017 W82 16.051 @ 2,810'
- Mouth fix: N35 34.079 W82 33.811 @ 1,970'

Size: large at mouth *(At its confluence at the source of the French Broad "Proper")*

Gradient: flat .7% source to mouth average *(24.5 miles / 840')*

Effort: easy

Pressure: none to slight

Fishing Quality: poor

Species: stocked trout *(all three),* bass *(large & small),* assorted pan fish, chain pickerel, catfish, chubs, etc.

Access: Detailed directions for all 24.5 miles aren't practical. The river is paralleled by major / secondary roads its entire length. Hwy 70 from Black Mountain parallels it most of the way to Asheville. A maze of city / surface streets provides access for the rest. A basic road map is all you need.

Swannanoa *(Proper)* Watershed Overview

I wish there were some nice things to say about this river in terms of fly fishing for wild trout. But I just can't think of any! As with the French Broad *(Proper),* I'm including just an overview here for the simple reasons that the Parkway crosses it in Asheville, it has great history, and it gets some hatchery support. Actually, the main reason is to avoid getting hammered for *not* mentioning such a well-known river – even though, aside from a few headwater pockets, it doesn't have a sustainable wild trout population. I question whether it can even sustain a population of holdover hatchery trout. Regardless, for better or worse, below is my take on the Swannanoa. After reading it, you can decide if you want to chase bass, suckers and pan fish and the holdover stockers that struggle to live here.

The Swannanoa River and the namesake valley through which it flows, has a rich history attributable to the peoples and enterprises that have called it home. The name *Swannanoa* has roots in the Native American names *Shawano* or *Shawnee* – referring to an early tribe in the area and/or a Cherokee word meaning *"beautiful river."* In 1776, before white man had settled the Swannanoa Valley, *General Griffith Rutherford* passed through the valley. His mission was to persuade or coerce *(whatever worked best)* the Indians from joining forces with the British. But there was just one problem with his plan: there were no significant Indian settlements in the valley at that time. So he left.

When the Revolutionary War ended, Indian Territory was declared open for settlement and the men who'd ridden with Rutherford remembered the beautiful Swannanoa Valley with its open fields, lush forests, natural food for livestock, ample water, craft breweries, etc., and returned to claim their spot in paradise. From that point in time, the Swannanoa Valley as well as the surrounding region, has continued to grow into the congested residential and commercial community we see today.

That unbridled growth, with a lack of consideration for its impact on the valley's ecology, is the primary reason the watershed is in the poor state it's in today. Most of this predicament is attributable to the effects of residential and commercial development that contributed high volumes of sediment runoff into the watershed. Additionally, water quality issues have been identified in several stretches of the Swannanoa that have now been listed as *"impaired waters"* because of the lack of biological integrity and turbidity issues. Again, these were linked

Sections of the Swannanoa are choked with sediment and moderate levels of trash. / *Image by Author / 2018*

to urban development. The *2005 French Broad Basin Plan* identified habitat degradation, damaged riparian buffer zones, nutrient enrichment, high temperatures, sedimentation, channelization and toxicity as water quality problems in the watershed. Geeezzzzzz! No wonder Asheville skipped over the main flow and turned to the Swannanoa's headwaters above Black Mountain for much of its drinking water!

Fortunately, a dedicated group of stakeholders took notice and hatched a scheme to rehabilitate certain sections of the watershed. The plan increased water quality monitoring, local ordinance development, and aggressive natural resource protection throughout the watershed. A regimen of best management practices *(BMP)* is being employed such as riparian plantings, invasive / exotic plant removal, conservation easements, bio retention cells, rain gardens, and a host of other methodologies. Progress is happening – but results are slow in coming. Healing will take a while.

So what does all this mean for trout fishing and the Swannanoa? Let me answer it this way - after reading the last couple of paragraphs, if you were a trout, would you want to live in the Swannanoa? I would say an emphatic *"No!"* At least not in any healthy and sustainable habitat the main flow could support. Yet there are exceptions. Don't count out the isolated pockets of wild trout in the remote, high-elevation tributaries and headwaters – like the *Burnett* and *Bee Tree Reservoir* watersheds that are protected! Also, the 11,000 or so stockers the state puts in between Ridgecrest *(east of Black Mountain)* and Azalea Park / Wood Avenue in Asheville four or five times each year. Most of these trout are quickly caught by the kill & grill crowd. And the ones that escape are hanging on to dear life in a less than ideal habitat. In short – a wild trout habitat doesn't exist on the Swannanoa *"Proper"* – at least in water you and I can access legally and fish. With all the above negativity out of the way – let's consider the Swannanoa's main flow. Even though I usually start at the mouth and work upstream, for this *Overview* of the Swannanoa's main flow, I'll start at its source and move downstream.

Swannanoa's source is at 2,810' in *Swannanoa Gap* on the west slope of *Blue Ridge* across the road from *Ridgecrest Baptist Assembly* in Black Mountain. It bubbles up just a stone's throw from I-40 / Hwy 70 and just yards from the Pisgah National Forest boundary – the closest it will get to NFS land throughout its entire flow.

From that point it begins a 24.5 mile flow at a flat average gradient of just .7%. Perhaps this very low gradient and slow flow accounts in part to the river's inability to flush the excessive sedimentation the surrounding developments have dumped into it over time. For the next 9.2 miles, from Black Mountain to the community of Swannanoa, it's shadowed by I-40 / Hwy 70 and a busy railroad track. It also flows through working farms and commercial / residential developments. Its bed is covered mostly in sediment and moderate amounts of urban debris.

In the community of Swannanoa, alongside I-40 / Hwy 70 and the ever-present 200 car freight trains carrying coal to Duke Power *(soon to end when Duke closes that plant)*, the Swannanoa is joined by its largest tributary – the *North Fork*. From its exit point below the *Burnett Reservoir Dam*, the North Fork flows 4.7 miles to its confluence with the Swannanoa. Along this route, it drops only 240' in elevation, giving it a flat and slow 1% average gradient. Along this stretch it flows through cow pastures and plowed farm land, as well as residential / commercial developments that have choked its bed with sediment and some amounts of urban trash. It is joined along the way by several feeders that surely hold wild trout – but they are all on private lands. I have never fished any of the 4.7 miles of water between the dam and the mouth. Regardless, it does not look like healthy trout water to me.

I think the real trout fishing for the Swannanoa and / or its North Fork is in its headwaters coming off the Parkway above the reservoir. The problem is that the entire watershed is *off limits* - protected by the *Asheville Water Authority*. The actual source of the North Fork comes off of *Walker Knob* on the Parkway at about 4,840'. From there it flows for 4.9 miles down to *Burnett Reservoir* through a huge funnel-shaped watershed with multiple tributaries and feeders. Given this elevation and remoteness, I'm sure all of them contain trout – but you can't fish them because they're protected. What a shame. Of all the water in the Swannanoa River Watershed, this is surely the finest. Perhaps one day we'll be permitted to fish it.

After the Swannanoa's main flow leaves the community of Swannanoa, it makes a 7.6 mile northern arc through even more pasture, residential / commercial developments. About 1.4 miles into that arc, it picks up additional volume from *Bee Tree Creek*, flowing out of *Bee Tree Reservoir*. Bee Tree has several tributaries of its own coming from high up off the Parkway. But apparently all its water is protected too.

At the end of the 7.6 mile northern arc, the Swannanoa turns southward and passes under Hwy 70, then turns west as it makes its final 7.7 mile run to the French Broad. At that point, it is flanked on the north by Hwy 70 and to the south by I-40 as it enters east Asheville. In about a mile, the Parkway passes over head on its way into the mountains above Asheville.

As the river continues west, it passes through *Azalea Park / Asheville Recreational Park Complex*. Much restoration has been done to clean and protect the river from further damage. From there it continues through even heavier urban development in Biltmore Village before reaching its mouth at 1,970' on the French Broad across from the rail yard / Arts District. Along this final stretch, the river's bottom and banks are eroded and covered with sediment – urban trash levels increase and a faint waste water odor can often be detected. I haven't fished it in years – perhaps it's better now.

Ironically, with the exception of a few county and city parks and recreational areas, the Swannanoa flows most of its 24.5 miles through highway right-of-ways and private / protected lands. None of it flows through Pisgah National Forest. *Perhaps that's the problem...*

Carter Creek

At a Glance

Sam's Rank: 👍👍👍👍
GPS Fixes:
- Source fix: N35 42.792 W82 22.890 @ 4,765'
- Mouth fix: N35 44.464 W82 24.506 @ 2,510'

Size: very small at mouth
Gradient: steep 12.9% source to mouth average *(3.3 miles / 2,255')*
Effort: difficult to extreme
Pressure: none to slight
Fishing Quality: good
Species: Rainbows & Brookies
Access: From the Parkway at Craggy Gardens *(MP 355),* turn onto Stony Fork Road – it's gated and can be closed from time to time. Go 5.5 miles to Carter Creek Road on the right. Turn and parallel Carter Creek for the next 1.5 miles until you reach the NFS Boundary. The first ½ mile looks like someone's yard and / or a junk yard! Nonetheless, after about ¼ mile, turn left across the wooden bridge and continue to the NFS boundary. Parking is available inside the boundary – don't park outside the boundary. Headwaters access can be gained at Craggy Gardens via Trail #440 and #162. You will walk about an hour before you reach water. I did this one time, and I don't recommend it.

Overview & Description

Carter Creek is the quintessential, small high-elevation, blue liner. Although small, the fishing experience is BIG. I've jumped off the Parkway several times to hit this little mountain gem that's managed as *Catch and Release / Artificial Lures Only.* At the end of the day, I may be worn out and scratched up, but the fishing is always worth the effort I expend.

Although you'll pass wide open water on the way up to the NFS Boundary, the upper stretches of the creek are much smaller and will test your skills and choice of gear. Short rods *(7' and under),* 6X and smaller tippets, and stealthy approaches, sling shot / bow & arrow casting techniques are best suited for this stream. Fishing is tight from start to finish as you climb between one drop / plunge pool to the next while attempting to negotiate the increasingly steeper gradient. It is technical fishing for some of the prettiest little specs you'll see anywhere.

Carter seeps out of ground at about 4,765' just north of *Craggy Pinnacle* on the Parkway. From there it starts a 3.3 mile downhill ramble from between *Sprucepine Ridge* and *Bullhead Ridge* through the *Pisgah Game Lands* and *Craggy Mountain Scenic Area.* Along the way, it averages a steep 12.9% gradient. On the upper 1.8 miles on NFS land, it reaches an extreme 18.3%. Along its run, it picks up added volume from several feeders with names like *Waterfall Creek, Bearwallow Branch* and *Peach Orchard Creek.* Several hold brook trout! Carter's mouth is at about 2,510' where it joins *Mineral Creek* at the intersection of *Stony Fork Road* and *Carter Creek Road.* There they form *Stony Creek's* source.

Moving upstream from the mouth, the lower 1.5 miles of Carter Creek is about 15' – 20' wide. The first ¼ mile runs through a junk yard. Above that to the boundary the creek is beautiful with wide and deep runs, drop pools and runs through open forest. This stretch is prime trout water. Unfortunately, it's through private land. Don't fish without permission. *And I doubt you'll get it... I tried!*

Just upstream from the NFS boundary, *Peach Orchard Creek* joins creek left. This feeder is small but definitely fishable. On up another .6 miles you reach *Waterfall Creek* also

Carter Creek as it exits Pisgah National Forest and begins its run through private holdings. / *Image by Author / 2014*

entering creek left. Its headwaters source is even higher than Carter's at 5,170'. This creek is steeper, tighter and marginally fishable for the small specs that live there. I've fished about 1,000' up both of these feeders and caught specs in the 4" – 6" range. On up the main flow another .2 miles is tiny *Bearwallow Branch* entering creek right. I don't consider it reasonably fishable.

Along those first .8 miles above the NFS boundary to *Bearwallow*, Carter Creek's main flow is small, 5' – 8' across at *Peach Orchard Creek.* It's also steep and tight with a low canopy. Small stream wading, casting and good presentation skills are required to catch fish, while climbing and bushwhacking as much as fishing. I found myself doing a mix of 50 / 50 fishing and rock climbing. This .8 mile stretch is a progression of smaller and smaller plunge / drop pool and runs, with occasional stretches too clogged with flora to fish effectively. By the time you get to *Bearwallow*, Carter is only 3' – 5' across at best. Fishing the pocket water will deliver the best results – and will be the easiest! I've never caught anything over 5" as I approached *Bearwallow*.

Above Bearwallow the main flow gets more rugged and smaller. At this elevation, the creek is just a few feet across and only inches deep, with an occasional pool and undercut bank offering a place for a small trout to hold. Up there the gradient exceeds 20%. But there are hungry trout to be had!

Carter Creek Tributaries

Peach Orchard Creek
A Tributary of Carter Creek

At a Glance

Sam's Rank: 👍👍👍
GPS Fixes:
- Source fix: N35 43 357 W82 21.618 @ 4,765'
- Mouth fix: N35 44 281 W82 23 172 @ 3,030'

Size: very small at mouth
Gradient: extreme 17.9% source to mouth average *(1.9 miles / 1,735')*
Effort: difficult to extreme
Pressure: none
Fishing Quality: average
Species: Bows & Specs
Access: From the Parkway at Craggy Gardens *(MP 355),* turn onto Stony Fork Road. It is gated and can be closed from time to time. Go 5.5 miles to Carter Creek Road on the right. Turn and parallel Carter Creek for the next 1.5 miles until you reach the NFS Boundary. The first ½ mile looks like a junk yard. After about ¼ mile, turn left across the wooden bridge and continue to the boundary. From there, wade Carter Creek a hundred feet to Peach Orchard entering stream left. I know of no trail access. Do not park outside the NFS Boundary.

Overview & Description

Peach Orchard is the best Carter Creek feeder. Being the *"small creek freak"* I am, I included it because of the really nice runs and drop pools that make for surprisingly good spec fishing. It's small, steep and tight, about 3' – 5' wide at its mouth. But it is definitely fishable if you will bushwhack your way upstream between its frequent runs and pools. I've only fished about 1,000' up and caught bows and specs in the 4" – 6" range – *and a bunch of them too!*

The creek scrambles down the north face of *Bullhead Mountain* from about 4,765' at a high rate of speed for about 1.9 miles at a bone crushing 17.9% gradient before converging with Carter at about 3,030'. This convergence point is about 1.5 miles above Carter Creek's mouth. Along the stretch I fished, its flow was joined by several very small feeders that are not at all fishable in my opinion.

Curtis Creek

At a Glance

Sam's Rank: 👍👍👍👍
GPS Fixes:
- Source fix: N35 43.879 W82 11.708 @ 3,990'
- Mouth fix: N35 38.157 W82 09.438 @ 1,350'

Size: small at mouth
Gradient: mild 5.7% source to mouth average *(8.8 miles / 2,640')*
Effort: moderate to difficult
Pressure: slight to moderate
Fishing Quality: good
Species: Rainbows, Browns & Brookies
Access: From the mouth: Take exit 73 off of I-40 to Old Fort. Go about ½ miles on Catawba Avenue and turn right onto Hwy 70. Go about 2 miles and turn left at the Curtis Creek sign *(Hwy 1227 – Curtis Creek Road).* This road parallels the creek most of the way to the Parkway. After 2.6 miles the pavement ends and at 3.7 miles the road changes to FSR 482. Roadside parking is available everywhere.

From the source: At Big Laurel Gap *(about MP 347.5)* on the Parkway, turn south onto FSR 482 and follow it about 3.1 miles to the creek. From there it tracks the creek all the way to its mouth. It will eventually change to Hwy 1227 before reaching Hwy 70. If you continue across Hwy 70, the road changes to Hwy 1246 and in about .5 miles turn left and parallel I-40. Curtis Creek's mouth on the Catawba River is about .3 miles on the other side of I-40.

Overview & Description

Curtis Creek holds a significant place in history. The creek and the 8,100 acres surrounding it have the distinction of being the very first National Forest land purchased east of the Mississippi. This first *"eastern"* tract was purchased for the National Forrest Service from the Marion, NC based *Burke McDowell Lumber Company* under the authority of the newly passed *Weeks Act of 1911.* This tract is now a part of the *Grandfather Ranger District* of *Pisgah National Forest.*

Named after the U. S. Representative from Massachusetts, John Weeks, the Act authorized for the first time, the purchase of private property for inclusion into the National Forest System. The primary reason was to restore and protect watersheds of navigable streams and improve fire protection and fire fighting in the eastern U.S. For years national forests' land in the West had been set aside from land already publicly owned. But no such lands had been set aside in the Eastern U.S. because most all lands were privately held – in other words they had to be purchased. The Weeks Act became law on March 1, 1911 and for the first time, allowed National Forests to be established in the eastern U.S. through the purchase of private land. Curtis Creek was the first of those purchases.

Entrance sign commemorating the first tract of land purchased for Pisgah National Forest by the National Forest using the Weeks Act of 1911. / *Image by Author / 2018*

Aside from flowing through some historically significant forests, Curtis could easily stand on the merit of just being a fine trout stream. Managed under *Delayed Harvest* and *Wild Trout Water* regulations, it sports a wide variety of high-elevation blue-line waters, as well as miles of bigger and flatter lower elevation water – all with healthy populations of all three trout. As if that's not enough, it has great access from Hwy 70 and I-40 at its mouth and from the Parkway to its source. It even has a campground where you'll find yourself surrounded by some old growth forests at the site of an old Civilian Conservation Corp *(CCC)* camp – with interpretative markers. It's a great place to spend a day chasing trout in whatever type of water you like, or just catching up on local history.

Curtis squirts out of the side of the mountain at about 3,990' just south of *Big Laurel Gap* on the Parkway. From its source, it begins an 8.8 mile run from between *Laurel Knob* and *Buckeye Knob* through the *Pisgah Game Lands* at a mild 5.7% average gradient. During that run, it gathers more water from several feeders with names like *Big Camp Rock Branch, Bear Drive Branch, Slick Rock Branch* and *Newberry Creek* – Newberry and Big Camp Rock being the largest and most fishable. As Curtis approaches its mouth, it leaves Pisgah National Forest and slides under Hwy 70 and I-40 before joining the Catawba River at 1,350'. The river is about 30' wide and 3' - 5' deep at its mouth.

Fishing Curtis' first 4.7 miles upstream from its mouth can be tricky because of the intermittent private / public land through which it flows. The first 1.3 miles are outside the NFS boundary and on private land. About .6 miles up Hwy 1227 from Hwy 70, you will see a NFS boundary sign - this is also the start of the Delayed

Harvest section. Public water runs for 1.7 miles up to the parking area at tiny *Deep Branch* entering river left at about 2.3 miles above Hwy 70.

The *Delayed Harvest* stretch is super easy to fish - and it gets pounded by visitors and locals alike looking for their share of the 8,250 trout that get dumped in each year. I've heard from many people, including state and federal authorities, that this section is heavily poached by locals. That makes sense given the easy access and number of empty corn cans and worm buckets littering the bank. Be sure to pay attention to the signage and get permission if you fish or park on the private stretches. I've heard some land owners can be aggressive with outsiders.

Most of the next 1.7 miles above the end of DH section at *Deep Branch* is also a private carve-out that is posted up to about 4 miles above Hwy 70. Of this last 1.7 miles of private water, only a .2 mile section starting just above *Tantrough Branch* is open to the public. Right in the middle of that last private section, *Newberry Creek*, the river's best fishing tributary, enters river left. There is no more private land above those 1.7 miles. In other words, the rest of the river is open for business!

A Brown caught just above the campground. / *Image by Author / 2014*

The entire first 4.7 miles of the creek averages 15'- 25' wide and a couple of feet deep in most places. Its flat gradient makes for easy wading, and the large trees offer a high and wide canopy that make casting open and easy. Large rocks litter the river bed and a wide variety of run and riffle patterns, laced with long and deep pools, long and shallow flats and rock-faced banks provide plenty of cover for trout. I fish extra hard under the bridges and culverts all along Curtis Creek – most hold nice fish.

Starting at about 4 miles above Hwy 70 all the way to the headwaters, the river is managed as *Wild Trout Water*. At about 4.9 miles up is Curtis Creek Campground. It has adequate amenities with lots of CCC history stuff and serves as a good base camp while fishing this part of the Parkway. Two tributaries, *Hickory Branch* and *Long Branch*, flow into the campground river right within feet of each other – a rare site. Both have nice little waterfalls and have pocket waters that actually hold rainbows in the 4" – 6" range.

Along this campground stretch, the river starts getting a bit smaller and tighter – about 7' – 9' wide on average, although it's still plenty deep and open enough to fish well. However, fishing this stretch can be challenging in warm weather due to the bikers, hikers, bathers, rock hoppers and the kill & grill, worm-dunker crowd.

The upper 3.2 miles above the campground to the source is my favorite place to fish. The fish are wild, and the river trims down to about 5' – 7' across and takes on the character of a true Appalachian mountain stream with all the usual flow features that attract and hold wild and feisty trout. On the way up, several tributaries enter river left. The largest of these are *Big Camp Rock Branch, Licklog Branch* and *Bear Drive Branch.* All three are steep, difficult and marginally fishable for small bows and an occasional spec. Of the three, *Big Camp Rock Branch* is the one I recommend fishing if you have a mind to. This stretch of Curtis is a progression of plunge / drop pools and runs, with many stretches having a tight / low canopy. When you get to *Bear Drive Branch*, Curtis is only 3' – 4' across.

I've never fished any of the last 1.6 miles of Curtis above where the road crosses *Bear Drive Branch* – still quite a way up to the source. This headwater flow is even smaller, steeper, tighter and more remote and looks only marginally fishable if at all. You'll be climbing and bushwhacking as much as fishing.

Curtis Creek Tributaries

Newberry Creek
A Tributary of Curtis Creek

At a Glance

Sam's Rank: 👍👍👍
GPS Fixes:
- Source fix: N35 41.485 W82 13.616 @ 2,485'
- Mouth fix: N35 40.520 W82 11.866 @ 1,675'

Size: small at mouth
Gradient: steep 14.3% source to mouth average *(2.4 miles / 1,810')*
Effort: moderate to difficult
Pressure: none to slight
Fishing Quality: average to good
Species: Bows & Brookies
Access: From Hwy 70, drive up Hwy 1227 for 3.6 miles to Newberry Creek Road #1463 on the left – an old grist mill is located there. This road or trail tracks up the creek about 3.5 miles to its source. It then tracks up to a headwater stream entering from the left - *Chute Creek.* There is a gate about 1.3 miles up from the start that may or may not be open. Above the gate, the road changes to FSR 482A. The first 1.1 miles up the creek is private with numerous dwellings close to the

road and creek. Do not park in the 1.1 mile private section. Go above it and park near the gate on public lands. Curtis' headwaters can also be accessed from the Parkway via Trail #210. Its trailhead is near MP 352.

Overview & Description

As of this writing Newberry Creek is the only stream managed as *Catch & Release / Artificial Lure Only* in McDowell County, NC that I know of. It is highly prized for having a really healthy population of brook trout. As Curtis Creek's largest and most productive tributary, it is also very accessible for the angler who hankers to fish for Southern Appalachian Brook Trout without the bushwhacking and rock climbing required of most brookie waters. But keep in mind, these are brookies, and as usual, to get the most out of this stream, you'll need to use your Neanderthal predator instincts to sneak up on them. Some of my buddies do well at that. If the fish see you or your shadow, they'll be gone. Stealth is critical.

Newberry springs to life on the south slope of *Deep Gap* on the Parkway along both sides of *Big Fork Ridge*. Two tiny headwater streams, *Chute Branch* and *Left Prong*, descend on opposite sides of that ridge for about 1.5 miles each at moderate gradients – each picking up additional volume from at least one additional feeder before they converge at about 2,485' to form Newberry's source.

From its source at 2,485', Newberry starts a 2.4 mile downhill run at a steep gradient of 14.3%. Along the way to its mouth, it picks up additional volume from several small feeders. At about .8 miles above Newberry's mouth, *Horse Branch* is the largest and most fishable. Newberry's

Small dam on Newberry Creek once used to power the mill standing just downstream near its mouth. / *Image by Author / 2011*

mouth is at 1,675' just beside an old grist mill at the intersection of Hwy 1227 and Newberry Creek Road.

From the grist mill at its mouth and moving upstream, the first 1.1 miles of water up to just below the gate on Newberry Creek Road is private. A hundred yards up from the mill, there is a silted-in dam with piping that provided water to the mill. This stretch is really nice; open water at about 10' – 15' across with lots of natural structure to hold fish. It is definitely fishable, but don't without the permission from the owners. At about .8 miles up, still in the private section, *Horse Branch* enters creek right. It's very small and its pocket water is also fishable, but you'll need to hike upstream about 150 yards to get into National Forest land. Keep in mind you'll be hiking 150 yards through private land to get there.

The next 1.3 miles, from just below the gate, up to the source is public water. Along that stretch the creek is about 8' – 10' across and a foot or so deep in most places. The creek bed is littered with large boulders and frequent runs, riffles, drop pools and dead falls that all hold trout. Surprisingly, the banks are low and wide in most places with an open canopy that makes casting easy. *And*, the 8.1% gradient along there keeps wading relatively easy as well. Along this stretch I have consistently caught brook trout in the 6" – 10" range - some even bigger.

At about 2.3 miles above Newberry's mouth, two *"blue line"* headwater streams, *Chute Branch* and *Left Prong*, enter the main flow. Both have small brookies in the 4" – 6" range. Fishing is very tight and hard fought the ¼ mile of each I have fished. Although FSR 482A is helpful when fishing the main flow, neither *Chute Branch* nor *Left Prong* have improved trails – it's all bushwhacking.

Big Camp Rock Branch
A Tributary of Curtis Creek

At a Glance

Sam's Rank: 👍👍 👍
GPS Fixes:
 - Source fix: N35 42.950 W82 12.855 @ 3,700'
 - Mouth fix: N35 42.033 W82 11.766 @ 2,150'

Size: very small at mouth
Gradient: moderate 18.3% source to mouth average *(1.6 miles / 1,550')*
Effort: difficult to extreme
Pressure: none
Fishing Quality: average
Species: Bows & Brookies
Access: From Hwy 70, drive up Hwy 1227 for 5.6 miles up to where Big Camp comes under the road. Its mouth is off to the right on Curtis Creek. Park anywhere along the road you can. As far as I've seen, there's no improved trail system.

Overview & Description

Of all the four or five sizeable tributaries at and above the campground, this one is the longest, largest and seems to have a more consistent flow than the others. *And*, I've caught more fish on it than any of the others. It has a really nice population of small brook trout too. Its biggest drawback is that it's a witch to fish – no improved trail, small, overgrown, and steep as heck. Other than that – it's a blast to fish.

Big Camp Rock Branch starts on the south slope of *Green Knob* on the Parkway at about 3,700'. From there it starts a straight 1.6 mile rocket sled downhill plunge to its source at a blistering average gradient of 18.3%. Along that run, it doesn't pick up volume from any other sizable feeders – rare for mountain streams of any sort. Big Camp's mouth is at 2,150' just off the right side of Hwy 1227.

There's not a bunch of public data about Big Camp – only the occasional blog. So what I write below is based purely on my experience of fishing the lower .5 miles a couple of times over the years.

Tiny Big Camp Rock Branch falling from high up on the mountain. Image taken from bridge. / *Image by Author / 2000*

From its mouth and moving upstream for .5 miles, the creek is about 3' – 6' across and a foot deep. The bed is choked with moss covered boulders and dead falls, with the ever-present quick runs and drop pool features that always hold trout – and they're definitely there! As you'd expect on a flow this high, it's small, very steep and the banks are narrow. In most places, the flora crowds the banks, and the canopy is relatively low. You'll be climbing more than wading and high sticking more than casting. Sound like fun?

I've caught mostly brook trout and a few bows – all in the 4" – 7" range. The fishing is very tight and hard fought, but the experience is always worth it. The couple of times I've fished it, I stopped at the campground for a few hours and poached beers off campers and other anglers and rested a spell. Big Camp is classic *"blue line"* water for sure. I can only imagine what the flow is like above the .5 miles I fished. If you fish it, give me a report of what you saw and caught.

South Toe River

At a Glance

Sam's Rank: 👍👍👍👍👍

GPS Fixes: The mouth fix below is not the official *mouth fix* of the South Toe – that's another 26.5 miles downstream between Spruce Pine and Burnsville where it converges with the North Toe. The fix below is the northern most point on the public section I'm including. This fix is before it enters a confusing patchwork of private / public lands – including the Mount Mitchell Golf Club just below this fix. The *source fix* I'm using is what most folks consider the South Toe's actual source:

- Source fix: N35 43.350 W82 14.835 @ 3,470'
- Mouth fix: N35 45.720 W82 12.411 @ 2,890'

Size: medium at mouth

Gradient: flat 2.6% source to mouth average *(4.3 miles / 580')*

Effort: easy to moderate

Pressure: slight to moderate

Fishing Quality: good

Species: Rainbows, Browns & Brookies

Access: *From the mouth:* At about MP 347.5 on the Parkway, take FSR 2074 north for about 2.2 miles down to FSR 472. Turn right and go about 1.3 miles to the South Toe's mouth. Roadside parking is available everywhere.

From the source: At about MP 351 *(Deep Gap)* on the Parkway, turn north onto FSR 472. About .5 miles down the road will parallel Left Prong. Continue about 1.8 miles to the bridge at Right Prong. South Toe's source is about .2 miles downstream where Right Prong and Left Prong converge. Park at the bridge.

Overview & Description

The South Toe flows through some of the most beautiful areas of the *Appalachian Ranger District* of *Pisgah National Forest*. That's the scenic description. But consider too that it sources up on the southeastern slope of *Mt. Mitchell* – at 6,684 feet above sea level, it's the tallest mountain in the eastern half of the U.S. and also designated a *Registered Natural Landmark*. This makes for some of the coldest and cleanest water in the southeast. Add in the fact that the South Toe routinely rewards anglers with multiple bows, browns and specs in the 6" – 12" range, with some much bigger. And if that's not enough, it has great road and trail access directly from the Parkway and offers abundant primitive and improved camping up and down its main flow. With all those positives, no wonder it's on so many fly anglers' *"must fish"* list.

I've heard all kinds of yarns about how the Toe River got its name. One local told me of an early settler named *Jonathan Nail* who lived on the river. One day he was splitting logs and the ax slipped and cut his toe off – after which his dog grabbed it, ran off and purportedly ate it. From that day on, he became known as

"*Toe*" Nail by his neighbors and the local Indians. After some time, he'd apparently had enough of the name shaming and went crazy and jumped off a cliff on the back side of Mt. Mitchell. Apparently people took their names danged seriously back then.

There are several other explanations just as believable. The one that's gotten the most traction over the years insists that "*Toe*" was most likely taken from the river's original name "*Estatoe*" – pronounced "*S-ta-toe.*" This was an

Official elevation medallion at exact summit point of Mount Mitchell. / *Image by Author / 2018*

Indian name associated with the Estatoe trade route leading from the North Carolina highlands down through Brevard and into South Carolina where a village of the same name was located. In fact, there is a plaque in Brevard with a description of the actual route, and it seems to corroborate this version of the Toe's name origination. White men shortened the name over the years to just "*Toe*" for easier pronunciation. I like the Toe Nail story better – it makes for more interesting campfire fodder. Who knows - perhaps each story has some of the real truth.

The South Toe is part of the larger Toe River system. About 31 miles downstream from the South Toe's source, it is joined by the *North Toe* which sources up near Newland. The combination of these two forms the Toe River *(Proper's)* main flow. This main flow lasts for only a short distance before converging with the *Nolichucky River*, which eventually flows into the *Tennessee River*. On up the *Nolichucky* is where Davy Crockett was born. As a heads up: nearly all of the flows in the South Toe watershed show the effects of past hurricanes and floods. Wide-graveled banks, boulders and cobbles line the sides along with runs of solid bedrock in some places. It affected the fishing initially. But generally, the river has returned to its previous beauty and fishing quality.

The South Toe's source is the result of two almost identical headwater streams crashing down the southeastern slope of Mount Mitchell. *Left Prong* and *Right Prong* both start at more than a mile above sea level – *Right Prong* as a seep from a few hundred feet south of the *Mt. Mitchell* access road and *Left Prong* as an actual flowing spring from *Pinnacle Springs* at about 5,300' just a few hundred yards south of the Parkway. Its clear water can be seen flowing along the Parkway shoulder at about MP 354.4. As *Left Prong* and *Right Prong* descend at very steep gradients, they pick up just enough flow to become small streams by the time they

South Toe just north of its source point above Mount Mitchell Golf Club. Notice the bank repair on the right side from flooding several years ago. Fishing is good along there. / *Image by Author / 2018*

converge at about 3,470'. That convergence point is the South Toe's source just below the bridge where FSR 472 crosses the Right Prong.

The South Toe's main flow *(source)* comes to life at 3,470' and starts a 4.3 mile slow run to its mouth at the *Pisgah National Forest Boundary* along FSR 472 above *Dicks Gap*. At its source, its water is pristine clear and cold. In the first mile or so, it flows from between *Chestnut Knob* and *Lost Cove Ridge*. Along its 4.3 mile run it collects additional water volume from tributaries with names like *Upper Creek, Lower Creek, Camp Creek, Setrock Creek, Big Lost Cove Creek*, and several other lesser flows. In my opinion, the two most fun to fish, are *Upper Creek* and *Lower Creek*. From its source to its mouth fix at about 2,890', the South Toe averages a very low 2.6% gradient. Below the mouth, the river enters the private lands of the *Mount Mitchell Golf Club* and then continues north.

Starting at its mouth just above the Golf Club, the first 1.7 miles up to *Black Mountain Campground*, the river is about 25' – 30' wide and has the look and feel of a cold and clear mountain river. An interesting area just above its mouth is the stretch along FSR 472 that had to be completely reengineered *(image above)* after several floods of the last decade. It now has a 20' high-stacked boulder wall along its left side. This is a particularly great run to fish – especially in dry months when the trout hold up in the boundary water against the boulders. At about one mile up, *Big Lost Cove Creek* enters river left – a very fishable tributary. All the way up to *Black Mountain Campground*, the river has mostly wide and open-cobbled banks, deeper runs and riffles, dead falls with wide-open canopies. This makes wading and casting easy. Two tributaries enter river right around the campground – *Little Mountain Creek* and *Setrock Creek*. Both are very small and marginally fishable.

At the campground, a bridge crosses the river. This area becomes crowded in the warmer months, and I usually quit fishing about 50 yards downstream from the bridge and start back about 25 yards above it. One thing I do like about the South Toe is the numerous first-come first-serve camping sites along FSR 472, as well as the Black Mountain Campground with all its amenities. It's a great place to go if you're looking to set up a base camp in close proximity to other Parkway fishing locations. This stretch of the river is managed under *Wild Trout Waters* regulations, and most of what I have caught up to the campgrounds have been bows and browns in the 8" to 12" range, with many exceeding 14".

The next 1.7 miles of river above Black Mountain Campground is still flat, but as you go further up it starts getting a bit steeper and more narrow – about 15' to 20'. The canopy will begin to close in on you as well up there. *Camp Creek* enters river right about .8 miles above the campground. It is also relatively small and only marginally fishable. About 1.4 miles above the campground, *Lower Creek* enters river right. It is definitely fishable and worth the effort – perhaps my favorite. At about 1.7 miles up, *Upper Creek* enters river right. This tributary is relatively large as headwater streams go and has an extensive feeder network. It is by far the largest and most fishable of all the other flows above the campground.

As you continue upstream, the river changes and takes on a more fishy nature with ledges, boulders, slides and drop pools. Trout congregate in all these pocket waters in dry seasons. I find the fishing in this stretch to be quite good and have regularly scored days with 10 to 15 bows and browns in the 8" – 12" range. This stretch of the river is also managed under *Wild Trout Waters* regulations. The river in this upper stretch above the campground starts to get very steep and is far below the road.

The Toe above the Campground. / *Image by Author / 2018*

So getting on and off the river can become problematic without planning.

The last mile above *Upper Creek* to the South Toe's source, the river turns into a typical blue-line mountain flow – about 5' to 8' and is choked with the usual line up of trees, dead falls and bushes. The customary high-elevation stream features create pocket water that can be technical, but productive if effective blue-line fishing techniques are used. The stream falls at a steep rate and consists mostly of short plunges and runs into small pools. I have caught a mix of wild rainbows, browns and some wash down brook trout – most in the 5" to 8" range. This upper last mile is rugged and difficult to access in many places because of the extreme water / road elevations. So plan carefully how you will get on and off the river.

All of the South Toe's headwaters above *Upper Creek*, including *Upper Creek* and its tributaries, are managed as *Wild Trout Water – Catch and Release / Artificial Flies Only* regulations. Everything below Upper Creek is managed under *Wild Trout Water* regulations. Most of the South Toe's wild trout water is not heavily fished because the leisure crowds typically stay in the easier to get to stocked waters of the lower sections. Consequently, many days you will have all the wild trout water to yourself.

South Toe Tributaries

Right Prong & Left Prong
The South Toe's Two Headwaters

At a Glance

Sam's Rank: 👍👍👍 *(Not so much from the fishing, but rather the exotic nature of the experience)*

GPS Fixes:
- Mouth fix for both: N35 43.350 W82 14.835 @ 3,470'
- Right Prong's source fix: N35 43.671 W82 16.991 @ 5,330'
- Left Prong's source fix: N35 42.307 W82 16.337 @ 5,300'

Size: both are small at their mouths

Gradient:
- Right Prong: steep 15.3% source to mouth average *(2.3 miles / 1,860')*
- Left Prong: steep 15% source to mouth average *(2.3 miles / 1,820')*

Effort: both – difficult to extreme

Pressure: both – none

Fishing Quality: both – average

Species: Bows & Specs

Access: *From the mouth of both Prongs:* At about MP 351.8 *(Deep Gap)* on the Parkway, turn north onto FSR 472 *(Big Laurel Gap)* and follow it about 1.8 miles down to the bridge at *Right Prong. Right* and *Left Prong's* converge *(mouth)* about .2 miles downstream. About .9 miles down from the Parkway, FSR 472 will cross the headwaters of *Left Prong* and its feeder *Hemphill Creek*. It then parallels *Left Prong* all the way to the bridge above the mouth. Parking is around the bridge.

From Left Prong's source: At about MP 354.4, *Left Prong* flows from its source at *Pinnacle Springs (a few hundred feet on the south side of the Parkway)* down onto the Parkway on its way to the bridges on FSR 472. Its feeder *Hemphill Creek*, bubbles out of the ground at *Hemphill Springs* about 250 feet south of the Parkway, then crosses the Parkway about MP 353.5. Roadside parking is easy.

From Right Prong's source: About .6 miles up the Mt. Mitchell approach road, Trail # 191 leads off to the right. About 500' down the trail is the source fix. But that's the source – you'll find no trout there. I know of no other *practical way* to get to and fish the Right Prong's headwaters. Parking is available on the roadside.

Overview & Description

As with other rivers in this Guide, source waters often result from the combination of several headwater flows. In South Toe's case, it's the *Right Prong* and *Left Prong*. Both begin their flows well above a mile above sea level and each is very remote, steep, rugged and beautiful. Neither has improved trails that follow them for any distance. Other than their names, they're darn near identical in length, gradient, structure, size, difficulty level, trout species, and access. These high elevation headwaters are fun to fish if you're into remote and exotic places. Just the fact they run down the east slope of Mount Mitchell makes them special.

Left Prong bubbles out of *Pinnacle Springs* just south of the Parkway at about 5,300' on the east side of the geological feature named "*Pinnacle.*" From there it flows down to the Parkway and begins a 2.3 mile run to its mouth at a steep 15% gradient. There it converges with *Right Prong* at about 3,470'. About 1.5 miles below its source, it is joined below the bridge on FSR 472 by its only sizeable feeder *Hemphill Creek*, which is also spring fed from up on the Parkway. Left Prong's twin *Right Prong* comes off the east slope of *Potato Knob* on the south slope of Mount Mitchell from about 5,330'. From there it runs for about 2.3 miles at the same blistering 15.3% gradient to its convergence point with *Left Prong* at 3,470'. Along the way, it doesn't gain additional volume from any sizeable feeders. The convergence of these two prongs forms the South Toe's source.

I fished up *Right Prong* about .5 miles and up *Left Prong* about the same distance several times. All I caught were brookies and rainbows in the 4" to 6" range - par for these high-elevation streams. Occasionally, I lucked up on a 12" trout in a larger than average pool. Once, I really wanted some punishment and fished up *Hemphill Creek* above FSR 472 for about 500 feet. There I caught brookies in the 3" – 5" range, as well as a bunch of scratches and bruises. Each stream resembles a *"drop pool ladder"* up the mountain side. Both are small and tight, and you'll do a lot of climbing and bushwhacking to the very small runs and pools. They're barely large enough to get a fly into, but a trout will be waiting. The experience is worth the effort.

Upper Creek
A South Toe Tributary

At a Glance

Sam's Rank: 👍👍👍👍
GPS Fixes:

- Source fix: N35 43.941 W82 15.026 @ 3,510'
- Mouth fix: N35 43.838 W82 14.306 @ 3,230'

Size: small at mouth
Gradient: mild 6.6% source to mouth average *(.8 miles / 280')*
Effort: moderate to difficult
Pressure: none to slight
Fishing Quality: good
Species: Bows & Brookies
Access: At about MP 351.8 *(Deep Gap)* on the Parkway, turn north onto FSR 472 and follow it about 2.8 miles down to the bridge crossing *Upper Creek.* Its mouth is about 200' downstream. FSR 472 crosses several headwater streams along the way. Upstream access is via an unmarked timber tote road / trail that leads about halfway up the main flow. Parking is around the bridge.

Overview & Description

Upper Creek looks to be the largest tributary in the South Toe's upper headwaters. It starts the *Catch & Release - Artificial Lures/Flies Only* managed waters that include this creek and extend upstream to all the other headwaters. This is a first-rate trout stream with relatively easy access and a healthy population of wild trout that don't see many humans. As most creeks go, it's rather short at only .8 miles. Its main flow has a mild gradient with an assortment of drop pool and runs. And it's wider than you might expect – making it easy to wade and cast. A trail / timber tote road offers access up the main flow. But when the trail ends, you'll need to use the streambed to get around. Past its source fix at .8 miles, two headwater tributaries offer additional high-elevation fishing. In most places, there's barely room to cast, but they do hold trout!

Two small headwater streams, *South Fork-Upper Creek* and *Grassy Knob Branch*, are the feeders that make up Upper Creek's headwaters. *South Fork - Upper Creek* sources up over a mile above sea level and descends at a scalding 18.6% gradient for about 1.9 miles to its mouth. Along the way, it gathers more volume from *Middle Fork*, which is another small but fishable feeder that enters about .5 miles above its mouth at 3,510'. Both of these flows are very small and tight and will give you a workout. Bushwhacking and / or the stream bed are the only access up the endless maze of drop pools and boulders you must traverse. I caught mostly brookies in the 4" – 6" range, with an occasional 8" overachiever.

The other headwater, *Grassy Knob Branch*, sources up just under a mile above sea level. From there it screams downhill for about 1.2 miles to its convergence with *South-Fork Upper Creek*. Believe it or not, its average gradient is a bone crushing 25.2%, *the highest of any flow in this Guide – I think!* It does not receive any additional flow along the way. Aside from being vertical, this creek is small and very tight – *a real challenge to fish!* Because of the gradient, bushwhacking is out. Consequently, the stream bed is the best access up the drop pool staircase you'll be climbing. Pocket waters are the best opportunities, and brooks are what I encountered most as I fought my way up it.

As far as *Upper Creek's* main flow goes, from its source at 3,510', it begins its abbreviated .8 mile run to its mouth at an average mild gradient of 6.6%. Along the

The Author on Upper Creek. / Selfie *Author / 2018*

way to its mouth, it doesn't pick up additional volume from any sizeable feeders. Upper Creek reaches its mouth on the South Toe at about 3,230' - about 200 feet below FSR 472.

From its mouth and moving upstream to its source, most of the main flow's .8 miles is what I'd consider first-rate blue-line trout water. The stream bed is about 7' – 10' wide in many places and the forest is open enough for reasonable casting. There are lots of boulders and shelves, along with frequent runs, riffles, drop pools and dead falls that all hold trout. Along this main flow, I have caught mostly brook trout in the 6" – 8" range, as well as a goodly number of bows about the same size. This creek fishes well; has great access, and is a must fish destination.

Lower Creek
A South Toe Tributary

At a Glance

Sam's Rank: 👍👍👍👍
GPS Fixes:
- Source fix: N35 45.611 W82 16.004 @ 5,995'
- Mouth fix: N35 44.013 W82 14.075 @ 3,185'

Size: small at mouth
Gradient: extreme 18.3% source to mouth average *(2.9 miles / 2,810')*
Effort: difficult to extreme
Pressure: none
Fishing Quality: good
Species: Bows & Brookies
Access: At about MP 351.8 *(Deep Gap)* on the Parkway, turn north onto FSR 472 and follow it about 3.1 miles down to where it crosses *Lower Creek*. Its mouth is about 200' downstream. FSR 472 crosses several headwater streams along the

way. Upstream access is via an unmarked trail / timber tote road that leads about .7 miles up the creek. There is no trail beyond that. Parking is at the bridge.

Overview & Description

Lower Creek's source is on the southeastern slope of Mt. Mitchell just below its summit at a location above a spot named *Camp Alice*. That spot was a bustling logging camp back in the early part of the last century, and the center of activity on the mountain. The camp's cook was named Alice – so for some reason they named it Camp Alice. "*Alice's Restaurant*" was where everyone ate. Next, it was a song by Arlo Guthrie and then a Hollywood movie. Not really the same place at all…

A logging railroad passed through Camp Alice over what is now the approach road. Later, after logging operations ceased, the rails were ripped up, and the rail bed became a road to carry paying tourists to just below the summit of Mt. Mitchell. The tourists would park at Camp Alice and hike to the

One of many small, but feisty Brookies caught on the upper stretches of Lower Creek. / *Image by Author / 2016*

summit. Some of the logging buildings were converted to restaurants, motor lodges, souvenir shops, etc. Today, it's supposedly just the site of the water operations for the Welcome Center up top. However, satellite imagery shows several suspicious buildings at the site. Who knows? It might be another secret "*black site*" where the government has the Area 51 Martians on ice, or where some other "*dark*" operations take place. Regardless, it's worth a visit, and Lower Creek's headwaters become legally fishable just below there at the Park boundary.

At about 6,000', Lower Creek has the distinction of sourcing higher up on Mt. Mitchell than any flow on the entire mountain – or any other mountain east of the Mississippi as far as I can tell. And I don't expect that to change anytime soon. The source fix is about 600' below the summit of Mt. Mitchell. This creek's flow profile resembles the track of a rocket sled down the side of a mountain – high, steep, narrow, straight, long – and fast. Although fishing is *NOT* permitted in Mt. Mitchell State Park, the section of the stream below the Park boundary can be fished and is managed as *Wild Trout Waters*. This little South Toe tributary has a healthy population of small wild rainbows and brooks. I love fishing it!

Three or four times over the years I've fished the lower one mile of this creek. So that's all I can accurately describe. Each time I was determined to fish up to the Park boundary, but the difficulty of doing so broke my will. In the lower first mile, bows and brookies in the 3" – 5" range were what I caught each time. They were beautifully colored and very healthy and fun little critters to catch. As you move up the mountain, you'll break out of the forest into what resembles a bald at about .7 miles below Camp Alice. As *Commissary Shelter Trail* crosses the creek at about 5,640' *(about .4 miles below the source)* you'll cross the *Park boundary* - no fishing is allowed beyond that point. Along that *"no fishing"* stretch you'll spot 2" – 5" brookies in the tiny pocket waters of this very high headwater stream.

The creek is essentially 2.9 miles of very steep, tight and small water, with the typical high gradient plunges and runs that create the pocket waters where the trout congregate. In the lower stretches, it can become so tight that there's barely room to cast. There's an old road / trail that offers access up the lower .7 miles of water. But after that, streambed is all you'll have. Lower Creek is certainly worth fishing if for no other reason than just to say you did it. But it ain't easy!

From its source at Camp Alice, Lower Creek begins that 2.9 mile rocket sled run down the side of the mountain at a steep 18.3% gradient. Along the run, it picks up a little more water about halfway down from only one tiny feeder – which doesn't appear fishable. It reaches its mouth

Lower Creek one mile up on the high country and thin air. / *Image by Author / 2018*

on the South Toe at about 3,185, about 200' below the bridge on FSR 472.

From the mouth moving upstream, you will find Lower Creek to be the perfect definition of a *"blue line"* headwater stream. It's small and difficult fishing for small trout, and it will continue to get smaller as it gets above the lower 1.1 miles. I have fished this first 1.1 miles, and I concentrated on the pocket waters – which are about all you can fish. The fishing is very tight, hard fought and technical. Every move must be calculated. You'll find the trail / tote road helpful for access to the first mile of pocket water. Without it, I wouldn't have gotten very far.

Big Lost Cove Creek
A South Toe Tributary

At a Glance

Sam's Rank: N/A
GPS Fixes:
- Source fix: N35 43.810 W82 13.496 @ 3,755'
- Mouth fix: N35 45.041 W82 12.835 @ 2,975'

Size: small at mouth
Gradient: moderate 8.7% source to mouth average *(1.7 miles / 780')*
Effort: N/A
Pressure: N/A
Fishing Quality: N/A
Species: Bows & Browns
Access: At about MP 347.6 *(Big Laurel Gap)* on the Parkway, take FSR 2074 north and go about 2.1 miles to where the road crosses *Big Lost Cove Creek*. This point is about .4 miles above the mouth and about 500 feet before you dead-end into FSR 472. Given the fact there is private land between the mouth and this point, this is a good place to start. Park and fish up from here or just past where you cross the creek. An old road / trail on the left tracks the creek's main flow upstream. Roadside parking is available at the bridge.

Overview & Description

In spite of its name, Big Lost Cove Creek is not big at all – in fact it's quite small! I haven't fished it, but I have some almost reliable buddies that claim they have, and a couple of them highly recommend it. It may not be the sexiest trout stream in the world, but it is convenient to the Parkway, has good source to mouth access, and does have hungry trout. So I'll provide you with the following basic information. Then, you can make up your mind as to whether or not to fish it.

Big Lost Cove Creek sources up at about 3,755' on the north slope of *Green Knob* north of the Parkway. From there it starts a 1.7 mile run along *Lost Cove Ridge (probably the creek's namesake)* to its mouth on the South Fork at an average moderate gradient of 8.7%. On its way down, it adds water from only two sizeable feeders – a *"no name"* flow, and its largest, *Neals Creek*. The mouth is at 2,975' on the South Toe.

Moving upstream from its mouth, the creek enters private land in about 350 feet and continues as private land to about .2 miles upstream. Above that, you're back on public land again. The first feeder, *Neals Creek*, enters river left at about .4 miles. *Neals Creek's* confluence with Big Lost Cove Creek is river left, just above where you cross on FSR 2074. It is small and has only a 1.1 mile flow down from its source at about 3,880'. It does have a couple of nice waterfalls with pools. These are always worth checking out.

On up at about .7 miles above the mouth, a second *"no-name"* feeder enters river left. It is also small with only a one mile flow down from its source at about 4,560'. It has good access via a road / trail that follows it to the source.

None of my buddies have fished either of the two feeders. But they did fish the main flow and claimed to have caught mostly rainbows and a few browns – all in the 4" – 7" range. If you believe them, Big Lost Cove Creek is probably worth a shot. It is managed under *Wild Trout Waters* regulations.

Rock Creek
A South Toe Tributary

At a Glance

Sam's Rank: N/A
GPS Fixes:
- Source fix: N35 46.047 W82 13.731 @ 3,355'
- Mouth fix: N35 46.877 W82 12.350 @ 2,815'

Size: small at mouth
Gradient: flat 4.1% source to mouth average *(2.5 miles / 540')*
Effort: N/A
Pressure: N/A
Fishing Quality: N/A
Species: Bows & Browns *(perhaps specs in the upper headwaters)*
Access: From the Parkway, take Hwy 80 north about 5.6 miles to Colbert's Creek Road / Hwy 1158 on the left. Turn and go about .7 miles to Hwy 1159. Turn left and go about one mile. Then cross Rock Creek and turn right onto FSR 5521. Beyond the gate, this small road / trail will track the creek for about .7 miles through what appears to be private land and then into the public land where you can fish. Along the first .5 miles or so of FSR 5521, the NFS / private boundary lines are very close to the creek. So use you own judgment and obey the signs. Parking is available up and down the road or at the end. A trail picks up at the end of the road and offers access upstream.

Overview & Description

This is another South Toe tributary I have not fished. But once again, my almost reliable buddies claim to have done so and twisted my arm to include it. It is actually below the *"Mouth Fix"* I chose for this section of the South Toe, but it is one of the largest South Toe headwaters in the area, so I decided to include it. As with *Big Lost Cove Creek*, it is also close to the Parkway, has reasonable up and down access and is known to have a healthy population of wild rainbows. That's all I know about it. You decide whether it's worth your time and effort.

Rock Creek's source waters, *Thee Creek* and *Middle Fork*, represent a maze of high-elevation flows pouring out of a big funnel formed by several mountains and ridges northeast of *Mount Mitchell*. With *Mount Mitchell's* northeast slope as the center of the funnel, the western and northern boundaries are formed by *Mount Craig, Balsam Cone* and *Maple Camp Bald*. Its southern and eastern boundary is formed by *Little Mountain* and *Open Ridge*. This funnel represents a large watershed with many miles of water that needs to be explored and fished!

From the top of the funnel, *Thee Creek* from about 5,890' and *Middle Fork* from about 5,615', flow roughly two miles at a blistering 23.5% average gradient to their convergence point at about 3,355' to form Rock Creek's source. *Thee Creek* receives no additional volume on the way down. But *Middle Fork* does gain more water from two feeders, *North Fork* and *Bill Autrey Branch*. *North Fork* is the larger of the two and is probably very fishable.

From that source point at 3,355', Rock Creek runs only 2.5 miles to its mouth on the South Fork at 2,815'. There on the South Fork, there's a swinging bridge and ford within sight just upstream from Rock Creek's mouth. *(I've driven across that ford many times in my Rover just for the fun of it)*. Along Rock Creek's 2.5 mile run to its mouth, the gradient is a flat 4.1%, which makes wading relatively easy according to my buddies who have fished it. It does pick up a few feeders along the way, but none appear to be particularly promising for our selfish purposes based on topos and satellite imagery. Of the 2.5 miles, only the first 1.2 miles below the source point is definitely on NFS lands. There appears to be a farm with several houses on the west side of the creek along that first .5 miles beside FSR 5521. In fact, the lower 1.3 miles to the mouth is in a patchwork of private / public land. So fish with caution and observe the signs.

Moving upstream from the mouth, Rock Creek's main flow and headwaters are managed as *Wild Trout Waters*. My buddies who fished the public stretch of the main flow up to the source, claimed they caught mostly bows and a few browns in the 6" – 8" range. None of them fished any of the headwaters. Personally, after studying satellite images and some reputable topo-quads, I arrived at the conclusion that the best fishing is probably about one mile above the source point where *Middle Fork* is joined by its feeders. Experience tells me that the combination of remote and extreme topography, as well as the observable water reflection returns in the satellite imagery, yields fishable water. *"There's trout in them there waters!"* And I'd bet you a Kosher hotdog they will most likely be brook trout. If you fish it before me, shoot me a fishing report.

Section III

63 miles

MP 343 *(just north of where Hwy 80 crosses the Parkway below Crabtree Falls)* to MP 280 *(just south of EB Jeffress Park)*

This section includes many of the "*High Country*" flows above and below Boone and Blowing Rock along the Parkway. With Grandfather Mountain anchoring the middle of this section, it offers some of the most varied, productive and storied fly fishing destinations along the Parkway. From easy, step out of the car into the water flows, to those heart pounding waters requiring climbing and bushwhacking, there's something for everyone.

www.wildbearings.com will have *lodging, campsite, outfitter, restaurant* and *brewery* recommendations to help plan your trip along this Section of the Parkway.

Linville River
At a Glance

Sam's Rank: 👍👍👍👍

GPS Fixes: The *mouth fix* below is the location at which the southern boundary of the Linville Gorge Wilderness Area crosses the river at the gorge's southern end. The river continues through private lands for another 2.1 miles to Lake James.
- Source fix: N35 07.391 W81 50.742 @ 4,065'
- Mouth fix: N35 48.691 W81 54.442 @ 1,320'

Size: large at mouth *(As it enters Lake James)*

Gradient: flat 2% source to mouth average *(35.4 miles / 2,745')*

Effort: upper section - easy to moderate / gorge section - difficult to extreme

Pressure: upper section - slight to moderate / gorge section - none to slight

Fishing Quality: upper section - poor to fair / gorge section - average to good

Species: Bows, Browns & some Specs

Access: I've divided the river into an *Upper Section* and *Gorge Section*. There are numerous access points, but the following are the ones I know best.

~ *Upper Section (top of the gorge to the source at Tynecastle):* To get to the source at the top of the Upper Section, from the red light in Linville, take Hwy 105 North for 4 miles to Tynecastle. Turn left at the light on Hwy 184 toward Banner Elk. Linville's source waters are along the first .4 miles on the left about 500' from the road. Parking is anywhere you can find it.

To get to the southernmost fix of the Upper Section, from Linville Falls take Hwy 221 North .6 miles until you reach the Parkway. Go north on the Parkway for about 1.2 miles until you cross the river at about MP 316.5. Take the first left onto Camp Creek Road and go about .7 miles – the river will be on your left. You are near the Parkway's Boundary at that point which serves as the bottom of *Upper Section*, and top of the *Gorge Section*.

~ *Gorge Section (from the mouth above Lake James to the Parkway's boundary just above Linville Falls):* To get to the top of the Gorge Section *(same directions as to the bottom of Upper Section)*. The start of this section is actually 3 miles above the gorge. From Linville Falls take Hwy 221 North .6 miles until you reach the Parkway. Go north on the Parkway for about 1.2 miles until you cross the river. Take the first left onto Camp Creek Road and go about .7 miles – the river will be on your left. You are near the Parkway's Boundary at that point which serves as the bottom of *Upper Section*, and top of the *Gorge Section*.

To get to the southernmost fix for the Gorge Section, from downtown Marion, take Hwy 50 East for about 5 miles to Hwy 126. Turn left and go about 9.7 miles, crossing Lake James, until you reach FSR 1239 on the left. Turn left and pick you way along the 1.7 miles up to the Linville Gorge Wilderness Area Boundary. The river will be along your right as you go in.

The trailhead for Trail # 231*(Linville Gorge Trail)* that tracks the river up through the gorge, is upstream. Park anywhere at the boundary you can find a space. The falls is about 14.5 miles upriver.

To get into the gorge at the falls as well as up and down the gorge, from Linville Falls, take Hwy 183 about .7 miles to FSR 1238 / Kistler Memorial Highway. Turn right and in about .1 mile on the left will be parking and the trailhead for Trail #248. This provides access to the falls which is about .4 miles down the trail.

NOTE: *(I'm only providing access points from the western side of the gorge – cause that's all I've used - there are eastern access points too – but I believe they are more difficult.)* For trail access up and down the river, from Hwy 183, take FSR 1238 / Kistler Memorial Highway south about .7 miles south to Trail # 231 trailhead *(Linville Gorge Trail)* on the left. The river will be about .4 miles down the trail. River access from where the trail meets the river back up to the falls is easy – about 1.3 miles.

Starting at Brushy Ridge just below the falls, Trail #231 tracks the river for 13.5 miles to the southern boundary of the Wilderness Area near Shortoff Mountain. It offers access up and down the river. FSR 1238 / Kistler Memorial Highway runs down the west rim of the gorge, and at least seven other trails originate from it and connect with Trail #231.

Overview & Descriptions

To be flowing through North Carolina's so called "*High Country*", literally in the shadow of *Grandfather Mountain*, the Linville River is not at all what you'd expect a mountain river to look, act and fish like. I often speak of rivers having personalities, and if you apply that thinking to the Linville River, you could only conclude that it is schizophrenic. It's only one river; but depending on the section, it looks, acts and fishes like two completely different rivers.

Its headwater / *Upper Section* is flat and slow as it flows through a patchwork of private / public lands with some stretches stocked with trout by the land owners or by the State. Easy access makes it popular with the power bait and canned corn crowd. At best, it is just marginal trout fishing, especially for wild trout. On the other hand, its lower / *Gorge Section* churns through the renowned *Linville Gorge Wilderness* – also known as the *Grand Canyon of North Carolina*. This remote stretch has everything you'd expect from a mountain river, including miles and miles of rugged and beautiful landscapes with torrents of big water, very little pressure, and lots of stream raised fish. Although the gorge is a difficult place to get into and fish, the experience is well worth the effort you will expend.

Given its split personality, I have divided the river into two sections. The fact that they are polar opposites makes this easy and sensible. The first 17.7 miles below its source to the Parkway boundary, I call the *Upper Section*. From that boundary south for the next 17.7 miles through the Parkway property and to the lower boundary of the *Linville Gorge Wilderness Area*, I simply refer to as the *Gorge Section.* It's purely coincidental each section is exactly 17.7 miles long.

As far as some river lore, prior to the colonization of North America by the Europeans, most of western NC was inhabited by the *Cherokee Indians* and a few lesser known tribes. The Cherokees called the river *"Ee-see-oh"* which means *"river of many cliffs"*. As it turned out that name didn't suit the early white settlers, so they re-named it the *"Linville River"* in honor of explorers *John* and *William Linville.* The name change

Linville River as it flows through the falls and begins its run through the gorge. Fishing the drop pool is usually good, and well worth the risk and effort to get there. / *Image by Author / 2017*

apparently made the *Shawnees,* one of the lesser tribes mad. So, one day in 1766 they caught the two *"Linville"* explorers in the gorge and scalped the top of their heads off. I would have thought the Cherokees would have been the ones doing the scalping! But this time anyway, it was the Shawnees. Regardless, with or without scalps, the Linville River was the name that stuck with the settlers and us today. A century or two later, descendants of those white settlers who lived upstream in the tiny town of *Linville* felt a bit guilty and named their Country Club *"Eseeola."* There's some threads of truth to all of that – I just don't know which part.

Aside from the interesting origin of its name, as well as the fact that it's one of the few NC *"rivers"* that actually flows underneath the Parkway, the Linville River would not be much of a trout fishery were it not for the *Gorge Section.* Of the two sections, it's the Gorge that offers some of the most remote, rugged, beautiful and productive fishing along the entire 469 miles of the Parkway. In my opinion, the *Upper Section* is worth fishing only if you can't get into the Gorge, or if you get invited to some of the privately stocked waters around the Linville community. As for the river in general, it has a very low flow rate for a river of its size and range most of the time – often just creeping along. And, it's extremely shallow when compared to rivers of similar size. It also lacks sizable tributaries to add volume.

The Linville sources at 4,065' in *Linville Gap* between *Flat Top Mountain* and *Peak Mountain* in the crossroads community of *Tynecastle*. Its source is literally across the road from *Inver Lochy Lake* – the source of the famed *Watauga River*. At the Tynecastle source, multiple flows join together in a flat marsh where they flow under Hwy 105. From there it begins a 37.7 mile run to Lake James.

From Tynecastle, its initial 4.2 mile flow to the community of *Linville* goes through *The Grandfather Country Club* where it is impounded, then released

Linville's headwaters in Tynecastle going under Hwy 105 before running to Grandfather Golf & Country Club Lake. / *Image by Author / 2019*

before continuing. From Linville, it flows southward another 5.6 miles to *Pineola* where it is again impounded by *Land Harbor Lake*. From Pineola, it flows another 7.9 miles to the *Parkway Boundary*. This point is the bottom of the *Upper Section* and is the top of the *Gorge Section*. A few miles below Pineola, the river slows down even more as it continues downstream to the Parkway Boundary.

From the *Parkway's Boundary*, it flows south about 3.2 miles to *Linville Falls* and the start of the *Linville Gorge Wilderness Area*. This is the beginning of the river's violent alter ego I spoke of previously. From the falls, it drops into a deep gorge and begins a 14.5 mile rubicon of cascading, dangerous, heart-pounding, hang-on-for-dear-life topography and water. It's some of the wildest and most beautiful water you'll see east of the Rockies. At about 35.4 miles below its source, it reaches the gorge boundary marker at about 1,320'. Along that entire 35.4 mile run, the river only attains a flat 2% average gradient – unbelievable for a river of this type. Below is a description moving upstream from its mouth to its source.

The Gorge Section: Before I describe this section, my neighbor Bill, the crooked lawyer, recommended I offer a few initial cautionary warnings due to the rugged and remote nature of this *Gorge Section*. It is true backcountry fishing, and it can be particularly intimidating and dangerous. The difficulty is in its remoteness, ruggedness, and steepness of the entry and extraction points. These points all require a steep rappel / climb to get to and from much of the water. If you start at one point and you don't know where you're going to get out, you're in for a rough time. Plan your entry and exit points carefully as if your life depends on it – *because it might!* Make a point to reduce back tracking by "*through fishing*" each

~ Linville River ~

Downstream view of the spectacular twin arched stone bridge the Parkway uses to cross the Linville just a mile or so above the gorge. Most people cross it and never even know its there. / *Image by Author / 2013*

stretch and using a different extraction trail from where you started. With that said, you'll need to make a serious commitment in time and effort between those two points. Generally, it's not easy to fish any stretch of the gorge in just one day. I recommend dedicating at least two days for each stretch.

The gorge section of the river flows through the 11,786 acre *Linville Gorge Wilderness Area* – a place you need to know more about to fully appreciate it. It's the third largest wilderness area in North Carolina behind *Shining Rock Wilderness* and *Joyce-Kilmer / Slickrock Wilderness*. It is one of only two wilderness gorges in the Southern United States along with *Bald River Gorge Wilderness* in Tennessee.

When the *Wilderness Act* was approved by Congress and signed into law by *President Lyndon B. Johnson* in 1964, this gorge was a prime target for inclusion. It had been purchased initially with funds donated by *John D. Rockefeller*, which allowed it to become formally protected in 1952. And it was one of the first formally designated Wilderness Areas of the new *National Wilderness Preservation System*. Its 11,786 acres are contained inside *Pisgah National Forest* and are managed by the *Grandfather Ranger District of the US Forest Service*.

The gorge runs on a north / south axis. It is hemmed in on the west by *Linville Mountain* forming the western rim and several amazing rock formations that frame its eastern rim named *Jonas Ridge, Sitting Bear, Hawksbill, Table Rock* and the *Chimneys*. In places, the river can be as much as 1,800' below the rims. That steepness and depth has helped protect the gorge over the years. In the early 1900s, logging was a major industry in the area, but thankfully the gorge was spared. The gorge's extremely rugged terrain made timber and mineral removal difficult and unprofitable. Therefore, no large scale logging took place, which is the reason it's one of the few remaining examples of old growth forests in the Appalachians. Of the four major gorges in NC, Linville Gorge is the only one without a road along its bottom – only a trail system.

Starting at the southern boundary of the *Gorge Section* and moving upstream, the river can be a good 50' – 75' wide, but is still shallow enough to wade easily. For the next 9.7 miles upstream to where a small *"no name"* feeder enters river right on the southern slope of *Brushy Ridge*, the river's flow is basically straight north. Along the way it remains wide and open with shoals, low drop pools, ledges and shallow runs – some deep water, but not a lot. With this stretch's flat gradient of only 2.6%, wading and hiking your way up is not difficult. This particular stretch has only two feeders that enter river right - *Cambric Branch* and *Chimney Branch*. Neither feeder adds any significant volume or seems worth the time to mess with. The main trail is close to the river all the way, and several spurs on each side lead up to the east and west rims. Access is there – but it's danged hard going!

As you get above 9.7 miles, starting at the south base of *Brushy Ridge*, the river begins to snake and undulate its way up the next 5 miles to *"The Falls"* – in some places looping back to within 450' of its course. At this point, it's about 30' – 40' wide and still flowing at a flat 1.9% gradient. As extreme as the topography is, casting, wading and hiking are relatively easy. The flow deepens along this stretch due to the narrowness of the walls, and it has lots of deep runs and pools, small falls and drop pools - but is still wide and open. Along this stretch, only two feeders, *Bull Branch* and *Gulf Branch*, enter river right. Neither has any real fishing potential as far as I can tell. There are many places along this stretch where you'll climb over or around truck-sized boulders, navigate over or around waterfalls, drop pools and slides, and get around long and deep pools with little or no banks. The main trail parallels this stretch and several spur trails lead up to the rims. As the river approaches the two-tiered falls, it constricts down to 10' – 12' as it passes through, and at its base you'll find an incredible drop pool surrounded by sheer vertical rock walls. Swim or fish – that's the question… *why not do both?*

The look and feel of the 3.2 mile stretch above the falls to the Parkway's northern boundary is a stark contrast to the look and feel of the gorge. As you move upstream from *"The Falls,"* the river is about 30' – 40' wide with shoals, low drop pools, ledges and shallow runs. The river is very slow along this stretch with much of its substrate coated in silt. With this stretch's flat gradient of only .3%, wading is not an issue. This stretch has two tributaries entering river right – *Duggers Creek* across the parking lot from the Parkway's spur down to the gorge and *Camp Creek* at the Parkway's upper boundary. I have fished *Duggers* once, but have not fished *Camp Creek,* although it is definitely fishable. As the river reaches the Parkway, a beautiful arched stone bridge comes into view. It is a work of art and typically holds a few nice size trout in its shadow. As you reach 3.2 miles above the falls you'll be at the Parkway's northern boundary. From there down to the falls the river is on Parkway right-of-way.

To summarize the Gorge Section, getting into and navigating it is not for the inexperienced and out of shape casual angler. But if you're not one of these types and are willing to dare the risks of rugged topography and a wild river, your adventure and angling expectations will be richly rewarded. Most likely you won't see anyone else on the river – save a hiker or two. Not many people are willing to expend the energy and risk the dangers to fish this section. The river runs relatively slowly through this section, but there are many runs, waterfalls, slides, pools and dark holes that are home to some very large browns, bows and brookies – many in the 12" to 18" class – and larger. The state apparently still stocks this section with fingerlings, so the fish grow up thinking they're wild - and act like it. I

The Linville flowing along Hwy 221 between Altamont and Crossnore. / *Image by Author / 2017*

feel the upper stretch of the gorge up to the falls has the best fishing. In fact, the large pool at the base of the falls is where I caught my largest trout on the river – a 19" rainbow on a #16 Prince Nymph dropped underneath a # 12 Elk Hair Caddis indicator.

Upper Section: This section above the Parkway's northern boundary is a stark contrast to the Gorge Section. It is every bit as tame and timid as the Gorge Section is wild and rugged. Being the river's headwater stretch, it's not the typical fast flowing river you'd expect it to be. It flows slowly at best in its upper stretches and even more slowly in the lower stretches as it approaches the Parkway boundary. In fact, it virtually creeps and meanders along in many places as if it were going to come to a complete stop. This is unusual given its headwater status and sourcing at over 4,000'. To add insult to injury, much of its upper flow passes through privately owned commercial / residential developments and agricultural land. If that's not enough, it's impounded three times. These factors add up to a river with a high level of sedimentation over much of its flow and a marginal ability to maintain an acceptable wild trout habitat – save a few stretches that are privately maintained, stocked and fed. For all these reasons and a few unspoken ones, I'm not a fan of this Upper Section. But you might be, so below is my overview of it with as much lipstick as I can put on this pig – which ain't much.

The *Upper Section* starts at the Parkway's northern boundary at 3,225' and heads upstream for 17.7 miles to the river's source in *Tynecastle*. Moving upstream over the first 7.9 miles up to *Pineola*, it's about 20' – 25' wide and runs mostly through private land where it is basically flat with no more than .7% flat average gradient. On its way to *Crossnore*, the river forms several islands and is very sandy and silty. There are a few large obstacles such as boulders, slabs, falls, etc. to obstruct its flow and create habitat. Between *Crossnore* and *Pineola,* it has a bit more bottom structure to mix up its flow, and it passes over an old decommissioned dam. I am not sure what the dam was used for.

Along this initial 7.9 mile stretch, it picks up additional flow volume from several tributaries, with *Stamey Branch, Bill White Creek, Mill Timber Creek* and the largest, *Stacey Creek*. With the exception of *Stacey Creek,* all of these source outside of the National Forest on private property before they join the Linville River. *Stacey* is within the confines of the National Forest, but still appears to be on a private carve out. Given the marginal look of their ability to support healthy habitats and their private status, I have not fished any of these tributaries.

Just north of Hwy 221 in *Pineola*, the river leaves the National Forest and for the next 5.8 miles up to the mountain community of *Linville*, flows on private land – most all posted with *"No Trespassing-No Fishing."* Along here the river is about 15' – 20' wide, shallow and slow moving – in some stretches constricting to just a few feet. Just .6 miles above *Pineola* it flows through the large gated residential development of *Land Harbor* and is impounded by *Land Harbor Lake*. From the lake it continues up another 4.2 miles to *Linville*. From Pineola to Linville, I'm not aware of any sizeable tributaries that add any significant volume.

The final 4.2 mile stretch of the river's Upper Section is from *Linville* upstream to its source in *Tynecastle*. As it leaves Linville, it re-enters the National Forest and at 2.3 miles upstream it enters the *Grandfather Country Club* development where it is once again impounded by the development's lake. Above the lake, it continues up 1.8 miles along the golf course to *Tynecastle* - its source. Most of the land from *Linville* to the source seems to be posted *"No Trespassing-No Fishing."*

Linville River Tributaries

Duggers Creek
A Tributary of the Linville River

At a Glance

Sam's Rank: 👍👍👍
GPS Fixes:
- Source fix: N35 57.904 W82 54.392 @ 3,605'
- Mouth fix: N35 57.344 W82 55.750 @ 3,185'

~ Linville River ~

Size: small at mouth *(At its confluence with Linville River)*
Gradient: low 5.3% source to mouth average *(1.5miles / 420')*
Effort: moderate to difficult
Pressure: none
Fishing Quality: average
Species: Rainbows
Access: From MP 316.5 on the Parkway, take the Linville Falls Road / Parkway Spur south for 1.5 miles to the parking lot for Linville Gorge. You cross the creek as you enter the parking area. Parking is free.

Overview & Description

It is danged depressing that *Duggers Creek* is the only tributary of the Linville that I'm including. Other than the fact the Linville has but just a few accessible tributaries that even qualify as legitimate trout waters, this is the only one that I believe is worthwhile and have actually fished. *Camp Creek*, upstream at the Parkway Boundary and *Gulf Branch* and *Bull Branch* in the gorge just below the falls, are the others that could also be considered candidates.

I stumbled onto Duggers when I was at the *Linville Gorge Falls* parking lot at the end of the *Parkway's Spur*. I thought it looked interesting, so I fished it and was pleasantly surprised with both what I caught and the scenery.

Duggers sources at about 4,605' on the southwest slope of *Ball Ground Mountain* and works downhill at a mild 5.3% average gradient for about 1.5 miles to its mouth on the Linville at 3,185'. It starts small and by the time it gets to the parking area, it's still small. But don't let that 5.3% gradient fool you! The upper half of the creek is relatively flat, but the lower half is a lot steeper that the 5.3% creek average – so it can sneak up on you. Other than a few seeps and springs, it picks up no addition flow from feeders.

Moving upstream from its mouth, the lower stretch features a series of small falls and drop pools, slides and ledges that all create pocket water. The thinly layered rock along the sides is unique and is covered in green moss. Its canopy is open and the water is shallow between pools making wading and casting easy. When I fished it, I used the streambed as my trail, but often found myself bushwhacking and rock hopping to get around. You'll use small stream tactics such as high stickin', sling-shotting, dapping, flick casts, etc. to present your bugs.

I only got about .5 miles up. My efforts were rewarded with rainbows in the 4" – 6" range. Every now and then I encountered a larger than normal pool holding a larger than normal trout in the 5" – 8" range. It's a pleasant little stream.

Wilson Creek

From Mortimer & Edgemont to Its Source

At a Glance

Sam's Rank: 👍👍👍👍👍

GPS Fixes: Only the top 9.8 miles *(Upper Section)* of Wilson Creek's 22.9 mile flow is included here. The Mouth Fix below is the point I selected at the bottom of the 9.8 miles of Upper Section headwaters. This Mouth Fix is in Edgemont, about half way down the river to its true mouth on the Johns River.

- Source fix: N36 06.327 W81 48.433 @ 4,812'
- Mouth fix: N36 00.091 W81 46.455 @ 1,570'

Size: large at mouth *(At Lost Cove Creek bridge in Edgemont)*

Gradient: upper section – mild 6.3% *(9.8 miles / 3,242')*

Effort: upper section – difficult to extreme

Pressure: upper section – none to slight

Fishing Quality: upper section – good to excellent

Species: upper section – Bows, Browns & Specs

Access: Wilson Creek's watershed is quite large. To make things easier, I've sliced it into three sections based on its numerous characteristics, access, and my twisted logic considering the vast amount of water to be covered. I will refer to the first 9.8 miles below its source down to Edgemont as the *Upper Section.* Below Edgemont for the next 6.4 miles to Craig Creek is the *Mid Section.* And finally, the 4.5 miles below Craig Creek to Hwy 1337 will be called the *Gorge Section*:

   ~ *Upper Section:* Several access points are available via road and / or trail. Most require some hiking.

   To get to the Upper Section's northernmost fix at its Source: At about MP 303.5 on the Parkway, park at bridge and hike below it to the creek's headwaters. The source is about .6 miles above the Parkway on Grandfather Mountain State Park property.

   To get to the Upper Section's southernmost fix at Edgemont: From about MP 305.3 on the Parkway, take Hwy 221 east towards Blowing Rock. After about .5 miles, bear right onto FSR 1514. Continue about 12.6 miles to Edgemont / Lost Cove Creek – the Upper Section's southernmost fix. The road parallels the creek for much of the last 1.3 miles. Be aware that along that 12.6 miles the road will change from FSR 1514 to FSR 45 and finally to Hwy 90. Starting at Lost Cove Creek nearly all of the creek through Edgemont and up to Crusher Branch is private or club controlled – observe all *No Fishing / Posted* signs. Park only in designated places.

To access other points along the Upper Section:

- About 2.1 miles after turning off Hwy 221 onto FSR 1514, you will cross Wilson Creek for the first time. Continue on for about 11.4 miles until you cross Wilson again just above Edgemont.

- About 3.9 miles after turning off Hwy 221 onto FSR 1514, you'll reach FSR 192. Turn right and in about 1 mile you'll cross Wilson Creek.

- About 3.9 miles after turning off of Hwy 221 onto FSR 1514, you will reach FSR 192. Turn right and in about .5 miles you reach the northern trailhead for Trail #258 on the left. This trail leads down to the Wilson Creek / Stack Rock Creek confluence in about 1.2 miles and then parallels the creek the next 3.6 miles to just before Crusher Branch. It then ascends up to FSR 1514 / FSR 45 in about .9 miles.

- About 9.1 miles after turning off of Hwy 221 onto FSR 1514, you'll reach the trailhead for Trail #264 on the right. It leads down 1.1 miles to where Wilson Creek and Mountain Laurel Branch meet.

- About 10.7 miles after turning off of Hwy 221 onto FSR 1514, you reach the southern trailhead for Trail #258 on the right. This trail leads down to Wilson Creek at about .9 miles and then continues up the creek to the northern trailhead on FSR 192.

~ *Mid Section:* From this 6.4 mile section's start at Edgemont / Lost Cove Creek, Hwy 90 continues south along the creek for about 1 mile to where it crosses Wilson at Mortimer Recreation Area, and at about 2 miles reaches Mortimer / Brown Mountain Beach Road. Turn right onto Brown Mountain Beach Road and continue down to the section's end at Craig Creek at about 5.9 miles. These roads parallel the creek through most of this section. There is a mix of private / public lands, so observe all *No Fishing / Posted* signs. Park only in designated places.

~ *Gorge Section:* From this section's start at Craig Creek, Brown Mountain Beach Road parallels the creek for about 4.5 miles down through the gorge, all the way to the end of the section at Hwy 1405. Although the road is in sight of the creek, elevations in some cases will be danged extreme. This will require a dicey hike over steep slab rock. Parking is everywhere.

Overview & Description

This is one of my favorite rivers to fly fish in the entire eastern half of the country - *and I really mean it this time!* For starters, its headwaters are on the south face of *Grandfather Mountain* – one of the most beautiful stretches of the Parkway's entire 469 miles. It is also the location of some incredible history *(more below)*, two ghost towns, it's officially designated a *National Wild and Scenic*

River, and because much of its 49,000 acres are within the *Pisgah National Forest.* To top it off, it offers a variety of wild and *Delayed Harvest* fishing opportunities to satisfy any fly fisher's taste. There are miles and miles of wild, rugged and remote waters that require physical ability, determination and skill to get on and fish, to flat, accessible and stocked *"assisted living waters."* Finally, a wild and woolly western style stretch that passes through a steeply-walled gorge with deep pools, slab bottoms and pan fish. The best part is that the entire river fishes well – from stocked waters, to wild waters, and those in between. What else do you want?

Due to the complexity of this watershed, I am only including the *Upper Section* in this edition, with just summary information about the two sections. After all, you could fish the *Upper Section* every day for years and never fish all the water that's there. Perhaps if I live long enough, I'll include the *Mid Section* and *Gorge Section* in future editions.

The Wilson watershed has a rich but tragic history involving logging, fires, floods and snakes. *Mortimer* and its companion community *Edgemont* just upstream are located about halfway down the watershed – with Mortimer as the larger of the two. Mortimer was a hurriedly built town to accommodate workers of the *Ritter Lumber Company* which bought most of the watershed's timber in 1904. It consisted of a company store, a blacksmith's shop, a church, a school, a hotel, a small

National Forest Service efforts to reforest the Wilson Creek Watershed were successful. / *Image courtesy of Special Collections, UNC Asheville*

cotton mill and numerous houses for the workers at the mill and their families. There was even a *Civilian Conservation Corps (CCC)* camp located there. By 1906, the newly incorporated town of roughly 800 residents also had a movie house and the *Laurel Inn,* which Teddy Roosevelt is said to have visited.

Substantial logging took place throughout the entire Wilson watershed, and the trees were hauled to the mill via Ritter's narrow gauge railroad. This route followed Wilson Creek much of the way before ending in the village of Edgemont. In addition to this line, The *Hutton-Bourbonnais Company* operated various other narrow gauge logging railroad lines that fanned out from Mortimer.

Tragically, in 1916 a disastrous fire burned the clear-cut forest from *Grandfather Mountain* down to and including upper Wilson Creek. The fire was followed immediately by a flood *(still considered the worst in Caldwell County history)* which destroyed the railroad lines and broke the *Lake Rhodhiss Dam* upstream. These two occurrences devastated Mortimer and Edgemont, as well as the Ritter Company's operations. The Ritter Company left the town of Mortimer entirely about a year later.

The ruins of Mortimer and Edgemont lie near what is now a stretch of prime trout water. Some portions of the saw mill's boiler room and a few intact boilers from a former cotton mill are still visible. There is also a white maintenance building constructed by the CCC during the 1930s, as well as other CCC building foundations that remain not far away. Today, these silent remnants are all that's left of that vibrant by-gone era.

United Mills Company, a cotton mill, opened in 1922 and revitalized the towns for a brief time. By 1933, the CCC Camp F-5 at Mortimer that opened during the Great Depression had repaired many buildings damaged by the 1916 tribulations. Then in 1934, *O.P. Lutz* began a

Plaque commemorating the location of CCC Camp F-5 in Mortimer. / *Image by Author / 2015*

hosiery mill in the cotton mill buildings. But it too survived only briefly. The *Carolina & Northwestern Railway* brought in mail every other day, but closed the route for good in 1938.

On August 13, 1940, Wilson Creek jumped its banks again due to the remnants of a coastal hurricane. The creek reached a flood stage of 94 feet and engulfed both towns once again. This second flood, coming only 24 years after Edgemont and Mortimer's first horrific experience, was enough to drive most of the remaining families and businesses from the area.

The CCC remained engaged in the area until the start of World War II in 1941. The railroad tracks that ran through Mortimer were taken up and melted down for the war effort. With the industries, railroad and the CCC gone, the valley essentially was left unchanged for the next several decades.

Today, there are only about sixteen permanent families living in the area. Much of the mountain property in the northwestern part of Caldwell County is now U.S. Forest Service land. The once active town of Mortimer has been reclaimed by nature and fishing clubs that control much of the river through Edgemont.

Aside from Wilson's tragic history, there's also an urban legend you should know about.... the *Brown Mountain Lights*. These are a series of ghost lights reported near *Brown Mountain*, just west of the gorge section of Wilson Creek. The lights can be seen from the Blue Ridge Parkway at MP 310 and 301, and from the *Brown Mountain Overlook* on Hwy 181 between Morganton and Linville. The best time of year to see them is September through early December.

~ Wilson Creek ~

One early account of the lights dates from September 24, 1913. A fisherman claimed to have seen *"mysterious lights just above the horizon every night"* in red with a circular shape. This prompted a formal *US Geological Survey* study in 1922 which determined that witnesses had misidentified automobile or train lights, fires, or other area luminaries. But strangely enough, a massive flood struck the area soon after the USGS study and all electrical power was lost, and trains were inoperative for a long period of time. Still the lights continued to appear.

The lights inspired the bluegrass song *"Brown Mountain Lights,"* by Scotty Wiseman and later performed by The Hillmen, The Kingston Trio, Sonny James, Roy Orbison, Tommy Faile, Tony Rice, and the Country Gentlemen. In this ballad, a light is being carried by *"a faithful old slave who's come back from the grave searching for his lost master."* A 1999 episode of the paranormal drama show *The X Files*, featured a case of missing hikers that were found dead in the vicinity of Brown Mountain. The show's main character, Fox Mulder, believed it was due to UFOs. I don't know about any of these claims, but I do know residents in the Wilson Creek area who will swear the lights are real. Trust me. You'll think about all of this when you're solo camping on Wilson.

Okay, enough history and lore – back to Wilson and fishing. Wilson Creek's *Upper Section* comes to life at 4,812' on the south slope of *Calloway Peak* from about .5 miles above the Parkway. At 5,919' Calloway's summit is the highest elevation of the entire *Grandfather Mountain* ridge. From its source, Wilson screams the .5 miles down to the Parkway at a blistering 28.4% gradient, and then continues down 9.8 miles to the end of its *wild* Upper Section at the *"ghost town"* communities of *Edgemont* and then *Mortimer*. This section's upper stretches are for the most part on National Forest Service lands. However, starting just above Edgemont down to *Lost Cove Creek*, it's mostly private club water. Along the way, Wilson's *Upper Section* is joined by several tributaries with names like *Little Wilson, Stack Rock Creek, Bucks Timber Creek* and *Lost Cove Creek* – all of which add considerable volume and are highly fishable. Along this entire section, the creek flows at a mild 6.3% average gradient. At about 1,570' and 9.8 miles below its source on Grandfather Mountain, Wilson reaches *Lost Cove Creek* and the bottom of its *Upper Section*.

From Edgemont and Mortimer, Wilson begins its *Middle Section* run down through the next 6.4 miles at a much flatter gradient with wider stream beds. Its .5% average gradient is extremely flat for a sizeable mountain stream. Much of this section is managed as *Delayed Harvest*. It runs for 3.5 miles from the *Game Land Boundary* downstream of the *Lost Cove Creek Bridge* on Hwy 90 and follows Hwy 1328 to the *Phillips Branch Bridge*. This section is a patchwork of private / public lands, but there is plenty of *Delayed Harvest* water available. Along this run, Wilson is joined by only a couple of sizeable tributaries – *Harpers Creek* and *Craig Creek* add some volume and both are very fishable.

~ Wilson Creek ~

Below *Craig Creek*, Wilson's *Gorge Section* starts and flows for 4.5 miles to where it goes under Hwy 1335. Although this section starts out rather tame, in about a mile it enters *Wilson Creek Gorge*. This gorge is renowned for large, deep pools, long slides and truck-sized boulders as well as runs flowing over a concrete smooth solid granite substrate at an average gradient of only 1.4%. This section is managed as *Hatchery Supported* and is similar in appearance and structure to many western rivers. The actual gorge is about two miles long and the creek is rather large, with deep pools and short sections of runs and riffles. In this particular

section, it is not joined by any sizeable tributaries that are fishable. This ends the source to mouth description of the creek's main flow. Now back to the focus of this chapter – the *Upper Section.*

Moving upstream from the *Upper Section's* southernmost fix where *Lost Cove Creek* enters Wilson at Edgemont, the river is flat for the next 2.6 miles up to just above *Crusher Branch*. The valley opens up into a perfectly wide and open target for a flood, and there have been several horrific ones over the years. The evidence is everywhere - abandoned or trashed buildings, factory foundations and walls, large numbers of bent trees, debris piles, exposed rock and gravel

Wilson's Middle Section below Mortimer and Edgemont opens up and becomes wide. / *Image by Author / 2015*

beds and large piles of boulders. The creek along here is about 50' wide, shallow with large rocks and frequent runs and riffles. The water is beautifully clear.

Within sight of the creek are scores of cabins, a church, school house and a general store / museum where artifacts and pictures offer stark evidence of the severity and deadliness of the flooding. The creek along this stretch is controlled by private landowners and fishing clubs. At about 1.2 miles up from the *Lost Cove Creek Bridge*, *Laurel Creek* enters river right. This is a beautiful and fishable tributary once you get upstream and off of private land. Along this lower civilized stretch of Wilson, it is followed closely by the road for the first 1.3 miles or so. The road heads up into the forest along *Laurel Creek* for a bit before pulling away.

On upstream about 2.5 miles to just above *Crusher Branch*, Wilson finally gets above private property and lives up to its *National Wild and Scenic River* title. It is also managed as *Wild Trout Water - Catch and Release Artificial Lures Only*. About one mile above *Crusher Branch* is *Laurel Mountain Branch* - a marginally fishable flow. On up another .8 miles is *Turkey Branch,* also small, and up another .8 miles is *Bucks Timber Creek.* All three enter creek right. *Bucks Timber* is the best of the three and very fishable, the other two are not large enough to be worthwhile. I'm sure there's some wild trout on both of them – but their pocket waters are tiny and the trout would be tiny as well. The browns and rainbows that I have caught in the main flow of this stretch are in the 8" to 12" range, with occasional stockers from downstream much larger – 16" or more.

The 2.6 miles between *Crusher* and *Bucks Timber Branch* is a series of long runs and slides interspersed with stretches of wide gravel beds and banks, long runs and riffles and boulder fields, as well as large shallow pools. The creek averages 20' to 25' wide in most places and in several stretches has split and runs in parallel beds. There are

A small Brown caught with a #14 March Brown in Wilson's Upper Section under FSR 192. / *Image by Author / 2014*

several unusually large and deep pools along this stretch. These are very fishable and in times can be difficult to get around without leaving the creek and hiking around them. Although this stretch is not particularly steep, it is definitely remote and rugged enough to get your attention. Thankfully, Trail #258 parallels it up to where *Stack Rock Creek* comes in creek left.

It's about one mile from *Bucks Timber* upstream to the fishy *Stack Rock Creek.* Trail #258 also comes down from FSR 192 and starts its southward tracking of the stream from this point. This one mile stretch is where the wild and wooly nature of Wilson becomes really apparent. The gradient gets steeper, huge boulders litter the bed, the creek narrows to about 10' to 15' in most places, and the banks and canopies close in quite a bit to create a more typical mountain stream feel. Additionally, the gradient creates a solid pattern of drop pools, runs and riffles. Most of these hold colorful browns and bows in the 6" to 10" range.

Little Wilson Creek enters *"Big"* Wilson on the right about .9 miles above where *Stack Rock* enters. *Little Wilson* is not big, but it is fishable and worth the time and effort. Along that .9 mile, Wilson is much the same as it is below – but the gradient steepens to a mild 6.5%, and the bed narrows and becomes a bit more challenging to navigate. For the most part, it is a continuous ladder of drop pools with runs in between, with large boulders and shelves and slabs turning the water into a white froth. The creek is still about 10' to 15' wide at this point. It fishes well – but it's dang hard fishing!

Wilson Creek passes under FSR 192 about .5 miles above its confluence with *Little Wilson*. Along that stretch, it steepens, becomes smaller still, and earns its rugged, small mountain trout stream reputation. There're several primitive campsites where the creek passes under FSR 192. This area always has a bunch of wild people hanging around doing strange things to each other and themselves.

Above FSR 192, Wilson starts a 1.3 mile climb up to FSR 1514 just under the Parkway and Hwy 221. Along this stretch the creek takes on an even steeper gradient of about 11%. It's also very remote with no improved trail system for portage - only the streambed and bushwhacking. The creek is a continual series of large and small drop pools, shallow runs and riffles, car-sized boulders and several falls with pools that will get your attention. One notable feature along this stretch that I don't see in many other flows is the number of perfectly round, deep and clear swirl holes worn into the solid granite by the current. These are perfect tubs that are deep *(4' – 6')* and cold. These do hold fish, but they're best used for

stripping off and jumping in at the end of a hard day of fishing. The fish along this section are bows and browns in the lower areas – mostly in the 6" to 8" range. Up closer to Hwy 221, lots of specs in the 4" to 6" range hang out. Most all of the pools and runs along this stretch of Wilson hold fish. That's the reason I like it as much as I do.

Fishing Wilson above FSR 1514 can be difficult, but productive if you are willing to climb rock. / *Image by Author / 2015*

The .5 miles above FSR 1514 up to Hwy 221 is more of the same, except smaller and steeper – about 17.2% average gradient to be exact. Up there, the creek is about 8'-10' wide and shallow. Pocket water fishing is the game up there, and all I have caught are specs in the 4" to 6" range. It is hard fishing for small fish, but it's also a lot of fun, especially as you get higher and can hear the traffic on Hwy 221 and the Parkway.

There is only about 750' between Hwy 221 and the Parkway, but it's at a blistering gradient, and the fishing becomes even tighter and pocket water based. The creek is only feet across in most spots, with small drop pools and short runs in between. The water is tiny, and the 4" specs are just as tiny along this stretch. Once again, it is hard fishing, and I've only done it a few times. As for the .5 miles above the Parkway to the source, I've never caught a fish up there. I think it freezes solid in the winter. At least I think it does - probably why I haven't caught anything.

Wilson Creek's *"Upper Section"* Tributaries

Little Wilson Creek
A Tributary of Wilson Creek

At a Glance

Sam's Rank: 👍👍👍👍
GPS Fixes:
- Source fix: N36. 06.116 W81 47.832 @ 4,605'
- Mouth fix: N36 04.280 W81 47.330 @ 2,610'

Size: small at mouth *(At its confluence with Wilson Creek)*
Gradient: steep 15.7% source to mouth average *(2.4 miles / 1,995')*
Effort: difficult to extreme
Pressure: none
Fishing Quality: average to good
Species: Rainbows & Browns
Access: There are several access points. The following are the ones I know best:

~ *To access the source:* At about MP 302.7 on the Parkway, park at the bridge and hike below to the creek. The source is about .3 miles above the Parkway. Park along the Parkway.

~ *To access points below the Parkway between the source and mouth:*

- From about MP 305.3 on the Parkway, take Hwy 221 east toward Blowing Rock. After about 3.2 miles, you'll cross Little Wilson Creek. Parking is easy.

- From about MP 305.3 on the Parkway, take Hwy 221 east towards Blowing Rock. After about .5 miles bear right onto FSR 1514. In about 3.4 miles, you'll cross Little Wilson Creek. Parking is easy.

- About 3.9 miles after turning off Hwy 221 onto FSR 1514, you will reach FSR 192. Turn right and in about .7 miles you'll cross Little Wilson Creek. About .4 miles downstream is its mouth on Wilson Creek. Parking is easy.

Overview & Description

Little Wilson Creek is the first tributary of any size entering Wilson Creek below its source. It's a productive little trout stream depending on where you fish it. Although it can be hard fishing for small trout, there's at least reasonable access to its lower stretches where the fishing is best. It's blue-line trout fishing for sure, but I think it's worthwhile given its proximity in the watershed.

The creek comes off the southeastern slope of *Calloway Peak* perched atop *Grandfather Mountain's* ridge line from 4,605'. From that noble source, Little Wilson starts a 2.4 mile run at a steep average gradient of 15.7%. Along that run, it receives additional volume from only one or two feeders – neither with any size or fishing quality. Along its descent, it flows under no less than four roads – the Parkway, Hwy 221, FSR 1514 and finally FSR 190. All of these serve to provide the only access other than hiking through open forest – no trails. At about 2,610' it meets Wilson Creek about .4 miles below FSR 190.

Starting at its mouth and moving upstream through the .4 miles to the FSR 190 bridge, the creek is only 6' to 8' across at best, and is shallow with frequent boulders and drop pools that create pocket water. This stretch is the best fishing on the creek just because the water is larger with nice pockets where trout can hold. And, it's a bit more open than the stretches above it.

Because it's sandwiched between two roads – FSR 190 and FSR 1514 – the .6 miles stretch between the bridges is the easiest to get to and fish. At about 6' wide this stretch is still fishable, but it's very small, shallow and tight, and just plain painful to ascend, navigate and cast. But if you can handle the bushwhacking and rock climbing, it can be worthwhile. All of the trout I have caught along the one mile between the mouth and FSR 1514 have been in the 4"– 6" range – mostly rainbows and a few browns.

Above the FSR 1514 bridge up to Hwy 221, there is some pocket water that can be fished for the small bows and specs tough enough to live there. However, this stretch is marginally productive, and is at best hard fishing. I've never caught anything larger than a cigar up there. Having done it several times, I personally don't think the payoff is worth the effort. From Hwy 221 up to the Parkway and on up to the source is not really fishable in my opinion. I'm sure there's some small pocket water trout along those stretches, but they would have to be tiny given the fact the creek probably freezes solid in the winter. And in dryer months, there's hardly any meaningful water to sustain a trout habitat.

Stack Rock Creek
A Tributary of Wilson Creek

At a Glance

Sam's Rank: 👍👍👍👍
GPS Fixes:
- Source fix: N36 05.542 W81 49.260 @ 4,480'
- Mouth fix: N36 03.593 W81 47.207 @ 2,300'

Size: small at mouth *(At its confluence with Wilson Creek)*

Gradient: moderate 12.1% source to mouth average *(3.4 miles / 2,180')*
Effort: moderate to difficult
Pressure: none
Fishing Quality: average
Species: Rainbows, Specs & Browns
Access: There are several access points. The following are the ones I know best.

~ *To get to the source:* At about MP 304.6 on the Parkway, park at the bridge and hike below to the creek. The source is about .1 miles above the Parkway. Park anywhere you can.

~ *To access points between the Parkway and the mouth via road or trail:*

- From MP 305.3 on the Parkway, take Hwy 221 towards Blowing Rock. At about 1 mile you'll cross Stack Rock. Parking is easy.

- From about MP 305.3 on the Parkway, take Hwy 221 east towards Blowing Rock. After about .5 miles bear right onto FSR 1514. After about .7 miles you will cross Stack Rock, continue on and at 3.9 miles from Hwy 221 you'll reach FSR 192. Turn right and in about 2.1 miles you cross Stack Rock Creek. Parking is easy.

- From about MP 305.3 on the Parkway, take Hwy 221 east towards Blowing Rock. After about .5 miles bear right onto FSR 1514. After about 3.9 miles you'll reach FSR 192. Turn right and at .5 miles you reach the northern trailhead for Trail #258 on the left leading down 1.2 miles to Stack Rock's confluence with Wilson. Parking is easy.

Overview & Description

Stack Rock Creek is similar to *Little Wilson* in that it comes off the south face of *Grandfather Mountain* and is highly fishable. It's different in that it's longer and larger by the time it reaches Wilson. And, it has better access via roads and improved trails. As Wilson's second sizeable tributary, it's a productive trout stream. Its lower waters are bigger and better in terms of access, and known mostly for bows and browns. Its higher stretches are typical blue-line fishing and known for small specs. This is definitely a worthwhile creek given its attributes.

Stack Rock comes off the southern slope of one of the peaks of *Grandfather Mountain* named *Raven Rocks*. From about 4,480' it begins a 3.4 mile plunge along the eastern slope of *Gabes Mountain* and *Yancey Ridge* at a moderate 12.1% average gradient. Along the way, it gets additional volume from *Andrews Creek,* which is decent size and very fishable. About 1.4 miles below FSR 190, Stack Rock meets Wilson at about 2,300'. It also flows under four roads along its run to its mouth on Wilson - *Parkway, Hwy 221, FSR 1514* and *FSR 190.*

From its mouth and heading upstream along the 1.4 miles up to the FSR 190 bridge, the creek has a mild gradient and a respectable 8' to 12' width on average, with an open canopy. Its structure is the typical large and small drop pool, run and riffle pattern, with huge boulders of all sizes and shapes strategically stacked by nature to provide the best flow features. Generally the water is shallow, but the boulders and drop pools create some unusually large and deep pocket waters. All seem to hold fish, and I think this stretch offers the creek's best fishing. About .9 miles

Stack Rock lives up to its name. Fishing it can be challenging, especially above FSR 192. / *Image by Author / 2011*

up from Stack Rock's mouth, *Andrews Creek* enters creek left. It comes down from 2.5 miles above, just under Hwy 221. It offers additional trout fishing opportunities with adequate road and trail access. My friend Monte really likes this feeder and has been fishing it since he was a kid living in the Wilson Watershed.

Over the next 1.6 miles, Stack Rock is sandwiched between two roads, FSR 190 and FSR 1514, just like *Wilson, Little Wilson* and *Bucks Timber Creek*. The creek's basic structure is more of the same from below – just smaller and tighter, but now with a steep average gradient of about 13.5%. Along this stretch, the creek is about 5' to 8' wide and is definitely fishable, but it's getting smaller and shallower. The first .6 miles of this stretch is the best fishing. But be prepared for rock hopping and bushwhacking – there are no improved trails. It's pocket water fishing at its finest. Most of what I have caught along the .6 miles above the FSR 190 bridge have been rainbows and specs in the 4"– 6" range. Above that first .6 miles up to FSR 1514, the creek starts to get really tight and difficult to fish.

Above the FSR 1514 bridge up to Highway 221, the next .1 miles is at an extreme average gradient of 35%. I don't consider above Hwy 221 to the Parkway and above to the source to be very fishable – at least not at a 35% average gradient!

Bucks Timber Branch
A Tributary of Wilson Creek

At a Glance

Sam's Rank: 👍👍👍👍
GPS Fixes:
- Source fix: N36 05.141 W81 47.306 @ 3,370'
- Mouth fix: N36 13.106 W81 46.426 @ 2,055'

Size: small at mouth *(At its confluence Wilson Creek)*
Gradient: moderate 8.3% source to mouth average *(3 miles / 1,315')*
Effort: moderate to difficult
Pressure: none
Fishing Quality: good
Species: Rainbows, Browns & Brookies
Access: There are several access points. The following are the ones I know best.

~ *To get to the source:* From about MP 305.3 on the Parkway, take Hwy 221 east towards Blowing Rock. After about .5 miles bear right onto FSR 1514. After about 3.7 miles you will cross the extreme headwaters of Bucks Timber Branch. Park in any available space.

~ *To access points between FSR 1514 and the mouth via road or trail:*

- From about MP 305.3 on the Parkway, take Hwy 221 east towards Blowing Rock. After about .5 miles bear right onto FSR 1514. After about .3.9 miles you will reach FSR 192. Turn right and in about .2 miles you cross Bucks Timber Branch. Park in any available space.

- From about MP 305.3 on the Parkway, take Hwy 221 east towards Blowing Rock. After about .5 miles bear right onto FSR 1514. After about 5.5 miles you will reach the trail head for Trail # 257. This trail leads down, crossing *Cary Flat Branch* along the way, until just before its confluence with *Bucks Timber Branch* on the northern side of a private carve out. From that point it's bushwhacking and in-stream wading and climbing up to FSR 192 – no improved trails. Parking is everywhere.

Overview & Description

When I get around to it, I plan to petition the National Forest Service to change the name of this creek from Bucks Timber Creek, to Bucks Timber "*Rattler*" Creek. Over the years I've encountered no less than five Timber Rattlers and at least the same number of Banded Water Snakes - three of which were eating trout. That sight gives me the creeps. Not only do water snakes look like copperheads, or skinny Timber Rattlers, they're just downright sinister if you ask me.

Some of the locals around New Hopewell Baptist Church on FSR 1415 tell a story about one of the original landowners on Bucks Timber Branch - we'll call him Buck. After he sold the timber on his property to Ritter Lumber Co., he had a tidy sum of money. That money attracted a gypsy woman from Florida who set out to seduce him – she did, and they eventually married. Being from Florida, his wife had always wanted to own a Snake-a-Torium. So the newlyweds started a snake raising business. A few years passed and the business was doing well - especially with Floridian tourists wearing Bermuda shorts and black knee socks. But then came the fires and floods of 1916. The snakes escaped and the business failed.

With his fortune lost, Buck reportedly slid into a deep depression and eventually jumped off a cliff. His gold-digging gypsy wife, seeking warmer weather and another sugar daddy, returned to Florida and married a Cuban cigar smuggler. Unfortunately the dang snakes stayed! All that's supposed to be mostly true...

Other than snakes, the other bad news about this creek is that its access downright sucks. The headwaters are accessible, but they are very small and not very fishable. And, to get to the larger fishable waters above the mouth requires a killer hike. Other than that, it's a great little trout stream with lots of rainbows, browns and a smattering of brookies. So if you have a hankering for a hike and a *"snake around every corner"* experience – knock yourself out!

Bucks Timber Creek sources up at about 3,370' on the southwestern slope of *Pilot Knob*, between *Rough Ridge* to the west and *Pilot Ridge* to the east. From there it starts an almost straight 3 mile downhill run to its mouth on Wilson Creek at a moderate average gradient of 8.3%. Along that run, it is joined by *Cary Flat Branch* and *Flat Land Branch* - both are marginally fishable. Bucks Timber's confluence with Wilson is at 2,055'

At its mouth, the creek is only 8' to 10' across and shallow with the typical boulders and drop pools that create pocket water with occasional runs and riffles in between. During the first .1 miles upstream, *Flat Land Branch* enters creek left. This creek is small, and its pocket waters are almost, but not easily quite fishable. It's not really productive in my opinion. On up above the .1 mile mark, you enter private water for the next .5 miles. Just before you exit that private land, *Cary Flat Branch* enters creek right. This feeder comes down from about 1.5 miles above from several trout ponds in the community of *Gragg,* just off FSR 1514. This feeder is definitely fishable after you get about .3 miles up and back on public land. It yielded 5" to 7" rainbows the two times I fished it.

Above the private land on Bucks Timber, and on up the 2 miles to FSR 192, the creek is a typical mountain stream. This stretch is the best fishing on the creek and features several small 8' to 12' waterfalls with nice pools underneath, scores of pools and runs, and countless boulders, slabs and slides of most every size. Most create nice pocket water where trout can and do hold in good numbers. I have fished about 1.5 miles up this stretch and caught browns and bows in the 6" to 9" range – large for a creek this size. I also caught several specs in the 5" class. The hike out was a killer. Of course all the time I was being stalked by Timber Rattlers and Banded Water Snakes.

Approaching FSR 192 and on up to FSR 1514 and above, the creek is only a few feet wide, shallow and very tight. Personally, I don't think it's worth investing the time to mess with. But all in all, the lower stretches of Bucks Timber are worth fishing if you can handle the hiking, bushwhacking and danged snakes.

Laurel Creek
A Tributary of Wilson Creek

At a Glance

Sam's Rank: 👍👍👍

GPS Fixes:

- Source fix: N36 02.189 W81 44.611 @ 2,320'
- Mouth fix: N36 00.745 W81 45.790 @ 1,630'

Size: small at mouth *(At its confluence with Wilson Creek)*

Gradient: mild 5.7% source to mouth average *(2.3 miles / 690')*

Effort: moderate to difficult

Pressure: none

Fishing Quality: average

Species: Rainbows & Browns

Access: There are several access points. The following are the ones I know best.

~ *To get to the mouth at Edgemont:* From about MP 305.3 on the Parkway, take Hwy 221 east towards Blowing Rock. After about .5 miles bear right onto FSR 1514. Continue about 11.5 miles to just past the bridge crossing Wilson Creek. This is all private land and the mouth is on the left behind a cabin and outbuildings. Parking is limited – obey the signs.

~ *To access various other points of the creek above private land:*

- About .5 miles above the bridge is the end of the private land and the start of public fishing. The road parallels the stream for about .8 miles upstream. Park anywhere you can.

- From about MP 305.3 on the Parkway, take Hwy 221 east towards Blowing Rock. After about .5 miles bear right onto FSR 1514. Continue about 9.9 miles to FSR 4068 *(gated)* on the left. This road begins crossing Laurel Creek's headwaters and feeders within a mile or so. Parking is everywhere.

Overview & Description

Let me begin by stating that I have not fished this creek. But several of my so called "*reliable*" buddies have and they like it. I've driven past it many times on my way up and down Wilson and it looks good to me too! The biggest challenge to this creek is getting above its private stretch above its mouth. You then rappel down off the road to fish. Other than that, my buddies say it's worth the effort.

Laurel Creek starts north of *Edgemont* along FSR 45 at about 2,320' between *Bark Camp Ridge* and *Wilson Ridge*. It begins a 2.3 mile run to its mouth on Wilson at a flat average gradient of 5.7%. In the mile below its source fix, it passes under FSR 4068, then picks up volume from three small feeders – *Poplar Springs*

Branch is the only one that's fishable. Other than road access, on the one mile of water above the private land, and up to the confluence of its feeders, there are no improved trails. Laurel Creek meets Wilson Creek at about 1,630' on private land.

Above the private land the creek is about 8' to 10' on average. According to my buddies, the one mile above the private land up to *Poplar Springs Branch* is the best fishing. They reported catching bows in the 7" to 12" range and a few browns slightly larger. Several of their catches in some of the larger pools were over 12".

Along that mile above the private land the creek has a very mild gradient, with lots of drop pools, runs and pools that are fishable. Its canopy and banks are also unusually open most of the way up, making wading and casting easy for such a small creek. My buddies reported that there are several small waterfalls that must be traversed, each with nice pools at their base holding larger than normal fish. Apparently many of the stocked *"pigs"* from the private and *Delayed Harvest* waters below find their way up this stream – which might account for the larger than normal fish they caught. At about one mile above the private land, *Poplar Springs Branch* enters creek left. The pocket water of this small feeder was fished by my buddies and yielded bows in the 4" – 6" range.

Lost Cove Creek
A Tributary of Wilson Creek

At a Glance

Sam's Rank: 👍👍👍👍
GPS Fixes:
- Source fix: N36 00.106 W81 46.454 @ 3,700'
- Mouth fix: N36 00.156 W81 52.640 @ 1,565'

Size: medium at mouth *(At its confluence with Wilson Creek)*
Gradient: flat 4.2% source to mouth average *(9.6 miles / 2,135')*
Effort: moderate to difficult
Pressure: none to slight
Fishing Quality: good
Species: Rainbows & Browns
Access: The first 2.9 miles of the creek is on private land. To get above that, go about .2 miles below the Hwy 90 Bridge crossing Lost Cove Creek in Edgemont. Turn right on FSR 464 and go about 2.7 miles until you reach the Trail #263 trailhead. This trail leads down .6 miles to Trail # 262 which parallels Lost Cove Creek. From there you can hike downstream .7 miles to the private land boundary and Gragg Prong, or upstream about 2 miles until it leaves the creek. The source and first mile or so of upper headwaters are accessible via Hwy 1518 from MP 311.3 on the Parkway. Other than these two points, access to the remainder of the creek and its feeders is by bushwhacking, wading or jetpack.

Overview & Description

Lost Cove Creek is the last and largest tributary entering *Wilson Creek's Upper Section* at Edgemont – and just might be the largest for the entire Wilson Creek watershed as far as I can tell. It's a great medium-sized trout stream with a surprisingly long and large main flow with open canopies and wide banks. It also has several feeders that qualify as exceptional trout streams themselves. If there is one drawback, it would be access to its public water. Fortunately, there is reasonable access via a road and trail above the private land of its lower stretches where fishing is best. I highly recommend it. Given the effort to get on it, and the amount of water to cover, plan to pack in and stay a day or so.

Just one of many young browns brought to hand on Lost Cove Creek. / *Image by Author / 2014*

It is managed as *Catch and Release - Artificial Fly Only.*

The creek sources at about 3,700' between *Big Lost Cove Ridge* and the south side of MP 312 on the Parkway. It flows northeasterly, paralleling the *Parkway* and *Big Lost Cove Ridge* for about 2 miles before *Breakneck Ridge* forces it to make a hard right to the east. During that first 2 miles, it's never more than a mile or so from the Parkway – sometimes as close as .3 miles. Along its rather long 9.6 mile run to its mouth on Wilson Creek at Edgemont, it does so at an average flat gradient of about 4.2% - which makes it surprisingly easy to fish for such a remote stream. Along the way, several feeders with names like *Sassafras Creek, Little Lost Cove Creek, Gragg Prong* and *Rockhouse Creek* contribute additional volume. All of these offer exceptional blue-line, small-creek fishing with the possible exception of *Little Lost Cove Creek,* which is really small. Finally, at about 1,565', it reaches its mouth on Wilson Creek.

Moving upstream from its mouth, the first 2.9 miles flows through private land. Along here the creek is about 15' to 20' wide, flat, with deep and long pools, wide open sides and canopies and gravel banks. The water is gin clear allowing you to see fish on the bottom. FSR 981 starts at the bridge on Hwy 90 and parallels Lost Cove the first .5 miles before turning away and heading north.

At .5 miles up from its mouth, Lost Cove's first feeder, *Rockhouse Creek* enters creek right. Rockhouse's first .6 miles is also on private land, but beyond that it enters the National Forest. FSR 981 parallels it for about the first 1.4 miles above its mouth on Lost Cove. At 1.4 miles the road veers left and heads up to *Gragg Prong* and *Webb Creek* and eventually the Parkway. Rockhouse is 5.3 miles long, rugged and with exceptional trout fishing. I've caught bows and browns in the 6" to 8" range - and in good numbers. I have not fished past where FSR 981 leaves it.

As you move up Lost Cove Creek and approach the top of the private land, you will reach *Gragg Prong*, the second sizeable feeder entering creek right at about 2.8 miles. This creek is also fishable and worth the time and effort. The few times I have fished the lower section just above Lost Cove, I caught bows in the 6" to 8" range. The first 500 feet or so is private, but above that you're good to go. This creek is about 5.6 miles long and its headwaters source up just .3 miles south of MP 306 on the Parkway. Its mid and upper stretches are accessible via several FSRs and trails. About 2.4 miles up Gragg Prong, *Webb Creek,* enters creek left. It is also an excellent trout stream.

About 6.2 miles up Lost Cove you'll come to *Sassafras Creek.* The stretch above the private land at *Gragg Prong* up to this *Sassafras* is where I have fished the most. This 3.3 mile stretch has a flat 3% gradient and has wider than normal banks and canopies. The creek is about 10' – 12' wide along this stretch, with the typical runs and riffles and the occasional drop pool you see in most creeks of this size. The fishing is always good along here and the trail helps with navigation. I'm always rewarded with at least one larger than expected brown or rainbow – *sometimes both!* Also along this stretch, *Little Lost Cove Creek* enters creek left at about 5.1 miles. It's about 1.3 miles long, very small, tight and steep, and its pocket water is marginally productive fishing.

At the 6.2 mile point, *Sassafras Creek* enters creek right. This creek is also very small. It is only 1.3 miles long and is the last feeder of any size. Its pocket water is fishable if you are willing to brave its extreme 18% gradient. I have never fished it, but I know people who have. They caught bows and specs in the 6"– 8" range.

For the next 1.4 miles above *Sassafras Creek*, Lost Cove runs below the southern slope of *Breakneck Ridge*. It is small and steep, with numerous small feeders entering it - but none appear to be fishable. At 7.6 miles the creek makes a hard turn to the south and parallels the Parkway to its source. This stretch is even smaller and tighter and close to the Parkway, but I have not fished it. *So go for it!*

Watauga River
From Valle Crucis to Its Source

At a Glance

Sam's Rank: 👍👍👍👍

GPS Fixes: I'm including only the initial 12.8 miles of the Watauga River. So I'll use the end of the second Delayed Harvest section downstream in Valle Crucis as the "*unofficial*" Mouth fix.

- Source fix: N36 07.270 W81 50.094 @ 4,000'
- Mouth fix: N36 12.992 W81 47.170 @ 2,655'

Size: large at mouth *(At Valle Crucis)*

Gradient: flat 2% source to mouth average *(12.8 miles / 1,345')*

Effort: easy to moderate

Pressure: moderate to heavy

Fishing Quality: good

Species: Bows, Browns & Specs

Access: The Watauga River can be accessed from numerous points:

~ To access the river's upper 8.8 miles starting at its source, down to the end of the Delayed Harvest section at the intersection of Hwy 105 and Hwy 1112, begin at Tynecastle at the intersection of Hwy 105 and Hwy 184. Head north towards Boone on Hwy 105 which parallels the Watauga for the next 8.8 miles to the bridge at the intersection with Hwy 1112. There are numerous access points on the right side of the road all the way down. Park where you can.

~ The river can also be accessed from the Parkway by taking Hwy 1559 north from MP 298.5. This is a several mile ride which will bring you to Hwy 105 and the Watauga at the community of Foscoe.

~ To access the river's lower 4 miles, from the bridge at the intersection of Hwy 105 and Hwy 1112, down to the end of the Delayed Harvest section in Valle Crucis, turn onto Hwy 1112 and head toward Valle Crucis. The road follows the river most of the way. The Valle Crucis Community Park, just behind Mast General Store, offers excellent access and parking.

Overview & Description

When I think of the Watauga River, or the "*Watagi*" as the Native-Americans called it, a word that meant *"the land beyond,"* I can't help but think too of the *Linville River* that sources up just across the road – *literally*. What's the chance two iconic rivers should source in the shadow of Grandfather Mountain only a few hundred yards apart? Yet, the Watauga flows north and into the Gulf of Mexico, and the Linville flows south into the Atlantic. For those reasons, and because its Boone Fork tributary crosses the Parkway, I consider it a good trout fishery.

~ Watauga River ~

I'm including only the first 12.8 miles of the Watauga's headwaters in this description. Most all of that stretch is on private land, save a few public access points and parks. This stretch is great for novice and experienced anglers alike because it is a wide stream, it's *Hatchery Supported*, and has two *Delayed Harvest* stretches. Additionally, it has several high-elevation, cold-water tributaries for those who seek a challenge. So... the issue is not about finding trout, but rather legally negotiating the patchwork of private / public land. So what should one do?

There are several approaches to the legal access conundrum. *First*, stop at a local outfitter along Hwy 105 or in Banner Elk and tell them where you want to fish – *AND* you want advice on which bugs work best. Ask which areas, private / public, along the river you can access. Most of the time, if you buy bugs they'll give you the scoop. *Second*, just fish the two *Delayed Harvest* sections – they're always open to the public. *Third*, approach the land owner with a bad limp, and ask if you can fish their stretch because it's easier for you to get around – *catch and release of course!* You'll be surprised how many will say "*yes.*" Heck, I've even had some ask me if there's anything they can do to help! *Fourth*, much of the water is posted, but much of it is not. So just play naïve and fish the non-posted water, especially around the bridges where lots of trout hang out. One or more of these "*responsible*" tactics will work. I've never been shot at! Correction: I've never been shot at and hit when employing one or more of these shameless tactics. But I have been talked to real ugly a couple of times.

It's hard to picture a river as large and long as the Watauga sourcing from a small spring-fed private lake in *Tynecastle* called *Inver Lochy Lake*. But that's exactly where it starts. It begins life as an impounded flow, and ends almost 79 miles later in another Tennessee impoundment called *Boone Lake*. It's in Linville Gap at about 4,000', between *Peak Mountain* and *Flat Top Mountain*; the Watauga escapes *Inver Lochy Lake* and flows under "*Pedalin Pig BBQ*" to the south side of Hwy 105. You can pull off the road across from "*The Pig*" and see the river trickling out of a pipe under the road into a small pool - *hardly looks like a river!*

From this tiny pool, the Watauga begins a 12.8 mile flow at a tame 2% gradient through a highly- civilized landscape to *Valle Crucis*. Along that stretch, it's joined by a dozen or more tributaries that add more cold water volume. *Green Ridge Branch, Moody Mill Creek, Boone Fork, Laurel Fork* and *Dutch Creek* are five of the largest. And all five are at least marginally fishable, but only three are reasonably accessible. Two *Delayed Harvest* sections provide about 2.25 miles of additional public fishing opportunities. At the end of the second *Delayed Harvest* section in *Valle Crucis* at about 2,655', the river reaches the end of the 12.8 mile stretch covered by this chapter. From there the Watauga continues another 65.7 miles into Tennessee, where it is impounded twice by the *TVA* before finally joining the *South Holston River* in *Boone Lake* near *Johnson City*.

~ Watauga River ~

Starting at its mouth at the bridge on Hwy 194, just below *Mast General Store* in *Valley Crucis* and moving upstream, the Watauga enters the first of two *Delayed Harvest* sections. Its first fishable tributary, *Dutch Creek*, also enters river right at the bridge. Dutch is good water and drains a large watershed a mile to the west just below *Valle Crucis Conference Center* and *Holy Cross Episcopal Church.* The 1.2 mile *Delayed Harvest* section runs from the bridge up to its end at the Hwy 1114 bridge. It flows through a wide open pastoral setting in an almost flat valley where the *Valle Crucis Community Park* offers easy access and is a

A respectable rainbow caught below the first Delayed Harvest section on the Watauga River. / *Image by Author / 2015*

great place to rest and hang out. I have seen naked female wood fairies in this area too, so be careful! Along here the river is 25' to 35' wide and other than a few islands, has minimal topographical features to impede flow. Wading and casting are easy. The river is very shallow in most places with beds of gravel and smooth river stone. Frequent long runs and pools offer holding lanes for both stocked and hold over trout. In this section, you'll find productive fishing for rainbows, browns and some brookies – all good sized.

Along the 2.8 miles above the *Delayed Harvest* section up to the Hwy 105 bridge, the river has much the same character as the lower *Delayed Harvest* stretch below – and even more residential / private property. You'll see evidence of this by the many posted signs and neighborhood / driveway bridges. Much of this stretch is posted, but a lot is not - at least with signage. It flows through pasture and farm land as well as residential developments, with only the last quarter mile or so just before Hwy 105 being somewhat undeveloped. This stretch of the river is still wide and open, but several islands and a few more in-stream features such as boulders, dead falls and ledges break up the flow. Most of the curves are wide and covered with gravel and stone. Frequent pools and runs offer good habitat to the wash downs from the upstream *Delayed Harvest* section, as well as those that come up from below – there are some large pigs that live here! As you get closer to Hwy 105, the river tightens to about 15' to 25', with deeper runs and in-stream features offering a more typical mountain stream character. At 4 miles above *Valle Crucis* as you reach the bridge at Hwy 105, *Laurel Fork*, the second fishable tributary, enters river left. This is a productive trout stream worth the time to fish.

Above Hwy 105, for the next mile or so up to Hwy 1557 / Shulls Mill Road, is the second *Delayed Harvest* section. The character of this stretch could not be more different from the one below the Hwy 105 bridge. Here the river is wide and features huge truck-sized boulders, steep banks, long, deep and smooth pools and a slow flow. It calls for pocket water and

Looking upstream towards the old dam alongside Hwy 105 below Foscoe. The pools offer excellent fishing. / *Image by Author / 2019*

dredging techniques. About .9 miles up from the Hwy 105 Bridge are the remains of an old concrete dam. This is an interesting place, and the pool behind it holds an occasional trophy trout. Generally, the *Delayed Harvest* fishing all the way up to the golf course at the *Shulls Mill Bridge* is usually productive and worth your time. In the off season, there are plenty of large holdovers if you are patient.

About .4 miles above the second *Delayed Harvest* stretch ending at the Shulls Mill Bridge, *Boone Fork*, which is the third fishable tributary enters river left. This is the same *Boone Fork* that crosses the Parkway at MP 299.9, and it is my favorite Watauga tributary. Above the *Boone Fork's* confluence, the river re-enters private land for the next 1.2 miles up to the Hwy 1580 bridge in Foscoe. At about 15' to 20' across, the river gets smaller here. There are lots of trout – but access sucks!

The remaining 5.3 miles above Hwy 1580 up to its source at *Tynecastle*, the Watauga is managed as *Wild Trout Waters*. Along this stretch the river closes in and gets smaller and shallower with slower flows and mostly pocket water. The occasional small run and riffle feature all tend to hold trout. This stretch is characterized by a cobble / rocky bed, relatively wide banks that have been scourged by flooding, and the canopies are wide open most of the way up.

About .5 miles above Hwy 1580 is the Watauga's fourth fishable tributary – *Moody Mill Creek*. This creek is small but does offer some fishing opportunities. Unfortunately, all of it is along private land too. On up at about 3.9 miles above Foscoe is *Green Ridge Branch*. This is the first sizeable and fishable tributary entering the Watauga below its source. Access is limited, but there are stretches in its headwaters you can fish and not get shot at. Much of the Watauga's upper stretches are flowing through commercial / residential property – yet many stretches are not posted with signs. All along the main flow, as well as the tributaries, there are lots of wild trout to chase. Some of the most colorful and feisty browns I have caught have been in these small waters.

Approaching the source the river is very tight and overgrown. But it still holds fish all the way up. I never fail to catch lots of small bows and browns in the 4" to 8" range, as well as an occasional spec. At 12.8 miles above *Valle Crucis*, you reach the source of the Watauga flowing out from under Hwy 105. From source to mouth, by the time it reaches *Valle Crucis*, it has flowed through golf courses, gated communities, townships, trailer parks, camp grounds, horse farms, dams, two delayed harvest sections and crossed by bridges no less than seventeen times.

Watauga River Tributaries

Boone Fork
A Watauga River Tributary

At a Glance

Sam's Rank: 👍👍👍👍👍
GPS Fixes:
- Source fix: N36 07.024 W81 48.129 @ 4,835'
- Mouth fix: N36 10.122 W81 44.846 @ 2,925'

Size: medium at mouth (At *its confluence with the Watauga*)
Gradient: flat 4.4% source to mouth average (*8.3 miles / 1,910'*)
Effort: moderate to difficult
Pressure: slight to moderate
Fishing Quality: good
Species: Rainbows, Browns & Specs
Access: I've divided the creek into four sections to make describing it easier. The first 1.2 miles of private water from the mouth on the Watauga up to Bee Tree Creek is the "*Lower Section*" - I'm skipping it altogether. The next 2.3 miles from Bee Tree Creek up to the dam at Price Lake on the Parkway will be the "*Mid Section*." The next 2 miles from the Price Lake dam, up to and through Sweet Grass Lake and on up to Hwy 1559 will be the *Upper Section*" - I'm skipping it too. Finally, the 2.7 miles from Hwy 1559 up to its source above the Parkway will be the "*Headwater Section*."

~ To access the *Headwater Section's* source fix, go to the bridge crossing Boone Fork at about MP 299.9 on the Parkway. The source fix is about 1.2 miles upstream. Park in the improved parking lot about 75 yards north - upstream access is by unimproved trails.

Access to the *Headwater Section's* bottom fix can be had by heading south on Hwy 1559 from the Parkway for about .5 miles to the creek.

~ To access to the *Mid Section*, go to MP 296.5 on the Parkway and park in the Julian Price Memorial Park parking area just behind the dam. The flow coming out of the dam represents the upper fix of the Mid Section. Several trails lead from the parking area for the 2.3 miles down to Bee Tree Creek and the Mid Section's bottom fix.

Overview & Description

I mentioned earlier that the Boone is my favorite Watauga tributary. The main reason is that I just like the name "*Boone*" because it reminds me of Fess Parker – and it fishes well too. It's also unique in that it is the only Watauga tributary that actually sources near the Parkway and then crosses it twice before heading north to join the Watauga. The *Headwater* and *Mid Sections* included here are the most public and fishable of its waters. You'd think they are a thousand miles from nowhere – and the fishing is outstanding! Along the other two sections, the creek flows through a

Boone Fork as it goes under the Parkway and begins its long ramble to the Watauga in Foscoe. / *Image by Author / 2015*

convoluted mess of residential / commercial lands, state parks, two warm-water lakes, and even cultivated land.

Boone Fork sources on the eastern side of *Grandfather Mountain Ridge* on the east slope of *Calloway Peak* at about 4,835'. From about 1.2 miles above the Parkway, it starts an 8.3 mile run to its mouth on the Watauga at a flat 4.4% average gradient. But don't be fooled by 4.4%, because the first 1.2 miles above the Parkway is a butt-kicking 14.9% gradient! For the first 4.3 miles of its run, it doesn't pick up a single feeder. But it is impounded twice: first by *Sweet Grass Lake,* and then the larger *Price Lake*. Below Price Lake it does pick up additional flow from several feeders with names like: *Sims Creek, Cannon Branch, Green Branch* and *Bee Tree Creek* – all are small and several offer additional water to fish. Along its 8.3 mile run, it flows through a maze of public / private land, beaver dams and a mix of topographies – all containing trout. At about 2,925' the Boone meets the Watauga just below the community of *Foscoe* on Hwy 105. What follows is a description of the *Mid Section* and *Headwater Section*.

Mid Section: As you hike down the trail from *Price Lake* to *Bee Tree Creek* *(the start of the Mid Section)* and then start upstream, the creek is about 12' – 16' wide and flows out of what looks to be a small gorge. *Bee Tree Creek*, entering creek right is small and marginally fishable in my opinion – especially in dry weather. Moving upstream over the next .6 miles, Boone is a mix of huge boulders and slabs that create large pools and runs. It also has a mild gradient, wide banks and open canopies. I've caught all three species of trout in this stretch – mostly in the 6" to 10" range. It's hard going just getting around and over the huge rocks.

At about .6 miles up, *Cannon Branch* enters creek left. This feeder is a bit bigger and sources about 1.5 miles up the mountain. About halfway down that mountain, it's impounded in a pond. I found it to fish well over the first .5 miles. The next .7 miles above *Cannon,* Boone first continues through a rugged boulder field and slide stretch with large and deep pools and pocket waters. Along here the river is a roaring cascade, thundering through a garden of cracked granite boulders. It's beautiful and the fishing is hard and often dangerous, but productive.

Above the gorge, Boone flows through a relatively flat landscape. There it becomes placid and flows through floodplains that can be covered with wildflowers in the summer months. Taking up residence along here is a rather aggressive pack of sharp toothed beavers that have created a series of ponds. The creek is wide, silted and somewhat void of a canopy. The dams come and go, so the fishing is different each time. Generally, fishing is difficult because of the flat and slow pools.

Green Branch enters creek left about .7 miles above *Cannon* - just above beaver town. It's small and not worthwhile in my opinion - beavers have invaded it too. Although most of the feeders don't offer great trout fishing, they do add cold water which helps the Boone to support trout habitat in its lower stretches.

The .6 miles upstream from *Cannon Branch* to *Sims Creek* is about 10' – 12' wide, shallow, silted and wide open in many areas - possibly from past beaver activity. There are few in-stream features to add character to this stretch, and siltation is evident on the creek bed and the banks are wide. Although this section is *Hatchery Supported*, it's not what I call the best trout habitat. I avoid it for the better water downstream. This "*park*" stretch, all the way up to the dam, can get danged crazy with hoards of people in warm months. I've even seen naked female wood fairies along here too – *needless to say that can, and does, lead to trouble!*

When you reach *Sims Creek* on the left, it's the largest feeder in the *Mid Section*. From its source, it flows over a mild gradient for about 2 miles. Then it is impounded in a pond, has beaver issues as well, and crosses the Parkway twice before joining the Boone below *Price Lake*. I've fished several stretches of *Sims* near its mouth and along the Parkway below the impoundment and caught a nice mix of all three trout.

The .4 miles from *Sims Creek* to the end of the Mid Section at the dam has not made my "*Got to Fish*" bucket list. Water temps, crowds, picnickers and stocked trout are not my thing. All in all, the lower stretches are my favorite. You just have to be willing to make the hike and tolerate beavers. This section is *Hatchery Supported* and managed as *Catch & Release*.

Headwater Section: I like this section of the Boone because it's managed as *Wild Trout Waters*, and it's secluded and easy to access and fish. The first .8 miles upstream from the start of the *Headwater Section* at Hwy 1559 and up to Hwy 1561 is private. However, most is not posted with signage and is flowing through forested land or pastures. Along this stretch the creek is about 8' to 10' wide, very shallow with lots of deadfalls, medium-sized boulders and rocks and the short runs, ripples and pool features you expect from a headwater. Some years ago I asked for and received permission to fish this stretch. I was rewarded with an eighteen fish day that included all three species - all in the 8" to 10" range.

Just .1 miles above Hwy 1561 the creek enters the Parkway's right-of-way, and then parallels it for the next .7 miles upstream until it reaches the Parkway Bridge. *Along that stretch the creek is absolutely beautiful!* Along there it's about 8' to 12' wide, plenty of pools, relatively shallow, and has a mild 6.7% gradient. It is littered with many boulders from Parkway construction - so much so that in places the creek disappears into the rocks, then re-appears in large pools and runs. Bows, browns and specs inhabit this water. Wading and casting is easy.

As you get above the Parkway bridge, the creek makes a steep 14.9% gradient uphill run to its source 1.2 miles up. I've only fished the first .5 miles above the Parkway using the trails for access. Along that stretch the creek opens up wider than you'd expect, and has the same scourged bank features from the flooding that most of these high elevation creeks have. As with the stretches below, it's mostly pocket water fishing for the small 6" to 8" bows and specs that hang there.

Laurel Fork
A Watauga River Tributary

At a Glance

Sam's Rank: 👍👍👍
GPS Fixes:
- Source fix: N36 11.190 W81 43.168 @ 3,665'
- Mouth fix: N36 11.678 W81 44.737 @ 2,750'

Size: small at mouth *(At its confluence with the Watauga)*
Gradient: flat 3.6% source to mouth average *(4.8 miles / 915')*
Effort: moderate
Pressure: none to slight
Fishing Quality: average

Species: Rainbows & Browns

Access: To get to its mouth: go to the intersection of Hwy 105 and Hwy 1112. Laurel Fork enters the Watauga just a few yards below the bridge on Hwy 105 – river left. Parking is tight along the road.

To get to its headwaters and source: from the intersection of Hwy 105 and Hwy 1112, head towards Boone on Hwy 105 for about 2.7 miles to Hwy 1557 on the right. Turn right and follow the road which roughly follows Laurel Fork for about 1.6 miles up close to the source. Parking is anywhere along the road.

Overview & Description

As a *Hatchery Supported* stream, the only part of Laurel that I consider productive is its lower stretches. So I'm including just the first 2.2 miles from Hwy 105 towards Boone, to just behind the concrete plant and quarry across the road. Rainbows seem to dominate this creek, and there's a good population of them each time I've fished it. Above the concrete plant, the creek gets small and is surrounded by private land and developments. Interestingly, none of its feeders seem large enough or accessible enough to waste time messing with. So… focus on the first 2.2 miles. It even has a fly shop within yards of its mouth.

Laurel Creek scrambles out of the valley at *Poplar Grove* from about 3,665' and flows at a slow speed for about 4.8 miles at a flat 3.6% gradient. Along the way, it picks up volume from a few feeders, with *Upper Laurel Fork* being the only one of any real size – even though it's very small too. There are other feeders, some being piped under large developments. Laurel converges with the Watauga at about 2,750'.

The Author fording the Watauga just above Valle Crucis - no snorkel needed. / *Image taken by a bystander.* / 2019

Moving upstream from its mouth, Laurel is about 8' to 10' wide and shallow with a nice mix of large rocks, gravel beds and open banks. All the way up to the take out point at 2.2 miles, Laurel has nice runs and small drop pools that make fishing worthwhile. Some of this stretch is posted. At about .9 miles up, *Upper Laurel Fork* enters creek left. Although the flow is marginal, the creek unfortunately takes up residence in back yards and golf courses – so count it out. For the next 1.3 miles upstream the creek gets smaller still, but the low gradient and adequate flows keeps the fishing easy for the bows and occasional browns you'll catch. I've fished the creek five or six times and caught trout in the 5" – 8" range. I've not fished above 2.2 miles.

This creek is definitely fun to fish if you like small streams in urban / commercial settings. Besides, where else can you hear a dynamite charge go off in a quarry across the road when you're standing in a trout stream?

Dutch Creek
A Watauga River Tributary
At A Glance

Sam's Rank: 👍👍👍
GPS Fixes:
- Source fix: N36 09.447 W81 49.042 @ 4,160'
- Mouth fix: N36 12.991 W81 47.165 @ 2,655'

Size: small at mouth *(At its confluence with the Watauga)*
Gradient: flat .5% source to mouth average *(5.6 miles / 1,505')*
Effort: easy to moderate
Pressure: none to slight
Fishing Quality: fair to average
Species: Rainbows & Browns
Access: To get to its mouth: from the intersection of Hwy 194 and Hwy 1112 in Valle Crucis, continue north on Hwy 194 about .7 miles to the bridge crossing the Watauga. Dutch Creek flows in from the right at the bridge where it joins the Watauga. Parking is along the road.

To get to its headwaters and source: from the intersection of Hwy 194 and Hwy 1112 in Valle Crucis, head south on Hwy 194 for about .7 miles to where the road reaches the open valley in front of the Valle Crucis Conference Center and Holy Cross Episcopal Church. Bear right and continue about .5 miles to Hwy 1134 *(Dutch Creek Road)* on left. Take Hwy 1134 for about 2.8 miles to just below Dutch's source – which is about .7 miles upstream. Parking is along the road.

Overview & Description

The first time I fished Dutch Creek back in 1999, I was wearing a Scottish Kilt. At the time I was attending a week long bag piping school at the *North American Academy of Piping and Drumming*, held each year at the *Valle Crucis Conference Center*. After classes one day I decided that since I was in trout country I should go chase trout. So, being the good Scotsman I am, I slipped into my kilt, Columbia PFG shirt, wading boots, grabbed my 7' / 3w Granger bamboo, and headed out to Dutch Creek in front of the conference center. It was a magical time fishing up that creek and catching little rainbows and an occasional brown. All the while, the majestic sound of bagpipes was drifting out from the hills above me. Every trout I caught that day seemed appreciative of the pipe music and being caught by such a gentlemanly and stylish angler. Yet I've never even gotten one thank you card from any of them. Next time I'll keep a few and eat them! It was a great experience and one I have not since fully replicated – although I've tried on several occasions.

Dutch Creek comes out of the valley between *White Rock* and *Hanging Rock Ridge* just west of *Valle Crucis* from about 4,160'. From there it starts a 5.6 mile run to its mouth on the Watauga at a flat .5% average gradient. Along that run, it passes through forest land, at least one big waterfall, open valleys, cow pastures, Mast General Store, and residential developments. Nearly all of it is on private land, although most is not posted. It receives added volume from three feeders – *Pigeonroost Creek, Clark Creek* and *Crab Orchard Creek.* All are small, but two offer some additional fishing, although access can be problematic. Along the entire 5.6 mile run it is shadowed by Hwy 194 and Hwy 1134. At about 2,655' it meets the Watauga about .7 miles below *Valle Crucis* at the Hwy 194 Bridge.

Moving upstream from its mouth, the creek flows for about a mile through the flat pastureland behind *Mast General Store* and along the *Valle Crucis Community Park.* The creek is 10' to 12' wide along here with lots of siltation and few features to break up its flow. It's picturesque, but I've not caught a lot of trout along there. When it reaches the intersection of Hwy 194 and Hwy 1112, it begins tracking southwesterly along Hwy 194 for about .7 miles to where Hwy 1136 comes in from the left at the valley in front of the *Valle Crucis Conference Center.*

At this point *Crab Orchard Creek* enters creek right. This is a fishable feeder and is followed by Hwy 192 and then Hwy 1152 for some distance up the mountain. It holds small bows as far as I can tell. On up Dutch's main flow another .2 miles from the bridge on Hwy 1136, *Clark Creek* enters creek left in the middle of the valley. This creek is small but somewhat fishable along several stretches. Simply follow Hwy 1136 which will zigzag it up to near its source. I've not fished it but the locals told me it has small bows and browns.

About .5 miles up from where *Clark Creek* enters, *Dutch* goes under the Hwy 1134 bridge at the west end of the valley. For the next 3.3 miles up to its source, the creek is easy to track along Hwy 1134 through mostly private land. Above the bridge the creek starts to get very tight, shallow and small - about 6' to 8' across at best. However, it begins to take on some character and structure you'd expect from a mountain creek – typical pocket water and an occasional run and pool. I've caught bows and browns mostly in the 5" to 8" range. Dutch is managed as a *Hatchery Supported* stream, not great trout fishing, but it is trout fishing…

Middle Fork
/ *South Fork of the New River*
At a Glance

Sam's Rank: 👍👍👍
GPS Fixes:
- Source fix: N36 08.077 W81 39.248 @ 3,675'
- Mouth fix: N36 12.245 W81 38.995 @ 3,110'

Size: small at mouth *(In Boone as it joins the South Fork)*
Gradient: flat 1.1% source to mouth average *(9.6 miles / 565')*
Effort: easy to moderate
Pressure: moderate to heavy
Fishing Quality: fair to average
Species: Bows, Browns & Brook Trout
Access: I'm including only the lower 6.2 miles of the Middle Fork that runs from the Parkway northward to where it meets the East Fork to form the South Fork of the New River in Boone. Access along the river's first 5.5 miles north above the Parkway to Boone is via Hwy 221 as well as the finished sections of the Boone Greenway Trail. Both parallel the river most of the way except the last .9 miles to its mouth. Closer access for that last .9 miles is via Deerfield Road.

Overview & Description

The Middle Fork is a 9.6 mile long headwater of the South Fork of the New River. It actually flows under the Parkway, is *Hatchery Supported*, and has decent access via road and the *Boone Greenway Trail*. Those are the reasons the Middle Fork made it into this Guide – not necessarily because it's a *"great"* troutery.

After the Middle Fork and the *East Fork* converge in Boone to form the South Fork, the South Fork meanders on a northeasterly trajectory for another 89.2 miles through *Watauga* and *Ashe County*. It eventually joins the *North Fork of the New River* to form the *New River (proper)* in northern Ashe County. The New River is reportedly one of the oldest rivers in the world. But I can't vouch for that – they all look old to me. I don't know how anyone could possibly know that for sure. Besides, if it was that old, why would it be named New River? You can't make this stuff up!

The Middle Fork is old as well, but it has several *"modern"* issues. *First*, it's short, small, and sources in highly-urbanized Blowing Rock. Then, it flows north into Boone which is another highly-urbanized area. Both towns have golf courses, private / public land, multiple lakes, dams, roads, neighborhoods, etc. *Second*, as a result of its environment, the first 3.4 miles of its headwaters in Blowing Rock are actually considered impaired water by the *North Carolina Department of Environmental Quality / Division of Water Resources*. The impaired title is given to waters that are too *polluted* or *degraded* to meet the strict water quality standards outlined in *Section 303(d) of the Clean Water Act*. This 3.4 mile stretch of "*impaired*" water runs from its source to 1.2 miles below *Chetola Lake* at *Sumpter Cabin Creek* near the intersection of US-321 / Edmisten Road. Fortunately, the river is now being managed under a strict plan to return it to acceptable quality standards.

Now don't get all worked up over this impaired thing – there's a silver lining. The 6.2 miles of water *below* the impaired headwaters up to Boone is in relatively good shape in terms of water quality, hatchery supported trout populations and fishability. My crooked lawyer neighbor Bill just suggested I make sure you knew all the negatives in case you caught a trout with three eyes, or ate enough of them to develop brain cancer, or form a third eye of your own. Whatever…

The Middle Fork sources at about 3,675' on a small farm in east Blowing Rock just off the Parkway. It quickly enters a residential area, and then moves on through the *Blowing Rock Country Club* golf course. From its source, it begins a 9.6 miles flow to the *South Fork of the New River* in Boone at a tame 1.1% gradient. Along that run, it receives additional volume from several feeders with names like *Flat Top Branch, Penley Branch, Sumpter Cabin Creek, Payne Branch* and *Aho Branch* – most are marginally fishable. At about 2,655', the river reaches Boone and the end of its 9.6 mile run through a highly-urbanized watershed. In Boone it meets the *East Fork* and *Winkler Creek* and forms the *South Fork of the New River*.

Moving upstream from the Middle Fork's mouth at the *Boone Golf Course* and *Watauga Recreational Complex IV*, the first .8 miles is along the golf course, a small farm and other urban structures until it goes under Hwy 221. Along that stretch the river is about 20' to 25', sandy, shallow and with few in-stream features. Much of it is highly silted from development and with minimal riparian protection. Not until just before going under Hwy 221 does it gain more riparian buffering. I've not found the initial .8 mile stretch to that productive. But then watching some of the ASU co-ed golfers along there can sure make up for it.

Moving upriver from the Hwy 221 bridge, the river changes and starts to look more like a mountain river with the typical large rocks, ledges, undercut banks and occasional long runs. It arches away from the road and enters a more rural / pastoral stretch for a short distance. I have found the fishing in this stretch pretty good for the *Hatchery Supported* trout that hang out there. As the river returns to Hwy 221 about 1.4 miles up, it gets even more rugged with large boulders and pools where trout tend to accumulate. Along that stretch, the river has constricted to about 15' to 20' with many deeper pools and runs. I have caught respectable quantities of 12" bows and browns along this stretch over the years.

Remains of the power plant dam built in 1923 just below Payne Branch. The fishing below the dam always seems to be better than above it. / *Image by Author / 2013*

At about 1.7 miles upstream from the mouth are the remains of a decommissioned power dam. In 1923, the *Appalachian Training School*, the forerunner of *Appalachian State University (ASU)*, purchased land at the confluence of *Payne Branch* and the *Middle Fork* from the Shore and Tate families. There they built a 26' concrete dam to harness the river to generate electricity for the school. The *South Fork Dam* as it was called *(even though it's on the Middle Fork)*, and its power station lit up the school, as well as the town of Boone. A major flood in 1940 destroyed the dam which was quickly rebuilt and operated until 1972. After the dam's retirement, *New River Light & Power* dynamited holes in it to set the river free again. The structure was so sturdy that it was only partially destroyed, and its remnants are visible today. The dam's pool is silted in for the most part, but I have found lots of fishing opportunities above and below the dam's ruins. A *Facilities Use Agreement* between *ASU* and *Watauga County* allowed the *Middle Fork Greenway Association* to create a park above the dam. On October 2, 2005 it was dedicated *Payne Branch Park.*

Above the dam, at about 2 miles up from the mouth, *Payne Branch* enters river right. This small branch sources about 1.1 miles up and does hold a population of rainbows that are worth the diversion to chase. I found them to be in the 6" to 8" range. Access is good along its entire length. Just be mindful of posted water.

For the next 2.8 miles up to *Aho Branch*, the river closely shadows Hwy 221, crisscrossing it at least three times and passing in front of the *Tweetsie Railroad*, developments and open pastures - all with minimal riparian protection. Along here, it constricts to about 15' in most places and is shallow and flat with minimal in-stream features. Nonetheless, hungry *Hatchery Supported* trout hold there and are easy to find and toss a fly to. Most of what I have caught along this stretch was in the 8" – 12" range.

At 4.8 miles up, *Aho Branch* enters river left at a small park. This stream flows down from about 2.5 miles over private land and is a marginal trout habitat. It has

a lot of siltation from residential and agricultural use. However, its confluence with Middle Fork is a place trout like to hang out – as well as a place where locals feed them corn and worms. I usually fish through to the Parkway and the less congested waters above the park. Occasionally, I stop at the park and play pitiful in order to poach food and drink from curious tourists.

This Rainbow caught below the dam appears to be actually watching me remove the fly. / *Image by Author / 2011*

For the next 1.4 miles up to the Parkway, the river continues to parallel Hwy 221 except one short stretch where it loops along *Roaring River Drive*. Along this stretch, the river is getting smaller and is only about 10' across and relatively shallow. There are several runs with nice drop pools, riffles and undercut banks along the road that hold trout.

At 6 miles up, *Sumpter Cabin Creek* enters river right. This small creek, only 6' to 8' wide, comes down from about 1.3 miles above through mostly private land. It is paralleled with roads most of the way. There are some stretches along the road that actually hold small 6" trout in the mid and upper reaches. Be sure you mind the posted signs.

At 6.2 miles from Boone, the Middle Fork flows from under the Parkway after escaping the *Chetola Lake* dam in *Blowing Rock*. I usually stop fishing here and go drink and smoke cigars in *Blowing Rock*. All in all, Middle Fork's main run is a fun river to fish. But if you want to fish on up into the *"impaired waters"* of the headwaters and possibly catch a trout with three eyes, knock yourself out!

Laurel Creek

At a Glance

Sam's Rank: 👍👍👍👍

GPS Fixes:
- Source fix: N36 10.643 W81 32.375 @ 2,000'
- Mouth fix: N36 09.741 W81 30.155 @ 1,410'

Size: medium at mouth *(As it joins Elk Creek)*

Gradient: flat 3.4% source to mouth average *(3.3 miles / 590')*

Effort: moderate to difficult

Pressure: none to slight

Fishing Quality: good to excellent

Species: Bows & Browns

Access: From the intersection of Hwy 221 / Hwy 421 in downtown Boone, take old Hwy 221 east *(not the new four-lane highway)* for about 5.6 miles until you start to parallel the Parkway. Hwy 1508 will cross old Hwy 221 along there. Take the right onto Hwy 1508, go under the Parkway and continue on for about 8.4 miles until you cross Laurel Creek as it dumps into Elk Creek. As you reach the valley floor, you'll parallel Elk Creek. Park anywhere off private property.

Overview & Description

Laurel Creek looks to be the largest *"upper"* tributary of the much bigger and longer Elk Creek – which flows for more than 21 miles before joining the Yadkin River west of Wilkesboro. It flows through a mini-gorge with surrounding peaks towering 300' to 500' above in places. It's remote and wild, and you won't see another angler on it or its two headwater creeks while you're there. As far as I can tell, it can only be accessed with unimproved trails, bushwhacking and wading. Perhaps that's why Laurel is overlooked by most people in favor of the bigger and easier to access Elk Creek. But I consider it a gem of a trout creek – albeit somewhat difficult to get on and off.

Elk Creek on the other hand, flows through a highly-populated valley and is very accessible. Elk's upper and mid sections are popular fishing venues and offer both *Hatchery Supported* and *Delayed Harvest* sections. It flows through some beautiful topography that has become highly developed over the past 25 years into home sites and *"farmlets."* It offers a maze of tributaries and headwaters to fish – you just have to be careful of the posted land.

Laurel's source is the result of two headwater streams - *North Fork* and *South Fork*. Both seep out of the mountain and flow to their convergence point at a mild gradient. Neither receives volume from any sizeable feeders. At about 2,000', just south of *Poor Knob*, they join and form Laurel Creek's source.

Laurel approaching the bridge on Hwy 1508 above its mouth on Elk Creek. / *Image by Author / 2011*

From that source point, Laurel begins its 3.3 mile flow at a flat 3.4% average gradient down to Elk Creek along the north side of *Ben's Ridge*. Along the way, it picks up volume from a handful of feeders. The larger ones include *Flat Branch, Pine Knob Branch* and *Puncheon Cove. (Some maps refer to this creek as Level Fork)*. At about 1,410' Laurel meets Elk Creek about 300' east of Hwy 1508 between two home sites - one with a big dog that bites first and asks questions later.

Heading upstream from its mouth, Laurel is about 15' wide as you leave the bridge and enter the gorge. Along that first 1.4 miles, the ridges on the sides will get steeper, but the creek maintains its width and has relatively open canopies. Huge boulders, slabs and ledges litter the creek bed and create drop pools, runs, slides and riffles that all hold trout. The water volume was been low each time I have fished it, but the boulders and drop pools create some unusually large and deep pocket waters that definitely hold trout even in times of drought.

At about 1.4 miles up, *Flat Branch* enters creek left. And just beyond, that at about 1.5 miles, *Pine Knob Branch* enters on the left. Of the two, only *Flat Branch* is even close to the size that offers productive fishing. I'm sure both might have some good pocket water, but I have not fished them. I like the lower 1.5 mile stretch of Laurel and believe it offers the best fishing of the entire flow. Most of what I have caught along this stretch were wild bows and browns in the 6" to 9" range – respectful for a low-elevation, low-flow creek.

The next 1.8 miles up to Laurel's source has the same basic structure as the first 1.5 miles, just smaller and tighter. It's still wide enough at 8' to 10' to make for easy casting and wading between the pockets holding fish. Just be prepared for rock hopping, bushwhacking and negotiating some huge boulders, slabs and slides - the trails are rugged too. At about 2.1 miles, *Puncheon Cove* flows in creek left. This flow looks fishable although I haven't tried it yet. On up at about 3.3 miles above its mouth on Elk Creek, Laurel reaches the convergence of its two headwater creeks. Most of my catch along this upper stretch below the source were rainbows and browns in the 6" – 8" range. This creek can be fished in a hard day, and it is well worth the effort to do so. *Its headwaters are a different story!*

Laurel Creek Tributaries

North Fork & South Fork
The Two Laurel Creek Headwaters

At a Glance

Sam's Rank: 👍👍👍👍

GPS Fixes:
- North Fork's source fix: N36 10.733 W81 34.382 @ 2,780'
- South Fork's source fix: N36 09.670 W81 35.017 @ 3,055'
- Mouth fix for both: N36 10.643 W81 32.375 @ 2,000'

Size: both are small at their mouths

Gradient:
- North Fork: mild 6.4% source to mouth average *(2.3 miles / 780')*
- South Fork: mild 6.4% source to mouth average *(3.1miles / 1,055')*

Effort: both – moderate to difficult

Pressure: both – none

Fishing Quality: both – average to good

Species: Bows & Browns

Access: There are probably easier access points if you study maps and figure it out. But the only way I know is to hike up Laurel Creek to the mouth fix of both headwater creeks. From the intersection of Hwy 221 / Hwy 421 in Boone, take old Hwy 221 east *(not the new four-lane highway)* for about 5.6 miles until you start to parallel the Parkway. Hwy 1508 will cross old Hwy 221 along there. Take the right onto Hwy 1508, go under the Parkway, and continue on for about 8.4 miles until you cross Laurel Creek. Hike up from there to the confluence of both creeks.

Overview & Description

Both of these small and rugged headwaters begin their flow at a relatively low elevation. Other than in name and length, they're darn near identical in gradient, structure, size, difficulty level, trout species and access. Neither is followed by improved trails - but both offer some worthwhile trout fishing.

North Fork sources at about 2,780' between *Poor Knob* and *Tar Ridge*. From there it begins a 2.3 mile run at a mild 6.4% gradient. Along the way it picks up

A Brown caught on the North Fork, one of Laurel Creek's two headwater creeks. / *Image by Author / 2013*

more flow from *Bee Branch* and *Bearpen Branch* – neither one is of any significant size. At about 2,000', it converges with *South Fork* to form Laurel Creek's source.

Its slightly larger and longer twin, the *South Fork*, seeps out at about 3,055' between *Tar Ridge* and *Mast Knob* and runs for 3.1 miles to its mouth at the same 6.4% mild gradient as the *North Fork*. It receives no additional significant flow volume along the way. It joins the *North Fork* at about 2000'.

I've fished the South and North Forks several times and caught rainbows and a few browns in the 6" to 8" range. I fished up *North Fork* about .6 miles. About .7 miles up it flows through a remote home / farm compound that restricts access to the higher reaches unless you are able to drop in from the maze of roads that runs the area's ridges. I've fished about 1.5 miles up the *South Fork*. It has no development or barriers along its entire flow. Both of these streams have rocky beds and numerous pools and runs all the way up. And they both eventually get smaller and tighter. You will be climbing and bushwhacking to the runs and pools that hold trout.

Stony Fork
The Hatchery Supported Stretch
At a Glance

Sam's Rank: 👍👍👍

GPS Fixes: Just the 1.5 mile hatchery supported stretch.
- Source fix: N36 13.619 W81 29.843 @ 2,115'
- Mouth fix: N36 11.263 W81 27.950 @ 2,000'

Size: small

Gradient: flat 1.5% average for entire section *(1.5 miles /115')*

Effort: easy

Pressure: none to slight

Fishing Quality: average to good

Species: Bows, Browns & Brooks

Access: Stony's Hatchery Supported stretch can be reached from MP 276.5 on the Parkway by taking Hwy 421 south for about 2.5 miles to Hwy 1500 *(Mt. Zion Road)* on the right. Turn right and at about .7 miles you will cross Stony Fork coming from the right. Hayes Welburn Road also comes from the right and offers upstream access to Stony's source. From where Mt. Zion Rd. crosses Stony, it continues to parallel it for most of the 1.5 miles of the Hatchery Supported stretch, and then turns into Flowers Branch Road just before the Wilkes Co. line. Much of this water is private, but is open for fishing. Park anywhere away from traffic.

Overview & Description

Although Stony Fork flows over 16 miles from its source just under the Parkway to its mouth on the Yadkin River, only the 1.5 mile *Hatchery Supported* section of its headwaters is included here. There are several reasons for this. *First*, the upper *Hatchery Supported* stretch is higher elevation, mostly forested, close to the Parkway, and easy to get to. *Second*, the middle section flows through forested areas and has good elevations, and probably has trout – but I haven't fished it. *Third*, the lower stretch flows through developments / agricultural lands, and low elevations *(just over 1,000')* not typically considered good for a trout fishery.

Stony sources from about 2,900' just under *Deep Gap* on the Parkway about 2.5 miles north of the *Hatchery Supported* stretch. It flows down the west slope of *Ivy Point Ridge* and picks up more water from several feeders before it reaches the *Hatchery Supported* stretch at 2,115'. Stony is about 10' – 12' across and shallow at the start of the *Hatchery Supported* stretch. Over the next 1.5 miles, it flows at a flat 1.5% gradient. By the time it reaches the end of the supported stretch, it has picked up more volume from two feeders – one that's as big as it is and fishable, the other not so fishable. At 2,000' at the end of the supported stretch at the *Wilkes Co. line*, it has turned into a respectable trout creek worth fishing. From the county line, it continues another 12.3 miles to its mouth on the *Yadkin River.*

Moving upstream along Hwy 1500 / Flowers Branch Road *(just above the Wilkes Co. line)* from the bottom of the *Hatchery Supported* section, the creek flows beside the road under a forest canopy. Along the first .5 miles the creek is about 15' – 20' wide, relatively shallow and has some waterfalls and pools. Assorted sizes of rocks litter the bed to break up the flow, and numerous riffles and long flat runs offer trout places to hold and feed. The fishing is good along this forested stretch, and on two occasions, I've had twenty trout mornings. About .3 miles into this initial stretch, *Flowers Branch* enters creek left - not worth much time and effort.

Stony emerging from under the Hwy 1500 bridge and beginning its Delayed Harvest run. / *Image by Author / 2013*

About .5 miles up, the creek breaks away from the road, leaves the forest and enters pastures - complete with cows and one bull with a bad ass attitude. Forget the pit bull barking at the house nearby, it's the dang bull you can't turn your back on! Along this .3 mile *"high alert"* stretch you're fishing in open pasture with cows.

At about .8 miles up, the creek rejoins the road and flows under forest canopy for the next .4 miles. The creek's personality here is much the same as below – and it fishes about the same. As mentioned before, much of this water is on private land that is not posted and seems to be open for fishing. In either event, I've never had anyone get after me except for that one attack bull.

Over the next .4 miles, the creek goes in and out of forest/pasture land and has the same features and fishing qualities as the water below. About 1.4 miles up another *"no name"* feeder enters creek right. Just past *"no name,"* Stony veers left and at 1.5 miles above the county line goes under the Hwy 1500 bridge – the end of *Hatchery Support.* From there Stony continues another 2.5 miles to its source.

Section IV

63 miles

MP 280 *(just south of EB Jeffress Park)* to MP 217 *(the NC / VA state line)*

This section starts with the Parkway running along the steep, high-elevation ridges from just above Deep Gap at EB Jefferies Park, all the way to the NC/VA state line. However, along the final 17 miles or so of this section, the Parkway dives off of those high ridges above *Thurmond Chatham Wildlife Management Area, Doughton Recreation Area* and *Stone Mountain State Park*, and begins its final run to the state line at well below 3,000' in most places. Section IV is unique among the other four sections in that it has a mix of large and small watersheds sourcing in the higher elevations, as well as several that source in lower elevations and run along beside the Parkway for quite a distance. Most all of the water is along the steep slopes south of the Parkway.

www.wildbearings.com will have *lodging, campsite, outfitter, restaurant* and *brewery* recommendations to help plan your trip along this Section of the Parkway.

Fall Creek

At a Glance

Sam's Rank: 👍👍👍
GPS Fixes:
- Source fix: N36 14.813 W81 28.165 @ 3,680'
- Mouth fix: N36 11.810 W81 25.678 @ 1,480'

Size: Small at mouth *(As it joins the South Prong of Lewis Creek)*
Gradient: Mild 6.6% source to mouth average *(6.3 miles / 2,200')*
Effort: moderate to difficult
Pressure: none to slight
Fishing Quality: average to good
Species: Bow, Brown & Brook
Access: The mouth of Fall Creek, which is on the South Prong of Lewis Creek along Hwy 421, can be reached from MP 276.5 on the Parkway. Take Hwy 421 south for about 4.9 miles to Hwy 1301 *(Fall Creek Road)* on the left. Hwy 1301 tracks up the creek for about 2.7 miles. The creek then flows away from the road for the next mile or so. At several points the road / creek elevations can become extreme. At 2.7 miles, Hwy 1301 connects with Hwy 1300 *(Summit Road)*. This road crosses Fall Creek another .9 miles up. From that point, the creek is accessible only by trail or bushwhacking. Parking is wherever you can find it. At about MP 274.7 on the Parkway, a trail leads up the creek from the overlook to its source.

Overview & Description

Fall Creek is a worthwhile little 6.3 mile long *Hatchery Supported* trout stream that is really easy to get to from the Parkway – in fact the Parkway crosses its headwaters. It is a headwater creek of the *South Prong of Lewis Creek* – another *Hatchery Supported* fishery. The unusual thing about this creek is that it is fed by at least three feeders – none of which have formal names that I have been able to confirm. This is unique among rivers, streams and creeks in this part of the country. As far as I can tell from official USGS maps and websites, no names were ever assigned. Apparently, the locals take exception to this...

One day I was chatting with an old codger who runs one of the local gas stations, and I mentioned the *"no name"* issue to him. He spit a load of chewing tobacco into the Coke bottle he was holding, paused a few seconds, and then asked where I had been fishing. I told him, and he then said; *"Well hell boy, everybody knows that there's Intercourse Prong."* I didn't know whether to believe him or run – and I sure as heck didn't want to ask any follow-up questions such as how'd it get that name, etc.? After all, he was spitting into a Coke bottle, and he looked a bit weird. *(My buddy Chris spits tobacco into a Coke bottle too – but he's okay).* So, that was the end of the chat about names – I changed the subject! Nevertheless, rainbow, brown and brook trout live in Fall Creek, and it's worth the effort to fish.

~ Fall Creek ~

Fall Creek's source is about .3 miles north of *Thomkins Knob Overlook* on the Parkway at about 3,680'. After a short run to the culvert under the Parkway at about MP 274, the creek reveals how it most likely got the *"falling"* part of its name. Over the next one mile, it drops more than 1,200' – a gut busting gradient of over 22.2%. Contrast that with the mild average gradient of 6.6% over its entire 6.3 mile run to its mouth on the *South Prong of Lewis Creek*. Along the way, it gets additional water from the three or four *"no name"* feeders mentioned above – with *Intercourse Prong* being the largest, and perhaps my favorite. At least two other feeders look large enough to be marginally fishable –but I haven't fished them. At about 6.3 miles and at 1,480' the creek reaches the culvert going under Hwy 421 and then on to its mouth on the *South Prong of Lewis Creek.*

Moving upstream from Fall Creek's mouth on the South Prong, the first 2.6 miles parallels closely and crisscrosses *Fall River Road.* It passes minimal development and pastureland and flows mostly through forest along the road. The creek along this stretch is littered with large boulders, drop pools and long runs and riffles. At about one mile, its first feeder enters creek left, and it appears to be large enough to fish, but I have not tried it. On up at about 2.5 miles, the creek enters what I'll describe as a *"small"* horseshoe-shaped gorge for about .7 miles. This is the best fishing on the creek in my opinion, and I have caught bows and browns in the 8" – 12" range in there. Just up from the gorge, the second feeder enters from the left at about 2.6 miles. I fished up this no name creek a hundred yards and caught small bows in the 6" - 8" range – in good numbers. All along the first 2.6 miles of the main flow, the gradient is mild and wading is easy. It is about 15' – 20' wide and relatively shallow, and the bed has sufficient large rocks, riffles, long runs and drop pools to support a productive troutery. In several areas the canopy and sides close in a bit. But all in all, this stretch is easy to fish – and productive.

At 2.6 miles up, the creek veers to the right away from the road and into the wild. The road tracks north some distance until it intersects Hwy 1300. For the next 1.3 miles, up to where the creek goes under Hwy 1300, it gets smaller and requires a heightened degree of stealth to continue catching fish. Nearly all of this stretch is pocket water fishing, with frequent pools and ledges providing cover for the trout. At 3.7 miles, the largest feeder, *Intercourse Prong,* per my source, enters creek right. This small *Hatchery Supported* flow continues up until Highway 1300 crosses it. I have not fished it. The .3 mile stretch of Fall Creek beyond *Intercourse* up to Hwy 1300 is not *Hatchery Supported*. This section of Fall Creek, crisscrosses developed and forested land most of the way. I have not found the fishing to be easy or worthwhile along its approach up to Hwy 1300.

The 1.7 miles above Hwy 1300 up to the Parkway, begins in a residential area and numerous pastures. For the first .7 miles, it winds up through an open forest to a point where it begins a steep climb to the Parkway. This is not a Hatchery Supported stretch. Along here the creek is very small, only 5'– 7' wide at best, and a foot or so deep. Since development along here is minimal, the creek's structure and look begins to resemble a mountain stream. And the trout behave as wild trout because they are! No Hatchery Supported fish along here either. Fishing is easy and productive with 6" trout common – bows and specs.

At 4.6 miles up, the creek begins that extreme 22.2% gradient mentioned earlier all the way up

A feisty rainbow caught about 2.5 miles up Fall Creek just as you enter the horseshoe-shaped gorge. / *Image by Author / 2002.*

to the Parkway. Along this upper stretch several cabins sit high up on the ridges looking down on the valley and creek. The fishing along here is reduced to pockets of water that are caught in the ledges and rock formations created by the rugged topography along this stretch of the Parkway. It's hard fishing to say the least. In places, the creek is just a trickle and then it disappears for a bit only to reappear as a vigorous creek cascading from one pool to the next. These pools are loaded with rainbows and specs – mostly in the 5" to 6" range.

Just below the Parkway is *Cascade Falls* where the creek negotiates one of the more extreme elevation changes. This falls looks benevolent, but take it from me; you can royally bust your butt there. *Trust me!* Use one of the trails around the falls to get around it - I wish I had the last time I fished it!

When you reach the Parkway at 5.6 miles, the creek runs under it and on up another .7 miles to its source. The water is very small along here and the foliage thick. I've hiked it, but not tried to fish it. I'm sure at least some small trout live there.

Meadow Fork

At a Glance

Sam's Rank: 👍👍👍
GPS Fixes:
- Source fix: N36 25.838 W81 11.278 @ 3,255'
- Mouth fix: N36 23.826 W81 15.324 @ 2,800'

Size: Medium at mouth *(As it joins Laurel Fork to form Cranberry Creek)*
Gradient: flat 1.8% source to mouth average *(5.7 miles / 555')*
Effort: easy
Pressure: slight to moderate
Fishing Quality: average to good
Species: Bows, Browns & Specs
Access: From MP 248 on the Parkway, take Hwy 18 north. In about 500' you'll cross Meadow Fork. Continue about .7 miles, and a gravel road on the left offers access in about .2 miles to its mouth at the confluence of Meadow Fork and Laurel Fork - the source of Cranberry Creek. Park where you can along the main road.

To get to Meadow's source from MP 248 on the Parkway, take Hwy 18 north for about .1 miles, turn right onto Hwy 1145 and continue about 1.9 miles to where Hwy 1193 enters on the left. Go left on Hwy 1193 about 3 miles to the source – which will be about 200' on the right. Park anywhere you can.

Overview & Description

Meadow Fork's mouth is in the tiny mountain community of Laurel Springs just north of the Parkway. It flows past what the local authorities describe as a couple of *"overactive"* motorcycle resort motels, as well as a campground. It's an all leather crowd with no affinity for bicycle Spandex! During the 2019 Memorial Day weekend, a friend and I were fishing Meadow Fork through Laurel Springs and discovered at least 700 bikers and their *"babes"* were packed into that place celebrating the holiday - and life in general. There was live music all weekend, and bikers were directing traffic on a state road that was almost shut down due to volume. The libations were free flowing and the crowd was having more than a large time. Fortunately, I had my bagpipes in my truck and got adopted by a platoon of Vietnam vets who took me and my friend under their wings and supplied us with food, beer and cigars for as long as I played for their lost comrades. It's the kind of place where a corporate dude needs to be part of a local group to survive. I caught a bunch of wild trout that weekend, but I also saw some unusually wild stuff and lived to tell about it. It was memorable to say the least!

In addition to bikers, Meadow Fork is unique in that it parallels the Parkway for about 2 miles – within sight the entire time. Other bodies of water cross under the Parkway as it matriculates through the mountains, but few actually parallel it for any distance. It has great access, is *Hatchery Supported* with over 1,400 bows, browns and specs annually, and has a flat, medium-sized flow. When you total it up, it's good trout fishing.

Along with *Laurel Fork, Meadow Fork* is one of two headwaters of *Cranberry Creek.* Cranberry is also *Hatchery Supported,* larger, easily accessible, and very popular with the local corn & wiggler, kill & grill crowd, which takes the pressure off the smaller Meadow. Even though Meadow flows mostly through a populated valley, it offers more solitude, wild fish, and a better angling experience than *Cranberry.* I like this creek for those reasons alone.

Meadow Fork sources on the west slope of *Wildcat Rock* just .3 miles west of the

Meadow Fork as it flows beside the Parkway is shrouded in a canopy of trees and bushes. / *Image by Author / 2018*

Parkway at about 3,255'. From there, it begins a 5.7 mile flow down to join *Laurel Springs* at a flat 1.8% average gradient. Along that run, it adds volume from five or six small feeders - none look fishable to me. At about 2,800' it joins *Laurel Fork* to form *Cranberry Creek's* source. From that point, *Cranberry* continues for several miles before joining the very large and long *South Fork of the New River.*

From its mouth at Laurel Springs and heading upstream for the first .7 miles up to Hwy 18, Meadow is about 10' – 12' wide, shallow *(6" to 18")*, flat, sandy and has relatively open sides and canopies. Along that stretch, it passes a Christmas tree farm, gravel dump, campground and the biker motels. This adds up to sketchy fishing at best along this stretch. I've had little luck along here with the exception of a few undercut banks and the Hwy 18 culvert where I coaxed a few bows to come out and suck down a caddis.

From the Hwy 18 Bridge, upstream for the next 2 miles the creek parallels the Parkway through a series of open pastures – complete with row crops, hay fields, cows, sheep, goats, etc. For the most part, the creek is shrouded with trees and bushes. Several stretches offer open casting – but not many. Along this stretch, the creek passes under several bridges and is still about 8' – 10' wide, shallow, flat and sandy. There are not many large boulders, rocks, drop pools and runs. Even so, I like fishing through the pastures. I've had good luck along this stretch dredging deep outside curves, undercut banks and bridge abutments. Several trout were 10" to 14" – all were bow and brown stockers.

As Meadow Fork departs the Parkway, the next three miles to its source is a chain of home sites, farmlets, tree farms, row crops, pastures, etc. Along here the creek has the same basic character as the "*pasture stretch*" below it. But at this location, it's smaller and tighter at about 6' to 8' wide, and due to agricultural usage and development it has a large amount of sand loading on its substrate. Yet wading and casting to the pockets holding fish are easy. Most of what I have caught along

Meadow Fork as it departs the small community of Laurel Springs just above the Parkway, and heads up to its confluence with Cranberry Creek. / *Image by Author / 2018*

this stretch was rainbows and browns in the 6" – 8" range and even an occasional brookie. On up at about 5.7 miles above its mouth, Meadow reaches its source. Appropriately, it sources on one of those domesticated farmlets. Meadow is not like most mountain streams, but it is convenient and fun to fish. And, if you're up to it, the Memorial Day biker crowd can add a bit of *risk* to that fun for you too!

Joshua Creek
Thurmond Chatham WMA Waters Only
At a Glance

Sam's Rank: 👍👍👍
GPS Fixes:
- Source fix: N36 22.366 W81 13.238 @ 2,995'
- Mouth fix: N36 19.883 W81 13.522 @ 1,450'

Size: small at mouth *(As it joins Mulberry Creek)*
Gradient: moderate 9.1% source to mouth average *(3.2 miles / 1,545')*
Effort: moderate to difficult
Pressure: none to slight
Fishing Quality: average
Species: Bows, Browns & Specs
Access: From MP 248 on the Parkway take Hwy 18 south. Continue about 4.3 miles until you reach Hwy 1729 on the left. Turn and go about .3 miles to unmarked Creek Ridge Road *(covered in white gravel)* on the right - this road is gated about .2 miles up. If the gate is closed – park and hike. If open, go about 1.1 miles down to the main flow of Joshua just before the 3-way intersection of Creek Ridge Road / Osborne Road / Joshua Ridge Road. From this intersection you have access to Joshua's entire 1.8 miles of water inside the WMA. Park anywhere.

This access intersects the creek's main flow and several of its feeders about midway up the WMA section. From here, you can fish up or down the entire 1.8 mile flow by using Osborne Road / Trail. *Note:* maps show Osborne Road continuing below the WMA and connecting to Hwy 1728. This would be an easier access point, but I've never found it. A house with a big dog with a mouth full of sharp teeth is sitting where Osborne Road's entrance on Hwy 1728 is shown to be.

Overview & Description

This trout stream is pretty easy to get to from the Parkway, yet quite remote and wild once you get on it. This 1.8 mile section represents Joshua's main flow and four headwater feeders in the *Thurmond Chatham Wildlife Management Area.* Although the main flow in the WMA is only 1.8 miles long, Joshua's five feeders are also in the WMA, and most can be fished as well. So there's plenty of water with good access to keep you busy. They offer excellent wild, blue-line fishing, despite the fact the main flow, headwaters and feeders are small.

Joshua Creek sources at about 2,995" on the south slope of *Little Grandfather Mountain* along the west slope of *Osborne Ridge.* From there it begins a 3.2 mile flow to its mouth on *Mulberry Creek* at a moderate 9.1% average gradient – *its headwaters are considerably steeper.* Joshua receives added water from five feeders within the WMA, including one from a small pond beside Creek Ridge Road. All these feeders are small, and most are fishable. *Dungeon Creek* is its sixth and largest feeder and adds the most flow. But it is below the WMA and on private land. About 1.4 miles below the WMA at about 1,450', Joshua joins *Mulberry Creek* alongside Hwy 18 and from there *Mulberry* flows south for many miles before joining the *Yadkin River* in North Wilkesboro.

Disregarding the 1.4 miles of private water below the WMA, we will start from the WMA boundary point on *Osborne Road / Trail* just above the farmstead with the big bad dog on Hwy 1728 at the bottom of the valley. From there heading upstream .8 miles to the intersection of *Creek Ridge Road / Osborne Road / Joshua Ridge Road*, the creek is about 6' - 8' wide in most places, shallow, and has the typical large rock / boulder and slab features that create lots of drop pools, small falls and short runs along undercut banks. The forest canopy is dense, but the sides are relatively open, making casting and wading somewhat easy.

About .4 miles up, a *"no name"* headwater feeder enters creek left. This one starts at the pond you passed alongside *Creek Ridge Road*. I have never fished it either, although both look fishable. Another *"no name"* comes in about .6 miles creek right – but is looks too small to fish. This entire initial .8 mile stretch is blue-line fishing between the various features where fish can hold. Nearly every drop pool, undercut bank and root ball holds at least one trout. I have caught mostly rainbows and a few browns, both in the 6" – 8" range along this stretch. Although this stretch averages a moderate 7.1% gradient, it gets steeper the closer you get to the intersection. But it can still be fished in a long morning. I usually eat lunch when I reach the intersection and ponder the steepness of the headwaters and whether I want to keep fishing, or just make camp and start drinking and smoking – it usually ends up the latter.

Above the intersection, the headwaters and main flow come together to form what looks like a large funnel-shaped watershed – with the spout of the funnel at the crossings on *Creek Ridge Road* just below the intersection. To fish the upper mile of Joshua's main flow, as well as one of its headwaters, start at the first crossing on *Creek Ridge Road* just below the intersection. The second crossing offers upstream access to two more headwaters. All of these flows are fishable – some more than others. They are all very small and tight with high-gradient flows. Unlike the lower .8 miles, all of these headwaters sport a blistering 18.4% gradient. So count on lots of hand-over-hand climbing and calculating your approach between the endless drop pools and other assorted pocket waters of this stretch.

I've only fished about .5 miles up the main flow and only .2 miles up its *"no name"* feeder. It's danged hard bushwhacking fishing, but worth the effort for the wild rainbows and brookies that seem to cohabitate these headwaters. All were 6" class with a few surprises in the 8"–10" range.

Pike Creek

Thurmond Chatham WMA Waters Only

At a Glance

Sam's Rank: 👍👍👍👍

GPS Fixes:
- Source fix: N36 22.919 W81 11.951 @ 2,410'
- Mouth fix: N36 21.320 W81 11.185 @ 1,570'

Size: small at mouth *(As it joins West Prong Roaring River)*

Gradient: mild 6.5% source to mouth average *(2.4 miles / 830')*

Effort: moderate to difficult

Pressure: none to slight

Fishing Quality: good

Species: Bows, Brookies & Browns

Access: From MP 248 on the Parkway take Hwy 18 south. Continue for about 6 miles until you reach Hwy 1728 on the left. Turn left and go about 3.4 miles to Pike Creek Road *(marked with an "Access to Game Lands" sign)* on the left. Turn onto and track up Pike Creek Road to the gate. If the gate is closed, park anywhere you can and hike up. If the gate is open, continue tracking up the creek and in about 1.4 miles up, the main flow turns north, and the road continues tracking along a feeder. Access up the remaining stretches of Pike and its feeders is by trail. At 1.2 miles up Pike Creek Road, Log House Road branches off to the right and tracks up one of the *"no name"* feeders for about .6 miles to Pike Creek Pond.

Overview & Description

Pike Creek is another small, relatively low elevation, blue liner in the *Thurmond Chatham Wildlife Management Area*. Its main flow is *Hatchery Supported*, and both of its feeders are managed as *Wild Trout Waters*. It's well known by many of the locals because it is a pretty productive little fishery. As with Joshua Creek on the far west side of the same ridge, it's easy to get to from the Parkway. However, unlike Joshua, Pike's 2.3 mile main flow section, along with its headwaters and feeders, are wholly contained in the WMA – except for the posted first .2 miles as it leaves the WMA, crosses Hwy 1728 and joins *West Prong Roaring Fork*. It even has a small, high-elevation pond on one of its feeders. With that said, Pike offers some interesting fishing for dedicated blue liners. I've also observed some interesting human activity on it too…

As for some of that human activity, there's an old cabin about 200' up the creek from where it crosses Hwy 1728. It's a secluded place with wild flowers covering the bank of the creek in front of it, wind chimes and folk art in the trees, etc. The last time I fished by it, a couple *(male / female)* was on the creek bank doing things to each other that would make a pirate blush. They were so *"involved"* they didn't even see me, and I was fishing within 10' of them - but I sure as heck saw them!

I'm sure a lot of wild times must happen amongst the wildflowers of that bank. That episode made my trout fishing look kinda tame...

Pike Creek's source is at about 2,410' up on the southern slope of *Flat Rock Ridge,* just under MP 245 on the Parkway. It seeps out and begins a short 2.4 mile run to its mouth at 1,570' on *West Prong Roaring Fork.* During that decent, it flows at a mild 6.5% average gradient. However, as with other creeks on the Parkway, its headwaters can be considerably steeper. It receives additional water from only two very small feeders along the way – the first flowing out of a tiny pond. Both feeders are small, yet appear to be fishable. About .2 miles below the WMA boundary gate just below Hwy 1728 at about 1,570', Pike opens its mouth into the *West Prong of the Roaring Fork.*

The start point for Pike

Pike Creek as it passes the old "*outdoor events cabin*" about 200 yards above Hwy 1728. / *Image by Author / 2019*

Creek is at the *WMA boundary gate* on *Pike Creek Road.* Moving upstream past the "*outdoor events cabin*" for 1.2 miles to the intersection of *Pike Creek Road* and *Log House Road,* this *Hatchery Supported* section of the creek is tiny, only about 8' - 10' wide at best. Along this lower 1.2 miles, even the main flow is overgrown much of the way, but it does open up a bit past the outdoor events cabin. The gradient is just enough to create lots of plunge pools, secluded deeper pools and undercut banks. There are very few long runs, riffles, falls and slides. The fishing along here is pocket water style so be prepared to use the road and trails to spot those features, bushwhack into them, and then use some creative wading and casting techniques to sneak up on the unsuspecting trout. Along this lower section of the main flow I have caught all three species of trout in the 8" – 10" range. In addition to stockers, I've also caught what were obviously stream-raised trout. So it seems to be a nice mix of tame and wild trout – especially in the higher reaches of the main flow.

About 1.2 miles up, the first of Pike's two feeders enters creek right. This feeder is tiny and has a very high gradient. I've not fished it, but I did walk up *Log House Road* about .6 miles to the pond. This pond is overgrown and is actually *Hatchery Supported* with all three trout. I'd like to come back and spin cast it, but I haven't done so yet. I have no idea why that pond is there – probably a good story.

If you continue on up Pike Creek for 1.4 miles above its mouth, the main flow turns north and away from the road. Its second *"no name"* feeder enters creek left and is followed by *Pike Creek Road* for a short distance. From this point Pike heads north and goes feral. Along this upper section you'll be using trails to get around. I've only bushwhacked up for about .1 miles, and it was not worth the

effort. Pike becomes even smaller, more overgrown and very hard to get to and get a bug on with any degree of accuracy. There's just not that much fishable water up there.

The second *"no name"* feeder (the one followed by Pike Creek Road for a short distance after the main flow heads north) has a big

A really nice Brown Trout caught about 1.2 miles up Pike Creek. / *Image by Author / 2019*

watershed – yet is still very small and tight with a high gradient. Although the road will help you navigate, you'll still be climbing and picking your way between the pockets that hold trout. I've fished the .3 miles along the road several times, and it's worth the effort for the 6" to 8" wild rainbows and brookies. I've not fished the higher reaches of this feeder.

Garden Creek

At a Glance

Sam's Rank: 👍👍👍👍

GPS Fixes:
- Source fix: N36 25.656 W81 06.310 @ 2,840'
- Mouth fix: N36 23.358 W81 04.143 @ 1,340'

Size: Small at mouth *(As it joins East Prong Roaring River)*

Gradient: mild 6.3% source to mouth average *(4.5 miles / 1,500')*

Effort: moderate to difficult

Pressure: slight

Fishing Quality: good to excellent

Species: Bows, Brookies & Browns

Access: From MP 229.5 on the Parkway, take Hwy 21 south for about 4.5 miles until you reach Hwy 1100 *(Oklahoma Road)* on the right. Turn right and stay on Hwy 1100 for about 3 miles to the intersection of Hwy 1784. Turn right and continue as the road loops through the park for about 4.4 miles until you cross Garden Creek – coming from the right. Garden Creek Baptist Church is just past the bridge on the left. After you enter the park, Hwy 1100 will turn into Hwy 1739 / John P. Frank Parkway and will eventually parallel Stone Mountain Creek. A bit later, just before reaching Garden Creek, you'll parallel the East Prong Roaring River. Parking is easy and the creek's trail head is across the road.

Overview & Description

Garden Creek is a wild trout stream with decent populations of all three species along its first three miles – fishing is even better farther up. However, it requires hiking to get to those better waters. Fortunately, a good trail system helps. Of the three *larger* streams on *Stone Mountain State Park's* north side, *Garden Creek* is in the middle, size wise. *Bullhead Creek* is the largest, and *Widows Creek* is slightly smaller. *Bullhead* and *Widows* are popular with hikers and anglers alike – Garden not so much with the hikers.

Garden has the typical characteristics and structure of any mountain trout stream. It has several waterfalls, including one very large falls in its higher reaches with a fine pool that's worth the hike just to fish it. Brook trout seem to dominate the waters above the falls all the way into its headwaters and main feeder. Of the three main *Stone Mountain State Park* creeks mentioned above, Garden is my favorite because of its size, structure, trout populations, and the hike minimizes fishing pressure.

Stone Mountain State Park is worth noting. It's located on more than 13,500 acres in *Wilkes* and *Alleghany* counties. Established in 1969 and designated a *National Natural Landmark* in 1975, the Park is bounded on the north by the *Parkway* and to the west by *Thurmond Chatham Game Lands*. Long before it became a state park, the area was settled by people of English, German, Irish, French and Scotch-Irish descent who built the homes, farms, mills, churches and schools they needed to be self-sufficient. A restored mid-19th century mountain farm and an old Baptist Church are some of the major landmarks.

The park has more than 20 miles of designated wild trout waters, and in my opinion, the best are the three mentioned above. All three flow into either the *East Prong Roaring River,* or one of its headwaters, *Stone Mountain Creek.* Both are managed as *Delayed Harvest* for several miles. Aside from trout water, the Park's most spectacular feature is *Stone Mountain,* a 600-foot granite dome that dominates the landscape. This amazing feature is part of a 25-square-mile "*pluton,*" an igneous rock formation beneath the earth's surface formed by molten lava. Over time, wind and water eroded the softer layers of soil and rock atop the granite block and exposed the massive outcrop we see today.

From an ominous sounding place called *Devil's Garden* just under the Parkway at about 2,410', Garden Creek oozes out and begins a 4.5 mile run along the west slope of *Scott Ridge* to its mouth. During that run, it loses only 1,500' in elevation which accounts for the mild 6.3% average gradient. Above the largest falls about 3 miles up, that gradient jumps to a steep 14% - still not crazy for a headwater flow on the Parkway. Along the way, Garden gets additional water from a couple of small "*no name*" feeders – the largest being the one highest above the falls. Neither appears to me to be more than marginally fishable. At about 1,340', just below Hwy 1728, Garden Creek flows into the *East Prong Roaring River* and forms a large pool. Located very close to its mouth is *Garden Creek Baptist Church,* which still has some "*fire and brimstone*" services occasionally.

Starting at the big pool at the mouth and moving upstream above Hwy 1728 over the first mile, the creek forms a big "V" shaped curve that points southward. At its mouth, the creek is about 10' – 12' across, shallow and actually looks smaller than it does further upstream. Just above Hwy 1728 two very small feeders enter creek right, but neither looks to be fishable. Along this first mile in the "V", fishing can be difficult given the fact there's not a good trail. Dead falls litter the bed, and places in the creek are really difficult to wade. You really have to work to get around them, so many people skip this stretch by using the trail that cuts across the top of the "V" and reconnects with the creek about a mile upstream. From there it parallels the creek pretty much all the way to its source. I've fished this first mile several times and had good luck mostly with browns as well as bows - all in the 8" – 12" range. The fishing was good, but it improves as you move upstream.

Above the first mile, and along the creek up to the big waterfall 2 miles up, the creek opens up and looks and feels bigger than it was at its mouth. However, it's still only 8' – 10' wide and no more than a foot or so deep in most places. The canopy and side flora closes in along some stretches, but generally it's plenty wide enough for easy casting and wading all the way to the falls. Along this stretch, the

The Author stalking an unsuspecting Brown Trout at the approach to the waterfall about two miles up Garden Creek. / *Image by fishing buddy who wishes to remain anonymous. / 2002.*

creek has a goodly number of small to large drop pools, rock gardens, small falls, pools of all sorts, and gravel beds as well as all the typical runs and riffle features trout love. About 1.6 miles up, the first sizeable feeder enters creek right. It is still small by any account, and I have not yet taken the time to fish it. The trail crosses the creek at least 18 times along those two miles up to the falls.

The two miles below the big waterfall is in my opinion the best fishing on the creek, with browns throughout most of lower Garden, with bows and an increasing number of brookies up to the falls. The number of pools and runs offer lots of opportunities to fish. In fact, there're so many features, don't waste time chasing that one trout that you keep missing. There're scores of other runs and pools to fish. The one exception is the pool at the base of the large waterfall. There're some "*bully*" trout in there, and you should throw everything you have at them. The largest trout I've caught on this creek was here – a 14" brown.

Above the falls, both the trail and creek become steep – about 14%. I have fished up another .3 miles to where the last headwater feeder creek enters on the left, and the main flow heads north to its source. Above the falls, it's entirely a brook trout stream in the 4" – 6" range – and a bunch of them. It's one of the few creeks where I've caught so many specs that I actually got tired of catching them. By that point on the creek, I was exhausted, needed water, food and a beer, and just felt it wasn't worth going further up. I'm sure I was probably wrong...

Bull Head Creek

At a Glance

Sam's Rank: 👍👍👍👍
GPS Fixes:
- Source fix: N36 26.367 W81 05.658 @ 3,220'
- Mouth fix: N36 23.857 W81 03.686 @ 1,385'

Size: medium at mouth *(As it joins Stone Mountain Creek)*
Gradient: moderate 8.9% source to mouth average *(3.9 miles / 1,835')*
Effort: moderate to difficult
Pressure: slight to moderate
Fishing Quality: good to excellent
Species: Bows, Brookies & Browns
Access: From MP 229.5 on the Parkway, take Hwy 21 south. Continue for about 4.5 miles until you reach Hwy 1100 *(Oklahoma Road)* on the right. Turn right and stay on Hwy 1100 for about 3 miles to the intersection of Hwy 1784. Turn right and continue as the road loops through the park for about 3.5 miles until you cross Bull Head Creek – coming from the right. At some point after you enter the park, Hwy 1100 will turn into Hwy 1739 / John P. Frank Parkway. In the park you will be tracking along Stone Mountain Creek before you reach Bull Head. There's plenty of parking at the creek's trail head across the road.

Overview & Description

Bull Head is located south of the Parkway in *Stone Mountain State Park* and is managed as *Wild Trout Waters*. There's a lot of chatter about Bull Head concerning what it was back in its so-called heyday, as opposed to what it is today. Most of what I know started out as second or third hand hearsay from some of the locals, as well as several fishing blogs and websites – *and we know how accurate those are!* So, to get to the truth, I filtered the hearsay through several *Stone Mountain State Park* rangers who seemed to have the facts. As best as I can tell, the story of Bull Head Creek goes something like the following…

Bull Head is named after the unusually shaped Bull Head Mountain just over the ridge on the north side of the Parkway. The watershed was originally privately owned by a family / group who kept it stocked with pigs *(trout)*, fed them regularly, protected them under the threat of death, sweet talked to them, and even tucked them in each evening. For a while everything was dandy! The humans were paying reparations to the trout in an effort to right all the terrible things that had been perpetuated on their trout ancestors by the logging industry in the last century. And, the trout enjoyed what amounted to an *"assisted living existence"* where their every need was taken care of. Humans and trout were both content. Then, as fate would have it, the humans decided they'd paid enough reparations and made the decision to convey ownership of the watershed to the state for inclusion into Stone

Bull Head Creek emerges from under bridge and joins Stone Mountain Creek *(top right)* to form the source of the East Prong Roaring River. / *Image by Author / 2018*

Mountain State Park. The only contingency was that the state would continue to protect and feed the fish on a regular basis. However, the state did push back on tucking the trout in at night. But in the end, a deal was eventually struck, albeit with some restrictions and modifications.

For some time the state continued to manage Bull Head as the previous owners wished. The state divided the creek into sections, and anglers could pay a fee and have an entire section, with all its pigs, to themselves. Humans and trout remained happy and the creek grew in popularity and fame. Then things changed. Some say at one point poachers began to sneak in and use nets and other sinister devices to harvest trout – severely damaging the *"pig"* population. Others say the state stopped feeding them and all the big fish were eventually caught out. Some say both things happened. In either event, the pigs seem to be gone now, and many old timers say: *"the creek just ain't what it used to be."* Regardless, today the creek is finally back to what it used to be. It's now managed as *Wild Trout Waters* – no fees. I'm glad…

Another fact that's fascinating about the Bull Head watershed was the *aerial tramway* that once crossed hundreds of feet above its headwaters. *Worth Folger* was the visionary who built the tramway in the late 1960s and named it *Mahogany Rock Cableways, Inc.* He located it just below MP 235.1 on the Parkway where it could span the 7/10 mile between the peaks of *Mahogany Rock Mountain* and *Scott Ridge.* At one time, there were restrooms, a visitors' center, and a gift shop on the Scott Ridge end. It was quite an attraction for a period of time. However, Folger was unable to put outdoor ads and directional signage along the Parkway. There was also unpredictable visibility and traffic congestion caused by gawkers trying to catch a glimpse of the cable cars. Eventually, the tramway had to close its doors, and the 250 acres once owned by Folger are now a part of *Stone Mountain State Park*. Huge concrete slabs are still there on both peaks.

I've fished Bull Head three or four times, and it fished well each time. However, I don't get into the water until I get above *Rich*

An aerial tramway crossed hundreds of feet above Bull Head's headwaters in the 1960s. / *Image courtesy of National Park Service, Blue Ridge Parkway*

Mountain Creek about .4 miles up. This gets me above the hoards of hikers, waders, rock hoppers and casual anglers and into waters where the fish are not as pressured and seem to be more plentiful. Of the three larger trout streams on the north side of *Stone Mountain State Park*, Bull Head is by far the largest. The way I look at it - being the biggest water coming off the Parkway means bigger trout and more of them. In fact, the further you hike up Bull Head, or any of its feeders for that matter, the better the fishing is. I highly recommend trying this creek, but only if you are willing to hike a bit.

Here's a bit about *Stone Mountain State Park*. It's located on more than 13,500 acres in *Wilkes* and *Alleghany* counties. Established in 1969 and designated a *National Natural Landmark* in 1975, the park is bounded on the north by the Parkway and to the west by *Thurmond Chatham Game Lands*. The park has more than 20 miles of designated *wild, hatchery-supported* and *delayed-harvest* trout waters. Aside from its trout waters, the park's most spectacular feature is Stone Mountain, a 600-foot granite dome that dominates the landscape and horizon. It's worth exploring while you're there.

Bull Head Creek seeps out of the ground at about 3,220' from the south slope of *Mahogany Rock Mountain* at about MP 235 on the Parkway. From there it starts its 3.9 mile run to its mouth while losing about 1,835' of elevation and in so doing, establishes a moderate 8.9% average gradient. Along that run it picks up additional volume from about four feeders – two of which are small *"no names"* and don't appear to be fishable, and then *Rich Mountain Creek* and *Horse Cove Branch* –

Stone Mountain as viewed from Cedar Rock dominates the landscape in Stone Mountain State Park. / *Image courtesy of Zachary Robbins, M.S.*

both plenty big enough to be fishable. Bull Head reaches its mouth on *Stone Mountain Creek* at about 1,385', just below the bridge on Hwy 1728.

I've found where Bull Head opens its mouth into Stone Mountain Creek to be a productive place to fish – it's a full three times as big as Stone Mountain Creek at that point. Bull Head is managed as *Wild Trout Waters*, and Stone Mountain Creek is *Delayed Harvest*. On several occasions when *Delayed Harvest* is closed, I've had good luck standing just enough inside Bull Head's mouth to be legal in *Wild Trout Water* and casting to the *Delayed Harvest* fish that tend to run up Bull Head from Stone Mountain Creek. It works - try it. You can do the same at the mouths of *Garden Creek* and *Widows Creek* just down the road.

If you start at Bull Head's mouth and move upstream over the first .4 miles, the creek is comparatively large - about 10' – 12' across in most places, wider in others. It has a goodly number of small falls, drop pools, slides, runs and riffle features scattered along that lower stretch. The hiking trail is wide and close to the water along there and is often busy with both hikers and anglers. For that reason alone, I wait to start fishing until I'm above *Rich Mountain Creek* at .4 miles up. Crowds thin out up there and thin even more for each ½ mile you go upstream.

Rich Mountain Creek enters creek right .4 miles up. This is Bull Head's largest feeder. It is about 2 miles long and is definitely worth the time and effort to fish. As you get above Rich Mountain, the 2.1 mile stretch up to *Horse Cove Branch* is what I'd consider the sweet spot for trout fishing on Bull Head. The crowds are gone, the creek has excellent structure, access is good, and there's wild brook, brown and rainbow trout in good numbers. Most of what I have caught along this stretch has been a mix of all three in the 8" – 12" range. As you might expect, the brookies become more plentiful as you get higher up the creek.

Along the 2.1 miles up to *Horse Cove Branch*, the creek is about 6' – 10' wide in most places, the canopy and sides get tighter, and there can be a lot of deadfalls. This stretch has a large number of drop pools, rock gardens, small waterfalls, swirl holes, pools of all sizes, gravel bottoms, and all types of runs and riffles. About 1.4 miles up, the second small *"no name"* feeder enters creek right. It looks fishable but I have not tried it. At 2.2 miles, the third no name feeder enters creek left. It too is small and not tested by me. About 1.9 miles up, the big trail turns into a smaller trail and continues all the way to the Parkway. Along the way, it crosses the creek many times. This is a long stretch of creek, and you should allow plenty of time for it given the topography and rugged nature of its features. Wading and casting will become much more difficult the further up you go.

As you reach Bull Head's fourth feeder, *Horse Cove Branch*, coming in creek right about 2.5 miles up, Bull Head turns to the left and ascends another 1.4 miles to its source under the Parkway. *Horse Cove* continues another 1 mile to its source. Both become steep – about 14%. I've not fished beyond this point on either one, but the water on both is large enough to fish. By the time I got to them, I was beat and threw in the towel. Back in the 60's and 70's, the aerial tramway would have been hundreds of feet above with gawkers watching you fish these headwaters.

Bull Head Creek Tributaries

Rich Mountain Creek

At a Glance

Sam's Rank: 👍👍👍
GPS Fixes:
- Source fix: N36 25.000 W81 02.107 @ 2,575'
- Mouth fix: N36 24.153 W81 03.733 @ 1,465'

Size: Small at mouth *(As it joins Bull Head Creek)*
Gradient: moderate 10.5% source to mouth average *(2 miles / 1,110')*
Effort: moderate
Pressure: slight to moderate
Fishing Quality: average
Species: Bows & Browns
Access: From MP 229.5 on the Parkway, take Hwy 21 south. Continue for about 4.5 miles until you reach Hwy 1100 *(Oklahoma Road)* on the right. Turn right and stay on Hwy 1100 for about 4 miles to the Stone Mountain State Park boundary. Continue on Hwy 1100 as it loops through the park for about 2.4 miles until you cross Bull Head Creek – coming from the right. At some point after you enter the

park, Hwy 1100 will turn into Hwy 1739 / John P. Frank Parkway. In the park you will be tracking along Stone Mountain Creek before you reach Bull Head. There is plenty of parking at the mouth of Bull Head Creek. The creek's access trail is across the road – follow it for about .4 miles up to the mouth of Rich Mountain Creek on the right. Another trail offers reasonable access up Rich Mountain Creek although at times, it is far above the creek.

Overview & Description

I've only fished up this creek for about .6 miles to where it takes a hard turn to the right and a small no name feeder enters creek left. Along that stretch it has a moderate 11.4% gradient – enough to get your attention and make wading and navigating less than easy. There was another mile of water that looked fishable above me, but I was too committed to go back down and continue up Bull Head and didn't take the time. I caught lots of bows and browns in the 6" – 10" range.

Rich Mountain Creek looks to be Bull Head Creek's largest feeder. It starts at about 2,575' between the ridge lines of *Rich Mountain* and *Ellis Knoll*. From that source, it begins a 2 mile run at a moderate 10.5% gradient. Along the way, it picks up minimal volume from a few small feeders, but none are of any size. The only one I saw was very small. At about 1,465' its mouth converges with Bull Head Creek.

Moving up from its mouth on Bull Head, I found the first .6 miles of the creek to be similar to most of the other feeders in the area. Being at a somewhat lower elevation, its waters seemed to be warm when I fished it in the early fall. But I did catch a smart number of bows and browns. The creek has a rocky stream bed with plenty of pools and runs all the way up the stretch I fished. At the .6 mile point, I turned back. The creek begins to get noticeably smaller and tighter. Toward the end on that stretch, I was climbing and bushwhacking between the runs and pools that held trout.

Above the .6 mile point, satellite images and maps indicate the creek runs in an almost a straight line for over a mile up the side of the mountain. I'm sure it gets even smaller and tighter and the fishing tougher. I'll let someone else try that stretch! All in all, to be honest, Rich Mountain Creek is kinda vanilla. But given the fact the trail really helped navigate this creek, and I did catch fish, I consider it worth the diversion.

Brush Creek
Blue Ridge Parkway Stretch Only
At a Glance

Sam's Rank: 👍👍👍
GPS Fixes:
- Source fix: N36 26.381 W81 03.700 @ 3,040'
- Mouth fix: N36 31.921 W81 01.822 @ 2,465'

Size: medium at mouth *(As it joins the Little River)*
Gradient: flat .6% source to mouth average *(19.2 miles / 575')*
Effort: easy
Pressure: slight
Fishing Quality: average
Species: Bows, Browns & Specs
Access: The .7 miles of Brush Creek included here flows under the Parkway from the south at about MP 227.5, then flows northwesterly along the Parkway before departing at about MP 228 and heading north to its mouth. Parking is plentiful.

Overview & Description

As with Meadow Fork, Brush Creek is another creek that actually parallels the Parkway for a distance – even if it is just a short .7 miles. It's just too darn convenient to drive past it and not stop. Plus, it's *Hatchery Supported* with over 4,200 bows, browns and brookies each year. That makes it a good creek to include in this Guide for those two reasons alone.

Brush Creek is managed as *Hatchery Supported* water from its mouth below the Parkway on the *Little River* all the way up past the Parkway to Hwy 21. Still, I'm only including only the .7 miles along the Parkway. The main reason is that above and below the Parkway the creek flows through a maze of forested, cultivated and developed private land, and its flow is exceptionally slow and sandy. The other reason is that there are so many other waters in *Section IV* that aren't private, and more productive. In short, blow through this .7 miles stretch and catch a few "*dumb & unsuspecting*" stockers, then head on to more challenging wild waters and catch some "*smart*" trout you can brag about around the fire.

To offer a perspective of Brush Creek, here's an overview of the entire stream even though only .7 miles of it is being included. It sources just north of MP 231.5 on the Parkway at about 3,040'. From there it quickly passes under the Parkway and begins a 7 mile, slow and looping flow through mostly private land down to the Parkway's .7 mile stretch included here. From this second Parkway encounter it continues another 11.5 miles to its mouth on the *Little River* at about 2,465'. Along its 19.2 mile source to mouth run, it gains volume from several feeders, *Little Glade Creek* being the one at the end of this .7 mile stretch. It averages a flat .6% gradient along its entire run. It's very fishy.

As far as the .7 mile section of Brush included here, if you start at the Parkway's downstream right-of-way boundary about 500' downstream from MP 228 and move upstream, the creek is about 20'– 25' wide all the way to the upstream boundary. The entire .7 miles of creek's bed is sandy with very few rocks of any size to obstruct flow, and lots of dead falls. The creek is shallow, except in several curves and long runs against the road bed where the flow speeds up and creates undercuts and gouged-out runs that offer holding / feeding lanes. Along the entire stretch, the canopy is high but the side flora can crowd in on some stretches.

Brush Creek as it flows under the Parkway bridge at MP 227.5. / *Image by Author / 2018*

At about .1 miles up from the downstream boundary, *Little Glade Creek* enters creek right. Managed as *Wild Trout Waters*, this feeder should be fished, and I did for 500' and caught bows in the 6" – 8" range. There's lots of large trout along here – I've seen 18" rainbows in the shallows – stockers for sure.

Moving upstream from the downstream boundary at about .5 miles, Brush passes under the Hwy 1496 bridge, and at about .6 miles up, takes a hard right and passes under the Parkway. Both of these bridge abutments fish well, and the sharp turn the creek makes to get to the Parkway is one of the better spots of Brush to fish. The outside bank is undercut, and the side flora offers cover for the trout – but there's plenty of room to maneuver and stay concealed. Float a #14 Elk Hair Caddis with a soft hackle dropped about 24" underneath, and I'll guarantee you someone will come out and play. This stretch between the Parkway bridge and the Hwy 1496 bridge is my choice location for the entire .7 miles.

About 500' upstream beyond the Parkway Bridge, Brush reenters private farm land. The *Hatchery Supported* water continues upstream for another 3 miles, but I have never fished above or below the Parkway right-of-ways. I think the water is marginal, and I don't want to fight worm dunkers and the power-bait crowd.

Big Pine Creek
Blue Ridge Parkway Stretch Only
At a Glance

Sam's Rank: 👍👍👍

GPS Fixes:
- Source fix: N36 29.373 W81 00.240 @ 2,895'
- Mouth fix: N36 31.407 W80 56.728 @ 2,550'

Size: small at mouth *(As it joins Brush Creek)*
Gradient: flat .1% source to mouth average *(7 miles / 345')*
Effort: easy
Pressure: none to slight
Fishing Quality: average
Species: Bows, Browns & Specs
Access: The southern access point for the 4.3 miles of Big Pine Creek included here is at the Parkway MP 225.4 / Hwy 1463 intersection. At this point the creek is flowing down the left side of the Parkway, and just a few yards north of the intersection it departs the Parkway's boundary as it heads northwest towards its mouth on Brush Creek several miles away.

Its northern access point is just above the Parkway MP 221.8 / Hwy 1461 intersection. The creek enters the Parkway's boundary about .1 miles up on the left. Access to all points is by pulling off the Parkway.

Overview & Description

Big Pine Creek is the distance winner of the longest section of trout waters with actual frontage on the North Carolina section of the Parkway. It boasts more than 4.3 miles of water within the right-of-way - more frontage than *Brush Creek, Little Glade Creek, Meadows Creek* and even *Yellowstone Prong.* The reason is simple. The other three North Carolina Parkway sections run along high-elevation ridges with an extreme topography that prevents water from running any distance along the road. However, the upper stretch of the Parkway's Section IV, up to the Virginia line, departs from those ridges and runs through a much milder topography where water can run beside the road. Because Big Pine holds the distance record, is convenient to fish, runs mostly through forest, and is also *Hatchery Supported,* I included it as the last fishery in this *North Carolina Section.*

The *NCWRC's* trout stream management map shows the lower 1.7 miles and upper 1 mile of Big Pine outside the Parkway's right-of-way as *Hatchery Supported.* But I am including only the 4.3 miles along the Parkway. The stream management map does not color the Parkway stretch *Green,* but I assume they stock it based on the upper / lower boundaries of what they indicate they stock. My reasoning for describing only the Parkway water is the same as for *Meadow* and *Brush Creeks.* Above and below the Parkway the creek flows through a patchwork of cultivated and developed private land with minimal forest cover. Here, the creek is slow, exposed and very sandy. However, the Parkway water is more forested and better protected, and for me I know it fishes better for wild and stocked trout. The entire creek gets only *1,700 browns, bows* and *brookies* each year. That's not a bunch of trout. But the fish that find their way into the protected Parkway stretch have many hiding places to grow and multiply. I've caught fish along there that were not stockers and appeared to be stream bred.

Although only the 4.3 miles of Big Pine on the Parkway's right-of-way is featured here, a quick overview of the creek's entire flow is in order. The creek sources at about 2,895' from the spillway of a small

Big Pine Creek from the Parkway bridge at MP #225. / *Image by Author / 2011*

pond in the middle of a cultivated field, between the Parkway to the east, Hwy 1444 to the west, and Hwy 1460 on the north. From there it dives into its first forest canopy for about a mile, and then reemerges at the Parkway. From there it continues a lazy 4.3 mile, southern, very slow flow, while paralleling and crisscrossing the Parkway multiple times before reaching the bottom of its Parkway run. From there it heads Northwest from the Parkway, and for the next 1.7 miles creeps through some forests, but mostly through cultivated fields, log jams and pasture lands until it reaches its mouth at about 2,550'on Brush Creek. Throughout its 7 mile run, it averages a flat .1% gradient, while receiving minimal added volume from ten or more very small feeders – none of any size or fishing quality. On paper, Big Pine doesn't look that good – at least on its upper and lower stretches. The Parkway stretch is another story.

Starting at the downstream access point at Parkway MP 225.4 / Hwy 1463, Big Pine is about 10' – 12' wide and shallow as it leaves the right-of-way and heads to its mouth downstream. There is also a small pond across the intersection on the east side of the Parkway that empties into Big Pine. I've never fished this pond, but several friends and locals say they catch pan fish and bass at this spot.

Over the next 2.6 miles upstream to Hwy 1486, the creek crisscrosses the Parkway no less than five times. I find the bridges and culverts to be some of the best fishing on the creek – especially on the upstream side of each bridge where the trout hold under the drip / shadow line looking upstream. Some of these bridges are fifty feet or more above the water. All the way up, the creek is completely covered by a high canopy. Its bed is mostly sand and gravel, with occasional rock features that channel the water to create deeper runs and pools. These are obvious holding / feeding lanes where trout tend to congregate, and I've found the fishing to be average to good in most of them. The mile or so below Hwy 1486 the creek goes through what I call the *"Big Bend"* – a big sweeping *"S"* curve that offers some good features and deeper water where trout hold. The outside curve undercut bank offers even more opportunities. Along this 2.6 mile stretch, I have caught a goodly mix of trout averaging 8" – 12" and one bow that was at least 14" and is the one pictured in *"Trout of the Parkway Waters"* chapter.

The last 1.7 miles of the creek above Hwy 1486 up to where it leaves the Parkway boundary above Hwy 1461, the creek is noticeably smaller - about 6' – 8' wide at best and getting quickly smaller as you move upstream. It continues with a good forest canopy the first ½ mile, crosses under the Parkway several more times, and then begins its final run up to the Parkway / Hwy 1486 intersection.

The final run breaks out of the forest and into open fields, and finally into another short forest run next to a travel trailer park. I have only fished above Hwy 1486 a couple of times – and each time I stopped fishing about ½ mile up when I exited the forest canopy. The creek above there is tiny, silted and a thicket of bushes that makes casting impossible, even if there was pocket water to fish.

My best fishing on Big Pine has always been under the culverts and bridges, the undercut banks in the curves, and the occasional short, deep runs. I have never fished Big Pine above or below the Parkway right-of-way. There are some areas below the Parkway that are supposed to be accessible. But again, I just think the

Entering Virginia just past Big Pine Creek and the end of the Parkway's NC Section. / *Image by Author / 2017*

water is marginal. The Parkway water is so easy to get to, and as I've said so many times, I don't like competing with power bait and worm dunkers.

~ **Big Pine Creek** ~

Forty More Watersheds

I've fished a bunch of the following waters, but not all of them. However, I know folks who have fished the ones I haven't, and we've decided they're worth mentioning. Be aware that some flow through both public and private land, so use your maps, search engines and judgment to find and fish them. The location notes are approximate. The list starts from the south end of the Parkway.

Section I

1. **Soco Creek** - *Cherokee*
2. **Woodfin Creek** - *Balsam Gap / North on Parkway*
3. **Scott Creek** - *Balsam Gap / Silva / Dillsboro*
4. **Tuckasegee River** – *Silva / Dillsboro*
5. **Richland Creek** - *Waynesville*
6. **Tanasee Creek** – *Hwy 215 / South of Parkway*
7. **West Fork of the French Broad River** - *Rosman*
8. **East Fork of the French Broad River** - *Rosman*
9. **Little East Fork of the Pigeon River** – *Shining Rock Wilderness*
10. **Hungry Creek (*Private*)** – *Hwy 276 / SR 1890 North of Parkway*

Section II

1. **Pisgah Creek** – *north of Buck Springs Gap on Parkway / SR 1888*
2. **Upper Bent Creek Watershed** – *north of Parkway at Bent Creek Gap*
3. **Shope Creek** – *south of Parkway at Lane Pinnacle*
4. **North Fork / Swannanoa River Reservoir Watershed** (*Restricted*) – *below the Parkway above Black Mountain*
5. **Hawkbill Creek** – *north of Parkway at Beetree Gap*
6. **Mineral Creek** – *north of Parkway at Beetree Gap*
7. **Cane River** (*Public & Private*) – *west of Mt. Mitchell / south of Burnsville*
8. **Roaring Fork** – *north of Parkway / off Hwy 80*

9. **Buck Creek** – *south of Parkway along Hwy 80*
10. **Licklog Creek** – *south of Parkway / off Hwy 80 / along Hwy 1188 & 1188A*

Section III

1. **North Toe River** *(Private / Public) – north of Parkway / Spruce Pine area*
2. **Armstrong Creek Headwaters** *(Private / Public) – south of Parkway / between Hwy 80 and Hwy 226 ALT*
3. **North Fork Catawba River** – *south of Parkway / Linville Fall / Hwy 221 South*
4. **Camp Creek** – *along Parkway north of Linville Falls*
5. **Grandmother Creek** *(Private / Public) – north of Parkway / below Grandmother Lake on designated USFS land*
6. **Sims Creek** – *west of Blowing Rock / both sides of Parkway*
7. **Johns River Headwaters** – *south Parkway / west of Blowing Rock*
8. **Flannery Fork** – *west of Blowing Rock / north of Parkway / along Hwy 1541 above Trout Lake Dam*
9. **Aho Branch Headwaters** *(Private) – east of Blowing Rock / north of Parkway*
10. **Goshen Branch** – *north of Blowing Rock along Parkway*

Section IV

1. **Middle Fork Reddies River** – *south of Parkway / east of Hwy 16*
2. **North Fork Reddies River** – *south of Parkway / east of Hwy 16*
3. **Basin Creek** – *south of Parkway / Doughton Recreation Area*
4. **Cove Creek** – *south of Parkway / north of Longbottom Road*
5. **East Prong Roaring River** – *South of Parkway / Stone Mountain State Park*
6. **Turkey Cove Creek & Upper Pond** – *south of Parkway / north of Longbottom Road / Thurmond Chatham Game Land*
7. **Camp Creek** *(Upper stretch) – south of Parkway / north of Hwy 1730 / Thurmond Chatham Game Land*
8. **Widows Creek** – *South of Parkway / Stone Mountain State Park*
9. **Little Glade Creek** – *along the Parkway at Hwy 21*
10. **West Fork Chestnut Creek** – *north & south along the Parkway at NC & VA State Line*